UNSETTLED LEGITIMACY

Other volumes planned in the Globalization and Autonomy series:

Global Ordering: Institutions and Autonomy in a Changing World
Edited by Louis W. Pauly and William D. Coleman (2008)

Renegotiating Community: Interdisciplinary Perspectives, Global Contexts
Edited by Diana Brydon and William D. Coleman (2008)

Empires and Autonomy: Moments in the History of Globalization
Edited by Stephen M. Streeter, John C. Weaver, and William D. Coleman (2009)

Cultural Autonomy: Frictions and Connections
Edited by Petra Rethmann, Imre Szeman, and William D. Coleman (2009)

Indigenous Peoples and Autonomy: Insights for a Global Age
Edited by Mario E. Blaser, Ravi de Costa, Deborah McGregor, and William D. Coleman

Property Rights: Struggles over Autonomy in a Global Age
Edited by William D. Coleman and John C. Weaver

Deux Méditerranées: Les voies de la mondialisation et de l'autonomie
Edited by Yassine Essid and William D. Coleman

Globalization and Autonomy: Conversing across Disciplines
Diana Brydon, William D. Coleman, Louis W. Pauly, and John C. Weaver

See also the *Globalization and Autonomy Online Compendium* at www.globalautonomy.ca

globalization + autonomy

UNSETTLED

Political Community, Power, and Authority in a Global Era

LEGITIMACY

Edited by Steven Bernstein and William D. Coleman

UBCPress · Vancouver · Toronto

20 19 18 17 16 15 14 13 12 11 10 09   5 4 3 2 1

Printed in Canada on ancient-forest-free paper (100% post-consumer recycled) that is processed
chlorine- and acid-free.

Library and Archives Canada Cataloguing in Publication

    Unsettled legitimacy: political community, power, and authority in a global era /
edited by Steven Bernstein and William D. Coleman.

(Globalization and autonomy, 1913-7494)
Includes bibliographical references and index.
ISBN 978-0-7748-1717-2

    1. Globalization – Political aspects. 2. Autonomy. 3. Legitimacy of governments. 4. Power
(Social sciences). I. Coleman, William D. (William Donald), 1950- II. Bernstein, Steven F.
III. Series: Globalization and autonomy

JZ1318.U58 2009   327.1   C2009-904087-5

Canadä

UBC Press gratefully acknowledges the financial support for our publishing program of the
Government of Canada through the Book Publishing Industry Development Program
(BPIDP), and of the Canada Council for the Arts, and the British Columbia Arts Council.

Research for this volume was supported by the Social Sciences and Humanities Research
Council of Canada through its Major Collaborative Research Initiatives Program, Grant No.
421-2001-1000, and by the Canada Research Chairs Program.

UBC Press
The University of British Columbia
2029 West Mall
Vancouver, BC V6T 1Z2
604-822-5959 / Fax: 604-822-6083
www.ubcpress.ca

Contents

Part 2: Legitimacy — Accommodating Difference and Autonomy

Part 3: Legitimacy, Autonomy, and Violence

Part 4: Legitimacy and Autonomy on Global and Regional Scales

Preface

The Globalization and Autonomy Series: Dialectical Relationships in the Contemporary World

THE VOLUMES IN THE Globalization and Autonomy series offer the results from an interdisciplinary Major Collaborative Research Initiative (MCRI) funded by the Social Sciences and Humanities Research Council of Canada (SSHRC). SSHRC set up the MCRI program to provide a vehicle to support larger projects with research objectives requiring collaboration among researchers from different universities and across a range of disciplines. The MCRI on Globalization and Autonomy began in April 2002. The research team involved forty co-investigators from twelve universities across Canada and another twenty academic contributors from outside Canada, including scholars from Australia, Brazil, China, Denmark, France, Germany, Slovenia, Taiwan, the United Kingdom, and the United States. Drawing on additional funding from the International Development Research Centre (IDRC), the project became affiliated with a separate interdisciplinary research team of twenty-eight scholars, the Groupe d'Études et de Recherches Interdisciplinaires sur la Méditerranée (GERIM). GERIM is based in Tunisia and includes members from France, Spain, Jordan, and Lebanon as well. Scholars from the following disciplines participated in the project: anthropology, comparative literature, cultural studies, economics, English literature, geography, history, music, philosophy, political science, and sociology.

The project was conceived, designed, and implemented to carry out interdisciplinary research. We endeavoured to put disciplinary-based theories and conceptual frameworks into dialogue with one another, with a view to developing new theories and understandings of human societies. Four conditions needed to be met if research was to be done in this way. First, we brought humanities and social science disciplines into a relationship of mutual influence, where perspectives were integrated without subordinating one to another. To achieve this integration, the team agreed on a set of core research objectives informed by existing writings on globalization and autonomy. Members developed a number of research questions designed to address these objectives and a research plan that would permit them to address these questions in a focused, systematic way. Second, team members individually were encouraged to think inside disciplines other than their own and to respect differences across disciplines in terms of how the object of knowledge is constructed. Third, team members were selected to ensure that the research was carried out using multiple methodologies. Finally, faced with researching the complex relationships involved in globalization, an interdisciplinary approach meant that our work would be necessarily pluri-theoretical. We held to the view that theories would be most effective when, in addition to applying ideas rigorously, their proponents acknowledged the limitations of any particular theoretical perspective and consciously set out to cross boundaries and use other, sometimes seemingly incommensurable, perspectives.

To ensure intellectual integration from the start, team members agreed on this approach at the first full meeting of the project and committed to the following core objective: *to investigate the relationship between globalization and the processes of securing and building autonomy.* To this end, we sought to refine understanding of these concepts and of the historical evolution of the processes inherent in both of them, given the contested character of their content, meaning, and symbolic status.

Given that *globalization* is the term currently employed to describe the contemporary moment, we attempted to:

- determine the opportunities globalization might create and the constraints globalization might place on individuals and communities seeking to secure and build autonomy
- evaluate the extent to which individuals and communities might be able to exploit these opportunities and to overcome these constraints
- assess the opportunities for empowerment that globalization might create for individuals and communities seeking to secure and to build autonomy

- determine how the autonomy available to individuals and communities might permit them to contest, reshape, or engage globalization.

In seeking to address the core objectives for the project, we moved our research in three interrelated directions. First, we accepted that globalization and autonomy have deep historical roots. What is happening today in the world is in many ways continuous with what has taken place in the past. Thus, the burden of a contemporary examination of globalization and autonomy is to assess what is new and what has changed. Second, the dynamics of the relationship between globalization and autonomy are related to a series of important changes in the locations of power and authority. Finally, the globalization–autonomy dynamic plays out in the construction and reconstruction of identities, the nature and value of community, and the articulation of autonomy in and through cultures and discrete institutions. In each of these three areas, the team developed and agreed to answer core questions to provide clear direction for the research. The full text of the questions is available at http://globalization.mcmaster.ca/ga/ga81.htm.

Over successive annual meetings of the team, our research coalesced around the following themes: institutions and global ordering; democracy and legitimacy; continuity and rupture in the history of globalization and autonomy; history, property rights, and capitalism; community; culture; the situation and struggles of indigenous peoples; and the Mediterranean region as a microcosm of North-South relations. The researchers addressing these themes tended to be drawn from several disciplines, leading to interdisciplinary dialogue within each thematic group. The themes then crystallized into separate research problems, which came to be addressed by the volumes in the series. While these volumes were taking form, the project team also developed an online publication, the *Globalization and Autonomy Online Compendium* (see next page), which makes our findings available to the general public through research summaries; a glossary of key concepts, organizations, people, events, and places; and a comprehensive bibliography. The ultimate objective of all of these publications is to produce an integrated corpus of outstanding research that provides an in-depth study of the varying relationships between globalization and autonomy.

Globalization and Autonomy Online Compendium

Readers of this volume may also be interested in the *Globalization and Autonomy Online Compendium* (available at www.globalautonomy.ca). The *Compendium* is a collective publication by the team of Canadian and international scholars who have been part of the SSHRC Major Collaborative Research Initiative that gave rise to the volumes in the Globalization and Autonomy series. Through the *Compendium,* the team is making the results of their research available to a wide public audience. Team members have prepared a glossary of hundreds of short articles on relevant persons, places, organizations, events, and key concepts and have compiled an extensive searchable bibliographical database. Short summaries of the chapters in other volumes of the Globalization and Autonomy series can also be found in the *Compendium,* along with position papers and peer-reviewed research articles on globalization and autonomy issues.

Acknowledgments

THE EDITORS WOULD LIKE to express their immense gratitude to Nancy Johnson and Sonya Zikic, the project editors for the MCRI on Globalization and Autonomy, for their excellent work, support, and committed professionalism. We are also grateful to Jennifer Clark, Sara Mayo, and Cassandra Pohl for administrative support throughout the project. We also thank Emily Andrew and Melissa Pitts of UBC Press for their guidance and unfailingly good advice. William Coleman acknowledges that the research for his contributions to the book was undertaken, in part, thanks to funding from the Canada Research Chairs Program. Finally, the editors and volume authors would like to thank the peer reviewers of this book for their helpful and insightful comments and suggestions.

Unsettled Legitimacy

chapter 1

Introduction: Autonomy, Legitimacy, and Power in an Era of Globalization

Steven Bernstein and William D. Coleman

THIS VOLUME ADVANCES UNDERSTANDING of the relationship between globalization and autonomy by examining it through the lens of legitimacy. Its premise is that contemporary globalization has unsettled the often taken-for-granted acceptance of relationships of rule between governing authorities and individuals and communities, whether in local, national, regional, international, or global settings. This unsettling of legitimacy — by which we mean the justifications and acceptance of that relationship of authority — raises questions and challenges assumptions about the relationship between political authority, power, and political community around the world. Our focus is on the practices through which individuals and communities have attempted to develop, reconfigure, or recapture shared rule under conditions of globalization — and on what might make such rule acceptable and justified. Democratic theory and variations of democratic practices are but two possible sources of legitimate authority. Exploring the unsettling of legitimacy also opens up space for an interrogation of the discursive practices that have legitimated (or delegitimated) reconfigurations of authority, sometimes producing morally suspect, unequal, oppressive, or, in the extreme, violent orders. It likewise allows for forward-looking analyses of the orders that nascent discourses of globalization may legitimate.

The individual chapters in this book collectively analyze the forces of globalization that have disrupted or led to reconfigurations of political authority, and they warn of the dangers of moving in a direction that is increasingly taken in the contemporary world: legitimacy for a permanent state of exceptionalism that justifies a suspension of rights in the name of security. Simultaneously, the chapters' authors demonstrate the possibilities and constraints of preferred responses to the challenge. Although no single label can adequately encapsulate the full range of the responses in the pages that follow, a discernable set of findings did emerge that might best be described as a global form of *liberal internationalism,* with apologies for the term's irony in a global age. Although this overall response offers no radical critique of globalization, it is morally uncompromising. Some might even call it conservative. We live in an era when political legitimacy at multiple scales of authority is under strain, and globalization creates demands for regulation, security, and protection of rights and expressions of individual and collective autonomy within and across multiple political and geo-graphical spaces. Accordingly, the balance struck here is, arguably, both ap-propriate and reasonable.

In this regard, three broad findings emerge that are captured by the de-scriptor *global liberal internationalism.* First, the assertion of state authority remains necessary for individual and collective autonomy, though with an important caveat. Namely, in light of struggles for the renegotiation of sovereignty, we warn against new configurations of authority that threaten, even more than traditional configurations of state sovereignty now under strain, to undermine both individual and collective autonomy. Second, the growth of an autonomous, yet often disenfranchised and frustrated, global civil society will constitute a danger for new configurations and sites of political authority if it continues to lack adequate opportunities for effica-cious political action. These opportunities depend in large part on the willingness of interstate institutions, global public authorities, and global sites of private authority to engage in political discussions of key issues. Third, there is a need to take far more seriously twentieth-century liberal values, especially human rights and citizenship and expansive (rather than solely property rights-based) notions of rule of law, democracy, and other expressions of empowerment and self-rule. Globalization has not dimin-ished the need to protect these values in domestic constitutions — and the particular historical circumstances of insecurity that mark the early twenty-first century have only increased this need. Nevertheless, globalization's consequent disruption and reimagining of political community unsettles legitimacy, thereby increasingly necessitating the entrenchment of these values in interstate, transnational, or global institutions.

To be clear, if state sovereignty is understood as the exclusive jurisdiction over territorial spaces, these findings do not endorse it as the sole appropriate form of political authority. Other sites of authority are emerging, as a companion volume, *Global Ordering: Institutions and Autonomy in a Changing World* (Pauly and Coleman 2008), in this series suggests. States are increasingly called on to share their monopoly, in theory or in practice, on the protection or legitimate expression of autonomy. To the degree that states fail in an era of globalization to satisfy new legitimacy demands, renegotiations of political authority are necessary. The contributors, nonetheless, see value in renegotiating new forms of sovereignty that involve the state and the continued importance of the state and interstate cooperation to achieve public goods.

These themes are explored from multiple disciplinary, normative, and geographical vantage points. Underlying them all is the question of legitimacy as it bears on the relationship between autonomy and political authority. Two core questions are addressed in this regard. First, under globalization, how or why do individuals and communities accept commands directed at them, or that affect them, as legitimate? Second, from the vantage point of autonomy, how do individuals and communities retain or gain influence and control over local and non-local decisions that affect them? By extension, we are interested in how such expressions of autonomy permit individuals and collectivities to shape globalization itself. Underlying these questions is the quest to understand how globalization disrupts the ways autonomy is maintained or promoted in relation to political order. We begin, then, with the nature of the challenge posed by contemporary globalization to legitimate political order.

The Context: Globalization's Challenge to Political Authority

Contemporary globalization has, arguably, led to increased uncertainty and insecurity as the givens of the old international order — premised on the security of the state and the bounding of political communities and justice therein — appear to be under considerable strain (Devetek and Higgott 1999; Ruggie 2007). A long digression on the meaning of globalization is unnecessary in this context, especially since that meaning, as one of our contributors, Nisha Shah, puts it, is so wrapped up in our experience of it. Although the implications of globalization are far from certain — indeed, that is the question addressed by our larger project — the material and social forces associated with globalization are fairly uncontroversial. Rising

levels of transactions, communications, and flows and the growth in what
Jan Aart Scholte (2005) has described as transplanetary connections — particularly ones that are supraterritorial and, thus, less constrained by the territorial boundaries of states — have been well documented, despite large
swaths of humanity being left behind. In addition to the usual focus on the
economic and social dimensions of these processes, events of the last decade
direct our attention to the military and security aspects of globalization.
New debates about the reassertions and reconfigurations of sovereignty
exist side by side with discourses of what Heike Härting describes in this
volume as localized transnational wars. Although globalization may encompass an unequal, power-laden, and fractured set of processes, few would
dispute that its reach, even as felt by those who cannot directly participate
in it, continues to increase.

The two great motivators of political life, fear and hope, rise to the
surface in such times. A desire or demand for autonomy underlies both.
Fears of disorder, insecurity, loss of control, and domination motivate the
drive to legitimate power and order precisely to protect autonomy. At the
same time, hope may spur individuals and groups dissatisfied with the old
political order to take advantage of such changes to push for more control
over their destinies, resist domination or oppression, promote social justice,
and pursue the good life. These efforts reflect the hope that autonomy may
be enhanced as authority is reconfigured. Pursuit of autonomy, particularly
in its collective form, has a complex relationship with legitimacy, as we
discuss below. For example, the push for more collective autonomy by
some Québécois or some Scots is based, in part, on an argument that political decision making in Canada and the United Kingdom, respectively, is
not legitimate. Efforts to redefine or renegotiate the political community
of relevance for the exercise of collective autonomy represent challenges to
the basis of legitimacy. Similarly, when it comes to individual autonomy,
demands for rights by women, the poor, or practitioners of minority reli-
gions might challenge the basis for how collective autonomy is exercised if
they are not included in decision making. In short, in creating the openings for such renegotiations and questions, globalization rapidly expands
the scope of questioning of legitimacy.

The challenge, then, is how to promote security and order while, at a
minimum, preserving autonomy or, more ambitiously, creating opportunities for those seeking new forms of enhanced autonomy. More generally,
does the legitimization of power — the central problem of political order
at whatever level it falls — require the protection and enhancement of

autonomy; if so, what kind of autonomy, and for whom? This question turns attention to the political dimensions of legitimacy, our primary focus.

Core Concepts

Legitimacy

We define legitimacy as the acceptance and justification of shared rule by a community. This definition is overtly political, as opposed to legal or sociological. Thus, legitimacy is not the same as legality, being in accordance with a body of recognized law. Law may be a source of legitimacy, and legitimacy may be one important underpinning of law, but the two do not always coincide. As Inis Claude (1966, 369) noted in his landmark study of collective legitimation in international politics, the legitimacy of positive law "is sometimes the precise issue at stake in political controversy." Indeed, many of our contributors demonstrate how globalization unsettles the relationship between law and legitimacy, exposing tensions between them. They explore this tension through various prisms, including an assessment of challenges to an increasingly legalized world trading system (Ostry, this volume; see also Howse and Nicolaïdis 2001), an investigation of contradictions in the emerging human rights law on the "responsibility to protect" doctrine (Nyers, this volume), and a questioning of the legitimacy of sovereign states' exclusive authority to make laws (see, this volume, Keating, McGarry, and Moore; Sunday; Feit; and Pal; see also Kingsbury 2007 for a broader discussion).

Political legitimacy should also not be confused with the legitimacy of an organization or institution, the targets of interest for many sociological accounts. In that literature, the term *legitimacy* refers to a collective audience's shared belief, independent of particular observers, that "the actions of an entity are desirable, proper, or appropriate within some socially constructed system of norms, values, beliefs, and definitions" (Suchman 1995, 574). Still, sociological conceptions of legitimacy may point to important bases of political legitimacy. In particular, sociological understandings of legitimacy usefully highlight that legitimacy is rooted in a society or community in which the rule or institution operates. They also point to processes in which practices become institutionalized or accepted as "appropriate" by the community in an ongoing process of legitimization and delegitimization. From this perspective, rules constantly interact with the social purposes and goals of relevant audiences or communities.

A focus on political legitimacy, however, shifts attention to authority relationships that empower actors and institutions that participate in those relationships and construct governing institutions through their inter-actions. In other words, political legitimacy concerns relationships in which commands ought to be obeyed. It reflects "a more general support for a regime [or governance institution], which makes subjects willing to substitute the regime's decisions for their own evaluation of a situation" (Bodansky 1999, 602). Political legitimacy requires institutionalized au-thority (whether concentrated or diffuse), power resources to exercise rule, and shared norms among community members. These norms provide justifications and a shared understanding of what an acceptable or appro-priate governing institution, or political order, could look like; they pro-vide the boundaries for what it can and should do. Virtually all of our contributors, though they may draw from different scholarly traditions or root their analyses in different epistemologies, are concerned in some way with the acceptance (or rejection) of governance relationships and, thus, with political legitimacy.

With its emphasis on acceptance and justifications, our definition of political legitimacy self-consciously straddles the traditional divide be-tween empirical measures of legitimacy and normative theory. The former have their roots in Weberian social science and serve to guide investiga-tions of whether actors accept a rule or institution as authoritative. The latter asks whether the authority possesses legitimacy, a view best reflected in contemporary political theory by Habermas's position (1973, 97) that a belief in legitimacy is assumed to have an "immanent relation to truth." That position also underpins theories of deliberative democracy, which now dominate the normative literature on political legitim-acy. Melissa Williams, who best represents this position in this volume, understands legitimacy as "the justification of actions to those whom they affect, according to reasons they can accept" or, more generally, as being rooted in reciprocal justification. Our definition of legitimacy, thus, may not capture the position of all contributors. It does recognize, however, that, as a practical matter, arguments about why actors should accept a de-cision or rule as authoritative (as opposed to being coerced) necessarily include possible reasons why the decision is accepted and vice versa.

Our group of authors explicitly rejected pre-judging on what basis legitimacy under globalization does or should rest. In particular, they re-fused to frame the volume around questions of democracy, the usual start-ing point for scholarship on the prospects and possibilities of governance under globalization. David Held is the most prominent scholar who organizes his thinking in this way. His work on globalization begins with the premise that "democracy bestows an aura of legitimacy on modern political life: laws, rules, and policies appear justified when they are democratic" (Held 1995, 1). Although no contributor dismisses the legitimating power of democracy outright, many identify potential tensions between autonomy, democratic practice, and political legitimacy in contemporary and emerging configurations of political communities and authority. Consequently, the volume frames the question of what constitutes the most appropriate form of political life in terms of achieving political legitimacy rather than democracy.

Our empirical chapters, in particular, begin not with democratic, deliberative, or rights-based theories of legitimacy but with the Weberian questions: What basis of legitimacy holds sway in a particular society? How does a prevailing political order generate an intersubjective belief in its legitimacy (Connolly 1984, 18)? And how is globalization unsettling these bases and associated beliefs? Even our theoretical chapters point to ways in which globalization opens up debate about what notion of autonomy ought to provide the basis for legitimate political order. Moreover, by complicating who counts as a citizen, or by forcing the renegotiation of the boundaries of relevant political communities, globalization forces us to pay attention to how the different audiences of states, global civil society, or marketplace actors may share different criteria or weightings of the elements of legitimacy that justify political domination. For example, some global civil society actors may highly value accountability, participation, transparency, and equity, whereas global corporations concerned with governance may give priority to the rule of law and fairness in the marketplace. In another context, a minority national community may base its understanding of legitimacy on protection of collective identities as much as on individual autonomy. In contrast, discourses of rights, global environmental stewardship, or traditional knowledge may play different legitimating roles in different local contexts, as the chapters by Tara Goetze and Harvey Feit suggest. There is no abstract mix of procedural, substantive, or performance criteria of legitimacy that can be known to produce legitimacy outside the context of particular political communities.

A loose analogy can be drawn between how globalization introduces these new problems of political legitimacy in global policy domains and how the expansion of the welfare state (into more and more areas of economic and social life) shifted the debate about political legitimacy domestically after the Second World War. According to Connolly (1984, 13), who is commenting on Habermas (1973), that expansion "enhance[d] the visibility of the conventional and political dimension of social life and encourage[d] citizens to ask the state to legitimize the particular conventions supported by its action." Similarly, as economic and cultural relationships become more transplanetary and supraterritorial and, thus, less "contained" by the boundaries of nation-states, a mismatch develops between some facets of the exercise of authority and these economic and cultural relationships. In the words of Reinicke (1998, 64), "Whereas the political geography that defines markets continues to be structured by mutual exclusion, the economic geography on the basis of which these markets function has become increasingly inclusive, defying the territorially fixed nature of the nation-state by creating non-territorial space." States increasingly seek to address the mismatch between economic processes and the territorial limits to the exercise of political authority by pooling sovereignty. In cases where they are unwilling or unable to do so, they often allow regulatory authority to shift to private or networked forms of governance in the marketplace. In sum, increased economic and cultural interdependence between states undermines the congruence between the people being governed and their supposed governors, thus unsettling legitimacy (Scharpf 1998, 5).

John Ruggie (2003a, 94) nicely sums up the problem of governance that results for international institutions designed for an earlier era and premised on states' capacities to intervene in their own economies to ensure social stability. These institutions, especially the economic institutions most frequently targeted by global justice protests, "presupposed an *international* world" and "the existence of *national* economies, engaged in external transactions, conducted at *arms length,* which governments could mediate at the *border* by tariffs and exchange rates, among other tools. The globalization of financial markets and production chains, however, challenges each of these premises and threatens to leave behind merely national social bargains." Consequently, institutions that operated largely invisibly in an international system now face increasing scrutiny — some might even say a legitimacy crisis — in a more global system in which they appear more authoritative to ordinary citizens. In addition to nation-state governments, civil society now looks to these institutions to provide social justice, equity, ecological integrity, and other societal values, not just functional goals such as financial stability (Devetak and Higgott 1999, 483; Smith, this volume).

Whether increased authority flows to existing international organizations or to new ordering institutions that operate partially or independently from states, the growing significance of the sites of authority involved can further circumscribe the individual autonomy of citizens by limiting their ability to contribute to decision making. This erosion can truncate the range of agency of citizens, thereby undermining notions of popular sovereignty associated with legitimacy. To the extent that the demands of citizens have difficulty entering the political processes that most affect their lives, the legitimacy of the authorities making such decisions comes into question. Notions of accountability associated with legitimacy include the idea that political leaders will explain to citizens how their actions have addressed the wants and preferences of "the people." The fact that the participants in sites of authority beyond the state frequently do not represent the full range of populations affected by their decisions compounds the problem of accountability. Again, the problem of defining the appropriate boundaries of political communities arises. If legitimacy always rests on shared acceptance of rules and justificatory norms recognized by the relevant community, defining membership in the given community becomes central. As globalization forces the renegotiation of community boundaries and memberships, issues of identification of community members and what share of norms of appropriateness must be present become central concerns. These issues are the focus of another volume in this series, *Renegotiating Community: Interdisciplinary Perspectives, Global Contexts* (Brydon and Coleman 2008). As these negotiations take place, long-standing rules and norms come into question, thereby unsettling how legitimacy is achieved.

Autonomy

In the Globalization and Autonomy project, researchers have worked with concepts of both individual and collective autonomy. These two notions of autonomy became increasingly common with the onset of modernity. The idea of the pure freedom of the individual based on her or his "natural" quality grew out of a rejection of the oppressiveness of medieval institutions in Europe. Gradually, there developed the idea that individuals (originally, propertied males) had the right to choose their own way of living, to decide which convictions they wished to promote, and to take steps to shape their own lives (Taylor 1991, 2). Notions of individual autonomy came to be understood as complementary to collective autonomy in the sense that, in modern societies, individuals decide on the rules and forms through which they will be governed.

Modern theories of democracy postulate that when decisions arise from the exercise of collective autonomy by individuals who themselves possess individual autonomy, they are highly likely to be accepted and, thus, legitimate. The exercise of collective autonomy is anchored by the condition that all members of a given political community have an equal right to participate in decision making. How they exercise that right will vary from person to person as each exercises her or his individual autonomy. As Habermas (1996, 130) writes: "Communicative and participatory rights must be formulated in a language that leaves it up to autonomous legal subjects whether, and if necessary, how they want to make use of such rights." Individual autonomy provides "a protective cover for the individual's ethical freedom to pursue his own existential life project or ... his current conception of the good" (ibid., 451). As long as they have this individual autonomy — and, thus, the capacity to shape collective decisions — these decisions are likely to be accepted. Securing legitimacy is facilitated by a sense of political community, cultivated and developed in a state.

Habermas (1996, 122), in these respects, sees collective autonomy and individual autonomy as co-original: together they form the basis of democracy and, thus, of legitimacy. "The idea of self-legislation *by citizens,* that is, requires that those subject to law as its addressees can at the same time understand themselves as authors of law" (ibid., 120). This co-originality, however, rests on certain conditions. The decisions are located in "a geographically delimited legal territory and to a socially delimitable collectivity of legal consociates, and consequently to particular jurisdictional boundaries. These limitations in historical time and social space result simply from the fact that legal subjects cede their authorizations to use coercion to a legal authority that monopolizes the means of legitimate coercion and if necessary employs these means on their behalf" (ibid., 124). And behind this reasoning is a further assumption: the given polity, in turn, makes the primary decisions for the members of that community.

Although these understandings of individual and collective autonomy are common in democratic theory, they are often challenged outside that body of theory. Feminists have argued that individual autonomy thus conceived reflects the dominance of social structures that favour the self-reliant male. They also note the powerful association between this conception of individual autonomy and neoliberal thinking (Code 2000). Some advocate for the adoption of a conception of relational autonomy: autonomy emerges through the social relationships between persons. Relational autonomy is the focus of another volume in this series, *Indigenous Peoples and Autonomy: Insights for a Global Age,* which addresses the research problematic of the project through the experiences and thought of indigenous peoples (Blaser, de Costa, McGregor, and Coleman, under review). This understanding of autonomy is also addressed in chapters in this volume by Goetze, Feit, and Smith.

Finally, although cast as universal ideas, these notions of autonomy generate considerable *friction,* to use Tsing's (2005) term, when introduced into many societies with cultures that have colonial histories and have resisted Euro-American domination. In these societies, struggles over autonomy, democracy, and legitimacy can take different forms, particularly when contextualized in formerly colonial and subsequently neo-imperial structures. These struggles and their implications for autonomy are examined in more depth in another volume in this series: *Deux Méditerranées: Les voies de la mondialisation et de l'autonomie* (Essid and Coleman, under review).

Challenges from the intensified globalization of the past three decades to the ideal relationships in democratic theory between individual autonomy, collective autonomy, political community, and legitimacy occur in several ways. First, there is a growing disjuncture between the legal territorial reach of nation-states and the world economy. The internationalization of production in some sectors and the rapid expansion of fully global financial markets reduce the capacity of most states to manage their own domestic economies in ways they had practised in the latter half of the twentieth century. In this respect, the collective autonomy of states is reduced, which may undermine, in turn, the willingness of citizens to support them and accept their decisions.

Second, companion processes of political globalization in the form of international laws and norms recognize the rights of individuals and, thus, open up spaces for the expression of individual autonomy, which is no longer constrained so fully by state sovereignty. For example, the core principles of the International Criminal Court (ICC) recognize that persons in their individual capacities are accountable for their actions to humanity and are no longer sheltered by state sovereignty. Thus, any political leader can be held personally accountable for any crimes committed within the jurisdiction of the court. Any citizen of any state has a right to call any leader to account for alleged crimes if her or his own state fails to do so. Admittedly, the ICC is a particularly strong example of how the co-originality of individual and collective autonomy can be pulled apart by globalizing processes. (Although even in this case limits still appear in practice, not least the ongoing resistance of major powers, including the United States and China, to allow their citizens to be subject to the ICC's jurisdiction.) Nonetheless, other examples in international law are also available (Held 1995, 101-7). Under these kinds of processes, for example, women in a country like Pakistan might imagine and even act on the idea that denials of basic rights in practices like honour killings are an infringement of individual autonomy as defined in international law and norms. In such instances, the heteronomy arising from an authoritarian state can be challenged in global sites of authority on legitimacy grounds through claims to individual autonomy formulated on the basis of international laws and norms.

Third, the emergence of regional and global sites of authority adds complexity to the process of securing acceptance for political decisions. Legitimacy is a question of the mutuality of individual and collective autonomy within the nation-state, but it also extends beyond the nation-state to sites like the World Trade Organization (WTO), the World Health Organization, and the European Union (EU). If these supranational sites of authority work in ways that do not permit individuals affected by their decisions to have a sense of being *authors of law,* to use Habermas's term, legitimacy may be undermined. Notably, Habermas has recognized this disjuncture even in the case of the EU. As he put it in 1990, "the democratic processes constituted at the level of the nation-state lag hopelessly behind the economic integration taking place at a supranational level" (Habermas 1996, Appendix 2, 491). Some even suggest that these supranational sites of authority, along with the body of law they administer, are creating an external constitution to the state that removes its decisions from the realm of politics and accountability; others dispute this contention, even in the most cited example of the WTO (compare Clarkson 2008 and Howse and Nicolaïdis 2001 to Dunoff 2006). What is less in dispute, however, is that any move to do so would be self-defeating, precisely because it would provoke a debate on the normative justifications and empirical legitimacy of a constitutional vision, which only a political debate could address (Dunoff 2006, 665). Legitimacy problems of this sort are independent of left-right debates, such as those over global neoliberalism. The danger of constitutionalization in the absence of mechanisms to produce political legitimacy is equally strong whether one wishes to constitutionalize a right to trade, institutionalize judicial review, or incorporate human rights into trade law.

Fourth, as the collective autonomy of states shrinks in a relative sense, individuals often come to identify with political communities that cross territorial boundaries, such as global communities of women, as the Pakistan example above suggests. Changes in identification with communities can then give rise to questions about the decisions of states and, thus, their legitimacy. Parallel processes take place within states as well. Cultural minorities might seek more collective autonomy in an attempt to widen the space in which individual autonomy by their members can be exercised. Julie Sunday's discussion of Hungarians in Romania in this volume and the analysis of such minorities more broadly in Europe by Michael Keating, John McGarry, and Margaret Moore outline these processes and note the challenges they imply for legitimacy within the nation-state.

These illustrations of the challenge to the logical interconnection of individual autonomy, collective autonomy, political community, and legitimacy as outlined by Habermas, among others, raise a final question. Is globalization likely to reproduce analogous interconnections on a global scale, or will these interconnections take rather different forms as globalization proceeds? Habermas's own position is closer to the former. He sees the need to reproduce a *demos* — that is, the "popular unit that exercises political rights" (Cederman 2001, 144) — that consists of a people sharing certain political, and perhaps cultural, norms at levels beyond the nation-state. Legitimacy also requires the functional equivalents of the institutions that he argues are necessary to recognize co-originality of individual and collective autonomy. For example, he has written that a European constitution voted on through referendum could catalyze "the emergence of a European civil society; the construction of a European-wide public sphere; and the shaping of a political culture that can be shared by all" (Habermas 2001a, 16-17; 2001b, 89-103). However, as we note below, the failure so far to gain popular support for a European constitution suggests that the challenges globalization poses to the ideal of co-originality may not be so easily resolved. Others, too, have commented on the challenge of creating a demos beyond the state, even in Europe, the most likely case for its appearance (e.g., Cederman 2001). The difficulty of this challenge does not mean collective autonomy beyond the nation-state is impossible (see, especially, Melissa Williams's chapter, this volume). Most of our contributors suggest, however, that it will occur not as a replacement of collective autonomy in the state but in new arrangements in which the relationships between individual autonomy, collective autonomy, and legitimacy are much messier (we borrow this descriptor from Harvey Feit's chapter in this volume) than the ideal of co-originality suggested in Habermas's political writings.

Power

How the relationship between political legitimacy and autonomy under globalization is worked out in practice is intimately connected to questions of power. In the most direct sense, political legitimacy, following Max Weber (1978, 953), relates to the justification of power in the form of authority, domination, or both. Although much of liberal political philosophy has been concerned with limiting power — especially the arbitrary exercise of coercion by the state — all political orders require power. And any exercise of power has potential implications for autonomy. The question of power, thus, has two facets: what requirements does globalization create for its exercise to be legitimate, and what is power legitimating under globalization? Put another way, how are particular orders legitimated over others, and what are the implications for individual and collective autonomy?

Our contributors employ at least two different understandings of power to address these questions. The first conceives of power as relational and rooted in material or ideational resources of actors or institutions to produce control or desired effects. Within this conception of power, themes of empowerment, ownership, and capacity emerge as the crucial links from autonomy to legitimate authority. Two chapters on the African experience of globalization offer the clearest illustrations of these linkages. In one, African elites interviewed by Rhoda Howard-Hassmann perceived globalization as a form of heteronomy, as a foreign imposition, and as a continuation of a history of exploitation dating back to colonization. The problem identified was usually not the power of global markets per se, which is potentially empowering; rather, interviewees pointed to a lack of autonomy — owing primarily to having to devote limited material resources and expertise in international forums when they were strongly needed domestically — to engage and shape global markets and political processes.

Howard-Hassmann, thus, describes Africa as being "missing" under globalization. Sylvia Ostry, using similar terminology, notes the missing cases of African disputes at the WTO. Ostry shows the ironic consequences of the legalization of the trade regime, which was supposed to level the international playing field and improve fairness compared to the system under the General Agreement on Tariffs and Trade (GATT). Instead, legalization increased corporate influence and the intrusiveness of international regulation in domestic governance, and it masked the underlying use of power capabilities by those states that possess them to achieve trade goals at the expense of weaker states. Legalization cannot produce legitimacy when many poorer state members are unable to fully participate in negotiations and African cases are conspicuously absent in the dispute settlement system. The problem is not simply material resources — though they are important — but also a significant gap in technical knowledge, lack of functioning institutions in which to generate policy domestically or transnationally, and weak legal infrastructure (Ostry, this volume; see also Adler and Bernstein 2005).

It would be easy to conclude from these analyses that global markets, universal norms of human rights promoted by the West, or the rule of law is to blame for Africa being missing from globalization. Howard-Hassmann and Ostry explicitly disavow such a position. Autonomy provides the missing link between globalization and empowerment. This empowerment requires, however, a real commitment to help Africans develop their own institutional capacity and ability to engage in decision making and participate, adapt, develop, and take ownership of these values in accordance with their own needs and experience. Taken together, these two chapters suggest that, at least in the African context, autonomy at multiple levels (individual, state, and perhaps even continental) is closely linked. As Howard-Hassmann puts it, "Continental autonomy is not possible without national legitimacy. National legitimacy in Africa, as elsewhere, rests on the capacity to create efficient, rule-bound, law-abiding democratic governments that can fairly deliver needed goods to their citizens. This capacity is crucial to Africa's ability to negotiate as a regional body on the global scene."

The actual practices of many international institutions, however, militate against the development of this type of autonomy. As Ostry put it in reference to trade negotiations during one of our workshops, there are two kinds of autonomy: the autonomy of the United States and the autonomy of the rest of world. In other words, the powerful have the luxury of protecting and defining their autonomy and sovereignty in ways they may not themselves accept when it comes to other states. Les Pal's chapter on governance of the Internet observes a similar pattern. The United States, he notes, gave up nothing at the 2005 World Summit on the Information Society, a result that thrilled US Ambassador David Gross (Washington File 2005). The outcome preserved the unique role of the United States government in ensuring the reliability and stability of the Internet. Pal questions whether such a situation is sustainable given its questionable legitimacy because the broader international community lacks a significant policy input.

A second conception of power presented in this volume views it as being productive of individuals' identities and practices (Foucault 1991; Barnett and Duvall 2005, 20-22). This conception resonates with Michel Foucault's (1991) notion of governmentality, the idea that disciplines or epistemes — the background knowledge that passes "the command structure into the very constitution of the individual" — extend into sites of authority, thereby empowering and legitimating them (Douglas 1999, 138). Accordingly, new sites of authority extend a process of diffusion and internalization of epistemes often associated with globalization — such as globalism, competitiveness, self-motivation, rapidity, agility, and so on — beyond the state (ibid., 152). Legitimacy is explicitly linked to power in terms of how background normative, ideological, technical, and scientific understandings produce specific modes of behaviour and interaction (Foucault 1991).

In this volume, Harvey Feit's account of the evolution of co-governance between the indigenous James Bay Cree Nation and various levels of state governance in Canada most directly shows productive power in practice under globalization. He traces dominant discourses associated with globalizing periods — first development and then neoliberalism — and the way they constituted and influenced practices of co-governance. These practices centred on partnerships between the Crees and the state that involved often "messy" arrangements among nested collective autonomies. The power of these discourses is profound. Thus, Feit sees neoliberal co-governance as a vision and a practice rooted in the universality of markets to shape governance and lives; he adds that it obscures the possibility of relationships with people and lands that are not encompassed by the market. In these respects, neoliberalism dehistoricized co-governance, which opened the way to overriding the Crees' collective autonomy and misunderstanding their subjectivity when it comes to those lived experiences that express the Cree way of life. There is nothing in co-governance itself that makes this outcome inevitable — it is but a mechanism. It is the productive power of market discourse, through its enabling and shaping of understandings of legitimate possibilities for co-governance, that structures the particular form partnerships of autonomy might take.

A focus on productive power, however, risks degenerating into a position that all legitimation must be resisted because authority in all guises is always a mode of normalization (Beiner 1995). Feit, conscious of this risk, assesses the indeterminacy of globalization rather than assuming it automatically produces a need for resistance. In particular, he notes that although neoliberal discourse disrupted earlier autonomy partnerships at the local level, it simultaneously provided new openings for the Crees to re-establish some co-governance by working directly with corporate institutions involved in resource development. Thus, the Crees were able to construct new avenues for political agency. These accomplishments came at the end of a period of global activism involving alliances with environmental organizations to put pressure on American investors in the major hydroelectric development project at James Bay (Bergeron, under review). These alliances led to political action in New York State (a potentially important investor and future customer) and at the Permanent Forum on Indigenous Issues at the UN, where they drew on discourses on indigenous and human rights to gain legitimacy for their claims to co-governance in Quebec.

Tara Goetze's chapter on natural resource management in Belize similarly illustrates the power, yet ambiguous influence, of another intersecting set of globalizing discourses: global conservation management and empowerment. The empowerment discourse includes norms of access to information, participation, accountability, and support for local organizational capacity. In other words, it is potentially a discourse of collective autonomy. In practice, however, these discourses undermined local power and autonomy by defining externally how and which marine resources were to be conserved and how these resources were to be "managed." At the same time, these discourses supported the creation of a locally based conservation non-governmental organization (NGO) that included active participation from community members in order to co-manage marine resources with the state. The design of the conservation NGO, it was hoped, would reduce friction caused by the external imposition of conservation norms and would introduce competing knowledge claims and justifications of alternative practices by scientists and local communities. Even as the empowerment discourse permitted the reconstitution of collective autonomy for local fishers, it had the ironic consequence of constructing them as powerless, as in need of external help, and often ignored their traditional local knowledge. The case study, therefore, shows how globalizing discourses directly empower new actors, but with complex consequences for the legitimacy and authority of the state and local communities.

Goetze's chapter highlights that although scholars in the Foucauldian tradition have often focused on how globalization is linked closely to a neoliberal economic discourse, we need not pre-judge the epistemic underpinning of globalization to see productive power at work as a legitimizing force. In this volume, Nisha Shah takes this insight the furthest, arguing that legitimacy is a discursive property embedded in the metaphors that constitute political communities and political authority. Which metaphor of globalization dominates is not preordained. Instead, she argues that different interpretations of globalization will produce different norms, promote different governing institutions, and advocate different policies, motivating certain types of political activity while excluding others. Using Rorty's (1989, 1991) idea of redescription, she argues that metaphors of globalization can redescribe and, therefore, transform institutions and political communities by specifying new legitimating principles.

The Volume: Putting the Pieces Together

Every chapter in this volume explores ways in which globalization unsettles knowledge about how legitimacy, autonomy, political community, and power are related. In an earlier era, that relationship was understood axiomatically for both domestic and international politics: the legitimacy of the liberal state rested on the choices of autonomous individuals; the liberal international order rested on the autonomy of states. Liberal international theory understood sovereign states as being the repositories of collective autonomy, because states bounded political communities. International legitimacy could, at most, reflect processes of collective legitimization by states, which were facilitated by institutions such as the United Nations that served a function of legitimating collective decision making (Claude 1966). Individual autonomy simply had no place in theories of international politics.

In this section we work through the organization of the volume to see how various authors understand the disruptive and reconstitutive impact of globalization on that settled knowledge. We begin, however, with a longer discussion of Peter Nyers' chapter on the new doctrine of responsibility to protect (R2P). Endorsed by the UN General Assembly, the doctrine essentially says that the international community has a right to intervene to protect individuals and communities when their state fails to act (or is complicit) in the face of gross human rights violations. It serves as an excellent entry point to bring together a number of themes raised above.

Nyers' chapter addresses how a new practice associated with globalization may undermine long-standing assumptions about the co-originality of individual and collective autonomy. He asks: "Can the autonomy of states be defied in the name of protecting the autonomy of individuals whose lives are at risk?" The R2P doctrine answers in the affirmative. It reflects an extension of liberal values and the internationalizing of the liberal constitutional basis of the state rooted in a notion of individual human rights. Its operationalization — though whether it will ever be implemented is an open question — throws into sharp relief the dilemma of how to reconcile a cosmopolitan notion of individual autonomy anchored in human rights that trump state sovereignty (and, thus, collective autonomy) with governing institutions that derive their authority from sovereign states.

Cosmopolitan in outlook, the doctrine's justifications have deep roots in the natural law tradition, which posits the sovereignty of the individual as the basis of all political order. These justifications implicitly depart, however, from that tradition in one important respect: cosmopolitan conceptions of the international, beginning with Kant, never, until now, extended those rights to grant an expression of collective autonomy beyond the state. Only in the context of globalization is there a notion that the sovereignty of individuals can be given over not only to the state, in order to provide the security necessary for individual autonomy, but also to sites of authority beyond the state.[1] Indeed, the mechanics and limitations of transferring sovereignty to other sites is a central preoccupation of the new cosmopolitan literature on democratic legitimacy. It views that problem as one of shortening the chains of delegation (Keohane and Nye 2001, 276) or creating new political communities unbounded by politically defined territorial borders, as if the state were but one forum for the exercise of collective autonomy. Much of that literature turned to an examination of pragmatic or constitutive features of democracy, not ontological questions of sovereignty and statehood. Thus, many discussions in the globalization literature focus on how to re-create the elements of democracy that legitimize rule, such as accountability to multiple, overlapping, or disconnected spaces of authority, as if the state held no privileged position.

The R2P doctrine falls far short, however, of the new cosmopolitanism that globalization supposedly enables. Like global cosmopolitanism, the doctrine focuses on the elements of political liberalism that legitimize political authority; unlike it, it reifies the state as the sole location of political community. The R2P doctrine simply reframes the basis of state legitimacy by stating that it does not automatically flow from individual to state sovereignty but is conditional on the state — and only the state — providing internal security and protecting autonomy. Reifying the state in this way closes off, unjustifiably, opportunities to recognize wider notions of global citizenship that are worthy of protection. The idea that liberalism entails a duty to protect individuals as bearers of rights has a long lineage, but there is nothing inherent in the liberal concept of citizenship that privileges the state in doing so (Williams, this volume).

Normative Foundations

This insight is at the core of Melissa Williams's chapter on citizenship under globalization, which leads off the volume's first section on the normative foundations of globalization and autonomy. She argues that globalization opens up space to disaggregate notions of citizenship, from which the idea of public autonomy as self-protection (as well as self-rule) stems.[2] Even if the requirements to achieve public autonomy as self-protection are high — for Williams they include the creation of institutional structures capable of securing the rule of law, the legitimate authorization of decision makers by the community, and the accountability of decision makers to the community — we can imagine new political communities under globalization emerging to produce these conditions. Although states certainly *can* continue to serve this function, Williams's argument challenges the position that *only* the state can be a site of citizenship.

This argument has implications for new humanitarian practices under globalization, including the R2P doctrine. The greatest limitation of this doctrine may be its failure to acknowledge that nothing inherent in its normative underpinnings limits the protection of citizenship to political communities that happen to coincide with state boundaries. The failure to move beyond a state-centric understanding of citizenship is compounded by the endorsement of a state-centric mechanism of protection. The doctrine privileges the UN Security Council, which is itself facing legitimacy problems, to make judgments about when rights are violated. Even setting aside that the Security Council reflects power asymmetries, its authority is explicitly based on the autonomy and sovereignty of states. Thus, states, as Nyers points out, retain their sovereign right to grant exceptions. The irony is that while the basis of exceptions may change — the doctrine takes the perspective of victims of "conscience-shocking" human rights violations — it explicitly rejects any movement of the authority to judge and decide to a new form of governance that would diminish the sovereign rights of states. The old political order is put in the position of implementing a new order designed, at least *potentially,* to undermine its own basis of legitimacy as the ultimate guardian of international order and governance. The attempt to shift the justificatory discourse to a new understanding of legitimacy, however, is made in the absence of any support for a new institutional mechanism to reflect the necessary reconfiguration of authority to implement the new doctrine. Even more troubling, the doctrine's practical effect is to reinforce the autonomy of the most powerful states — permanent members of the Security Council — while the autonomy of weak states is undermined. As Nyers notes, the doctrine involves the globalization of the autonomy of some states in the name of protecting the autonomy of individuals in others.

The practical lesson is that globalization is properly seen as potentially reconstitutive of relations between individual and collective autonomy, but with an indeterminate, and at times ironic, trajectory. In this regard, the three chapters on theory emphasize that new political orders are constructed, not preordained. Depending on how that construction unfolds under globalization, and depending on the understandings of autonomy and legitimacy that underlie those constructions, very different political orders, and justifications for those orders, can arise. Nisha Shah's and Ian Cooper's chapters explore alternative possibilities for these constructions.

Although they come from different theoretical traditions, Shah and Cooper each identify two alternative understandings of the relationship between globalization and autonomy that have the potential to produce (in Shah's case) or justify (in Cooper's case) different worlds. Cooper's analysis directly maps onto the potential tension between individual and collective autonomy addressed in the liberal-communitarian debate among political theorists. Globalization, he argues, forces that debate — with one side rooted fundamentally in individual autonomy and the other in collective autonomy — to the global level. For Shah, alternative metaphors of globalization produce a similar distinction: cosmopolis invokes individual autonomy; empire and its mirror image, multitude, invoke forms of collective autonomy, or heteronomy, depending on how they become manifest in history. Shah's point is that these metaphors of globalization inform the discourses of legitimacy that emerge as one or the other metaphor gains dominance.

These two formulations of the relationship between globalization and autonomy do not superimpose on each other exactly. Rather, they make a similar point about the potentially elemental significance of starting from different understandings of autonomy and the normative theory (Cooper) or legitimating discourse (Shah) that emerges. Cooper is interested in normative justifications and the appropriate location and relations of authority under multi-level systems of governance; Shah's focus is on language and the productive power of metaphors to potentially constitute new bases of legitimation for political authority, at whatever level it occurs. Moving from theory to practice, Cooper's elemental distinction does not foreclose the possibility that actual practices of legitimation are highly contingent on dominant metaphors and the discourses they generate.

Legitimacy: Accommodating Difference and Autonomy

The practical implications of how globalization exposes, but does not resolve, tensions created by conceptions of legitimacy rooted in different understandings of autonomy are explored most directly in two chapters on the challenge of minority nationalism in Europe (see Keating, McGarry, and Moore; Sunday). These chapters are grouped with those of Feit and Goetze because they also explore the effects of the complex interplay of globalizing forces on minority political communities. In all cases, the authors find that globalization disrupts the autonomy of minority communities *and* provides new avenues of political expression.

Regional institutions like the EU promise support for limited expressions of national autonomy by cultural minorities. Simultaneously, they send an ambiguous, even contradictory, message about the legitimacy of territorial sovereignty. On the one hand, their support of political liberalism in the form of a universal notion of individual rights and economic liberalism erodes, pools, or disaggregates state sovereignty (the outcome that applies depends on how one understands the operationalization of EU integration). Moreover, practices of integration enable non-territorial or transnational expressions of national autonomy in new political spaces only imaginable through EU institutions. Indeed, the EU has sponsored initiatives that have encouraged mechanisms such as cross-border partnerships in which national minorities exist in regions that overlap more than one state. On the other hand, the EU formally supports the territorial autonomy and integrity of existing states — except where secession is a fait accompli — over any claims of minority nationalities to their own territories. In sum, simple dichotomies that favour either individual or collective autonomies do not exist; rather, complex, and sometimes competing, interactions of legitimating discourses and practices that disrupt settled understandings of the relationship between them do.

Williams's chapter provides a theoretical basis to understand how notions of citizenship might adapt to these multiple and overlapping identities, just as political institutions have adapted to multi-tiered governance. For Williams, citizenship stems from political communities wherever they are found, even if institutions are ultimately needed to grant the protection of autonomy that citizenship requires. She borrows and expands on David Held's notion of "a community of shared fate" as being what defines the boundaries of community. This notion, she argues, applies equally well to the state as it does to the new imagined communities enabled by globalization. Political communities are constructed through two forms of political agency: imagining a set of human beings as socially related to one another in the past and the future and claims that the terms of the relationship should be subject to standards of a common good, including the fundamental good of legitimacy as reciprocal justification. Whereas public autonomy is explicitly expressed through forms of self-legislation for conceptions of citizenship rooted in the state, citizenships of globalization do not presuppose that total self-sovereignty is or can be the ultimate aim of democratic agency. Rather, Williams stresses, just as the functions of sovereignty can be disaggregated or parcelled out, so too can the functions of citizenship, which can be expressed within "multiple and overlapping communities of fate."

The chapters on minority nationalism, however, show that globalization does not provide ready-made solutions for how to translate new understandings and claims of citizenship in practice. This aspect of globalization is true even in Europe, where the institutional conditions for citizenship beyond traditional state boundaries are the most highly developed. European citizenship is, at most, a work in progress, with many signs that significant roadblocks and detours will continue to mark the journey. The failure of the draft European constitution — which Keating, McGarry, and Moore note is state-centric in any case — illustrates the challenge. Like the other chapters in this section, their analysis highlights that globalization catalyzes, and in some cases forces to the surface, the need to renegotiate collective autonomy with majorities and state institutions. This observation suggests again that processes of globalization interact with political agency to produce outcomes — and that legitimacy can be achieved only through those interactions.

Autonomy and the Legitimation of Violence

How violence is legitimated under globalization cannot be ignored in any project focused on autonomy and globalization. Like other contributions, the two chapters in this section — Peter Nyers on the R2P doctrine and Heike Härting on narratives of localized transnational wars — focus on disruptions to political order. Unlike the rest of the volume, however, they are specifically concerned with violent disruptions and the justificatory discourse that can legitimate violence — whether for ostensibly noble or less noble ends — as globalization proceeds. Whereas Nyers focuses on a doctrine that only globalization could produce, Härting turns global humanitarian discourse on its head by showing how it can add new justifications for ongoing atrocities that have their roots in the past, usually colonial systems of domination. Nyers flips the usual question posed by doctrines of humanitarian intervention. Instead of only asking the question, who has the responsibility to limit global violence? he also asks how is violence in the name of global norms legitimated?

In showing the ironies and contradictions in global humanitarianism, both chapters are especially adept at revealing how discourses of globalization embody and reflect power. Härting does so through an exploration of the productive power of narratives in legitimizing localized transnational wars. She is interested in how the mobilization and production of perceived cultural differences legitimates forms of extreme violence. This violence removes any possibility of individual autonomy and severely restricts any expression of collective autonomy. Like Nyers, Härting finds that contemporary practices of global protection, including those endorsed by R2P, limit collective autonomy. They serve the interests of powerful countries rather than those seeking protection, while overriding the sovereignty of targeted countries in patterns continuous with colonialism. She uses a short story about communal conflict in Sri Lanka to illustrate her argument. She shows that these legitimating narratives in the current context of globalization can justify the extreme violence of global communal warfare by defining its purpose in humanitarian terms. While globalization is not a cause — enactments of localized transnational war are better understood in terms of historical continuities of practices dating at least from colonialism — discourses associated with globalization "produce cumulative effects" (Balibar 2004, 126). Consistent with Shah's understanding of metaphorical redescription, however, literary fiction writing also has the potential to delegitimize existing discourses and to suggest paths towards new narratives. Read together, however, these two chapters suggest that new narratives rarely arise completely dissociated from older discourses and the power relationships that sustained them.

Legitimacy and Autonomy on the Global and Regional Scale

The final section of the volume investigates attempts to build legitimate global and regional governance institutions. It also addresses the resistance provoked when these attempts appear to threaten individual and collective autonomy at multiple levels or when they lose their connection to appropriate collective autonomies, which are the basis of their legitimacy.

The WTO is often cited as the prototypical example of an institution that faces a legitimacy crisis for both reasons. On the first count, critics claim that its rules threaten the autonomy of states subject to its disciplines because they require significant changes to domestic institutional, legal, and regulatory systems. As Sylvia Ostry points out, these new disciplines mark a significant shift in the trade regime. In effect, the trading system was transformed from the negative regulation of the GATT (what governments must not do) to positive regulation (what governments must do). On the second count, critics argue that the legalization and judicialization of the trade regime removes the WTO's most controversial decisions from the political domain and, thus, from their legitimate basis in state-based collective autonomy.

Even if politics continue to play an important role, the chapters by Ostry and Rhoda Howard-Hassmann convincingly show that many smaller developing economies, especially in Africa, lack the necessary autonomy to participate in the rule making and adjudication processes that affect them. Without the ability to participate fully in either political or legal processes, these states lack a sense of ownership required to overcome legitimacy deficits. To the degree that these deficits make the trade system as a whole appear unfair, they can fuel a broader crisis of legitimacy beyond those specifically disadvantaged states. Ostry's analysis suggests that the existing emphasis in the WTO on improving technical capacity for implementation is unlikely to increase a sense of ownership and improve fairness. Thus, she proposes that, in addition to those mechanisms, the WTO should support mechanisms to improve knowledge, consensus building, policy development, and the ability to participate and engage in the dispute resolution process and political debate and negotiations. Like Howard-Hassmann's conclusions noted earlier, Ostry's proposals put the emphasis squarely on strengthening domestic and international mechanisms that increase state autonomy as a starting point for building the legitimacy of international institutions. Both authors, however, also note significant obstacles to quick progress in these areas.

With their emphasis on autonomy and engagement with the state, the chapters in this section also depart from conventional wisdom in the global democracy literature, which pins much of the hope for improved legitimacy on efforts to engage global civil society directly (e.g., Scholte 2007). Instead, our contributors find that the answer lies in opening up avenues for members to engage with states — domestically and in multilateral settings — since states remain privileged as legitimate public authorities. Even Jackie Smith, who notes the suspicion with which the global justice movement views public authorities, argues that engagement with states and interstate institutions is necessary to democratize the global system. Observing the divisions in social movements associated with globalization, she fears that without such engagement the rejectionists, who hail from the extreme left *and* right, will gain the upper hand. The consequences are potentially disruptive to global democracy and governance, and they show signs of becoming increasingly violent. In other words, satisfying the demand for legitimacy requires engagement with public authority, not a rejection of globalization. This finding is perhaps less surprising in light of Williams's observation that, despite globalization's enabling of new expressions of citizenship, the state is still best equipped to supply the conditions necessary for collective autonomy.

Chapters in this section examine how much tolerance, or ability to resist, there is for dominant states asserting control of global governance. Les Pal's chapter on governing the Internet, for example, shows the state reasserting its authority in what should be a most likely case for cosmopolitan global governance. At least in a functional sense, the Internet has characteristics of a global public good that should point to limits on the state's legitimate claim to control it, although the same cannot be said for its underlying technology. Moreover, the Internet's potential impact on individual autonomy — both positively in its potential for building transnational and virtual communities and negatively in its subjection to government censorship and surveillance — is profound, no matter where people live. Pal shows that despite four innovative models of Internet governance that emerged from the World Summit on the Information Society process, the existing system of governance dominated by the United States prevailed. Although that system can claim some stakeholder involvement under the Internet Corporation for Assigned Names and Numbers (ICANN), its lack of input over the years has, according to Pal, compromised ICANN's struggle for legitimacy.

Pal's chapter also nicely illustrates that tensions may remain between global democracy, if rooted in the collective autonomy of states, and individual autonomy. The current configuration of ICANN is undemocratic by almost any measure because it is only accountable to the United States, even though its decisions potentially affect any connected country. The irony is that the most vocal opponents of ICANN were the governments of China and a number of Middle Eastern countries, many of which engage in Internet censorship and other Internet practices that undermine individual autonomy.

To sum up, the contributors to this section each found the state showing up in unanticipated ways. They highlight ongoing renegotiation with traditional state structures even as globalization contributes to the reconfiguration of political authority. In this context, Smith's warning of a shift in the struggle over what kind of globalization will prevail is highly relevant. The debate in the 1990s centred on democratic critiques of neoliberalism. Today, the struggle is over an engaged globalization that can build legitimate authority at appropriate levels rooted in expressions of autonomy, a globalization of competing moralizing missions, or simply a retrenchment to an inward-looking garrison state. As Smith argues in this volume, the latter two alternatives would justify violence that suppresses autonomy. To the degree that global institutions continue to decline in legitimacy, disenfranchised non-state actors may, too, be tempted to turn to violent alternatives.

To avoid such outcomes, new expressions of collective autonomy must find ways to connect with public authority, and public authorities need to pay greater attention to empowering those who are missing or left out. The hope is that experiments now underway in Europe, in co-governance arrangements, or in other creative reconfigurations of sovereignty elsewhere will be allowed to flourish.

Conclusion

One overarching conclusion of this volume — that a revived liberal internationalism that re-enfranchises civil society while respecting local expressions of collective autonomy and human rights — might seem quintessentially Canadian, a product of our project's particular place and time.[3] Nonetheless, two observations about Canada make us quite comfortable with this conceit. First, Canada is at the forefront of globalization by almost any measure. A leading statistical survey of globalization that looked at economic, technological, political, and social indicators ranked Canada sixth overall in the world in 2005 (*Foreign Policy* 2005). Questions about whether globalization has led to disruptions in understandings and expressions of autonomy are part of the lived experience for many of our contributors.

Second, Canada is a near archetype of a globalizing society that has evolved through a long and continuing struggle over multiple expressions of autonomy. The Canadian state's struggle for autonomy extends back to before its founding. Struggles included those for responsible government within the British Empire; the pursuit of national policies to buttress economic development against the grain of geography, with its pull to the south; the final political weaning from imperial Britain in the 1920s, 1930s, and 1940s; and, finally, attempts to construct an identity defined not solely in opposition to the US colossus. The struggles to build a modern nation-state came up against other autonomy claims, including those from Quebec nationalists, who argued they constituted a people and a nation with the right to self-determination. These struggles also involved the suppression of Aboriginal peoples' autonomies, usually accompanied by their forcible dispossession from their territories. Indeed, Harvey Feit's chapter on nation-state–indigenous co-governance in Canada traces one Aboriginal community's resistance to these processes and how that resistance took different forms as globalization advanced. Feit throws into sharp relief that globalization has meant it is no longer always appropriate to speak of idealized versions of democratic polities or clear boundaries of the demos, if it ever was. At the least, the opportunities for ongoing struggles with political expressions of collective autonomy have increased significantly.

Acknowledging the situatedness of the intellectual impulses of many of our contributors is not, however, a justification for the volume's conclusions. Rather, it is a privileged vantage point to explore and inquire critically into the themes of the volume. It militates against the idealist tendencies sometimes evident in cosmopolitan scholarship. Simultaneously, it encourages an outlook that engages with economic and social forces that increasingly operate globally and impinge on and reconfigure individuals' and collectivities' relationships to political authority and power. The result is perhaps also quintessentially Canadian: a refusal to embrace simple dichotomies, a struggle for compromise in a world of constraints and complexities, and a self-reflective and critical engagement with the opportunities and limits of any self-governing arrangement.

Part 1
Normative Foundations of Legitimacy and Autonomy

chapter 2

Citizenship as Agency within Communities of Shared Fate

Melissa S. Williams

To MANY ANALYSTS OF the phenomena we cluster under the heading "globalization," the concept of citizenship may appear beside the point, even rather quaint and outmoded. Our received understandings, after all, define citizenship as membership in a political community that is unified by a single order of law within a discrete territory. Citizenship, they might argue, remains a salient category of analysis within territorial states, which have not disappeared from the political stage despite the increased importance of transnational and international institutions of governance. As long as (and to the extent that) states remain significant players in these institutions, citizenship will persist as a relevant status within those states that have a democratic form. But it is quixotic or at least a category mistake (these analysts might continue) to use the concept of citizenship to make sense of the broad political dynamics that we associate with globalization.

The modern variant of the concept of citizenship is indeed connected tightly to the construct of the post-Westphalian state, sovereign within its boundaries and respected as such by other states. Historically, the theory and practice of citizenship laid largely dormant from late antiquity to the early modern era. To sum this up very crudely: Greek conceptions of citizenship gave way to subjecthood under the Persian Empire, were revived and revised in the Roman republic, then fell into decline with the rise of the Roman Empire. Citizenship re-emerged as a relevant concept only as a rather late chapter in the theories of state sovereignty first propounded (most significantly) by Bodin in the sixteenth century and Hobbes in the seventeenth century. The idea of the consent of the people as the foundation of the state's claim to legitimacy — an idea traceable to Hobbes and radicalized first by Locke and then by Rousseau — generated the idea of the sovereignty of the people as final judge and arbiter of state action. The doctrine of popular sovereignty blossomed in the age of democratic revolution of the late eighteenth century. As members of the legitimizing people, individuals were transformed from subjects of the state to democratic citizens, to joint authors of the state's laws and bearers of rights against its arbitrary power.[1] By participating directly and indirectly in the formation of the laws under which they live, and by authorizing and demanding accountability from the public officials who act in their name, citizens express their individual (or private) autonomy as rights-bearers and their collective (or public) autonomy as a democratic community (Habermas 1996, chap. 3).

My purpose in offering such a rough-and-ready history of the modern concept of citizenship is simply to highlight that it comes bound up in a package of concepts: state sovereignty; the territorial basis of sovereignty; peoplehood (or, in its dominant variant, nationhood); democracy; legitimacy; and legitimacy's close relation, justice. As John Ruggie suggests in his seminal 1993 article, this joining together of core political concepts (in which the concept of sovereignty functions as a keystone) is no coincidence. Rather, it is emblematic of the modern imagination itself, in which the human capacity to grasp the world — to exert both rational and practical agency in the world — is enabled by the adoption of a single point of view on that world. Just as single-point perspective took hold in the visual arts in Renaissance Italy, Ruggie argues, it also took hold in politics: "Political space came to be defined *as it appeared from a single fixed viewpoint*. The concept of sovereignty, then, was merely the doctrinal counterpart of the application of single-point perspectival forms to the spatial organization of politics" (Ruggie 1993, 159). With this innovation, the singular perspective of the sovereign becomes the vantage point from which all questions of political rule can be settled. The concept of sovereignty incorporates within it an account of unitary territory, a unitary people, and a unitary account of legitimacy and justice, just as the sovereign itself incorporates all the individuals that are subject to its authority (as in Hobbes's famous image on the frontispiece of *Leviathan*). *E pluribus unum*: out of many, one.

Ruggie seeks to understand the ways in which the social episteme of modernity — single-point perspective and its political expression in the concept of the sovereignty of territorially bound states — is undergoing a transformation as the multi-perspectivalism characteristic of "postmodernity" takes hold (Ruggie 1993). More specifically, he traces out the ways in which the unitary territoriality of the state is undergoing transformation through the emergence of spatially decentred economic relations (commonly referred to as globalization of production, trade, and economic regulation) and multi-centred political forms such as the European Union.

Although Ruggie writes primarily about the unbundling of territoriality, others thematize the unbundling or disaggregation of sovereignty itself. Notwithstanding the efforts of the Bush administration to reassert aggressively the doctrine of state sovereignty (at least on behalf of the United States, if not Iraq), it is plausible to claim that since the end of the Cold War the sovereign state's power of political decision is being parcelled out among a range of subnational, transnational, and supranational institutions. Or it is simply dissipating altogether, as when states relinquish their powers to tax corporations in deference to the naturalized forces of global competitiveness (Slaughter 2004b). We have all heard the argument that the neoliberal policies of the World Trade Organization (WTO), the International Monetary Fund (IMF), and the World Bank have sapped states' capacity to regulate their internal economies and set their own policy priorities. In the realm of international security, the idea that military force should not be used unilaterally, and preferably not without UN approval, may be gaining ground, despite the war on Iraq. NATO's interventions in Bosnia and Kosovo, world leaders' public expression of moral shame at the international community's failure to intervene during the Rwanda genocide, and the ongoing (though evidently pointless) debates over multilateral intervention in Darfur should the Sudanese government fail to stop the genocide there — all of these express a norm that fundamental human rights trump state sovereignty. Few, if any, serious scholars predict the total demise of sovereignty at the state level: the sovereign territorial state is undergoing a transformation, but it is not likely to disappear altogether for a very long time. But the sovereignty it exercises appears, increasingly, to be a qualified sovereignty in which the authority of supranational institutions and international norms to generate binding decisions in some areas of policy has a plausible claim to validity.

Unravelling Modern Conceptions of Democracy and Citizenship

One can tell the story of the unravelling of the neat package of democratic and autonomous political communities from various angles. In lieu of territoriality or sovereignty, for example, one might focus on the unsettling of the construct of a unitary people as the basis of democratic community that followed from the civil rights and feminist movements of the 1960s and 1970s and theoretical treatments of the politics of difference (including multiculturalism) of the 1980s and 1990s (see, for example, Young 1990, 2001; Kymlicka 1995; Taylor 1992). These strands of both movement politics and academic political theory laid bare the multiform exclusions by which the myth of a unitary people was constructed through the politics of nation building in Europe, North America, and elsewhere — a politics often based on a masculinist (as well as culturally or racially exclusivist) ideal of the citizen. Because many of the scholars who contributed to this body of work would resist the label of postmodernism (since, by and large, they advanced their arguments in the service of Enlightenment ideals of justice and equality), these tendencies, too, express a multi-perspectivalism that stands in tension with the unitary logic Ruggie identifies with modernity.

A defining theme of this volume is that the processes that unbundle sovereignty have generated new challenges for legitimacy, if not a new legitimacy crisis. The chains of authorization and accountability that bind state decision makers to the citizens in whose name they act are weak or absent in the new forms of transnational governance and the bodies that sustain and regulate global capitalism (see, for example, Ostry, this volume). The economic and political power of multinational corporations has grown, within both transnational regulatory institutions and the countries in which they operate. Yet they remain largely unaccountable to those whose life circumstances they profoundly affect (the workers whose labour they employ, the communities whose environments they transform, and the social inequalities they generate). Meanwhile, the internal legitimacy of Western democratic states is undermined by growing social inequality and called into question by proponents of a politics of difference. The weakening of legitimacy is evidenced by declining political participation and diminishing trust in government institutions and officials.

These stories of unbundling cast a rather gloomy shadow over the inspiring ideal of democratic citizenship sketched above. If our received ideals of citizenship are bound up in a conception of the state that is obsolescent, does it not follow that citizenship is obsolescent as well? And since the capacity for political agency that is expressed through the concept of citizenship is so indispensable for the modern account of political legitimacy, does the threat of the decline of citizenship leave individuals with a reasonable sense of powerlessness to make effective demands for justice against those who make political decisions?[2] Are we at a historical moment analogous to that of Greek democrats or Roman republicans, who lived when the dynamics of empire turned citizens into subjects? And is this moment not occurring long before the promise of justice and legitimacy through the active exercise of democratic citizenship was ever fulfilled in any actually existing state?

Intriguingly, such morose musings have not inhibited discussions of citizenship, even in the context of broader treatments of globalization. Indeed, we are now witnessing a burgeoning of languages of citizenship that attempt to grasp the new modalities of civic engagement that do not align with membership in a territorially bounded constitutional state (Isin and Wood 1999). The language of global citizenship is now in common currency, denoting everything from individuals' participation in the Battle of Seattle and subsequent anti-globalization demonstrations, the unprecedented coordination of anti-war marches in major cities throughout the world on 15 February 2003, human rights and humanitarian activism, and corporate departments aimed at countering the images of multinational corporations' exploitation of workers and of natural resources. Michael Hardt and Antonio Negri (2000, 400) also employ the term *global citizenship* to refer to "a first element of a political program for the global multitude, a first political demand ... All should have the full rights of citizenship in the country where they live and work."

Discourses of cosmopolitan citizenship are continuous with global citizenship in many ways but emphasize universal standards of human rights and a universal human interest in freedom. *Environmental citizenship* denotes mobilization aimed at combatting damage to local and global ecosystems by humans. The term *transnational citizenship* encompasses transnational social movements (women's movements, labour movements, environmental movements, movements for the rights of sexual minorities, indigenous peoples' movements, etc.) and their efforts to increase the responsiveness of transnational institutions (particularly the WTO and the Bretton Woods institutions) to the interests of economically weak actors affected by their policies. *Post-national citizenship* and *denationalized citizenship* denote the effort to exercise political agency in arenas that are not delimited by or oriented to the national state (e.g., Sassen 2005). Increasingly, scholars are employing the term *diasporic citizenship* to describe the efforts of diasporic communities to maintain communication and social links across national boundaries and to attain cultural recognition from the political communities in which their members actually reside (Isin and Wood 1999; Laguerre 1998). One can even find examples of the language of worker citizenship to express a departure from traditional class politics in the form of efforts mediated by non-governmental organizations (NGOs) to coordinate the interests of corporations and workers to attain better working conditions, eliminate child labour, and so on.

Some might find it tempting to respond to these new discourses of citizenship as perversions of the concept of citizenship as a formal legal status within a territorially bounded state. Historical usage of the concept of citizenship makes clear, however, that it is a role (and, hence, includes characteristic virtues of the performance of that role) as well as a status, and that status and role do not necessarily always go together (Soysal 2001). These recent reformulations of citizenship are focused not on status but on role, on the exercise of new forms of political agency aimed at some form of common good. Granted, there is still a great deal of terminological and conceptual ambiguity in these new languages of citizenship: some use the language of transnational citizenship to denote the same phenomena that others describe under the heading of "global citizenship." Yet each of them attempts to grasp in thought the transformations of the contours of political relationships and of political action that have been unfolding on the ground (and over the Internet) for the last several decades.

Many of these reconceptualizations of citizenship draw on the critique and reconstruction of conceptions of citizenship that we witnessed in the political theory of the 1980s and 1990s, which was led by feminist theorists, theorists of cultural recognition, critical race theorists, and the critical legal studies movement. For the most part, however, those innovations in political theory rested on the background assumption that democratic citizenship takes place within the framework of a territorially bounded constitutional order. These more recent efforts to rethink citizenship seek to suspend the supposition that territorially bounded community is a precondition of meaningful democratic agency, even as most acknowledge that citizenship in these communities remains vitally important.

Citizenships of Globalization

Suppose that they are right to do so: Is there a way of thinking of citizenship that can make sense of these new conceptualizations of citizenship *and* the conceptions of democratic agency embedded in our received traditions of citizenship theory? If so, what does this reconception of citizenship entail for our understandings of peoples and constitutions? Does it mean that we should jettison the concept of "the people" altogether in thinking about political agency? Does it mean that constitutions can no longer serve as the legal-institutional vehicle for democratic self-rule?

In joining the fray of theorists who are attempting to make new conceptual sense of the meaning of democratic citizenship in these changing circumstances, it seems reasonable to begin by leaning on that reliable standby, the concept-conception distinction (Hart 1961; Rawls 1971). Given the plurality of conceptions of citizenship, even before the recent explosion of literature described so briefly above, what can we say is the core of the concept of citizenship, the elements that every particular conception contains? I do not pretend that there is a single authoritative answer to this question, but the following may serve as a working definition: Citizenship is a form of political agency aimed at (a) *a common good* within (b) *a bounded community* in which the agent can claim (c) the *status of membership.* The exercise of this agency expresses (d) *a public role* of the citizen, which is fulfilled by the performance of (e) *activities or functions* characterized by (f) a set of *virtues,* where virtues are evaluative criteria for distinguishing better from worse performances of the roles and practices of citizenship.

In the story of modern citizenship sketched out above, we might fill in the content of this concept more or less as follows: the most important common good (a) realized through citizenship is freedom (or public autonomy) understood as self-legislation, or being bound only by those laws to which one could rationally consent and which one authorizes (directly or indirectly) through one's own actions. The bounded community within which self-rule is exercised constitutes the people, who are defined, at least in part, by a territorial boundary that separates them from other territories and the peoples that occupy them (b). The role of the citizen (d) is defined by the activities of authorizing public decisions (directly or through participation in processes of election and representation) and holding government officials accountable through participation in (at least some of) the institutions established by the constitution (e). The status of membership in this political community brings with it the public rights of participation as well as private rights against the state and against other social actors (c). The principal virtue of citizenship is active participation in the activities of self-legislation, which is constrained by a vigilant commitment to the common good and a concern to protect the rights of individuals (f).

In contrasting this conception of citizenship with emerging conceptions of citizenship sketched above — global, transnational, post-national, environmental, or diasporic — two elements stand out as especially divergent: the boundaries of community (b) within which the exercise of citizenship takes place and the activity of citizenship (e). The initial point of observation is purely negative: these new conceptions of citizenship do not presuppose territorial boundaries (though perhaps we might decide that the forms of community they do imagine may still warrant using the term *people*). Nor do they conceive of the activity of citizenship as being aimed at realizing self-rule through the holus-bolus of sovereignty and self-binding legislation. Rather, most often they seek to resist the power of dominant actors to make decisions that affect the fundamental interests of others without having to take those interests into account.[3]

Is it possible to articulate a single conception of citizenship that covers both these new forms of political engagement and the depiction of modern citizenship with which this chapter opened? If so, such a conception would have to articulate an account of the boundaries of community (b) and the functions or activities of citizenship (e) that excludes neither modern citizenship nor conceptions of global, post-national, transnational, or diasporic citizenship, the points on which the two visions diverge most markedly.

Let us begin, then, by unpacking the conception of the boundaries of community that is implicit in newly emerging ideas of citizenship. For simplicity's sake — while acknowledging the important differences among global, cosmopolitan, transnational, post-national, environmental, and diasporic conceptions of citizenship — let us bundle them together with a single label, say, "citizenships of globalization." What can we say, in general, about how these ideas of citizenship conceptualize the human relationships within which individuals seek to assert political agency aimed at a common good?

First and foremost, the citizenships of globalization stress relations of interdependence that exceed the boundaries of the territorial states. Many emphasize relations of interdependence that arise from global capitalism, the flows of finance, capital, consumer goods, and services that elude the regulatory control of the state. Some emphasize the environmental impact of industrial production, energy, and water consumption: pollution, climate change, natural resource depletion, and so on. Some stress international migration and its impact on both countries of emigration and countries of immigration as well as the emergence of new forms of cultural and political community that stretch across space. Transnational social movements of women, indigenous peoples, labour organizations, and sexual minorities reveal that these groups often face similar challenges in their struggles with very different states and that their local battles can be more successful if they join forces and learn from one another's experiences. Human rights advocates argue that the security of basic human rights in any particular location depends on the actions — or inaction — of international society as a whole.

What all of these views have in common is the claim that the actions of some agents — whether individuals, states, corporations, transnational institutions of governance, or non-governmental organizations — have an impact on others, even distant others. Whether that impact was intended, whether the agent was fully conscious of it, or whether the consequent relationships of dependence and interdependence were voluntary or involuntary — none of these considerations changes the fact of the impact or the facticity of the relationship that it creates.

These impacts and relationships, moreover, have temporal as well as spatial extension. They are not passing phenomena, but have their origins in the past and will extend into the future. A particular nexus of relations of affectedness may be shifting, but the broad contours of the relationship are more or less stable for the foreseeable future. They constitute systems of relationship that have emerged out of history and cannot be expected to disintegrate as a matter of course.

What makes these relationships potential sites of citizenship — possible communities that are capable of possessing a common good — is the possibility that they can be brought under conscious human agency aimed at rendering the relationships mutually advantageous, just, or legitimate. Thus, the citizenships of globalization bear important similarities to John Dewey's (1927, 15-16) theory of the public: "The public consists of all those who are affected by the indirect consequences of transactions to such an extent that it is deemed necessary to have those consequences systematically cared for."[4] They also resonate with the principle of affected interest that informs Ian Shapiro's (1999) conception of democratic justice and with Iris Young's conception of social connection as a basis of moral and political responsibility (Young 2003). In each of these conceptions, what relates individuals to one another is not necessarily a shared identity, a shared sense of membership, or a shared commitment to common values, it is a system of social interdependence, often characterized by inequalities of power in which individual-level actions generate effects beyond the parties immediately concerned.

The facticity of social relationships, however, is no guarantee that those relationships will be transformed into communities over which human beings exercise intentional political agency aimed at a common good. This transformation depends on a dual act of imagination. First, agents must develop a consciousness of the relationships as existing, ongoing structures of social interdependence. Second, they must imagine that the relationship can be made subject to conscious political agency, to regulation aimed at some common good. Although the first moment of imagination is logically prior to the second, it is not necessarily temporally prior. Often, it is the effort to exert agency over the unwanted consequences of unacknowledged patterns of relationship that brings the facticity of the relationship into view and sparks a changing consciousness of the scale and scope of interconnection. These two aspects of imagination stand in an iterative and mutually constituting relationship: the possibility of action generates a new understanding of relationship, which generates new possibilities for action.

Thus, although relations of interdependence have a quality of facticity, they do not by themselves generate political relationship. The formation of new forms of political community depends on the specific forms of human agency expressed in this dual act of imagination. Since we are enmeshed in a large number and a wide array of webs of relationship, the identification of one set of relationships as a site for political action — action aimed at bringing those relationships under conscious control — involves a choice that is not determined by the facts themselves. It also depends on persuasion: the ability to bring others around to seeing this set of relationships as salient and susceptible to intentional action aimed at a common good. Imagined communities (Anderson 1991), if they are to become sites of political agency, must be imagined together by a significant number of the people who are ostensibly involved in them.

This shared imagining as the basis of political community brings to the surface the discursive basis of any potential context for democratic citizenship. The constitution of political community through shared discourse is expressed through a variety of languages by democratic theorists: *publics* (Dewey 1927), *public spheres* (Habermas, multiple writings), *social imaginaries* (Calhoun 2002; Taylor 2002), *stories of peoplehood* (Smith 2003), or *civicities* (Pettit 1997). For our purposes here — attempting to rethink the meaning of the concepts of peoples — Rogers Smith's conception of constitutive stories of peoplehood is especially instructive, because it emphasizes the constructed character of political community and the importance of identifiable agents of construction — leaders as storytellers — in community formation (Smith 2003).

What I want to suggest is that we should understand the citizens of globalization — the mass demonstrators; the activists; the (often self-appointed) advocates for women, labour, and the environment; the more structured NGOs; and theorists — as storytellers of peoplehood, to borrow Rogers Smith's language. They are, most importantly, purveyors of new ways of imagining social relationships in the context of the diverse phenomena of globalization. Through their words and their actions, they attempt to persuade other parties to these relationships that the connections between them are real and that their actions have real consequences for others. Moreover, they seek to persuade others that these consequences can be brought under some form of rule aimed at a common good. In its most elementary form, the content of the common good they seek is (heightened) legitimacy, defined as most deliberative theorists now define it: the justification of actions to those whom they affect, according to reasons they can accept (Cohen 1989; Gutmann and Thompson 1996; Habermas 1991; Rawls 1996; Scanlon 1982, 1998).

Citizenships of globalization, then, define the boundaries of community in terms of that set of human beings who are related through the impact of some members' actions on others, wherein each member has standing to make claims of justification against the others and claims of legitimacy against the nexus or system of relationship as a whole.

If we like, we can call any such community a *people*. Because of the long association between conceptions of peoplehood and assumptions of either a shared territorial base or a shared ethnic heritage, however, I am inclined, instead, to use the tag *communities of shared fate* to denote such collectivities. Although the language of fate is problematic in several ways (as I discuss below), it is commonplace in discussions of globalization (Held 1995). What is appealing about the language of communities of fate is its connotation that the ethically significant relationships that exist among human beings are not all of conscious choosing. There are forces not of our own making that bind us to one another, like it or not. Colloquially, this understanding of *relationship* is often expressed by the declaration "we are all in the same boat." The forces that bind us certainly include the past exercise of political agency, as when we find ourselves connected through the laws and institutions of a long-standing constitutional order. Some of these forces are the unintended consequences of economic activity, as in the case of climate change, or of practices aimed at security, as in the case of the proliferation of weapons of mass destruction and the potential of rogue states or non-state actors to procure them. Unchosen relationships also result from historical patterns of human migration, colonialism, and conquest that have transformed the demography of a given territory. Communities of fate can also be constituted by bonds of culture, language, or religion. We do not choose to be born into such communities, and regardless of whether we embrace or resist the elements of identity that they constitute for us and for others, we may feel that we have little choice but to act within the set of relationships they structure. In each of these (and no doubt other) ways, we find ourselves thrown together into webs of relationship with near and distant others. These webs of relationship have a history, but they also extend into the foreseeable future. We find that if we can extricate ourselves from these relationships at all, it may be exceedingly difficult to do so on terms that could meet a basic standard of legitimacy. The language of fate, for all its pitfalls, captures this sense that the condition of political action is a world that has been shaped by forces other than our intentional agency.

This emphasis on fate does not, however, imply fatalism, the belief that natural or divine forces so determine our circumstances that there is little or no scope for creative human agency. To the contrary, the identification of a particular web of relationships as a community of shared fate is the logical first step in efforts to exert political agency over the terms and consequences of that relationship. Nor is *fate,* here, synonymous with *destiny,* a shared future willed or determined by a supernatural force or agent. Fate, as used here, has no mystical content. Despite the literal translation of *Schicksalgemeinschaft,* the concept community of fate, as it is articulated here, does not entail a belief in a people thickly connected by blood whose destiny is to realize their greatness as a people. I grant that the language of fate may carry such connotations, which is perhaps reason enough to avoid it — even if our language offers no satisfactory alternative for capturing the element of unchosen connections that I wish to emphasize.

Community Boundaries

Let us return now to the task I set myself above: to identify a definition of boundaries of community that could be shared by both the modern conception of citizenship and the newer citizenships of globalization. I suggest that the idea of a community of shared fate meets this task. It is a pragmatic and constructivist account of community, but there is nothing in it to exclude bonds based in a shared territory, a shared constitutional tradition, a shared commitment to certain moral principles or values, or a shared cultural or political identity — all the conventional markers of constitutional peoples. Nor does it require any of these particular bonds of relationship as the basis of citizenship aimed at a common good. The idea of a community of shared fate construes the formation of political community as the outcome of two forms of political agency: imagining a set of human beings as socially related to one another in the past and the future (and telling a persuasive story so that other parties to relationship can share in that imagination) and claiming that the terms of relationship should be subject to standards of a common good, including the fundamental good of legitimacy as reciprocal justification.

Of course, narratives of past and future relationship are hotly contested. But in the first instance what constitutes a community of fate is the agreement that there is a story to be told about this relationship — that as a site of contestations over legitimacy the relationship itself is significant and enduring. To agree that there is a story to be told is not to agree on which story is the right one or on what the terms of relationship should be. On this very thin reading of community, then, Aboriginal Canadians and non-Aboriginal members of settler society, or sovereigntist Québécois and Canadian federalists, do constitute a political community. To the extent that transnational regulatory bodies such as the WTO, the IMF, and the World Bank acknowledge the critiques of their legitimacy by NGO advocates for the environment, women, and labour, they accept that there is a story to be told about the impact of their decisions on these groups. Thus, they begin to participate in a community aimed at regulating trade and finance according to some standard of a common good.[5] The UN's Global Compact project, framed under the leadership of John Ruggie, seeks to engage multinational corporations in dialogues with civil society leaders (including NGOs such as Amnesty International and the World Wildlife Fund) and with UN and other international agencies (including the International Labour Organization). In signing the Global Compact, businesses agree to uphold basic principles of human rights, labour rights, and environmental responsibility. They also undertake to create projects aimed at one or more of these concerns.[6] In constructing these relationships, the Global Compact project seeks to constitute a norm-governed community that directly includes corporations as members.

Roles and Activities of Citizens

Let me turn now, much more briefly, to the second point of divergence between the conception of modern citizenship and the citizenships of globalization: the characterization of the role and activity of citizens. Recall that in the story of modern citizenship citizens contribute to public autonomy through their participation in the processes of collective self-legislation. In the citizenships of globalization, the functions and activities of citizenship are much more diffuse but are, in any event, less ambitious because they do not presuppose that total self-sovereignty is or can be the ultimate aim of democratic agency. Indeed, given its implicit assumption of territoriality, total sovereignty cannot even serve as a plausible aim of this agency. Rather, as I suggest above, the disaggregation or parcelling out of sovereignty seems to entail a correlative disaggregation of the functions of citizenship. The challenge is to see whether we can find a coherent way of thinking about citizenship that does not depend on assumptions of territorially bounded communities. At the same time, the goal is not to re-conceptualize citizenship *de novo* but to draw on our rich traditions of democratic thought to search for a conception of the functions and roles of citizenship that is consonant with those traditions while also being adaptable to changing forms of political agency.

The strategy here, then, is to abstract away from specific historical institutions and practices of citizenship to seek out a pragmatic or functional account of the roles of the citizen in broad terms and then to reconstruct an account of contemporary citizenship that makes sense of those roles within the legal–institutional context of the constitutional state and within the more diffuse nebulae of transnational and international or global structures of relationship. What is citizenship good for? What are the most important functions it serves in individual and collective life?

When we gaze at Western traditions of democratic citizenship, two broad functions stand out as crucial, and they are likely to remain so even if the contexts and institutions of citizenship change dramatically.[7] One of these — self-rule — is the legacy of classical and modern republicanism; the other — self-protection — is the achievement of modern liberalism. Beginning with Aristotle, citizenship has been understood as an integral part of the project of human freedom. To fulfill the human potential for freedom, we must learn to govern ourselves both as individuals and as collectivities. The role of the citizen is, above all, to participate with other citizens in collective self-rule by reasoning with them over what they, collectively, ought to do — what will be just and advantageous for the community and its members.

In the liberal tradition, citizenship entails being recognized as a bearer of rights that others are obliged to acknowledge and respect. The security of rights depends on active citizenship and, therefore, for several reasons entails a form of self-protection. First, governments can only be trusted to protect and enforce rights when they are accountable to those who live under them; the security of rights depends on the active vigilance and regular participation of citizens. Thus, a key instrument of citizenship as self-protection is participation in the authorization of decision-making officials and keeping them accountable to those affected by their decisions (e.g., by voting in contested elections in constitutional democracies). Second, the content of the rights that should be protected is itself worked out through citizens' participation in defining and contesting the legal and practical meaning of rights. In this way, the functions of self-rule and self-protection intersect through the distinctive procedures of political and legal institutions that give content and legal force to the broader concept of rights.[8]

From this very sketchy account of the functions of self-rule and self-protection, we can specify a bit further some of the activities through which these functions can be met. Some may be common to both self-rule and self-protection or entailed by their mutually constitutive character, while others may be specific to one function or the other.

I would also include among the activities of citizenship actions that are aimed at securing the conditions that make self-rule and self-protection possible. Three conditions or prerequisites of citizenship appear to be elemental to both functions. First, as I have emphasized above, citizenship as a form of political agency requires a shared understanding that systems of social relationship define the *boundaries of a community* that are significant and enduring and the site of an existing or potential common good, including the common good of legitimacy. The boundaries of community further establish *criteria of membership* through which agents are recognized as rights claimants or as those who have the standing to participate in deliberation over common ends. Second, both self-rule and self-protection require *physical security* — freedom from domination by the force of the community in question or its members. The boundaries of security must either coincide with or exceed the boundaries of community.[9] Third, both forms of agency depend on some degree of *economic security* — the capacity to generate sufficient wealth within the boundaries of community and to prevent the excessive outflow of that wealth. In this way, its members' basic material needs are met and there are sufficient resources to finance the institutions through which members exercise self-rule and self-protection.

Some conditions of citizenship appear to be specific to one function or the other. The function of self-rule depends especially on the existence of shared discursive spaces within which individuals can participate in deliberations about the good of the community and its members. Self-protection requires the creation of institutional structures capable of securing the rule of law, the legitimate authorization of decision makers by the community and the accountability of decision makers to the community.

The roles and activities of citizenship as a form of political agency, then, include direct participation in the activities of self-rule (deliberation and judgment) and self-protection (claiming rights, authorizing decision makers, and holding them accountable). But they also include action aimed at securing the conditions under which these activities are possible: persuading others of the existence of ethically significant relationships; providing physical security for the community and its members; achieving the necessary degree of economic security; constructing discursive spaces for deliberation about the good of the community; and constructing institutions for the rule of law, legitimate authorization, and accountability.

If we recognize each of these activities separately as instances of citizenship, then we have succeeded in disaggregating the concept of citizenship in a manner parallel to the disaggregation of sovereignty. Eventually, the hope is that this disaggregation of citizenship will enable more contextualized judgments about the relative importance of different forms of political agency and conditions for their realization. Where fundamental human rights are at stake, for example, the activities of self-protection may have greater salience than those of self-rule. Where issues of cultural self-determination are at stake, the activities of self-rule may have greater salience than those of self-protection. Perhaps most importantly, a disaggregated conception of citizenship enables us to understand individuals as being situated within multiple and overlapping (not only nested) communities of fate, with different issue domains, within which different modalities of citizenship are most salient for the realization of freedom.

This characterization of disaggregated citizenship remains, admittedly, quite vague and underspecified. My purpose here is limited to identifying a strategy for thinking through the meaning of citizenship beyond territorially bounded communities. The further specification of the forms and conditions of such citizenship, and of the possibility of realizing any meaningful degree of self-rule and self-protection beyond territorially bounded constitutional democracies, is a subject for further investigation. It may turn out that at least some of the institutional boundaries through which structures of self-rule and self-protection can be constructed depend, in the final analysis, on their coincidence with territorial boundaries. My reading of the literature to date does not persuade me, however, that this is necessarily the case. The forms of political engagement exemplified in the various citizenships of globalization clearly resist this supposition. Efforts are underway to construct boundaries of community, spaces for self-rule, and institutions of self-protection that are not necessarily territorially grounded, but these efforts are still in the early stages. A clear and final judgment on their prospects for success — and on the question of whether there is a necessary relationship between territory and meaningful citizenship — will rest, in part, on further research into specific cases of efforts at construction and, in part, on waiting to see the outcomes of these experiments. My efforts here have been aimed at making a plausible case for the claim that non-territorial citizenship is not impossible and rendering coherent the use of the term *citizenship* to cover both newly emergent forms of political engagement and received understandings of political agency.

Conclusion

Suppose, then, that the foregoing constitutes a defensible analytic account of citizenship as agency within communities of shared fate as a concept that covers both modern citizenship and the citizenships of globalization. In concluding, I want to draw attention to the fact that such an analytic account cannot answer some key normative questions about citizenship. More specifically, I wish to highlight that understanding the boundaries of citizenship in terms of communities of shared fate does not, by itself, offer much guidance for judgments about which relations of interdependence individuals should privilege as the sites of their citizenly exertions.

Indeed, understanding ourselves as immersed in broad and deep networks of social interconnection has the potential to be politically paralyzing. The late Iris Young posed this problem in her social connection model of moral and political responsibility for structural injustice:

Most of us participate in a number of structural processes that arguably have disadvantaging, harmful or unjust consequences for some people in virtue of our jobs, the market choices we make, or other activities. Surely it is asking too much, the objection runs, for each of us to worry about all these modes of participating in structures and how we might adjust our lives and relation to others so as to reduce their unjust effects. Our relation to many of these structural processes is so diffuse, and the possibility that our own action can effect a change in outcomes is often so remote, that it is more reasonable to limit our moral concern to matters where we stand in direct relation to others and can see clearly the effect of our action upon them. (Young 2004, 383)

Young's response to this political anxiety is, first and foremost, to re-mind us that our sense of being overwhelmed by the weight of our moral responsibilities does not relieve us of the burden of these responsibilities. She goes on to offer an agent-centred strategy for thinking through what actions we ought to take as individuals who seek to discharge these re-sponsibilities. Young suggests that in thinking through how best to direct our political energies we should note where we have greater power to in-fluence change and are especially privileged by existing patterns of struc-tural injustice. Furthermore, she argues, our political action should be guided by the interests of the victims of injustice, as they understand them, and the opportunities for effective mobilization around a particular injus-tice — that is, our collective ability (Young 2006).

As I have noted already, Young's social connection approach to respon-sibility for structural injustice is similar in spirit to what I have presented in the language of communities of shared fate. It calls on us to imagine our-selves as being enmeshed in social relationships that we may not have chosen and to exercise our agency to transform those relationships in the direction of a common good, with special emphasis on the common good of justice. For those of us who agree with John Rawls that justice is "the first virtue of social institutions," this emphasis is not difficult to endorse (Rawls 1971, 3).

And yet, sympathetic as I am to Young's approach and commitment to justice, I want to suggest that there is a limit to the possibility of deriving a political action orientation from the objective facticity of social connec-tion or interdependence. The objective dimension of mutual affectedness — our capacity to trace out, empirically, the impact of one agent's deci-sions on others — may get us a certain distance in making arguments about which nexus of relationships we should privilege as the focus of our agency as citizens. This decision is particularly true in cases where the principle of affected interests addresses humans' material interests and is connected to claims of distributive justice. It is certainly feasible, at least in principle, to track the impact of political and economic decisions upon the material conditions of individuals and, hence, their life chances. It is possible (I imagine) to plot the density of social relationships in terms of their propensity to affect individuals' access to the basic human needs of nutrition, shelter, physical security, education, and health care. And from there it is not difficult to make the leap from empirical analysis to the normative claim that dense relationships with strong negative impacts on individual well-being should be privileged as sites of citizenship in the form of resistance to injustice.

This argument is not a difficult one to make, but in making it one must not lose sight of the fact that it is a political argument, one that is aimed at persuading others to perceive their social connectedness and their citizenly responsibilities through the particular lens of social justice. It is an argument that aims to constitute the subjective dimension of community in a particular way, over and against the other ways in which individuals might imagine their relationships to others. Although the objective dimensions of mutual affectedness constrain the number of stories that might plausibly be told about social relationship, the facticity of social connection does not reduce the number of plausible stories to one. This complexity becomes particularly clear once we begin to layer accounts of material relationship on accounts of identity-based relationship, a process that seems inescapable when we try to make sense (for example) of the legacies of colonialism.

To put these points a bit differently: there is no Archimedian point, no view from nowhere (Nagel 1986), from which to assert a strong hierarchy among competing stories of shared fate. The facticity of social relationships and histories reduces the indeterminacy of the political choices we make when we privilege one story over another, but it does not reduce it to zero. The choice among plausible, fact-grounded stories is, therefore, an irreducibly political choice in the Arendtian sense (or, if you prefer, in the Aristotelian sense of *prohairesis*), determined not by necessity nor even by rationality but by shared political judgment. As Arendt argued, this space of indeterminacy is the space of political freedom, in which humans exert their agency, in concert with others, to shape the world according to the lights of their own imaginative judgment.

This space of indeterminacy is filled with danger as well. Most importantly, it carries the risk of confusion as to which stories of relationship are plausible and prevents any of them from becoming action orienting. It can produce anomie, passivity, and political paralysis. And to the extent that it does so, it leaves a political vacuum to be filled with the stories the powerful tell the weak — stories such as neoliberalism, one might argue.

The various citizenships of globalization assert different (empirically grounded) stories as they seek to fill in the indeterminacy of political space; they enjoin us to imagine ourselves in quite different communities of shared fate. Each is action orienting, but each prescribes a somewhat different object for the exercise of political agency. It is possible, even likely, that one could examine each in turn and argue for the greater or lesser plausibility of their accounts of shared fate on the basis of objective facts. What they have in common, however, is a refusal of political passivity in the face of the legitimacy failures of both state and transnational institutions of governance. Whatever their relative strengths and weaknesses, their assertion of the possibility of effective citizenship, even in an age of unbundled sovereignty, is salutary as an expression of human freedom, which is by no means to say that it is enough to secure that freedom. Securing freedom will depend, as ever, on moving beyond political imagining to the transformation of the structures through which humans order themselves.

chapter 3

Autonomy, Democracy, and Legitimacy: The Problem of Normative Foundations

Ian Cooper

THE PROBLEM OF LEGITIMACY, as it relates to the twofold study of globalization and autonomy, may be stated in the following way. The pressures of globalization give rise to new post-Westphalian governance arrangements in which political authority is vertically dispersed to levels both above and below the sovereign state.[1] This dispersion disturbs many of our settled concepts of political theory — such as legitimacy, community, and democracy — which are generally adapted to political practice at the level of the sovereign state. Therefore, to determine whether the emerging governance arrangements should be deemed legitimate, it is necessary to rethink, from first principles, the normative foundations of political authority. One possible starting point would be to base legitimacy on autonomy: the new arrangements may be judged to be legitimate according to how well they respect or safeguard this value. The crucial question then becomes, how should autonomy be defined?

Autonomy is an ambiguous concept. In political theory, it is sometimes cited as an attribute of individuals and at other times as an attribute of groups, ranging from the very small (the family or household) to the very large (the nation or state). This ambiguity is true of autonomy not only as an empirical fact but also as a moral value: there is a divide between political philosophies that only ascribe value to individual autonomy and others that attach some value to group autonomy. This ambiguity presents a serious obstacle to any attempt to construct a normative theory for a post-Westphalian world, because it represents a disagreement over what the starting point for such a theory should be. A working assumption of this chapter is that the distinction between individual and group autonomy is elemental and cannot be ignored or glossed over. Perhaps one way to address this distinction would be to devise a single grand theory of legitimacy that reconciles within it these two competing notions of autonomy. I intend, however, to do the opposite: I problematize the distinction between individual and group autonomy to draw out the contrast between the two normative theories on which they are based. This analysis highlights the choices at stake when we think about how to judge the legitimacy of the various governance arrangements that are emerging in response to globalization.

The ideas of cosmopolitanism and communitarianism are applicable in this context, because the contrast between these schools of normative international relations theory could be said to turn on their respective definitions of autonomy. In cosmopolitan philosophy, only individual autonomy has inherent value because the individual is ontologically prior to the group; group autonomy only has an instrumental moral value, insofar as it allows individuals to achieve their personal autonomy. In communitarian philosophy, by contrast, individual and group autonomy are not wholly separable because individual and group identity are mutually constitutive: therefore, group autonomy has an inherent moral value that is not reducible to the autonomy of its individual members. In other words, the building blocks of cosmopolitan theory are individuals and those of communitarian theory are groups. This basic difference has practical implications for the design of the institutions of political authority.

As it happens, the cosmopolitan-communitarian debate has largely developed as one between those who would attack the nation-state as the primary form of political organization and those who would defend it. The argument here, however, is that a post-Westphalian order in which political authority is vertically dispersed to many levels — that is, global, regional, national, subnational, and local — could be constructed on either cosmopolitan or communitarian principles. In each theory, the individual would simultaneously be a member of numerous communities of varying size, radiating out from her or him in concentric circles, though the nature of the individual–community relationship would differ between the theories. The cosmopolitan sees the individual as a bundle of interests, and the communitarian sees her or him as a bundle of identities; in each theory, these interests or identities would correspond to the various communities in which she or he is a member and would be represented at the various levels of political authority that govern those communities. Not only would these two theories rely on distinct notions of community — interest-based versus identity-based — their notions of democracy and legitimacy would differ in a parallel way, following from the choice of individual or group autonomy as a starting point.

This choice also has ramifications for institutional design. Specifically, there is the question of how the boundaries of each successive community should be drawn. Should they be in accordance with the contours of a particular issue or around a group of people who share some fellow feeling — that is, along functional or communal lines? Furthermore, there are a number of questions concerning the relationship between the levels of authority. In what manner should higher authorities govern in relation to lower authorities? Should they intervene to safeguard individual auton-omy, or should they exercise self-restraint out of respect for the autonomy of lower levels of governance? How should powers be allocated between the various levels? And, finally, who should have the power to make final decisions about boundary drawing and power allocation?

This chapter is animated by a normative question: if the sovereign state is giving way to some other kind of post-Westphalian order, then on what principles should this new order be constructed so that it may be considered legitimate? To begin to address it, the various normative elements, identity-based and interest-based, that are bundled together in the notion of sover-eignty must be disentangled from one another. This inquiry is similar to some recent empirically focused work that classifies types of multi-level governance (Hooghe and Marks 2003), but with a more normative focus, one that judges the arrangements not only by standards of effectiveness but also by standards of democracy and legitimacy. This analysis takes many things for granted, and the assumptions have requisite drawbacks. Even from a normative point of view, this analysis is incomplete: it does not as-sess, for example, the legitimacy of the constitutional process that would bring the post-Westphalian architecture into being. Furthermore, I am making the essentially liberal (in international relations theory terms) assumption that states will be willing to surrender some authority to agen-cies of regional or global governance and are, in fact, doing so. This as-sumption is at odds with realist arguments that the logic of anarchy (Waltz 1979) or other collective action problems present an insuperable structural impediment to such an outcome or that the norm of sovereignty has always been subject to violations and the current era does not differ qualitatively from the Westphalian era generally (Krasner 1999). Also, I am effectively

ignoring the problems of war and tyranny by making the even more uto-
pian assumption that the participants in these post-Westphalian governance
arrangements are part of a security community (Deutsch et al. 1957) — in
which war is not a contemplated policy option — and that all the authorities in question are broadly democratic. Despite these caveats, the analysis
presented here should provide some insight into the moral choices that
must be made in the construction of the architecture of post-Westphalian
governance.

The Cosmopolitan-Communitarian Debate

The principal difference between cosmopolitans and communitarians, as I
define them, is that whereas cosmopolitans claim that only individual autonomy has inherent value, communitarians attach some inherent value to
group autonomy. To divide these two camps in this stark way — according
to the essential difference in their treatment of the concept of autonomy
— has the virtue of simplicity but the disadvantage of obscuring a great
deal of the thoughtful nuance of the work of individual thinkers. For this
reason, I will present the two opposing philosophies in generic terms, as an
argument between a hypothetical cosmopolitan and communitarian, the
attitudes of whom will not necessarily perfectly match up with the leading
thinkers of the respective fields (for an overview, see Brown 1992, 1994). In
so doing, I realize that there are, variously, community-oriented cosmopolitans and liberal communitarians. But following the example of Molly
Cochran, I am presenting the communitarian and cosmopolitan positions
as "caricatures with which certain writers have a better or worse fit"
(Cochran 1999, 9-10). This blunt division necessarily leaves out those
thinkers who have endeavoured to reconcile the two philosophies (Bellamy
and Castiglione 1998) or who, for example, mount a defence of nationality
on essentially liberal principles (Miller 1995). Nevertheless, I think that this
is the most compelling way to draw out the distinction between the two,
and it imposes order on a disparate theoretical field because it captures
various strands of thought under two broad umbrellas. Under the umbrella
of cosmopolitanism, it is largely inclusive of not only contemporary theories of global democratic governance (Held 1995; Pogge 1992) but also more
venerable theories of global governance such as functionalism (Mitrany
1966). And under the umbrella of communitarianism, it largely captures
both those who might be called right communitarians for their defence of
the autonomy of traditional communities and values (Sandel 1982; Walzer

1983) and left communitarians who champion "difference" for its own sake (Young 1990) or the autonomy of indigenous or otherwise marginalized groups (Kymlicka 1989; Linklater 1998a).

The cosmopolitan-communitarian debate in international relations theory grew out of the liberal-communitarian debate in political theory that began with John Rawls's (1971) liberal theory of justice. In an updated version of social contract theory, Rawls argued in favour of a generous welfare state because this arrangement would have been chosen by hypothetical individuals in an "original position" who did not know which place they would subsequently occupy in society. The communitarian critique of Rawls was that his hypothetical original position had stripped the individual of the very attributes that make moral choices possible, leaving only an "unencumbered self" (Sandel 1982). Rawls's response (1985) was that his theory was "political not metaphysical" and was intended not to assert a philosophy of the self but to make a political point about the requirements of justice. Meanwhile, there arose a cosmopolitan critique that criticized Rawls for limiting his theory to justice *within* states. Beitz (1979) pointed out that if Rawls's theory was taken to its logical conclusion, then the demands of justice would require not only a national but a global redistribution of wealth, because the distinction between fellow citizen and foreigner is essentially arbitrary. Communitarians, in turn, responded with a principled defence of national community and an insistence that this distinction is ethically justified (Walzer 1983).

The cosmopolitan-communitarian debate may be summarized as a dispute over three interrelated questions, an observation for which I am greatly indebted to Cochran (1999), though I have adapted her ideas into my own typology, for my own particular purposes (see Figure 3.1). Whereas she seeks to bridge the gap between the two positions, my aim is to draw out their differences. Cochran argues insightfully that this debate is not simply a moral one; it also turns on ontological and epistemological disputes. Cosmopolitans and communitarians have a normative disagreement over the moral standing of states that stems both from an ontological disagreement over the nature of the self and an epistemological disagreement over whether values are universal or particular. Adopting an individualist ontology, cosmopolitans believe that individual human beings are the ultimate units of moral concern in political theory and that this status applies to all human beings equally, regardless of who they are or where they live (Pogge 1992, 48-49). In other words, they assume that the individual is ontologically prior to the political community. This assumption is most vividly illustrated in the liberal contractarianism of Hobbes and Locke, whose starting point is to imagine man alone in a state of nature. Rawls, with his conjectures about an original position, is heir to this tradition. For the communitarian, however, Rawls's depiction bespeaks a rootless atomism that is sociologically inaccurate and morally unattractive. Adopting a holist ontology, communitarians argue, instead, that individuals are inseparable from the communities in which they live and that the liberal–contractarian notion of a presocial human being unencumbered by communal ties is a theoretical construct that bears little resemblance to the true nature of interpersonal relations. The communitarian contends that each person is, in fact, embedded in a network of social ties that have a profound influence on the formation of his or her individual identity and that this notion of the person should be the starting point for political theory. Cosmopolitans accuse communitarians of making the potentially totalitarian mistake of asserting the ontological priority of the community over the individual. Communitarians respond that, in their schema, community and individual are mutually constitutive and neither has priority over the other.

The epistemological dispute, thus, centres on the question of what kind of value claims ought to be taken as valid and under what circumstances. The cosmopolitan contends that it is possible to make a priori, universally applicable value claims: specifically, he or she posits that individual autonomy is a political value of paramount importance, regardless of time or

Figure 3.1: The cosmopolitan-communitarian debate

	Cosmopolitanism	Communitarianism
Ontology (individualist vs. holist)	The individual is ontologically prior to the community.	The individual and the community are mutually constitutive.
Epistemology (universal vs. particular)	It is possible to make a priori universal claims (e.g., the value of individual autonomy) that are valid across space and time.	Reasoning about political morality is only possible within a political community.
Moral standing of states	The state has no moral standing: it is only valuable insofar as it represents the aggregate interests of its citizens.	The state has an inherent moral standing because it represents a particular national community.

place. The communitarian contends, by contrast, that values are always grounded in a particular community and, thus, the product of a particular time and place. Communal ties engender mutual obligations; human beings develop notions of right and wrong not alone but within a social context. And it is only within the political community that reasoning about political morality — and with it, the possibility of the criticism of prevailing values — becomes possible.

This disagreement relates to the above ontological debate because whereas the contractarian school presupposes that a person in the state of nature is capable of making moral choices, the communitarian insists that these choices may only be made by someone embedded in a community. This debate becomes most heated over whether, and on what basis, outsiders may critique community values or practices they find abhorrent. While not condoning human rights abuses, communitarians nevertheless are uncomfortable with the idea that universal values could be imposed on a community from without; they are skeptical of the notion that there is an Archimedean point outside community that provides a neutral moral ground upon which the philosopher would stand and formulate her or his critique. For this reason, cosmopolitans accuse communitarians of moral relativism; communitarians countercharge that cosmopolitans assert a hegemonic ideology that would impose uniformity of values on the diversity of communities, which would, in turn, homogenize the world and eliminate difference.

The upshot of these philosophical debates is a dispute over the moral standing of political communities — more specifically, states. Cosmopolitans ascribe only an instrumental value to the state, whose continued right to exist is utterly contingent upon the fact that it helps citizens to realize their own autonomously chosen ends. This philosophy has radical implications for political institution building because cosmopolitans would significantly modify the state or dispense with it altogether in favour of post-Westphalian governance arrangements if these were shown to better achieve this goal. Communitarians, by contrast, attest that the state can have inherent value in the sense that it is the repository of a collective national identity that comprises elements such as a shared history, language, and culture. The cosmopolitan considers this notion of an irreducibly collective identity to be dangerous mumbo jumbo: "It is unclear how states/nations can have interests or moral claims that are not reducible to interests and moral claims of their members (which can be accommodated within a conception of human rights). This idea smacks of bad metaphysics and is also dangerously subject to political/ideological manipulation" (Pogge 1992, 74). The cosmopolitan acknowledges that national feeling does exist, but only as an aggregate of individual loyalties; therefore, it may be accommodated within a framework of individual interests or rights. The communitarian counters that the notion of a person having a right or an interest in his or her community membership does not capture, in a rich sense, the degree to which the collective identity is constitutive of the individual.

Perhaps what is most unsatisfying about this debate is that it has been framed so that cosmopolitan theory challenges sovereignty and communitarian theory justifies it. The resulting conflation of communitarianism and statism leads to a rather one-dimensional notion of community and identity. On reflection, a multi-layered notion of personal identity should lend itself more to a critique than a defence of sovereignty. After all, the state has a tendency to subjugate all forms of community to one dominant form, that of nationality. A more complex notion of identity would be compatible with what might be called *multi-level communitarianism*. National identity would coexist with other identities that correspond to communities, both above and below the national level, that are all constitutive of personal identity to some degree. There is no reason to suppose that national identity should take precedence over these other identities; if anything, according to the logic that these identities are likely to play a larger constitutive role, priority should be given to those communities that are more local. From this perspective, both the cosmopolitan and the communitarian positions could be said to pose a significant challenge to sovereignty and an argument in favour of some new post-Westphalian arrangement. Nevertheless, the two theories would produce systems of multi-level governance that are markedly different, not only in their normative foundations but also in their institutional design. The remainder of this chapter is devoted to explicating these differences.

Competing Normative Foundations for Multi-Level Governance

The dilemma for devising a political theory for a post-Westphalian world is as follows: not only are most of our political theory concepts adapted to political practice within the sovereign state, the concepts themselves have always been, to some extent, cloaked in ambiguity, an ambiguity obscured by the concepts' subsumption within the broader notion of sovereignty. Democracy presents the most striking manifestation of this ambiguity: depending on one's theory of democracy, it is either an expression of collective will or a system for the aggregation and accommodation of individual interests. Similar points may be made about concepts such as legitimacy and community. In this way, the modern state could be said to be founded on ideas that are in part cosmopolitan (i.e., liberal) and in part communitarian. Indeed, one could even make the case that the genius of sovereignty has been its ability to bring together these disparate grounds for citizen loyalty within a single ideological framework. Although these grounds are not necessarily incommensurable, they are at least in tension with one another. In other words, the key to sovereignty's success as a political creed has been its ability to conflate not only nation and state but also the notion of the nation as a community of interest and a community of identity. The problem for the theorist is that if the state is indeed unravelling (Hooghe and Marks 2003), then this change exposes these ambiguities and raises serious questions about what the normative foundations of any post-Westphalian architecture will or should be.

In an ideal world, a global system of multi-level governance would be one in which political authority at each level would be legitimate, representative of a relevant community, governed democratically, and respectful of autonomy. My contention here is that a multi-level system could be founded either on cosmopolitan or communitarian principles, but it would be based on one of two quite different sets of definitions of the following key terms: legitimacy, community, democracy, and autonomy (see Figure 3.2). Within each theory these key terms are mutually dependent, and each will differ from its counterpart in the opposing theory in a parallel way. Thus, my aim is not to produce an exhaustive exegesis of the various possible meanings of these terms but to show how they fit into their respective theories. Furthermore, I am not attempting to reconcile the respective definitions but to contrast them to better elucidate the differences between the two broader theories. In each case, the starting point of the theory is its particular notion of the person, which in both cases is a divided, or at least multi-faceted, self. The cosmopolitan considers the person to be a bundle of interests, and the communitarian sees her or him as a bundle of identities. The difference between these contrasting notions of the self plays out in the contrast between the two theories' respective notions of autonomy, community, democracy, and legitimacy.

The divided self is the starting point for both theories. Both heuristically envisage the person as being at the centre of a series of concentric circles, each of which corresponds to a community of which the person is a member; each community is governed by a political authority at its

Figure 3.2: Two possible normative foundations for a post-Westphalian order

	Cosmopolitan	Communitarian
Basic unit of theory	Individuals	Groups and communities
Nature of the (divided) self	Bundle of interests, ranging in scale from local to global, to be represented at multiple levels of governance	Bundle of identities, ranging from the thick (local) to the thin (global), to be expressed at multiple levels of governance
Autonomy	Only individual autonomy has inherent moral value; group or community autonomy only has instrumental value	Group autonomy has inherent moral value as a necessary condition for realization of individual fulfillment
Community	Based upon common interest; organized along functional lines	Based upon common identity; organized along communal lines
Democracy	Each individual participates in several democratic communities, based on a principle of affected interests	Each individual participates in several democratic communities, based on collective expression of general will
Legitimacy	Political authority is legitimate insofar as it represents the aggregation of interests of individuals within its jurisdiction; it must respect the autonomy of individuals within it	Political authority is legitimate insofar as it is an expression of authentic group identity; it must respect the autonomy of smaller groups at lower levels

corresponding level. The major difference between the theories lies in the terms of membership. For the cosmopolitan, each circle, or level, of authority corresponds to one element of the individual's interests; for the communitarian, each circle corresponds to one element of the individual's identity. Thus, each theory reflects a competing notion of the self as either a bundle of interests or a bundle of identities. The principal difference between these notions of the self is that whereas interests inhere in the individual, identities are intersubjective and, thus, inherently collective and not reducible to the individual. It should be noted that these notions of the self are heuristic tools; they are useful for the purposes of constructing a governance model and not intended to be a complex portrait of the human character. Thus, against the possible criticism that the notion of the self as bundle of interests is morally bankrupt, the cosmopolitan may reply, like Rawls, that this depiction is political rather than metaphysical and conveys only what is relevant for the purposes of the construction of legitimate political authorities. Besides, interests may be defined expansively to include not only survival and material needs but also intangibles such as personal freedom and human rights — in short, all that makes individual autonomy possible. Similarly, the portrayal of the self as a bundle of identities is not intended as a strong empirical claim about the psychological state of every individual but, rather, as an observation that individuals are generally shaped by their environments, including the various communities to which they belong. Thus, political authority should be constructed in a way that reflects this pattern of belonging. To define identity in this way is not to assert that it is somehow primordial: I am assuming in effect that it is constructed and, by implication, mutable. With identities being intersubjective, however, they tend to be durable.

Two quite different notions of autonomy follow from these contrasting images of the self. Cosmopolitan theory is built on individual autonomy; communitarian theory is built on group autonomy. Cosmopolitans ascribe inherent value only to individual autonomy. Communitarians do not deny that individual autonomy has value but maintain that individual autonomy is only achievable within a network of social attachments: since the group is to some extent constitutive of individual identity, group autonomy has an inherent value. To the reader, what divides the two theories — the instrumental versus inherent value of political community, the reducibility versus irreducibility of autonomy — might seem slender and arcane differences. They are not. The basic building blocks of cosmopolitan theory are individuals, while the building blocks of communitarian theory are groups. The cosmopolitan asserts that political authority should be arranged so that individual autonomy is maximized; if this maximization is achieved by a vertical dispersal of power to many political authorities, then multi-level cosmopolitanism is the result.

In multi-level communitarianism, the demands of autonomy are more complex. If communitarianism is conflated with nationalism, it is only concerned with the autonomy of one relevant group, the nation, and autonomy becomes more or less synonymous with sovereignty. But where there are multiple levels of authority, each of which has a justified claim to autonomy because it corresponds to a group identity, then the crucial question becomes how the relationship between the levels should be regulated. In principle, what is required is that political authority at each level ought to have its autonomy respected by those at higher levels and, in turn, respect the autonomy of those at lower levels.

In both models of multi-level governance, the person would be a member of multiple communities, ranging from the local to the global; but each theory defines community in a different way, based on interest or identity. The cosmopolitan sees the community as a group of people that have a common interest. This notion of community is essentially functional, in that it is organized around a particular concrete problem or issue area. The communitarian sees the community as a group of people with a common identity, organized around communal ties and according to common bonds such as language, culture, religion, or ethnicity. These communities may be imagined, in the sense that their various members do not necessarily know one another on a personal basis (Anderson 1991), but they are, nonetheless, real insofar as the members themselves feel the attachment. In both theories, even a global community could be said to exist, but on different foundations. In communitarian theory, it exists by virtue of the fact that people feel a common bond based on a common humanity or global solidarity. In cosmopolitan theory, it exists because there are universal — that is to say, irreducibly global — issues that directly affect all human beings and the rights that all humans possess. Although at first glance a community of interest may seem to be held together by rather weaker bonds than a community of identity, it should be remembered that interests can be a powerful motivating force, particularly when they are defined expansively to encompass all aspects of individual autonomy, including survival itself. A community of interest may be thought of more evocatively as a community of fate (Williams, this volume).

In both models of multi-level governance, each level would be governed democratically — but again, the two theories define the key term *democracy* differently, in a way that reflects their different notions of the self and community. The cosmopolitan would claim that each person has a right to participate in any decision that could affect her or his interests — what might be called the principle of affected interests. The communitarian would claim that the members of each community have a right to collectively express their general will. In the cosmopolitan schema, democracy is the method by which a group of individuals addresses a common problem; in the communitarian schema, democracy is the method by which a community of identity expresses itself. In both cases, the danger of majoritarian democracy is the tyranny of the majority. Whereas the cosmopolitan worries that the majority will suppress individual autonomy, the communitarian worries that the majority will oppress the autonomy of minority groups.

This last point serves to demonstrate the contrast between the competing notions of legitimacy in the two theories. In both, legitimacy may be defined as encompassing what each political authority does and does not do: to be considered legitimate, a political authority must represent its community while not violating autonomy. For the cosmopolitan, this stipulation means that the authority must address the common problems faced by a community of interests without violating the autonomy of the individuals within it. For the communitarian, this requirement means that the authority would express the common identity of the community without violating the autonomy of the groups within it. In a multi-level system, a cosmopolitan would demand constitutional or other normative safeguards for individual rights, while a communitarian would demand them for group rights.

Two Models of Post-Westphalian Governance

Now that we have a more comprehensive understanding of the competing normative foundations of post-Westphalian governance, we can turn to questions of institutional design. Even if both theories endorse a global system of multi-level governance, with political authority governing successive communities at the various levels, the two theories would differ on three vital design questions. First, how should the boundaries for the exercise of authority be drawn? Second, how should power be allocated between the levels? And third, who should be empowered to provide an authoritative answer to the first two questions? In other words, at what level should the authority over matters of boundary demarcation and power allocation be located? Cosmopolitan and communitarian theories provide very different answers to these three questions (see Figure 3.3).

Cosmopolitan boundaries demarcate communities of interest; communitarian boundaries demarcate communities of identity. It is entirely an open question whether at a given level these boundaries will be coterminous. Only at one level, that of the global community, will there be easy agreement about how the boundary should be drawn, for the simple reason that it will include everyone. But for every other level — that is, for every community that is sub-global – it is likely that adherents of the two theories will disagree about how the boundaries should be drawn or, for that matter, even on how many levels there should be. Adherents of both

Figure 3.3: Two models of post-Westphalian multi-level governance

	Cosmopolitan	Communitarian
BOUNDARIES		
How boundaries should be drawn	Along functional lines; expansive, overlapping; subject to revision through functional redistricting	Along communal lines; non-overlapping; relatively fixed, "sticky"
Global	Moral basis: the need to address common issues that are irreducibly global	Moral basis: shared notion of universal humanity
Supranational	Transnational, functional	Cultural, religious, linguistic, civilizational
National	Moral basis: the need to address those issues that remain national in scale	Moral basis: nationhood — shared history, culture, language
Subnational	Functional; may be territorial (federalism, local or interstate special districts) or non-territorial (corporatism)	Communal; may be territorial (e.g., federalism) or non-territorial (e.g., consociationalism)
RELATIONS BETWEEN LEVELS		
How should powers be allocated between levels?	At the functionally appropriate level; forces of globalization will tend to push powers upwards	Powers should be allocated to the lowest possible level (the principle of subsidiarity)
How should each level relate to those below?	Interventionist — political authority at higher levels would intervene to protect autonomy of individuals at lower levels	Self-limiting — central authority would govern in a manner that respects the autonomy of groups at a lower level (subsidiarity as a norm of self-limiting governance)
Who decides how decisions about boundary drawing and power allocation should be made?	A central authority will be empowered by democratic processes to put in place a "rational" governance design that reflects the needs of all individuals	Each community must consent to having its boundaries changed (an existential issue), or to allocate power to a higher level (the principle of consent)

theories are committed to democracy at each level: for the cosmopolitan this commitment is based on the principle of affected interests, and for the communitarian it is a collective expression of the popular will. If the *sine qua non* of democratic practice is the bright line that separates members from non-members, those who are entitled to participate and those who are not (Walker 1991), then what is at stake in boundary drawing is not merely the efficient delivery of public services, as it is for Hooghe and Marks (2003), but fundamental democratic fairness.

The cosmopolitan would draw boundaries along functional lines, and the communitarian would draw them along communal lines. If, as a thought experiment, each were to utterly redraw the world's boundaries at all levels of authority, the two theories would likely reveal wildly different post-Westphalian maps.[2] In those policy areas in which there is a cultural component, their boundaries may well coincide; in policy areas that tend to spill across existing boundaries, such as the governance of economic activity or the environment, they are likely to diverge. A further complicating factor is that in both theories the boundaries are not necessarily territorial. It is possible to imagine non-territorial governance in which boundaries are drawn along communal lines (e.g., consociationalism) or functional lines (e.g., corporatism). The cosmopolitan map-maker is more likely to allow boundaries to overlap to capture the more varied outlines of policy problems; the communitarian map is more likely to resemble Hooghe and Marks's (2003, 236) Type 1 "Russian Doll set of nested jurisdictions, where there is one and only one relevant jurisdiction at any particular territorial scale." Furthermore, the cosmopolitan map must be continually revised because the shape of policy problems is likely to shift with circumstance; in general, its boundaries will have a tendency to expand to encompass the accelerating transboundary flows that are part of globalization. In contrast, the boundaries on the communitarian map are more likely to remain relatively fixed; although identities are constructed, and thus susceptible to change, they are, nonetheless, "sticky" and, therefore, likely to change only slowly.

These variations in boundary drawing have important implications for the practice of democracy. In the communitarian world, each citizen would be a member of multiple democratic communities, ranging in size from the local to the global; the boundaries of each would be stable, and each authority would have a bundle of competences. This type of world would at least be recognizable to the many Europeans who already cast their vote for democratic representatives at four levels — local, subnational,

national, and regional. From this perspective, adding one more democratic authority at the global level would not require a fundamental change in how democracy is practised, even though the voice of the individual citizen becomes progressively more diluted as the communities get larger (Dahl 1994). The implications of cosmopolitan democracy are more radical. If every person has a right to participate in decisions that affect her or him, and if every problem creates a community of interest, then the number of possible levels and communities is practically limitless. Sorting these problems out would involve determining what problems or issues are important enough to require management by a dedicated public authority and deciding exactly whom they affect. Thus, drawing the boundary, for example, must be done in a way that includes those significantly affected and excludes those marginally affected. In addition, these democratic authorities would be functionally specific; in contrast, democracy as we know it is practised mostly by authorities with bundles of competences. It should be noted, however, that functional democratic arrangements are not unheard of. For example, the European Coal and Steel Community had at its birth a quasi-democratic common assembly whose deliberations perforce focused on coal and steel issues; that assembly is the forerunner of today's European Parliament.

A further complication arises from the fact that the boundaries of communities of interest are likely to be constantly shifting. What this instability calls for, in effect, is functional redistricting, the continual adjustment of democratic boundaries to reflect the changing shape of the problem. If such a notion seems far-fetched, consider the monumental yet routine task of electoral redistricting, wherein a democratic government periodically takes a census of its population and redraws its electoral map to maintain the principle that all votes should have equal weight. Accordingly, if the principle of affected interests is to be taken seriously as the bedrock precept of cosmopolitan democracy, then it must entail some mechanism for the continual reassessment of the boundaries of communities of interest.

How would these differences play out at the various levels? As mentioned above, both theories could produce some form of global governance, though on a different moral basis. For the communitarian, governance would be a response to the emergence of a common feeling of global community; for the cosmopolitan, it would be a response to problems that are irreducibly global in scale. But the two maps' boundaries of the sub-global communities — those at the regional, national, and subnational levels — may vary widely. At the national level, the communitarian is likely to maintain existing national boundaries on the grounds that the nation is a legitimate community of identity. For the cosmopolitan, political authority at the national level should remain in place only insofar as there are problems or issue areas that are genuinely national in scale. At the regional level, communities of interest would address problems that are regional but not global in scale, such as regional trade or environmental issues. The boundaries of regional communities of identity would be drawn along lines that are, variously, cultural, linguistic, or religious. One possible example of how these boundaries could be drawn is provided by Huntington (1993), who interposes civilizations as a new level of analysis demarcated along cultural lines between the national and the global levels. It should be emphasized that at the subnational level traditional "federal" boundaries may or may not correspond to the shape of communities of interest or communities of identity. The functionalist David Mitrany (1966) lionized Franklin Roosevelt for his willingness to set aside the rigidities of federal constitutionalism to create interstate agencies, such as the Tennessee Valley Authority, organized around functional issues. Likewise, subnational communities may or may not correspond to the boundaries of federalism. They may be more congruent with non-territorial arrangements, such as consociationalism (Lijphart 1977), or asymmetrical arrangements, as in the United Kingdom, where power is devolved to Scottish and Welsh parliaments but England is still ruled directly by the central government.

After boundary drawing, the second question facing the architect of post-Westphalian governance is how the relationship between the levels should be governed. It has been noted that the two theories are likely to draw boundaries in widely divergent ways. If we bracket the matter of boundaries, however, then important questions concerning interlevel relationships emerge. The most obvious question is, on what basis should powers be allocated to the various levels? Both theories are likely to recommend that a power be allocated to its "natural" level — that which most closely coincides with the scale of the issue to be addressed. On the margin, however, when dealing with hard cases in which it is unclear whether the power should go up or down, the two are likely to diverge. On balance, following the logic of the principle of affected interests, the cosmopolitan will favour allocating powers upwards to capture externalities. Following the principle of subsidiarity, the principle from Catholic social philosophy and European Union (EU) politics that powers should reside at the lowest level that can still manage an issue, the communitarian will favour allocating powers downwards (Føllesdal 1998; Millon-Delsol 1992).

This difference is a logical consequence of the two approaches' notions of autonomy. The communitarian perspective favours group autonomy, placing particular emphasis on those communities of identity that are closer to the individual; this entails a presumption in favour of lower levels when deciding how competences should be allocated. The cosmopolitan perspective, by contrast, would more readily allocate powers to a higher level if this arrangement would better safeguard individual autonomy. There is something of a paradox here: the communitarian, adopting a holist ontology, defines autonomy principally as an attribute of the group, whereas the cosmopolitan, adopting an individualist ontology, defines autonomy as an attribute of individuals. In this way, the communitarian favours a higher level of association, in that groups are larger than individuals. Nonetheless, it is cosmopolitanism that tends to push powers upwards out of respect for individual autonomy and communitarianism that tends to push it downwards out of respect for group autonomy.

A closely related question is how each political authority should exercise its existing powers: should its manner of governance be regulated by a norm of interventionism or self-restraint? The communitarian would require self-restraint: political authority at each level must govern in a manner that respects the autonomy of communities of identity at lower levels. The cosmopolitan would be less inhibited, advocating governance most consistent with the maximization of individual autonomy, with no regard for a lower level's autonomy for its own sake. Their disagreement would be most pointed on matters in which individual autonomy is particularly at stake, such as matters of human rights. These norms that regulate the behaviour of political authority vis-à-vis lower levels may take the form of constitutional rules; a political authority's constitution may be framed to protect individual autonomy (e.g., a bill of rights), which entails interventionism, or group autonomy (e.g., federalism), which entails self-restraint. Alternatively, these norms may be largely political in character. For example, even in areas where it has the legal power to intervene, the EU is still constrained by the principle of subsidiarity. This principle operates as a norm of self-limiting governance: upper levels legislate only in certain circumstances — when member-state action is insufficient to address a given problem, making higher-level action necessary (Cooper 2006). The EU is, thus, a higher authority constrained, in accordance with communitarian philosophy, by a political norm to respect the autonomy of lower levels.

The third question that the communitarian and cosmopolitan are likely to disagree over is the most basic and in fact comes before the first two:

who should be empowered to make the final decisions about boundary drawing and power allocation? To this point we have only considered on what basis such decisions should be made. We have effectively bracketed the third question with a heuristic device, an exploration of how a hypothetical cosmopolitan or communitarian map-maker or architect would make such decisions. But at this point we must recall the epistemological differences between the two theories. The cosmopolitan is willing to make universal claims of value that are valid across space and time; the communitarian, by contrast, thinks that values are particular to a community of identity and is wary of adopting a universal point of view. This philosophical disagreement has practical implications for institutional design because it relates to the third question: should a central (i.e., global) agency be empowered to play the role of map-maker or architect who makes decisions concerning the demarcation of boundaries and the allocation of powers? The cosmopolitan, accustomed to adopting a universal point of view, is more likely to empower a central authority to rationally redraw boundaries to reflect communities of interest (i.e., to undertake functional redistricting) and to reallocate competences to their functionally appropriate level, all in the name of the better realization of individual autonomy. Although most cosmopolitans do not advocate world government — in this they follow Kant, who foresaw instead a world federation of free republics — their theory at least tends towards the centralization of authority over decisions about boundaries and powers in the name of the maximization of individual autonomy on a global scale.

The communitarian, by contrast, would doubt the ability of a global agency to competently and fairly make fundamental decisions in a way that would not violate the autonomy of the various communities of identity at lower levels. In fact, the communitarian would object to any project that involves a global redrawing of boundaries and reshuffling of competences between levels of authority — that is, any attempt to turn a thought experiment of this kind into reality. Instead, communitarians would advocate that local communities of identity make decisions about boundaries and competences. What this principle would mean in practice is that each community would determine its own boundaries — the boundaries of a community of identity being an existential matter — and that each community must consent to any transfer of competence to a higher level of authority. This approach would not lend itself to any particular overarching design. Whereas Hooghe and Marks (2003) argue that multi-level communitarianism (Type 1 governance) would have a system-wide architecture and multi-level cosmopolitanism (Type 2 governance) would be of flexible design, I come to the opposite conclusion. It is cosmopolitan theory that would lead to a world with system-wide architecture, because it lends itself to a rational redrawing of boundaries and a reshuffling of competences according to functional needs. Institution building in the communitarian world would be more ad hoc and flexible. In short, the cosmopolitan would reorder the world from the top down, and the communitarian would do so from the bottom up.

Conclusion

I am aware that there is a certain element of hubris involved in undertaking a thought experiment to utterly reconstruct all political authority in the world within the confines of a few pages. Voltaire wrote: "I am tired of all these people who govern states from the recesses of their garrets ... these legislators who rule the world at two cents a sheet" (cited in Durant 1962, 227). Despite this admonition, I have set out to sketch two quite different models of post-Westphalian governance, models that are based on two different notions of autonomy. Each theory, beginning with a distinct notion of the self, produces its own definition of autonomy, community, democracy, and legitimacy. The two theories produce systems of multi-level governance that are structurally similar — in both systems the individual would be a member of multiple democratic communities represented by political authorities on a number of levels. The systems would diverge on the crucial questions of how boundaries should be drawn, how powers should be allocated between the levels, and who should make these decisions. It may be thought that each model has its advantages and deficiencies and that the ideal solution would be to somehow combine them into a single model of multi-level governance that would incorporate the best of both worlds (e.g., Bellamy and Castiglione 1998).

I have not, however, tried to do that here. If anything, this work is a cautionary tale against such a project because I have tried to demonstrate the extent to which the two theories, if taken to their logical conclusions, would produce widely divergent outcomes. Nevertheless, if this study has any value, it is that it highlights the moral choices that are involved when we think about how a post-Westphalian order might be structured. In the face of the advances of globalization, this debate is unavoidable; indeed, it may be the most important political theory debate of our time. And the first step in joining this debate is making clear what we mean by autonomy because this meaning shapes how we understand legitimacy.

All that is left to do is to make explicit how the argument of this chapter responds to the questions that animate this volume: "First, under globalization, how or why do individuals and communities accept commands directed at them, or that affect them, as legitimate? Second, from the vantage point of autonomy, how do individuals and communities retain or gain influence and control over local and non-local decisions that affect them?" Because this chapter explores the problem of the moral foundations of a post-Westphalian order, it focuses more on the largely philosophical first question — particularly the why of it — than on the largely empirical second question. Furthermore, I have taken issue with these questions' premises — in particular the conflation of individuals on the one hand and communities (i.e., groups or collectivities) on the other. Although I accept that to some degree individual and collective autonomy are complementary, or even co-original, there remains a tension between them that has important ramifications for our notion of legitimacy.

As it turns out, two quite different notions of legitimacy emerge, depending on whether autonomy is defined in individual or collective terms. Moreover, this volume's apt definition of legitimacy as "the acceptance and justification of shared rule by a community" nevertheless begs the question of the basis for such acceptance and justification, which depends, in turn, on whether the relevant community is constituted on the basis of interest or identity. In this way, I have attempted to problematize the distinction between individual and collective autonomy to exacerbate the tension between them as far as it can go. The intent is not to be destructive but constructive. I am not seeking to destroy all prospects for reconciliation between the two notions of autonomy but merely to highlight the difficulties of such an enterprise. If such a marriage is possible, then I hope I have contributed to its establishment on firm foundations.

chapter 4　　　　　　Cosmopolis or Empire?
　　　　　　　　　　Metaphors of Globalization and
　　　　　　　　　　the Description of Legitimate
　　　　　　　　　　Political Communities

　　　　　　　　　　Nisha Shah

IN THE MIDST OF heightened levels of globalization, or even simply
heightened global awareness, the horizon of politics is contested terrain.
The real time effects of communications and finance provoke images, on
the one hand, of a seamless, global space with hope of unprecedented
human solidarity, a cosmopolis (Archibugi 2003; Brennan 1997; Cohen and
Vertovek 2002; Held 1995; Linklater 1998b; Zolo 1997). On the other, such
hope is met with fears of corruption of power and the unprecedented
reach of power and human subjugation, an empire (Balakrishnan 2003;
Chomsky 2003; Ferguson 2005; Hardt and Negri 2000; Ignatieff 2003;
Roy 2004; Steger 2005).[1] In both imaginaries, the traditional topoi of political theory are challenged. The belief that political life is rooted in the
confines of the sovereign territorial state is jettisoned either in hope or fear
of a future globality. Globalization evidently emerges not simply as a
technological or economic phenomenon but as a profoundly political one.
　　More than a concept, globalization is a normative vocabulary. In the
contest between hope and fear, the diverse processes that enable the conceptualization of the world as a single global space call for a political theory
without or beyond sovereignty.[2] In the twilight of sovereignty, the legitimating discourse of political life is thrown into disarray. Although *sovereignty*
denotes the physical geography of the state, it signifies a discursively constituted normative principle that legitimates a particular type of order. The
sovereign order designates a self-legislating and, accordingly, autonomous
political community. Not so much an empirical measure of autonomy, it

delineates what can be considered a political community and how it must function. This sovereign order also serves as the measure against which political authority within the state is evaluated. Subsequently, as sovereignty has evolved, the autonomy it legitimates has been further articulated by democracy. There is thus an intricate relationship between legitimacy, autonomy, and democracy that is encapsulated in the discourse of sovereignty and in the theory of the state. In disrupting sovereignty, the circumstances of globalization pose the following questions: What new legitimating discourses emerge as the field of politics moves from the sovereign state to the globe? And what are the consequences for the normative objectives of autonomy and democracy?

Cosmopolis and empire have emerged as the two dominant metaphors of globalized political community as political theorists attempt to construct a global political theory (Dallmayr 2005; Gills 2005). As metaphors, these images not only project future possibilities but also provide normative vocabularies through which the diverse processes associated with globalization can be understood. In this way, they provide narrative structures that not only delineate the problems and challenges raised by globalization but also legitimate the possible normative solutions. Taking on the motivating themes of this volume, I explore how these contending metaphors disrupt and reconstruct legitimacy, autonomy, and democracy in the context of globalization. In particular, I focus on how cosmopolis and empire challenge the metaphors typically invoked to discursively legitimate political community through the state and its sovereignty and seek to articulate political community in more global terms. I consider how each metaphor may help us understand globalization, how conventional relations of legitimacy, autonomy, and democracy as signified by sovereignty are destabilized, and what they might mean in new circumstances.

In other words, I explore how metaphors of globalization inform what we consider legitimate conditions of autonomy and democracy when political community is understood in global rather than territorial terms. I contribute answers to this volume's overarching questions by illuminating how cosmopolis and empire shape discourses of globalization and, in so doing, exert power by providing answers to the questions, what political possibilities are palatable and desirable? And what political choices are reprehensible or unfeasible?

My discussion undertakes a critical analysis of three key texts in the globalization debate: for cosmopolis, David Held's *Democracy and the Global Order* (1995) and for empire, Michael Hardt and Antonio Negri's *Empire*

(2000) and *Multitude* (2004). Held and Hardt and Negri explicitly take on the challenge of delineating the normative challenge and the normative possibilities heralded by globalization. They then provide novel articulations of political theory that move legitimacy beyond its conventional association with territorially bounded sovereignty and rearticulate it in more global terms. Although both assume autonomy and democracy as conditions of legitimacy, a comparative analysis of their arguments reveals that their different interpretations of globalization, and the crisis of legitimacy-cum-sovereignty it instigates, produce antithetical understandings of the referents of autonomy and the practice of democracy in a global context. These different metaphors show that the meaning of global politics is not a given: it must be constructed. In attempting to delineate the future globality, it is necessary to interrogate these metaphors of globalization and the understandings of political community they legitimate.

At first sight, conducting a textual analysis of metaphors seems far removed from the concrete and empirical dimensions of globalization that daily affect human societies. However, given the widespread popular and academic following that each of these texts has enjoyed, I treat them, in the spirit of Foucault, less as philosophical treatises and more as practical handbooks or manuals for living that "delineate for the individual certain values, standards and practices" (Clifford 2001, 70). It is therefore important to see not only how each of these theoretical positions is based on a metaphor of globalization that calls for new legitimate political orders but also how the metaphors are able to legitimate themselves as definitive accounts that inform how others might build strategies for autonomous, and democratic, global politics. What follows at one level may appear to be a familiar review of two popular accounts of globalization; however, by drawing out their metaphorical nature, I demonstrate their power — by instilling either hope or fear — to justify particular political beliefs and actions. I also show how they motivate us to find our way in a time when we can no longer be confident about the promises of sovereignty.

Metaphors, Globalization, and Political Community

By itself, the meaning of *global* is obvious — it denotes a physical, geographical space that is somehow transworld or transplanetary. However, when it comes to defining how *global* should be understood as a political community, the term's meaning is less clear. Although they are central features of globalization, empirical manifestations — be they trade or tele-communications — say little about its normative significance. Distilling the normative significance of globalization — how and in what ways it presents a transformation of political community — requires moving beyond specifying the empirical evidence to uncovering its normative logics and possibilities.

How political communities emerge — what they look like, how their boundaries are established, and how they function — is a matter of historical circumstance. The stories of their formation, however, are not simply about the course of events, such as wars. Näsström (2003, 819) argues that these historical and arbitrary forces do not remove the need "to provide a theoretical understanding of the political legitimacy upon which the new order [is] being created." Without grounding emergent orders in a doctrine of legitimacy, she asserts that "political decisions would run the risk of appearing arbitrary and illegitimate exercises of power" (ibid.). Näsström's comments highlight two crucial points: first, political communities are as much a product of history as they are matters of social construction and convention; and second, an account of legitimacy that allows spaces to take on normative significance and be accepted as appropriate sites of political authority and allegiance is crucial in establishing these conventions (see also Connolly 1984, 2-3).

Accordingly, no account — old or new — of the genesis of political community can escape contending with the precepts of legitimacy that become embedded within its community of belief. This volume is premised on a definition of legitimacy as "the acceptance and justification of shared rule by a community." Legitimacy is, as Lipset asserts, "the capacity of the system to engender and maintain belief that the existing political institutions are the most appropriate for the society" (quoted in Connolly 1984, 10). Based on this broad conceptualization, Bernstein and Coleman argue that legitimacy entails both an empirical measure of acceptance of rule and also a normative justification that garners allegiance.

However, the question remains, how do understandings of legitimacy constitute political communities? To explore this question, a number of scholars have examined the role of metaphors. Ricoeur (1984, 253), for instance, argues that regardless of whether it is the social contract or the nation, each metaphor, although virtual, founds a real community. By providing a founding myth that inscribes normative meaning onto an established or developing geographical space, each metaphor transforms it into a political one. Each metaphor therefore establishes different frameworks for individual and collective experiences within given spaces that promote particular kinds of social and political relationships.

Richard Rorty (1989) provides perhaps the most direct entry point into understanding the legitimating role of metaphors in establishing the normative foundations of political community. Rorty's notion of metaphor draws upon Davidson's pragmatist linguistic philosophy. Davidson (1979, 31) defines metaphors as "creative comparisons [that enable] us to attend to some likeness, often a novel or surprising likeness, between two or more things." From this perspective, the effect of the metaphor is not literal or even figurative, but performative. Metaphors provide non-verbal images or pictures that are not contained in the literal meaning of the metaphorical phrase itself. For instance, by saying "Juliet is the sun," attention is drawn to aspects of Juliet and the sun that were not noticed before. The point is not that metaphors reflect some pre-existing reality or truth — that Juliet has features like the sun in an objective sense. Rather, metaphors are constitutive — "Juliet is the sun" inscribes sunlike features onto Juliet and makes it impossible to understand Juliet outside of these features. The power and force of the metaphor, accordingly, rest in how it creates and embeds new imaginative possibilities that generate new understandings. Eventually, the metaphor's imaginative descriptions become so deeply entrenched and habitualized as part of the everyday way of speaking about the world that its metaphorical status is forgotten. When this happens, it ceases to be a metaphor — it is dead — and, instead, marks a "new stage of literal language" (Hesse 1987, 297). At this point the metaphor's descriptions define reality.[3]

Examing metaphors in relation to political societies, Rorty combines this understanding of metaphor with Wittgenstein's notion of language games. As the world comes to resemble the vocabulary of language games, Rorty argues that language games are prevailing cultural metaphors. As metaphors become entrenched, they provide the grounds for the creation of non-linguistic social institutions. For instance, taking the example of the French Revolution, the language of *liberté, égalité, et fraternité* at the core of the metaphor of the nation generated democratic institutions and practices. It not only transformed the understanding of the state, making it impossible to conceive of it outside of the nation, it also embedded this new kind of legitimacy in the people and not the divine right of the king, and opened the way for new institutions and practices. Rorty (1989, 5) therefore argues that individuals in a given social milieu come to understand their socio-political relations through the languages used to describe them. Description, however, should not be understood as a reflection of "reality out there," which is then reflected through metaphors. Rather, through the constitutive function of metaphors, political "reality" is constructed or created in a specific way; the field of description cannot be understood outside of the metaphor that inscribes it with meaning.

Consequently, more than literary devices that are tropes of resemblance, metaphors, by defining the scope and limits of political possibility, represent how spaces are understood as political communities. To put it a different way, the literalization of the metaphor explains how metaphors can, following Ricoeur, found a real community. The seminal role of metaphors in establishing the normative dimensions of political community is evident in discussions that range from Plato's notion of the polis as a soul to feudal society's great chain of being to Hobbes's "state is a man" (Williamson 2004). Given the normative significance that Rorty ascribes to metaphors, he contends that social and political transformation is a process of metaphorical redescription, one in which new metaphors, those that do not conform with established language games, are advocated for the adoption of new institutions of authority and associative relations. In essence, this redescription is a process in which constitutive language games seen as metaphors are fundamentally transformed. (New) metaphors therefore make it possible for us to change "ourselves and our patterns of action," our lives and our societies, by letting us step outside those areas of discourse "for which there are generally accepted procedures for fixing belief" (Rorty 1991, 163). Metaphorical redescription is a call to speak of, see, and, ultimately, experience political life in a different way (Rorty 1989, 9; see also Calder 2003; Deibert 1997).

Specifying the framework of political relations in a given space, metaphors legitimate particular constellations and relationships of authority — be they the virtue of philosopher kings, divine right, the rights of man, or the sovereign's absolute authority. Because legitimacy is a normative concept, one that outlines how human activity should be conducted, different metaphors of political community will differ with respect to the conception of legitimacy. Consequently, through metaphors, legitimacy is a discursive property embedded in the metaphors that constitute political orders. This account of metaphors and legitimacy relies on the productive power of metaphors. In contrast to more conventional accounts of coercive or institutional power, productive power is a constitutive dynamic that generates the system of social relations and political institutions through discursive practices. These practices, in turn, establish webs of meaning that normalize and naturalize particular relations of social interaction and association (Foucault 1972, 1977, and 1978). Applied to the study of metaphor, productive power defines the horizon of political possibility in a particular way: for instance, are we subjects in a kingdom ordained by God, or are we citizens of a nation? Metaphors are therefore inherently normative and legitimating — they provide a particular view of what the world should be like and then go on to enable and justify certain actions and discredit and suppress others. Principles of legitimacy are, accordingly, inseparable from the productive power of the metaphor itself. Metaphors may not be within the immediate consciousness of individuals in a community. To the extent, however, that institutions and practices (philosophers, kings, parliaments, elections, etc.) are considered essential, the metaphors are enacted and sustained. Over time the everyday practices and policies of authorities perpetuate what legitimates and constitutes political orders (ibid.).

Productive power also demonstrates that community is not distinct from or prior to the conception of political legitimacy. Rather, the understanding of legitimacy that comes to prevail constitutes political community. The nation, for instance, constituted a political community of equal members, which subsequently specified representative democracy as the valid measure and justification of political authority (see Näsström 2003). Thus, communities and legitimacy are not discrete entities. Communities do not adhere to or contest pre-existing criteria of legitimacy; conversely, communities do not exist prior to the precepts of legitimacy they come to adopt. Rather, metaphors produce particular configurations of political authority that are by definition legitimate. Legitimacy is therefore a contingent standard, one whose meaning and community of adherents will change across time and space. There is, accordingly, no affirmative theory of legitimacy, no ideal against which political orders are measured or evaluated. What appears is only a metaphor that has been absorbed so completely that its metaphorical status has come to appear transcendental, what some call a dead metaphor (Rorty 1989, 18; see also Lakoff and Johnson 1980). Political community and legitimacy emerge in tandem, forged through historically contingent and *sui generis* metaphorical discursive practices.

Metaphorical redescription and thus political change occur when legitimacy breaks down and reaches a point of crisis as social actors call into question existing forms of political community and promote others. What brings about the crisis is the contingent and arbitrary forces of history to which Näsström refers. What resolves the crisis is the need to find new grounds, new horizons of legitimacy for emerging orders. Responding to a sense that processes associated with globalization undermine the legitimating metaphors of the sovereign state through the emergence of a global sphere, metaphors of globalization seek to redescribe and, as a consequence, transform entrenched understandings and institutions of political community. They specify new legitimating principles and, in this way, new forms of political community (see Steger 2003, 2004, and 2005). Seen in this light, globalization is not merely a set of material and causal processes — it is a set of constitutive forces. Globalization is not simply about the physical transcendence of state boundaries but also about what these processes come to mean normatively and politically. In a word, as seen through its metaphors, globalization is not simply about the dismantlement or deconstruction of the state — it is also a reconstructive process, one that reshapes the normative foundations of political community.

Assessing the impact of globalization at this present juncture can only be speculative. Understanding the full normative significance of the changes we observe and experience will ultimately require a retrospective reflection with a much longer lens.[4] This constraint, however, does not dispute the need to interrogate emerging understandings and calls for action and to identify and examine the metaphors invoked to make sense of processes associated with globalization. Nor does it prevent us from advocating and justifying ways to construct political community in the future. Certainly, the global imaginaries that Held and Hardt and Negri articulate will not by themselves materialize into transformations of political community. To the extent that they raise normative questions about globalization, however, their articulations allow for an examination of the relationship between legitimacy, autonomy, and democracy and the transformations of political community that might result if these two metaphors were to become the basis for large-scale collective action.[5] A critical analysis of their arguments and the metaphors they employ can point to the different views of globalization, autonomy, legitimacy, and community that arise from one metaphor or the other. The point of my argument is not that political community is newly constituted. Rather, I explore what these popular signifiers of globalization as metaphors tell us about the kind of political communities we can associate with the global moniker and the characteristics that make them legitimate.

In summary, in the normative study of globalization, metaphors are significant for two reasons. First, at a general level, metaphors constitute political communities. Rather than being reflections of an objective reality, metaphors are constructions of political life rooted in particular perspectives. They are constructions of political space that legitimate particular structures of political authority. Studying political community in a global era thus requires interrogating the prevailing metaphors of globalization and the political orders they legitimate. Second, given their constitutive function, metaphors imbue global processes with certain meanings. The term *global,* as a descriptor of political community, can have multiple meanings that vary with the metaphors that construe the significance of globalization. Different interpretations of globalization will produce different norms, promote different governing institutions, and advocate different policies, motivating certain types of political activity and excluding others. As they become socially embedded, they begin to naturalize practices and conventions about political community. Consequently, it is crucial to interrogate the embedded metaphors of globalization by exposing their implications and their (potential) power to naturalize political assumptions and practices.

Sovereignty and the State of Nature

If globalization requires moving beyond the territorial state as the locus of political community, it is first necessary to outline the territorial state's underlying metaphors. Hobbes's theory of the state is perhaps the best starting point. If historical events transformed political geography, Hobbes's contribution was to establish the territorial state as the locus of political authority (Gauthier 1997, 27; see also Hinsely 1986, 155). Hobbes inscribes normative meaning onto the territorial state through the interplay of three metaphors: the state of nature between individuals, the state is a man, and the state of nature between states. Assuming a state of nature between autonomous individuals, Hobbes argues that in the absence of an overarching authority, the autonomy of individuals is a source of insecurity. In the state of nature, equal entitlements to, and responsibilities of, individual security result in the constant possibility of war (Hobbes [1651] 1996, 88). For the sake of their autonomy, individuals transfer their autonomy to the Leviathan. By transferring their autonomy, the state is individuated, vitalized by its sovereignty: the "great *Leviathan* called a *Common-wealth,* or *State,* (in latine *Civitas*)," Hobbes asserts, "is but an Artificall Man ... and in which, the *Soveraignty* is an Artificiall *Soul,* as giving life and motion to the whole body" (ibid., 9). This individuation inscribes the territorial state with all the desires, passions, and characteristics that Hobbes ascribes to human beings — autonomy, expressed as sovereignty, being the most significant.[6]

A concept with two dimensions, state sovereignty entails the internal autonomy of the state over its own affairs and external autonomy from a supervening authority. *Autonomy,* which comes from the Greek *autos* (self) and *nomos* (law), expresses the idea of making laws for oneself, or self-legislation or self-determination. Just as individuals must legislate or regulate for themselves in the state of nature, so also states, as sovereign entities that are similarly autonomous, must be responsible for determining their own policies independent of others. Like individuals, the state exists in a state of nature with other states because the autonomy-cum-sovereignty at the core of the "state is a man" metaphor gives way, or perhaps reverts, to a corporatized version of the "state of nature" metaphor: "Because of their Independency," states, much like men, "are in continuall jealousies, and in the state and posture of Gladiators; having their weapons pointing, and their eyes fixed on one another; that is, their Forts, Garrisons, and Guns upon the Frontiers of their Kingdomes; and continuall Spyes upon their neighbours, which is a posture of War" (Hobbes [1651] 1996, 90). Hobbes, however, does not advocate a global Leviathan.[7] States maintain their autonomy and are responsible for their own security. In turn, sovereignty — the soul of the state and the expression of its autonomy — becomes the foremost principle of international life. The autonomy of the individual is grafted onto, and in turn morphs into, the sovereignty of the state. The state, then, is legitimated by notions of sovereignty, because its individuation through Hobbes's metaphors makes autonomy a foremost concern. In a world in which political community is defined by the territorial state, legitimacy is a product of sovereignty (Biersteker and Weber 1996; Vaughan-Williams 2005; Walker 1993, 2003; Weber 1995).

Beyond Sovereignty and the State of Nature

From a purely geographical perspective, it is obvious why a territorial framework no longer captures the full spectrum of social and political activity.[8] However, where the challenge of globalization becomes salient is in how shifts in scale translate into normative dilemmas that necessitate the reformulation of the legitimating metaphors of political community. Accordingly, in the call for the transformation of political community, it is not sufficient that global processes transcend the physical geography of the state: they must challenge the Hobbesian metaphors and their legitimating principles of state sovereignty and redescribe them.

Whether globalization mandates this kind of normative shift is a matter of debate. Many scholars dispute that globalization generates normative dilemmas or any crisis of legitimacy (Hirst and Thompson 1999; Krasner 2001; Weiss 1998). In their analyses, sovereignty not only remains salient, it takes on greater significance in the context of globalization. These skeptical accounts of globalization fail, however, to consider the way in which the world is increasingly described in global terms: global media, global resistance, global economies, and global citizens. In some ways, whether states exist is irrelevant to this emerging "global" consciousness. Thus, crucial questions are, what does *global* come to mean as a space and site of political community, and how and why does it negate the privileged position of the sovereign state?

Held's cosmopolis and Hardt and Negri's empire similarly represent globalization as entailing a transformation in the understanding of political community. They also share the assumption that legitimacy in global politics rests on autonomy and democracy. However, Held and Hardt and Negri differ in their explanations of how state sovereignty as the standard of legitimacy is thrown into crisis by globalization. What legitimacy is and how it is related to autonomy and democracy take on very different meanings, depending on the metaphor that shapes understandings about globalization. The normative significance of globalization is thus revealed not only through metaphors and their construction of political community but also in the very power that metaphors have to determine understandings of what globalization is and what kind of political community it "legitimately" generates.

It is worth reflecting on the metaphorical status of the terms *cosmopolis* and *empire*. Read (2006, 1-2) argues that "something about globalization appears to compel the production of metaphors." Read makes this claim by arguing that *globe* and *global* are only geometric abstractions, things used to map and understand a physical space and not, by definition, a normative political order. Distinguishing between *world* (a normative-philosophical concept without a fixed spatial referent) and *globe* (a geometric abstraction used to understand a physical space), Read contends that the action of metaphor lies precisely in how a normative world is grafted onto the globe so that *global* is produced as a horizon of political order. In this reading, the metaphorical quality of cosmopolis and empire rest in the way they assemble the processes and events we call globalization as a particular kind of political order — cosmopolis or empire. This point relates to my argument that *global* by itself does not provide the blueprint for political action — it must be constituted as a political order through normative visions and ideals. Thus, to the degree that cosmopolis and empire provide normative vocabularies — language games, as it were — that construct the meaning of globalization, they attempt to found real global communities. Their literal descriptions of globalization must, accordingly, be read less as factual statements about globalization's political consequences than as the way a certain interpretation and narrative about globalization is legitimated. The inquiry into these metaphors uncovers the assumptions and theoretical moves their authors make so that global space can be defined as giving way to cosmopolitan or imperial constellations of power and authority.

It is important to note that metaphors of globalization do not imply that states no longer exist in a political or geographical sense. Redescribing political order only suggests that legitimating norms and practices of political community are no longer rooted in state-based authority structures in an increasingly global context. In other words, although states persist in the context of globalization, legitimacy can no longer be "described" through metaphors of sovereignty.

Cosmopolis

Although few authors explicitly use the word *cosmopolis* to denote their political projects and philosophies, cosmopolis has emerged as a popular metaphor to signify the revival of cosmopolitan theory in the context of contemporary globalization, as is evident in discussions of global democracy, global citizenship, global justice, and global public spheres, among others (Archibugi 2003; Beck 1999; Beitz 1979, 2000; Bohman 1997; Brennan 1997; Buchanan 2000; Cohen and Vertovek 2002; Colas 2003; Delanty 2000; Dower and Williams 2002; Held 1995, 2004, and 2005; Hutchings 1998; Kaldor 2000; Linklater 1998b; McGrew 1997; see also Nyers, in this volume). The most influential work in this regard is David Held's (1995) *Democracy and the Global Order: From the Modern State to Cosmopolitan Governance* (see also Held 2004 and 2005). Certainly, Held's work is not representative of the entire cosmopolitan oeuvre. However, he is the first to explicitly link cosmopolitanism with heightened levels of contemporary globalization. As a result, he has added new dimensions to the discussion of both globalization and cosmopolitanism. If not always garnering support, he has ushered in new debates about what it means to live globally.

Accordingly, by advocating or putting forward an understanding of cosmopolitanism as a description of global political community, Held's work is not only a watershed, it is the point of departure.

Like Hobbes, Held assumes that individual autonomy is the foundational principle of political life. Unlike Hobbes, however, sovereignty itself is not sufficient for autonomy: representative democracy is a necessary condition for individual autonomy. Accordingly, the legitimating condition of the state system is not simply the sovereignty of the state but rather a popular sovereignty in which individual and state autonomy are expressed through the democratic deliberation of its citizens, which is reflected in the actions and decisions of its leaders (see Held 1995, 29-141).

With globalization, Held (1995, 92) observes that "the modern state is increasingly trapped within webs of global interconnectedness permeated by quasi-supranational, intergovernmental and transnational forces" and is "unable to determine its own fate." As a result, "National communities by no means exclusively make and determine decisions and policies for themselves and governments by no means determine what is appropriate exclusively for their own citizens" (ibid., 16-17). This set of changes constitutes not only the internal sovereignty of a state, its policy autonomy, but also its external sovereignty, the legal independence of a state, because the far-reaching effects of globalization on a given population can be the product of decisions made by other governments or international institutions. By drawing individuals and communities into overlapping communities of fate, so that decisions and actions in one part of the world have significant implications for distant localities, the consequence of globalization is that the autonomy of individuals and national communities is compromised as choices are imposed on them.

Thus, sovereignty, as the delimitation of a community of fate bounded by territorial boundaries and its associated framework of democracy, is problematized by globalization: unable to ensure individual autonomy, the normative basis of legitimate governance is thrown into doubt. The crisis of legitimacy initiated by globalization is thus a crisis of congruence, whereby the autonomy of individuals is compromised as the democratic representativeness of state institutions is undermined. However, if democracy, rooted in popular sovereignty, is the only legitimate means to secure autonomy, then preserving and promoting autonomy and legitimate governance in the context of globalization is a matter of determining how democracy can be maintained if the sovereign territorial state is no longer an adequate framework for political community and practice.

Held's answer is to democratize global relationships by extending representative democracy to the global level through cosmopolitan democracy and cosmopolitan democratic law. Held's cosmopolitanism builds on Kant's (1996, 330) premise that states stand in relations that mutually affect one another so that "a violation of right in *one* place of the earth is felt in *all.*" Held adopts Kant's articulation of the all-inclusive principle of community as an all-affected principle in which cosmopolitan community is defined as one in which "individuals and states standing in the relation of externally affecting one another are to be regarded as citizens of a universal state of mankind" (ibid., 322). Kant's concern with the mutual affection problem is that it robs individuals of the capacity to be autonomous. By creating a system of cosmopolitan law that insists that individuals are citizens of a universal community, Kant attempts to solve this problem not only by outlining how individuals are interrelated and interconnected but also by creating norms and practices that ensure that individuals can maintain their autonomy through these interconnections.

From Held's perspective, in the context of globalization and its overlapping communities of fate, the contiguity between the all-affected principle and the all-inclusive principle only becomes more pronounced, as do challenges to individual autonomy. Following Kant, Held insists that individuals require institutions and practices that reflect the interconnectedness between individuals and groups and, at the same time, promote and preserve their autonomy. Making democracy a necessary condition for autonomy, Held reformulates Kant's cosmopolitanism to require not only cosmopolitan law but also cosmopolitan democracy and justifies this reformulation on the grounds that deliberation should include all those affected by a decision, event, or institution (Held 1995, 227). The crisis of congruence is resolved through the creation of a cosmopolitan political community in which individual autonomy is the foundation of political life and cosmopolitan democracy is the standard of legitimacy. By expanding democratic deliberation to the global level, individual autonomy is not only maintained through Held's directives, it is enhanced in a globalizing world.

Held does not have in mind the dissolution of states by the creation of a global government. He attempts to redress the limitations of state institutions through the creation of a new multi-layered democracy of regional and global parliaments instituting regional and global referenda and a series of other measures that would democratize the global sphere. A multi-level global democracy would give way to a multi-level global citizenship.

"People," Held asserts (1995, 232), "would come ... to enjoy multiple citizenships — political membership in the diverse political communities which significantly affected them. They would be citizens of their immediate political communities, and of the wider regional and global networks which impacted upon their lives." Accordingly, an evolving system of cosmopolitan global governance would be "an overarching network of democratic public fora, covering cities, nation-states, regions and the wider transnational order" (Held 2004, 109).

Quintessentially, Held (1995) proposes a project that would render our understanding of living globally for the sake of autonomy cosmopolitan. He argues that democracy and the global order require moving from the modern state to cosmopolitan governance. Highlighting the challenge or crisis posed to the "state as man" and "state of nature" metaphors as the legitimating principles of political life in a global sphere, Held's narrative of cosmopolitanism is not simply a depiction of the empirical dimensions of globalization but rather a metaphor that articulates their normative and political significance.[9] Certainly, cosmopolitan communities have been formulated, as in Kant, in the absence of heightened levels of globalization. However, for Held, given the patterns of interconnection and overlap that contemporary processes associated with globalization create, globalization both reflects and requires cosmopolitan purposes and objectives. At first a problem, globalization also becomes the solution. Globalization's overlapping communities of fate generate the crisis of congruence that undermines the normative framework associated with the state and its sovereignty. But it also heralds a cosmopolitan community — the cosmopolis — in which individual autonomy is the foundation of political life and representative democracy is the standard of legitimate politics.

Empire

For Hardt and Negri, the current moment of global politics is one of empire. Contrary to the argument presented in this chapter, Hardt and Negri (2000, xiv) explicitly state that their concept of empire is not a metaphor because that would imply a continuation of earlier imperialisms. Hardt and Negri extend the definition of *empire* beyond its earlier meanings to provide a new language of global politics (ibid., 8, 57). Indeed, although the imperial practices of the eighteenth and nineteenth centuries spanned the globe, they remained an extension of state sovereignty. Empire today, however, moves beyond entrenched state or territorial categories to create a single system of global sovereignty (see also ibid., 9, 43, 251-54, and 333). In line with Rorty's notion of metaphorical redescription, Hardt and Negri transform, through their new language of global politics, key political categories and promote new political horizons. Empire, despite their claims, is unambiguously a metaphor of globalization.

For many, empire today is synonymous with US power and foreign policy, especially in the aftermath of the attacks of 11 September 2001. Hardt and Negri (quoted in Szeman and Brown 2006, 386), however, situate the evolution of empire in a larger historical context, arguing that the attacks of 9/11 and the US response are symptoms of "an event that had already happened." They call this event empire and argue that it is not reducible to any state, not even the United States. They demonstrate the unique configuration of power that defines the contemporary global period, how it moves beyond the coercive authority of the state and gives rise not only to new political problems but also to new emancipatory possibilities. They therefore examine empire not as a specific set of actions by a given actor but as a fundamentally new field of politics. Thus, Hardt and Negri's articulation of empire — the questions it raises about how global political community might be configured, how it might be legitimated, and with what implications for autonomy and democracy — demands analysis.[10]

Hardt and Negri's discussion of empire is an attempt to delegitimize it, to call attention to its legitimating dynamics so that they can be overcome. Like Hobbes and Held, Hardt and Negri's motivating impetus is autonomy. But rather than individual autonomy, Hardt and Negri are concerned with the multitude's autonomy. Drawing inspiration from Spinoza, Hardt and Negri consider the multitude to be a dispersed and differentiated group of singular identities whose individual and collective identities cannot be represented or mediated by higher authorities. By invoking the notion of the multitude, Spinoza "renewed the splendors of revolutionary humanism, putting humanity and nature in the position of God, transforming the world into a territory of practice, and affirming the democracy of the multitude as the absolute form of politics" (Hardt and Negri 2000, 77). The multitude is, thus, an antidote to hierarchical authority and, during Spinoza's time, specifically to those structures legitimated by a transcendental principle represented by God. Although the multitude displaced God as the source of legitimate rule and obedience, it was ultimately overcome by another transcendent principle — sovereignty — which transferred "the autonomous power of the multitude to a sovereign power that stands above it and rules it" (ibid., 84). This struggle between the multi-tude and sovereignty represents for Hardt and Negri a battle between two legitimating principles: immanence and transcendence (ibid., 69-92). In the contemporary period, this contest continues, with empire representing a transfiguration, but nonetheless a continuation, of transcendent sovereign rule. Hardt and Negri therefore provide a dual metaphor of globalization: empire, the global configuration of sovereign power, and multitude, the potential for empire's defeat and the recapture of autonomous governance.

Empire emerges at the moment of the sovereign state's legitimacy crisis. Following Marx and Lenin, Hardt and Negri contend (2000, 221-34) that the state evolves with the emergence of capitalism and its imperial politics. Although capital is able to continue to realize profit through imperialism by acquiring new territories, capital eventually exhausts itself as all non-capitalist spaces are subsumed within its reach (Szeman 2001b, 180). Capitalism and its vehicle of power — the sovereign state — reach a mo-ment of crisis when there is no more "outside" to conquer. In this crisis of capital, capital abandons the state and assumes an autonomous power of its own to create a new global structure of authority and power. Capital no longer operates in a striated space of competing sovereignties; rather, its system of rule is the seamless space of the entire globe.

Although in this moment of globalization the sovereignty of the state is jettisoned for a new principle and institution of authority, it does not translate into the autonomy of the multitude. With globalization, "sover-eignty has taken a new form, composed of a series of national and supra-national organisms united under a single logic of rule. This new global form of sovereignty is ... [called] Empire" (Hardt and Negri 2000, xii). The power of empire is that its rule is both transcendent and immanent. It is transcendent in that it supersedes all other logics of political authority, subsuming them to the logic of capital. But it is immanent in that, when coupled with new forms of communications technology, it gives rise to new forms of immaterial labour that penetrate and encompass all facets of economic, political, social, and cultural life within its control (Bencivenni 2006, 27). Thus, empire emerges as a "*decentered* and *deterritorializing* appar-atus of rule that progressively subsumes the entire global realm within its open and expanding frontiers" (Hardt and Negri 2000, xiii). Empire is the ultimate realization of Foucault's notion of biopower and the epitome of Deleuze's concept of the society of control.

Through this penetration, empire does not rule through the conven-tional apparatuses of inclusion and exclusion (nationals over non-nationals, men over women, whites over blacks, etc.). Rather, imperial sovereignty rules through the contemporary celebration of difference, hybridity, and heterogeneity. While buttressing its authority on these immanent social discourses, empire legitimates its rule by showing that differences must be managed. Empire must intervene continuously to suppress potential challenges to the ordered totality over which it can rule and, as a result, governs in a sphere of perpetual crisis or omni-crisis, a ubiquitous state of emergency (Hardt and Negri 2004, 36; Ludmer 2001, 170). In this system exceptionalism emerges as the legitimating discourse. *Exceptionalism* often refers to Carl Schmitt's theory of the state of exception, in which the constitution is exempted in times of war or emergency so that the constitution itself can be preserved and protected. Under imperial sovereignty, exceptionalism becomes a global and an everyday condition. Empire's management suppresses the multitude's autonomy and, following Spinoza's notion of the multitude, any potential for democracy.

As the ultimate expression of capital's autonomous rule and inherent global scope, globalization is the continuation of the struggle between sovereign, transcendent rule and the immanent power of the multitude. By transcending the sovereignty of states, empire gives way to a global sovereignty. As this global transcendence operates through the immanent structures of society, however, it opens the moment for the multitude to realize its full autonomy by overturning empire with its vision of unmediated, non-sovereign global democracy.

Outlining the political order that the multitude can bring about, Hardt and Negri dismiss the common comparison between the multitude and the people. In their view, "the people" entails a vicious circular logic that precludes rather than promotes autonomy. Although the notion of the people transfers authority from the absolute sovereign to the population, this autonomy is ultimately transferred to representatives to act in the sovereign interest, which individuals are obliged to obey. "The people" is, thus, an ironic concept: although autonomy appears to be transferred from the transcendent to the immanent, it is ultimately co-opted by the collective sovereign will of the community. From this perspective popular sovereignty "inevitably poses power as the rule of the one" (Hardt and Negri 2004, 353), in which the people emerge as "a constituted synthesis ready for sovereign rule" (ibid., 103).

By contrast, the multitude is a constituted multiplicity made up of "innumerable internal differences that can never be reduced to a unity or a single identity — different cultures, races, ethnicities, genders, and sexual orientations; different forms of labour; different ways of living; different views of the world; and different desires" (Hardt and Negri 2004, xiv). Its immanence is both a descriptive category of the dynamic plane of the perpetual "production of differences, inventions, and modes of life" and a legitimating principle that substantiates this productive process and the multiple differences and realities it generates (cited in Brown and Szeman 2005, 378). Therefore, sovereignty — absolute or popular — defies the multitude, subsuming it within a transcendent principle that places the unity and autonomy of the collective over the multitude's diverse singularities.

As immanence of both embodied experience and the legitimating discourse of its multiplicity, the multitude represents a radical autonomy. Rather than seeing autonomy as an individual's status, one that is in the hands of the state, Hardt and Negri (2000, 407) argue that the autonomy of the multitude is captured in the term *posse,* a verb that reflects autonomy in action. This is a radicalization of autonomy in two senses. First, it makes autonomy a practice, not a status or right protected or granted by the state, as it is conceived in conventional accounts of sovereignty. Second, it destroys the assumed vertical distribution of power between the people and its ruler and locates power solely in the productive relations of the multitude. As a laterally organized process, not a status conferred by higher authorities, the multitude's autonomy is "what is left of reality once the conception of the people is freed from transcendence" (Negri 2002, 36). The multitude's autonomy is self-legislation in the truest sense of the term — not mediated, but solely in the immediate activity of the multitude itself. Freed from transcendence, sovereignty is undermined both for its system of legitimacy (vertical, hierarchical representation) and for its ontology of autonomy (individual rights).

To actualize this autonomy, Hardt and Negri argue that it is necessary to radicalize the practice of citizenship and democracy and detach them from conventional sovereignties. Given their view that autonomy is an active practice and not a status acquired through representation, Hardt and Negri argue that the "multitude must be able to decide, if, when, and where it moves. It must have the right also to stay still and enjoy one place rather than being forced to constantly move" (Hardt and Negri 2000, 400). They therefore call for a global citizenship based on rights of mobility rather than rights of representation to give the multitude the "power to reappropriate control over space and thus to design the new cartography" of political community (ibid.).

If representation no longer pertains to citizenship, then it is even less likely to pertain to democracy. Under empire, democracy is a near impossibility. By definition in a state of exception, democracy must be suspended until the crisis allows the constitution to assume its central political function. Invoking the notion of the people, however, does not emancipate the multitude and dethrone the absolute power of capital. The danger contained in representative democracy and implied by the term *the people* is that the claim of absolute representation only amounts to absolute rule. Rather than representative democracy, then, the defeat of empire requires absolute democracy, the invention of "different forms of representation or perhaps new forms of democracy that go beyond representation" (Hardt and Negri 2004, 255). Empire, governed by the logic of capital and the state of exception, which makes autonomy a near impossibility, must confront multitude, which seeks to redescribe empire, providing new possibilities of immanent autonomy through a mobile global citizenship and an absolute democracy.

Immanence therefore gives rise to the multitude as a political community. As both a descriptive category and a normative ideal, it legitimizes the radical conceptions of citizenship and democracy that are required for autonomy. This departure from existing categories and assumptions stands sovereign politics on its head. To the extent that modern logics of sovereignty have informed both political practice and political theory, political community has come to be understood as something unified by a singular identity, purpose, or objective. Hardt and Negri undercut these assumptions by delegitimizing sovereignty as a principle of rule, state or imperial, that defies rather than defines autonomy. Against empire, multitude suggests that in the global era the field of politics requires a global reach and an altogether different normative understanding of space and society.

Conclusion

Cosmopolis and empire are direct challenges to each other. The very schematic of legitimacy, autonomy, and democracy in cosmopolis is anathema to the multitude, and vice versa. In cosmopolis the insidious effects of globalization compromise the autonomy of individuals: it is the violation of the legitimacy of the representative democratic state. In empire, globalization is pernicious because it maintains and extends a system of sovereign authority that thwarts the autonomy of the multitude. Cosmopolis entails the extension of representative democratic structures beyond the state to enhance autonomy. From the perspective of the multitude, these representative institutions maintain a political system in which the autonomy of the multitude is transferred, compromising its immanent power. Cosmopolitan democracy is not a solution to the dilemmas of globalization. An absolute democracy, one that embodies the immanent political relationships of the multitude, is the only legitimate way to ensure its autonomy.

Despite these differences, what is striking is that for both readings of globalization, autonomy and democracy are closely intertwined with the notion of legitimacy. On the one hand, this commonality speaks to the salience of autonomy and democracy as key political objectives across different globalization projects. On the other, their very different articulations of autonomy and democracy reflect that they remain empty signifiers in the absence of a legitimating discourse, for instance, a metaphor that provides the context of its form and function. Accordingly, although empirical realities may ask us to reformulate our normative categories about political community, these reformulations engender certain interpretations of the world. Attention must, therefore, be directed towards the different narratives of globalization — the metaphors that situate current circumstances as a moment of normative crisis — and an exploration of the normative solutions they make possible.

Part 2
Legitimacy — Accommodating Difference and Autonomy

chapter 5

Governmental Rationalities and Indigenous Co-Governance: James Bay Cree Coexistence, from Mercantilist Partnerships to Neoliberal Mechanisms

Harvey A. Feit

THE CHANGING FORMS OF colonial governance that have been dominant during recent moments of globalization have had systematic but diverse effects on relations between European settler states and regional indigenous peoples. Exploring how to analyze these indigenous–nation-state relations affords an opportunity to address questions posed by the volume editors about legitimacy in the context of globalization, particularly in settings where multiple and diverse kinds of polities, including non-state polities, are interacting. These increasingly common settings also pose challenges to the analysis of colonial governmentality, which I see as an aspect of globalization. I use *globalization* to refer to the post-Renaissance extension to non-European lands and peoples of several interconnected and modern institutions and practices: nation-states, science, market-dominated societies, and colonial differentiation with the superordination of Europeans.

Relations of governance in colonial settings occur not only through direct and indirect rule but also through the distinct coexistence or co-governance relationships that are formed where colonial governance does not simply subsume or use local governance forms to its own ends. In these situations, the ongoing governance projects and visions of non-state peoples actively coexist with colonial forms. In many contexts, non-state peoples survive as societies and polities and continue to pursue an array, albeit often more limited than previously, of their own historical and concurrent projects. They pursue these forms, which are adapted to work in the changing contexts of globalization. They often seek to maintain these co-governance relations despite subordination and dispossession, suffering and loss. I argue that co-governance — which involves coexisting governance discourses, institutions, and projects — is important both in the historical record and in relation to the current forms of governance.

These diverse forms of globalization, colonial governance, and co-governance are each linked to fundamental issues of legitimacy in settler states. These issues arise because of the largely unexpected survival of indigenous societies in these states, which highlights the temporal priority of indigenous occupation and governance of lands claimed and encompassed by the states. The survival of indigenous societies and polities constitutes a continuing limitation on, and fundamental threat to, the legitimacy claims of settler states (see Alfred 1999). The priority of indigenous peoples' rights to the territory and governance of these domains has never been effectively dealt with — no less satisfactorily recognized, mutually negotiated, or enduringly settled — from the point of view of either settler or indigenous societies (see Tully 1995; Asch 1997; Alfred 2002; Scott 2004; Beier 2005; and Blaser et al., under review).

Legitimacy problems have been heightened in recent global governance settings partly because of the complexity of defining the extent of the relevant legitimating community, the compositional diversity of obvious community claimants, and the plurality of communications and world views among state and transnational non-state actors (Bernstein 2004). The legitimacy of settler states is problematic for similar reasons. In addition, problems arise because the colonial vision of an encompassing hierarchical community no longer carries the conviction it did when justifications for the supremacy of settlers were taken as more self-evident and authoritative than they are now.

Questions of legitimacy, in a political sense, are also closely implicated in the forms of governmental rationality and discourses that emerged in the modern history of Europe and in the ways Europeans formulated the constitution of individuals, society, political rule, and nation-states (Foucault 1991; Burchell, Gordon, and Miller 1991; Barry, Osborne, and Rose 1996). These governmental rationalities and mechanisms were developed not only within Europe but also in diverse settings of colonial governance. The colonial projects involved discourses legitimating the superordination of colonists over colonials, however mixed and inseparable these categories and persons were. These governmental discourses made certain kinds of colonial conduct and projects of domination appear normal and necessary, as well as legitimate.

The regional and temporal diversity of colonial settings and projects requires attention to the differing forms and effects of colonial governance in interaction with diverse pre-existing and emerging forms of regional and local non-state governance (see, for example, Escobar 1995 and D. Scott 2005, as well as analyses in Said [1978] 1991 and Bhabha 1994). Thus, although there are compelling continuities in the interrelated post-Renaissance histories of nation-states, science, market societies, and colonialism, there are also widely recognized and debated discontinuities, changes, successes, and failures in the histories of governance within and outside Europe. These complex relationships of diverse forms of governance at work in changing settings problematize how to analyze colonial governmentalities at particular times and places (D. Scott 2005).

These pervasive, diverse, and fragmentary processes also require setting colonial governance in relation to non-state peoples in ways that go beyond the latter's encompassment by and use in colonial governance. In David Scott's helpful account of analyzing colonial governmentality and his summary of its application to the analysis of colonial rule in Sri Lanka, he concludes by citing an 1830s call by Charles Trevelyan for a new form of rule to "set the natives on a process of European improvement ... They will then cease to desire and aim at independence *on the old Indian footing*" (cited in D. Scott 2005, 44).[1] Scott then formulates a project for analyzing colonial governmentality, "If we are to grasp more adequately the lineaments of our postcolonial modernity, what we ought to try to map more precisely is the political rationality through which this old footing was systematically displaced by a new one such that the old would now only be imaginable along paths that belong to new, always-already transformed, sets of coordinates, concepts, and assumptions" (ibid.).

This project is important and critical, but I think that it frames analyses of colonial governmentality too narrowly by limiting the scope to questions about how the "old footing" is displaced and how it comes about to "only be imagined" through the new. This formulation understates the problems of identifying long-term effects, and it limits the analysis of the relationships between other forms of governance and new governmentalities to the displacement or transformation of the former.

Colonial projects of displacement are often incomplete and disrupted. They have complex and contradictory consequences, and they involve relations to emerging forms of governance. In the contemporary world, including areas long subjected to colonial governmentalities and rule, we see numerous instances of situationally specific governance informed by

99

cultural, national, and religious projects as well as anti-colonial resistance. The projects are sometimes rooted in earlier visions and practices, albeit in complex ways. There are analyses in many of these settings of how old footings were transformed for new purposes, how old footings were invented in new contexts, and how these footings may be taken as "tradition" — that is, how the old comes to be imagined through the new. In my view, however, these accounts often do not demonstrate how governance can now *only* be imagined or even practised through the new.

This is the case especially among non-state societies, at diverse scales, even though they are being changed by and subordinated to colonial governance. I indicate below how contemporaneous forms of coexisting governmentalities and other forms of governance are not adequately analyzed solely by considering the effects of colonial governmentality.

There are other reasons for not excluding these relationships. If we ignore the distinctive trajectories and effects of other forms of governance as we develop critiques of the knowledge and power of colonial governmentality, we risk not examining the critical framework we ourselves use. We also risk ignoring alternative perspectives on governance that may arise from the ongoing and changing knowledge practices of those who are in subordinate positions.

Despite the long, widespread, and often harrowing successes and enduring effects of colonial governmentalities, it is important to consider the often diverse, fragmentary, hybrid, and contradictory, but also sometimes enduring mutual effects of the forms of governance with which they engage. These forms of non-state governance do not derive from the logics of colonial governmentalities. This understanding requires additional forms of analysis than those that are common in the study of governmentality in European history or its application to colonial rule. The analytical frameworks of colonial governmentality must be subjected to ongoing critical re-examination by considering other logics of governance and how these forms engage colonial governmentalities. In this chapter, I examine an example of these processes.

In my longer-term and ongoing research, I explore both the logics of a non-state form of governance and the forms of coexisting governance that develop between a non-state people and a colonial-settler state. I show how non-state governmental structures and projects are not solely imagined through new modern coordinates, concepts, assumptions, or subject identities; rather, they are effected through ever-changing old footings that serve modern projects. Here, I explore a part of that analysis, the relationships, and the diverse and sometimes hybrid governance visions and practices that have existed and developed between Canadian and Quebec governance institutions in northern Quebec and a regional indigenous people, the James Bay Crees.

The Crees (a term I will use here to refer to James Bay Crees) are a hunting and an indigenous people who number sixteen thousand and occupy over four hundred thousand square kilometres. They have been tied to European nations and to world markets, initially through the trade in fur pelts, since the seventeenth century. More recently, they have been drawn into new national, transnational, and globalizing relations by the joint impact of expanding state administrations, large-scale natural resource developments, and nationalist movements, as well as by engagements that they have initiated with encapsulating societies.

I show that in the 1930s and 1940s, as nation-state administrations established their first presence in northern Quebec, specific forms of colonial mercantilist governance were used by state and trading company officials and also that mutual forms of co-governance emerged as a result of Cree initiatives. In the 1970s, when large-scale natural resource developments were initiated in the region in the context of Quebec nationalist projects to ensure state legitimacy, the mercantile co-governance relationships changed. State negotiators and bureaucrats came to see them as the specific demands and requirements of the Crees, rather than as a part of ongoing state-Cree relations. As a result, the complex relationships of the earlier period were reduced or ignored as development governmentality was deployed. But Crees responded in terms of co-governance. More recently, with the emergence of neoliberal governmentality, state accommodations to Crees now occur in the context of the active promotion of neoliberal co-governance mechanisms. The assumption, then, is that market dominance in conjunction with satisfying the Crees' economic needs will finally ensure Cree modernization and their consistent support for conditions essential to the legitimation of the state and its resource exploitation projects.

The analysis, thus, extends not only to the discursive agency and institutions of states, markets, and civil society but also to relations between them and the discourses, logics, and projects of peoples who are not wholly encompassed by modern governmentality. I summarize how Crees significantly shaped mercantilist co-governance processes, and how their vision of co-governance gave it form (see Feit 2005). I note how in the 1970s they negotiated accommodations and modifications to developmental governance, introducing their ideas and needs into the modern structure of a highly legalized land claims agreement. Although this effort had diverse effects, many being part of colonial projects of governmentality, Crees also made this process affirm the continuity of their co-governance. The failures of the implementation of this agreement from Cree perspectives brought some of its adverse effects into clear perspective and led to Cree challenges to new neoliberal resource development and nationalist projects in the 1980s and 1990s. These challenges demonstrated to state institutions and corporations, among others, that Crees had not accepted new identities and conduct as citizens, which were attributed to them in the prevailing governmental projects. Also central to these conflicts were the developing international legitimacy needs of state projects and increasingly transnational state corporations. Cognizant of these needs, the Crees effectively carried their projects of opposition into transnational arenas in the 1990s.

Although neoliberal governmentality was increasingly the context for many of these conflicts, the dominance of neoliberal governance also opened new opportunities to Crees for specific forms of national recognition and participation in economic development through new neoliberal relationships. Neoliberalism also shifted the terrains of ongoing struggles for co-governance (see Feit, in press).

I undertake this analytical case study by using several shifting perspectives rather than by offering a general model of colonial governance or its analysis. The case study is ethnographic in that it implicates events and interpretations of daily lives as well as political-historical moments, although the ethnography is thin description.

I choose not to offer a general model because to do so would risk bringing the analysis within the globalizing histories and stories of progress or improvement, or within the knowledge practices of equally modernist universalizing critiques of improvement and modern governance. To develop a general model risks locating the presence and the possibilities of contemporary and historical non-state societies and actors in an analytical space shaped solely by modern histories, nation-states, transnational markets, and governmentality — that is, in universalizing discourses and practices. In these spaces, non-state societies seem tied to the past, implausible in the present, and with no real, enduring, and distinctive possibilities for the future. I do not fully avoid these risks, but I seek to moderate them by keeping to a situated and ongoing case and trying to offer an account that may be read, and hopefully used, by people in different polities and contexts.

Co-Governance and Legitimacy

In this analysis co-governance is any non-exclusive form of governance by which both a distinct non-state people or entity and a nation-state exercise control, albeit not equally, over the conduct of relations among their societies, within domains of action, or with nature. It can comprise discourses, practices, visions, and institutions.

For the non-state peoples that concern me here, this definition presupposes not only an effective governance capacity but also an enduring ability to reproduce social lives not founded on the presuppositions of modernity. For example, the radical distinctions between individual citizens and representational processes that characterize "Euro-American" forms of rule and democratic nation-states do not apply in James Bay Cree society. Crees envisage societies of inherently social individuals embedded in networks of family and kinship that make human lives possible. Indeed, for Cree hunters, social networks and kinship, and relations articulated by analogies to kinship, permeate all aspects of social life and the world, including governance and legitimacy. Like many other indigenous societies, Crees draw on traditions of direct and consensual, not solely representative, governance (see Alfred 1999). These differences are important and modifiable.

These practices also shape the way that distinctive capacities for self-governance and co-governance are envisaged in the context of relationships with nation-states. Co-governance in this sense does not depend on formal recognition or systematic reconciliation with state law or sovereignty. For this reason, co-governance might be called messy when it is looked at from the point of view of the system of nation-states. Co-governance in this sense can also be messy in other ways, because the governance logics that are in relationship are typically not commensurable. Co-governance is not often a project of state governmentality.

A variety of co-governing discourses, practices, and institutions can develop to express and give effect to the differing relations of governance that exist between state institutions and practices and non-state peoples. These may be new or they may be altered or emerging forms of what were previously state or self-governing practices that are now taken up in relational governance activities.

Here, co-governance is also messy in that there may not always be a clear separation between the discourses, practices, and institutions of co-governance and those of either the nation-state or non-state societies. They may not always be clearly distinguished or separable from state and non-state forms by their practitioners, nor may they always be separable in a grounded analytical sense, although anyone might make the distinction in a more abstract form.

In addition, these areas of convergence need not develop into an encompassment of non-state governance by the projects or visions of state governmentalities. Where this absorption has occurred, it would mean the existence of a form of state or colonial rule rather than a coexisting co-governance arrangement. This messiness partly explains why co-governance often is not recognized or acknowledged, why it is often denied when questioned, and why it can be a recurring site of contestation.

This lack of recognition and denial by practioners is reflected in analytical ambiguities. Co-governance is often assumed in analytical settings to be ephemeral and unimportant, a transition stage in the advance of state or colonial rule. But the analysis must consider what people are doing and saying in their everyday lives, not just when they express formal reasons or justifications. Nor can it be assumed that situations can be fit into pre-existing analytical categories. By this test, messy co-governance may prove to be surprisingly complex and important, as in the circumstances I analyze here. Indeed, the blurred boundaries between messy co-governance and state and non-state societies' governance may help to explain the durability and wide-reaching effects of co-governance.

This messiness of co-governance has important bearings on legitimacy. Nation-states and indigenous polities have different and diverse forms of legitimacy that follow differences in their forms of governance, all the while being tied to each other. When legitimacy involves claims that implicate relations to others who are partly outside the nation-state communities, ambiguities of state legitimacy readily come into focus.

Within indigenous polities, legitimacy is inevitably different. For Crees it is founded in kinship and personalized kinship-like relations and consensual processes. Although the legitimacy ideas and practices of Crees and many other non-state peoples can in many respects be characterized as normative rather than legal or rational, the foundations of their governance may not be fully encompassed by the ideas of normativity or law and rationality. Legitimacy for Crees, for example, is inseparable from personally lived histories of relationships. Many Cree hunters and elders do not radically separate themselves or their knowledge from the world that is known but understand themselves as embedded in it. As a consequence of this epistemology and cosmology, one that does not follow from post-

Renaissance ideas of modernity or social science, legitimacy is not simply about what should be or what is formally arranged in law or political thought; rather, it is historically and experientially rooted in what has been and is. Thus, Cree legitimacy statements about co-governance with the state are not simply about an "ought" or a "right," they are also about relationships that "are." Crees have experienced enduring co-governance; they do not just desire it, nor do they seek agreement with others through reasoned accord to promote it. Its history is known even if it was and is contested. Theirs is neither a claim to universal or rational truth nor a search for normative or constitutional agreement. Rather, they are making a statement about knowledge that is situated in relationships of particular times and places and true in the lived present. Moreover, this statement is always subject to change.

It is important, therefore, to consider not only how legitimacies of nation-state and non-state communities differ but also how they mutually implicate and complicate one another. Co-governance is a context in which these aspects of the messiness of legitimacy come to the fore. In the balance of this chapter, I explore issues of colonial governance and co-governance and the question highlighted by the volume editors in the Introduction: how do communities retain and gain influence and control over the non-local decisions and projects that affect them?

Governance and Messy Co-Governance: Historical and Ethnographic Perspectives

In preparing affidavits for a court case in 1999, elderly James Bay Cree hunters and women talked about the effects of commercial forestry on their hunting territories, the family hunting lands into which the Crees divide their region, and important forms of Cree governance.[2] They commented on how their tenure and governance were recognized by actions, institutions, and instruments of governments. Charlie Coon Blacksmith said,

> About 45 years ago a representative of the Department of Indian Affairs visited Simon [Metabie] and me and confirmed that we were Ndoho Ouchimauch [hunting leaders or, more literally, land bosses] of this territory.[3]
>
> I have never consented to any [forestry] cutting on my land. I did hear that they were coming into my land from our Band council but

I have had no word on where or how they cut. This is not right. As *Ndoho Ouchimau* I am responsible for the land. If they want to cut, then the company must understand that I manage the forest and I protect it. They must talk to me and listen to my expertise ...

As far as I can tell, none of the big companies operating in Eeyou Istchee [Cree land] are obeying the rules of the James Bay and Northern Quebec Agreement [1975]. Until they do so they should not be allowed to cut any more timber. It is simple to enforce this. The Agreement says the government and developers must consider our way of life and protect the environment. They have not done so. (Charlie Coon Blacksmith, 7 July 1999, trans. Charlie Mianscum)

This view that Cree tenure and the roles of hunting leaders in governing their lands were both recognized and also ignored by governments was echoed by others such as Christine Saganash, whose family lands were more remote and had not yet been cut. She recalled one of the earlier government recognitions of Cree tenure and governance:

I remember so many years ago when Indian Affairs [agents] came to draw boundary lines [i.e., to map the boundaries of the hunting territories for use of the Beaver Reserves system then being established jointly with the Crees]. Allen [her late husband] was already the tallyman [a Ndoho Ouchimau]. They gave him a badge to show he was a game warden. I still have that badge and carry it with me ...

They must listen to us and respect us. We are the owners of the land. We are part of it. To cut our land is to destroy us and our way of life. (Christine [Jolly] Saganash, 22 July 1999, trans. Johnny Cooper)

Crees, thus, see a continuity that stretches from the first active presence of government agents in the region and the setting up of beaver reserves between the early 1930s and the 1950s through to the James Bay and Northern Québec Agreement, a modern treaty negotiated by the Crees and the governments in the 1970s, and present conflicts over the use of lands and resources. This continuity exists through ongoing Cree control, use, and protection of the land; through ongoing conflicts; and through continuing, repeated, and renewed recognitions of Cree tenure and governance by governments. Some of these include the distribution of badges symbolizing Ndoho Ouchimauch authority for Crees, the mapping of their land tenure units for use by new joint conservation institutions, and the recognitions and protections declared in the five-hundred-page modern legal agreement that the Crees signed with the government in 1975.

These Cree histories shape the Crees' interactions with governments and nation-state institutions, and they highlight how government actions lack legitimacy because they fail to fulfill mutual obligations and Cree knowledge. During the period from 1931 to the 1960s, there were numerous recognitions in government records of Cree governance and contemporaneous co-governance by Crees and Canadian state institutions. The recognitions were expressed, albeit sometimes partially or with hesitations, in personal and official discussions and correspondence among government bureaucrats and fur traders and with Crees. They are also found in inter- and intragovernmental policy statements, reports to Parliament, legal documents, and Orders-in-Council (see Feit 2005).

Recognitions of Cree governance and co-governance were also part of the ongoing lived experiences of Crees and state agents. They were put into practice in a myriad of procedures and relationships through which government agents, fur traders, and Crees interacted year after year to bring about the recovery of beaver populations in the region. These were not only bureaucratic but also personal practices and experiences. For example, the meetings between government managers and Cree hunting territory leaders to mutually agree on the allocation of annual beaver harvest quotas to each hunting territory were social and personal. Decisions about allocations were partly joint and partly made among the Crees themselves. They required government administrators and Cree leaders to know the individuals they were dealing with well. The government agents had a limited understanding of how trapping was done and how it could be done to conserve beaver. Cree hunting leaders reported the number of beaver lodges on their territories, which was the basis for the agreed upon quota, but leaders were varied in their skill and the effort they put into gaining this knowledge. The individual hunters on a given territory were varied in their trapping skills and efforts and, therefore, in how many beaver they were likely to catch and how many their families needed. Each of these considerations affected how allocations were made. The families of hunters who hunting leaders agreed would use a territory then lived at the same camp site with the leader's family for up to nine months of the year. Thus, governance of beaver reserves not only required extensive co-operation, it also personalized the official government agents' relationships. In addition, it demanded the extension of aspects of state and trading company administration into some parts of the social and personal lives of the Crees.

Thus, the hunting territories and Ndoho Ouchimauch were key Cree governance institutions that became the central means of government initiatives for the conservation of beaver.[4] Governments developed modified administrative bureaucracies for beaver conservation by working closely with and adopting fur trade and Cree traditions and practices. Governance of lands and resources to promote beaver conservation was a process of state governance and an exercise of Cree governance, and it required the creation of new joint forms of hybrid co-governance, like the joint quota meetings and allocation processes. When a government agent met a Cree hunter to mutually agree on a beaver quota that the Cree hunters would respect and generally conform to over the course of the next year of trapping, the agreement was based on Cree knowledge. The hunting leaders still regularly adjusted the actual harvests to fit what they knew was happening on the land by using hunting leadership practices and institutions. Cree people could understand this arrangement as one of partnering and respecting government management, as well as exercising and sustaining older and continuing Cree forms of land governance. In these respects, it was a mutually respectful co-governance.

When the governments withdrew from the management of beaver reserves in some parts of the region in the 1960s and 1970s, Cree hunting territories and Ndoho Ouchimauch continued, and they are still being practised by Crees today, although the practices continue to be altered as circumstances change. These Cree governance practices have, thus, survived the long period of colonial governance.

Governance of Beaver: Mercantilist Governance as Limited Interventions and Personal Relationships, 1931-70

The idea of restoring beaver populations was suggested by Crees. The ideas and practices that emerged and made this idea attractive to governments and trading companies, however, were cost efficiencies, future profits, and defining territorial claims, as well as the management and pastoral care of the Crees and the beaver (see Feit 2005). The forms of governance developed had many features that were common to mercantilist forms of governance that were characteristic of pre-eighteenth-century Europe and colonization (Foucault 1991; Burchell, Gordon, and Miller 1991; Rose 1996; D. Scott 2005).[5] Among its characteristics, mercantilist governance aimed to preserve the wealth of governments, it depended on the use of laws and regulations, and it modelled its project on family economy (see Foucault 1991, 97-99).

The beaver conservation project was characterized by tension on the one side between a conception of preserving the Crees in a condition of economic and social self-sufficiency and self-governing autonomy, which included re-establishing the conditions of greater self-sufficiency that existed in the past. This objective was pursued through the support of long-standing Cree tenure and leadership institutions and the passing of laws that limited the access of outsider trappers to the region. On the other side, there was a more liberal project of improving the Crees by advancing their "inevitable development." But it was traditional self-sufficiency and the partly mercantilist rationales of economic extraction, limiting costs, accommodating state governance to local conditions, and expediency that prevailed.

The state project was, therefore, narrowly focused. There were no significant efforts to redeploy Cree labour or to take over Cree lands to exploit other resources. Using and strengthening Cree tenure and governance over hunting territories and leadership continued the long "traditions" of the fur trade compact of "partnership," which had emerged over three centuries. This partnership had endured because of the super profits it often provided to the traders and because of the conditions Crees negotiated for their energetic participation in the fur trade (see Francis and Morantz 1983). In short, mercantilist types of governance had a long history and were deeply embedded in the regional ideas and practices of both Crees and non-Natives. Neither sought to radically transform local tenures, local leaders and governance, the socio-religious universe, or the way of life of the Crees.

In the 1930s the partnership in conservation also reduced the costs of the centralized federal bureaucracy because increased beaver catches and meat and higher incomes from pelts lessened Cree demands on government assistance. In addition, managing beaver with Cree tenure and governance reduced enforcement costs and was a key to the Crees' active participation. Although nation-state institutions also claimed the land and resources as their own, government agents only occasionally tried to change Cree control of — or claims and access to — land and game (see Feit 2005). The governance project depended on and worked through the personalized social relations that Crees and government agents were developing.

Although there were visions and practices of governing the Crees as a society among state agencies and initiatives, the cooperation of the Crees could not be advanced by calling on them as citizens or as Crees or Indians per se. Indeed, only the term *Indian* would have been a jointly recognized category of self-reference for Crees during this period. Cooperation was secured through gaining the support of individuals within the community and through family leadership and kinship networks. This support was founded on recognizing and supporting a unique Cree relationship to the land and other Crees that was expressed in the governance of territories and consensual decisions, as Charlie Coon Blacksmith and Christine Saganash insist. As their views indicate, it was not an effective form of indirect rule. Crees exercised a strong sense of personal and collective autonomy.

In addition, it was a project whose subjects or objects, depending on one's perspective, were not only Crees but also beaver and the land. For government agents and traders, aiding beaver recovery was an exercise in managing natural animate objects and a means to economic ends. For Crees, aiding beaver expressed the inseparability of human societies and what modern Europeans call nature, the land and animal persons. Beavers were social beings and subjects for Crees. The distinction was obscured in the everyday practices of the governance of beaver — where they were treated as natural objects or social beings. But the difference is important because, for the Crees, these governance practices established relations to game and lands as social beings that had value distinct from human projects and a worth in and of themselves (as Charlie Coon Blacksmith indicates above). This key ontological difference reappears throughout many subsequent Cree-state relations (see below).

Thus, governance of beaver reserves did not create or depend on shared understandings of impersonal rules, nature as an object, abstract liberal individuals, or social conditions managed by experts. In this respect, too, the governance project did not dramatically reconstruct the society or the identities of Crees. Rather, Crees now extended their forms of relating to the land as a living society, relating to others in egalitarian ways, and treating individuals as socially connected, which they had been applying to traders during the fur trade, to interactions with the representatives of a nation-state. This limited but did not eliminate changes to themselves.

The personal and social autonomy of the Crees, and the histories and goals of state governance in the region, thus created the relations of governance that gave substantial form, albeit a messy one, to effective and enduring co-governance. A space of social partnership and spaces for autonomies, tensions, and conflicts developed that linked, but did not synthesize, the several distinct forms of non-state governance and governmental rationalities that coexisted. The legitimacy of this partly colonial co-governance partook broadly of both Cree practices and state forms, and many of its ambiguities were well recognized by Crees and government agents (see Feit 2005).

Developing Land and the Crees to Legitimate the State: Transforming Regional Governance, 1971-90

Co-government during the long period of beaver reserves shaped Cree responses to state and industrial projects that threatened their lands in the 1970s. While changes to forms of governance had been underway for several years in the region (see Feit 1985), a significant break occurred when the James Bay Hydro-Electric Project was initiated in 1971 without Cree involvement.

Since the story of Cree opposition to hydroelectric development plans, the court cases they initiated, and the negotiated treaty has been widely told, I will limit my analyses to the governance and legitimacy aspects (see, for example, Richardson [1975] 1991; Salisbury 1986; Vincent and Bowers 1988; Feit 1989; Grand Council of the Crees 1998; Gnarowski 2002; Gagnon and Rocher 2002; Blaser, Feit, and McRae 2004a, 2004b).

Developmentality: A Challenge to Co-Governance

When the Government of Quebec announced the James Bay Hydro-Electric Project, it legitimated its action by referring to the need for development. After the Second World War, development became a central discourse and practice of domestic and international governance. States abandoned the discourses of early twentieth-century colonialism in favour of ideas and practices that fit with the accelerating international decolonization movement and with the world leadership responsibilities of the United States and its allies, such as Canada, which saw themselves as never having had colonies (Sachs 1993a, 1993b; Escobar 1995; and, within this series, Streeter, Weaver, and Coleman 2009).

Development discourse made new states into underdeveloped ones, thereby legitimating as necessary and benevolent resource exploitation projects and economic intrusions that were already established or newly offered by developed states and international market institutions. Consequently, globalizing exploitation and domination continued through partly new governance instrumentalities (see Ferguson 1990; Sachs 1993a, 1993b; Escobar 1995). It was also a form of governance that was continuous with the developing governmental rationalities that Foucault called *governmentality* and described as emerging in European nation-states throughout the nineteenth and twentieth centuries (Ferguson 1990; Escobar 1995; Burchell, Gordon, and Miller 1991; Barry, Osborne, and Rose 1996).

Deployed within Canada, development discourses and governance envisaged the country as both a developing and a developed nation: it was a raw materials supplier to the expanding US economy on the one side and a home to businesses and middle classes that were expanding and drawing resources and sometimes labour from Canadian regions or hinterlands on the other. Inside Canada, development discourses and practices were also tied to national projects and regional development programs that transferred some federal economic resources to regions, including parts of Quebec, for social and economic development. These were intended, in part, to help bind a disparate and geographically challenged nation-state that existed adjacent to a powerful neighbour.

In Quebec, development discourses and practices readily joined with those of decolonization, which were accelerating with the Quiet Revolution of the 1960s. Quebec francophone elites actively moved into business, industry, finance, and state-owned corporations to wrestle control of the Quebec economy and state institutions away from a largely English Canadian class elite. The discursive practices were especially powerful from the 1960s onward, when Quebecers started to shed their rural and religious self-image and embrace the urban and industrial expansion that had already been underway for several decades.

The James Bay Hydro-Electric Project was initiated by a federalist Quebec government, in part to reassert the province's governance and legitimacy over its domain after the October Crisis. During this episode, separatist violence was countered by Prime Minister Pierre Elliot Trudeau sending Canadian army troops into the streets of Montreal (Gourdeau 2002, 18; Ciaccia, reported in Wilkinson and Masella 2002, 218).

Development as the rationality of governance, when addressed to Crees who were not fully part of national polities or identities, was a radical break with the regional histories of co-governance. It cast the Crees in ways that echo some of the effects of development discourse as it is deployed in the Third World (see Ferguson 1990). It redefined Cree hunting, land use, tenure, governance, and co-governance as underdeveloped and backward. It defined a massive industrial hydroelectric project as a response to the social and economic needs of twelve thousand Cree men, women, and children, most of whom lived on the land as subsistence hunters and fur trappers. To incorporate Cree society fully into national polities, the development discourse envisaged and initiated broad-scale transformations. It built transportation and communication infrastructures for resource development projects that facilitated government access to and increased control of James Bay lands for state and market purposes. It had the effect of significantly expanding governmental administration and services to all Crees in the region. And it made all of these changes appear to be an apolitical process of inevitable benefit that was done both for the region's Cree inhabitants and for the ordinary citizens of urban Quebec and Canada.

From a Cree point of view, the hydroelectric project was a direct challenge to long-standing relationships and reciprocal obligations and a denial of an effective Cree voice in the governance of the region. When the Crees presented their case in a court action against the project and governments in 1972 and 1973 (see Richardson [1975] 1991 for a sample of Cree witness statements), the presiding judge understood the thrust of their views. He ruled that Cree hunting and fishing constituted a "way of life" that the Cree wish to continue, that they "have a unique concept of the land" and that "any interference therewith compromises their very existence as a people" (quoted in ibid., 298; see also Malouf 1973). By taking up the discourse of a way of life and of its inseparability from the land (see Christine Saganash above), the judge effectively rejected the colonial discourses of underdevelopment and backwardness and the subordinating relations that they implied. His decision forced Quebec into negotiations with the Crees. Many Crees saw the court ruling as recognition of their unique ways of using, governing, and protecting their lands and as a reaffirmation of their co-governance relationships with Canada and Quebec.

Negotiating to Clarify State Legitimacy and Re-Envisaging Relationships as Governmentality

In the negotiations that ensued, Quebec's senior negotiator said the province's goal was legitimacy and territorial integrity. The aim was "to affirm finally Quebec's presence throughout its entire territory" so that Quebec's "jurisdiction will be established in a precise and definitive manner" (Ciaccia [1975] 1998, xiii, xv). The negotiations that developed in 1974 and

1975 were, thus, focused on clarifying and transforming both legitimacy and co-governance.

Part of the solution to the legitimacy problem for governments was an insistence, as in many of the much earlier Canadian treaties, that the Crees "cede, release, surrender and convey all their Native claims, rights, titles and interests, whatever they may be, in and to land in the Territory and in Québec" (Quebec [1975] 1998, section 2.1). This "classic" provision in the agreement was thought to reduce uncertainties about the legitimacy of settler states' rights within the law and the political regimes of sovereignty, but the fundamental problem of settler-state legitimacy was not removed because it was tied to the issues of coexistence and co-governance.

The senior negotiator for the state hydroelectric corporations retro-spectively highlighted the urgency of clearing threats to the construction of current and future development projects through the agreement and how this hinged not only on clarifications of legal recognitions or political sovereignty but also on broader relations. "The agreement was supposed to be global, lasting, and without appeal. It was supposed to put an end to Crees' Aboriginal claims and to give approval to the hydroelectric project ... Moreover, it was supposed to propose regulations for future develop-ment projects and ensure a satisfactory social climate" (Couture 1988, 51, trans. Lise Feit). The government sought to use the agreement with the Crees to remove the conditions for "a social climate unfavourable to de-velopment" (Couture, cited in Wilkinson and Masella 2002, 218). What governments sought was not active Cree participation and co-governance but to create a social contract, a new governmentality, the result of which would be that the Crees would not oppose development (Couture 2002, 67). This matter could not be settled by laws: it was a matter of Cree con-duct and, therefore, of relationships.

The governmental rationality implied by these broad goals was that Crees were now primary objects and subjects of the project of regional governance and transformation. Thus, schooling, health care, the judicial system, local government institutions, transfer and compensation pay-ments, forestry, and mining were discussed, often at the Crees' insistence, with the aim of modifying them to better meet Cree goals. For the gov-ernment, however, they were means by which the Crees would develop and change to accommodate government and market interventions in the region (see, for example, Ciaccia [1975] 1998). This change of governance was not systematically explicit to those who were involved on different "sides." It was these governmental rationalities, however, that significantly shaped government and corporate strategies during the negotiation of the James Bay and Northern Québec Agreement.

Cree negotiators saw the conflicting visions in the negotiations, and they spoke of these differences and constantly challenged them. For example, they contested the assumptions of government negotiators that final authority rested with the state and that expertise was possible without living extensively on the land.

Cree goals and visions were partly recognized by Quebec and Crown corporation negotiators, but they were not recognized as a differing vision of governance. Rather, they were cast as specific conditions that would "absolutely [have to] be part of an agreement," otherwise an agreement would probably not be possible with the Crees (Couture 1988, 51, trans. Lise Feit). This position did not recognize that Cree aims, understood broadly, constituted a renewed relationship that was still a partnership in co-governance.

According to a senior Cree negotiator, the agreement did include, at the Crees' insistence, "provisions respecting local and regional autonomy, self-determination, and lands" (Awashish 1988, 43), including self-government, protection of a traditional way of life on the land through recognition and support of hunting and trapping, socio-economic development, and modifications to the project aimed at limiting its impacts (ibid., 43 and 44). Crees thought that the concessions governments made in the agreement would allow them "to decide, to a large extent, upon the course of their future, to be self-sufficient and self-governing people and to have an important role in the development, management and administration of lands and resources within their homeland," as they had in the past (Awashish 2002, 161-62).[6] It "was meant to bring about the sharing of powers and responsibilities for the governance of *Eeyou Istchee*" (ibid., 163), and it, therefore, was thought to hold out the prospect that a partnership in co-governance could continue in the new arrangements.

But Crees also negotiated in the realization that "the hydro-electric project could be constructed with or without our consent," because court actions would drag on for years as construction continued (Awashish 1988, 44). Under these exceptional pressures, the Crees had to accept less than would have been the case under other circumstances. Nevertheless, Crees had confidence in their ability to sustain their governance, as Charlie Coon Blacksmith's 1999 comments show nearly twenty-five years after the agreement. His statement was made for both the courts and younger generations of Crees who must carry on today.

Each of these visions — Quebec, Cree, and that of some analysts — has been disappointed to date. Continuing co-governance, governments' and analysts' expectations for comprehensive modernization among Crees, and expectations of a "peace" with the Crees (attributed to the then president of the James Bay Development Corporation by Couture, cited in Wilkinson and Masella 2002, 218) have substantially failed.

But at the same time, many development projects have proceeded without systematic restraint, and Quebec and Canada government agencies as well as corporations have effectively occupied most of the lands they wanted. Nevertheless, Cree societies with daily ties to lands have survived, and not all state projects have succeeded as Crees have found continuing and new ways of asserting their role in governance.

Logics of Governmentality: Seeking to Govern the Crees while Ignoring Commitments and Relationships

There is little that at first look appears systematic in the implementation of provisions of the agreement. Diverse government agencies implemented some provisions carefully and cooperatively, failed to implement others, implemented some without Cree participation, and implemented and then subsequently abandoned still others. Government agencies ignored some judicial rulings that the Crees succeeded in obtaining to enforce the implementation of particular provisions, subverted other court rulings, and sometimes implemented a ruling only to ignore it when the next similar action or decision had to be made. Some of the implementation outcomes are clearly related either to particular strategies of direct or indirect control or to interest-group liaisons with governments. Other failures are the effects of everyday bureaucratic mechanisms of governmentality.

These dispersed non-mechanisms are standard liberal governance forms and practices, but many were also given renewed impetus, commitment, and legitimacy by the growing prominence of neoliberalism in the decades following the agreement. Actions based on neoliberalism led to a reassertion and prioritization, contra the previously prevailing mix, of the "natural" dominance of interests and economy over "artificial" legal recognitions, negotiated commitments, and social benefits.

Contrary to the earlier forms of co-governance, the general effect of the implementation of the agreement was to marginalize Crees from government agencies and processes. Overall, the implementation tended to have the effect of disrupting Cree efforts at both cooperation and opposition by

its mix of strategic and arbitrary non-compliance along with partial implementation, all of which was "normal."

After fifteen years of implementing the agreement, Billy Diamond, the
chief Cree negotiator, concluded: "If I had known in 1975 what I know
now about the way solemn commitments become twisted and interpreted,
I would have refused to sign the Agreement" (Diamond 1990, 28; see also
Moses, another principal negotiator, 2002, 231-33).

Philip Awashish (2002), another Cree negotiator, outlines the failures in
implementation, and he notes many that could be called failures of co-
governance in practice. Crees have been marginalized from decisions about
the land, and the agreement provisions for land have "led to their exclusion
in the overall governance of the territory and exclusion in economic and
resource development and benefits" (ibid., 156). According to Awashish,
the consultative and advisory bodies, such as those for the management of
game and hunting and for the protection of the environment, "have not
had any significant impact on the making of policies and enactment of
legislation by Canada and Quebec" (ibid., 158); the provisions for economic development are "another dismal failure as Quebec continues to
pursue and implement policies that exclude *Eeyouch* [Cree people] from
direct participation and full benefits" (ibid.); the provisions for projects to
remedy the impacts of hydroelectric projects and the "relationship between
the *Eeyouch* and the James Bay Energy Corporation simply permitted and
enabled the [latter] ... to control the type of remedial works necessary"
(ibid.); "*Eeyou* communities are suffering from the soul-destroying effects
of inadequate and ... [insufficient] housing, unsafe or lack of water supply
and rampant unemployment" (ibid.); and "capital projects and agreements
on funding arrangements have led to demands from the Government of
Canada for an outright release from treaty obligations and commitments"
(ibid., 158-59).[7]

Awashish goes on to say that "governments presently continue to exercise outright domination and control over lands and resources of *Eeyou
Istchee* with the exclusion of *Eeyouch* in the exercise of power" (2002, 162).
Reflecting on these lessons, Awashish writes: "Broken promises, lies and
deceit perpetuated by greed in pursuit of profit and the exercise of power
through exclusive domination and control are serious flaws of the heart
and spirit. These flaws of the heart and spirit cannot be rectified by laws,
treaties and constitutions of nations and governments. For the truth is that
the essential element in any righting of wrongs eludes law and morality
because justice lies in the will of the powers that be" (ibid.).

Along with his stinging condemnation, Awashish also notes that the agreement "has been beneficial, to some extent, in advancing *Eeyou* governance ... [through] institutions created pursuant to the Agreement ... controlled by *Eeyouch*" (2002, 162). "*Eeyouch,* through their local governments and other *Eeyou* authorities, are exercising a substantial control over their destiny and affairs ... In many instances *Eeyouch* of *Eeyou Istchee* have adopted a 'just do it' approach" (ibid.).

Globalizing Arenas, Neoliberal Governance, and a Renewed Prospect for Co-Governance?

Globalizing Arenas of National Development and Non-State Identities

The failure to implement the agreement created a crisis in co-governance for many Crees, who saw the failures as a denial of the enduring relationship between Crees and the state, which could not be cut simply by ignoring or denying it. These failures undermined the legitimacy of the new projects of the state because they ignored the multiple ways the Crees were related to, and were inevitably affected by and could also affect, those projects. The governments were ignoring not only norms but also history and Cree experience.

The Cree approach to doing it themselves, which itself was rooted in both Cree history and a response to neoliberalism, along with the organizational and political skills they developed and the limited but still significant financial resources they now control, allowed them to respond to major confrontations with the government of Quebec in the late 1980s and 1990s. The Quebec government sought to initiate new hydroelectric developments in the region and then to claim, in the midst of a referendum campaign on the separation of Quebec from Canada, that it could take the James Bay region and its inhabitants into an anticipated separate Quebec without the Cree having an autonomous collective decision in the process.

The hope of some government negotiators and policy makers that the Cree would acquiesce to a place in Quebec and Canada that denied them co-governance and accept extensive dependency on and subordination to state governance has not been fulfilled. This acquiescence did not happen, despite the opening of the territory to rapidly accelerated resource development and the resultant destruction and degradation of more and more of the most productive land; extensive socio-economic development that has incorporated part of Cree economic activities into a wider economy; the nearly full implementation of public schooling and health and social services for Crees on provincial models that are adapted to the Crees' circumstances and culture; the continuing and partial sedentarization of Crees, albeit with a continuing tradition of extensive mobility on the land; the inclusion of Crees in delegated governance structures for limited self-rule; the establishment of a significant Cree administrative bureaucracy and cadre; the expansion of communications and mass media from the south; increased Cree incomes and consumerism; and significant but always inadequate levels of funding for community services that provincial and federal governments interrupt at opportune moments.

Denied an effective voice in Quebec and Canada, Crees have taken an active lead in developing engagements with publics, politicians, markets, organizations, and social movements transnationally (Barker and Soyuz 1994; Niezen 1998, 2003; Bernstein and Cashore 2000; Gnarowski 2002; Bergeron, under review). They have developed and used new transnational linkages and partnerships to disrupt development projects despite the increasing dependence of Canadian and Quebec governments and resource developers on international arenas. This dependence includes international markets for funding and capital, transnational energy and resource markets, establishing and maintaining strong managerial reputations in transnational capital and product markets, effective project planning that depends increasingly on coordinating transnational suppliers and resources, and international political and public recognition of their market brand, national security, and stable governance (see Feit, in press).

Detailed stories of Cree opposition to the proposed Great Whale River Hydroelectric Project between 1989 and 1994 and Cree opposition in 1995 to the claim that the James Bay region would be included in a separate Quebec rather than stay in Canada have been told elsewhere (Posluns 1993; Coon Come 2004; Craik 2004; McRae 2004; and Gnarowski 2002). Here, I note only the relevant features.

At the heart of the Cree challenge to the new hydro project was a sophisticated international campaign that linked indigenous rights issues to the environmental movement. Unlike in the 1970s, the primary Cree strategy was not to fight mainly through the Canadian courts but to build a campaign in the United States, where the energy would be sold, and in the United States and Europe, where the international investors whose capital Hydro-Québec needed to supplement state funds were located. The Cree leaders thought that if US contracts for the purchase of Quebec electricity could be blocked, or if project timetables and cost projections could be disrupted, it would make the investment of capital in Hydro-Québec bonds more risky and less attractive to global financial markets, thereby making it harder for Hydro-Québec to profitably finance the project.

The Crees set out a multi-scale campaign and developed it as they went along. Many Crees and Cree leaders spoke to local and international environment groups in the United States, built campaign alliances with national and international groups that opposed the project on environmental and social grounds, and cultivated understanding, support, and long-term personal friendships with activists, politicians, and supporters. The campaign used the Cree experience of the effectiveness of personal relationships to build movement and organizational alliances (see Craik 2004; McRae 2004). The US environmental campaign was so successful that a significant number of new US members joined the environmental group that was the US campaign's lead organization (Craik 2004) and, thus, pioneered new linkages between indigenous issues and the environmental movement.

Some time after the New York Power Authority cancelled a large contract with Hydro-Québec, the premier of Quebec announced that the Great Whale project would be delayed indefinitely.[8] The failure of the standard panoply of state governmental rationalities to reshape and limit Cree conduct and identities to those of nation-state citizens was explicit in a public outburst by a Quebec government energy minister during the campaign: "Yes, I blame [the Crees] for what they've been doing. I blame them for discrediting Quebec all over the world. Do you think a Quebecer can accept that? I don't think so. Are they Quebecers or not? They live in our territory. They live with us, they work with us, and they're penalizing Quebecers ... That's what I cannot accept and I will never accept" (*The Gazette,* 1 April 1992; and the film *Power* 1996).

Since then, Hydro-Québec has opened permanent offices in New York and Europe. The Cree campaign changed the strategies of governments and corporations transnationally, as well as those of social and environmental movements.

Shortly after the decision that cancelled the Great Whale River project, the referendum campaign on whether Quebec should separate from Canada went into high gear, and the Crees were drawn into it. They argued that they could not be incorporated into an independent Quebec against their will and that they were a nation with indigenous rights. They also argued that their lands would not necessarily become part of an independent

Quebec should Quebecers separate from Canada (Grand Council of the Crees 1998), again asserting that they were not simply citizens.

The Crees commissioned a public opinion poll that showed that the percentage of Quebecers who supported separation would be significantly lower if a separate Quebec would not include the northern Cree and Inuit lands (Gnarowski 2002). Some Cree leaders were told that this survey was one of the factors that influenced the federal government to argue more publicly against separation. The Crees' challenge threatened the *intégrité territoriale* of a sovereign Quebec, a fundamental tenet of the Quebec nationalist project. Northern Quebec was also critical to Quebec sovereignty because it was a vital source of Quebec-controlled energy resources, and hydroelectricity is one of Quebec's major export commodities. The challenge from an indigenous group also threatened to affect international recognition that a separate Quebec would need to gain recognition and join the ranks of legitimate sovereign states, as an extensive Cree publication showed (Grand Council of the Crees 1998). When the referendum to separate was defeated by the narrowest of margins, the Cree leadership thought that its campaign had played an important role in that outcome (Gnarowski 2002).[9]

These campaigns expressed in new forms how Crees continued to assert their co-governance of northern Quebec, how their governance could not be radically separated or denied, and how they could succeed in making their governance role effective at critical junctures. Co-governance relations between the Crees and Quebec and Canada were ignored in many instances and subordinated by the daily operations of state institutions. But they could not be securely controlled at times that were critical for state institutions, when Crees strategically chose to have a say. Cree conduct was rooted in the longer history of co-governance, not by visions of the proper conduct of state and citizenry under neoliberal political thinking.

Neoliberal Governance, Participation, and Co-Governance

Neoliberal ideas and practices of governance that have become predominant since the 1980s significantly altered the forms and strategies of governance. In particular, they introduced new possibilities of devolved or shared governance between state institutions and non-state entities. As is widely noted, the neoliberal discourse of the market being the best way to run and organize human affairs shapes visions and practices that bring market mechanisms more directly into state governance and bring former state activities into institutions of the market and civil society.

In the late 1990s, more of the key decisions that affected northern Quebec and the Crees were taken by private corporations and paragovernmental agencies that sometimes exercised significant responsibilities that had been transferred to them by governments. Often the preference for dealing with the Crees was to try to strike private deals, investment partnerships, or agreements at the local level rather than with better-organized Cree regional entities or political bodies. Consultations, when they were needed, were carefully managed processes that sometimes had little more than the appearance of participation. Concessions that were made as a result of consultations were typically wrapped in constraints that limited their utility, undermined implementation and accountability, and, indeed, were often tokens of participation intended to release corporations and agencies from any further obligations. Cash was often offered in place of concessions and as a potential marker of consent (see Feit and Beaulieu 2001).

When Hydro-Québec offered the opportunity for discussions, joint ventures, contracts, and jobs to local Cree communities and entities that would be affected by its newly proposed diversion of the Rupert River to expand its original hydroelectric project, it was initially successful in creating community-by-community negotiations. However, the Cree community at the mouth of the Rupert River then said it would no longer talk about a diversion. Hydro-Québec and the Quebec government then sought to develop a new solution with region-wide Cree political, governmental, and corporate entities.

In 2001 the separatist premier Bernard Landry approached regional Cree Nation leaders to propose a new comprehensive agreement that would cover each of the main areas of conflict between the Crees and Quebec. An agreement was quickly negotiated and then ratified by Crees in 2002, albeit with partial support in Cree communities.[10] The accord agreed to several things that Quebec and Canada had refused to discuss with the Crees for twenty-five years. Its main provisions addressed each of the key Cree priorities set out at an annual General Assembly of the Cree People in 1997 (Grand Council of the Crees 1997).

The most important provisions included Cree participation in resource royalties or rents, substantially increased partnerships for Crees in regional economic ventures, the use of the Cree system of hunting territories for managing industrial forestry logging, Cree receipt and control of substantial funds from resource development rents, Cree acceptance of responsibility for the socio-economic development of their communities, and the application to Crees of the recent Quebec policy that the relationship of indigenous peoples to Quebec was one of nation to nation. In return, Crees agreed to give up court cases and claims against forestry activities and Quebec's failure to meet its economic and social development obligations under the James Bay and Northern Québec Agreement, and they agreed to the expansion of the existing hydro project, which would be subject to a social and environmental assessment and review of the plans. Quebec set aside its plans to develop another multi-river hydroelectric project that would include the now-diverted Rupert River (see C. Scott 2005 for an account of the agreement).

Contrary to the implicit structure of the 1975 accord, Premier Landry said at the signing of the 2002 agreement that "strengthening the Cree Nation does not weaken Quebec" (Landry 2002, translation by author), a point the Crees had been making as well (Moses 2002). The Crees, he argued, cannot close their eyes to the need to ensure economic development for their communities and, especially, their unemployed youth, for whom hunting and employment in public administration do not provide sufficient opportunities. The agreement, therefore, envisages accelerated development for the region (Landry 2002), with the qualification of respect for cultural differences and provisions that could moderate forestry impacts, which are described below. Nonetheless, the framework is still rooted in part in colonial development discourses that establish who is in crisis and in need and who has the solutions.

But under neoliberalism it is possible to recognize other nations within the territory of Quebec, so long as they are not sovereign states, and to transfer governmental functions and responsibilities to them. These practices, we have seen, have existed without wide recognition since at least the 1930s. This type of co-governance is not a threat to sovereignty, and it may even contribute under neoliberalism to projects for new national state sovereignties.

The neoliberal idea that governments should leave economic development more fully to market forces also provides a legitimating context for Quebec to turn responsibilities in this sector over to Crees who can work directly with corporate institutions that seek to develop the natural resources of the region. The new agreement provides capital with which Cree could develop resource-exploitation partnerships, but it does not include new recognitions of Cree rights that would strengthen their negotiations with corporations.

In his speech, Landry made it clear how the Province of Quebec thought the new agreement would work. He asserted that the Crees and the province would establish a new partnership and put aside their conflicts. This was possible, in the government's view, because the implementation of the agreement would lead to a convergence of objectives by Crees and the government (Landry 2002). The two common objectives that he identified were "an unshakable will, on both our parts, to ensure the full development of our respective communities" and "an equally firm conviction that the James Bay region has a potential which is not yet fully developed" (ibid., translation by author). Equitable participation in regional development is the best way to bridge the misunderstandings between the Crees and Quebec. Landry concluded that the goal that the province had sought for over a quarter of a century was now at hand, "We have signed a peace agreement" (ibid., translation by author).

From a Cree perspective, the agreement transfers sufficient financial resources over the long term to give Crees much greater opportunities to get on with improving the socio-economic conditions of Cree communities, with reduced direct state intervention and control. The rapid growth of the Cree population makes Crees deeply concerned about having economic development funds of their own to find ways to create employment and productive lives for the growing number of youth. However, the province retains the possibility of interrupting the annual flow of funds if Crees breach the expected "peace" too radically, and it is rumoured that the province has initiated these procedures as a threat on at least one occasion.

The forestry provisions of the 2002 agreement shift nation-state administration to new joint forums for decision making in which state institutions and Crees reach decisions either at a regional level or at the level of hunting territories, as is appropriate. The agreement mandates the use of small groups of Cree hunting territories as units for managing industrial forestry cutting and gives them government recognition in relation to an industrial development activity for the first time. Three to seven hunting-territory Ndoho Ouchimauch are to meet, assisted by local Cree administration staff, with local representatives of the Quebec Ministère des Ressources naturelles et Faune to negotiate and seek agreement on detailed logging plans according to rules established in the agreement (see C. Scott 2005 for a fuller discussion). The government still has final authority.

But Ndoho Ouchimauch can envisage, and do experience, this system as a functioning, if not necessarily satisfactory, form of co-governance. Moving many decisions to local face-to-face working groups is a kind of process and relationship that makes sense among Ndoho Ouchimauch and echoes some of the features of Cree models of co-governance that were created in relation to beaver reserves. The presence of these features contributed to the acceptance of the agreement among a part of the Cree people. Their implementation has, however, been delayed repeatedly as Quebec reorganizes its forestry sector.

So neoliberal governance is changing the terrain of negotiation and agreements. Many of these changes undermined the implementation of the early agreements, as has been indicated, but there are some that contribute to the recognition of co-governance in practice. But neoliberalism also defines how Quebec and corporations envisage the "new" relationship established with the Crees.

Neoliberal versus Cree Coexisting Co-Governance: New and Old Terrains of Governance

Many of the former state prerogatives that neoliberal governance makes available to Crees are offered as a form of co-governance that, in part, replicates and re-establishes personal-level relationships that are a central part of Cree forms of governance of hunting territories and communities. Nevertheless, neoliberal governance does not consistently fulfill the aspirations of Crees.

For example, the concessions Quebec made to Cree participation in forestry were in the expectation that they would involve a reorganization but not a reduction in forestry activity over and above that required by the then limited application of sustainable economic constraints. This logic was revealed in Quebec implementation strategies and in Premier Landry's claim that the objectives of the Cree and Quebec communities were the same: the full economic development of the resources of the territory and the development of the communities that occupy it.

If, in his view, peace can be achieved, it is because the government assumes that the Crees no longer have any needs, visions, projects, or autonomy that could not be encompassed by a system of governance that functions according to market and state goals. Quebec assumes that the old footings of Cree governance now exist only in the new.

If the Crees are not fully incorporated into the state, that can be accommodated, because, like corporations and paragovernmental agencies, all the Crees' current needs can still be fulfilled by the market. The need to create productive lives for Cree youths, it is envisaged, demands full engagement with market opportunities and constraints. A modern Cree culture can be accommodated because the experiences and non-market visions of hunt-ers and elders, such as those quoted above, are a part of the past but not the future.

Whereas in the past co-governance was messy in relation to nation-state sovereignty, the neoliberal Quebec view is that such ambiguities can now be readily accommodated. But what this process obscures is the dis-juncture between Cree governance and the market logic of neoliberal governance. Charlie Coon Blacksmith was not questioning or challenging the logic of the sovereignty of the nation-state because he claimed an al-ternative state-like sovereignty; rather, he was calling for co-governance based on history and coexistence, and on respect for the land. What he was challenging in present co-governance practices was the rationality of gov-erning lands and forests according to the logic of big companies. He wanted corporations to act in ways that took into account what was neces-sary to protect the land, the Cree way of life, and the jobs now needed by many Crees and, by implication, non-Crees.

This is the multi-faceted risk of neoliberal governance. Cultures can now be diverse, nation-states can coexist with non-state nations without threatening sovereignty, activities of the state can be decentralized and de-volved, modernization need not be an explicit or totalizing and trans-forming goal, and direct interventions in encapsulated societies can be reduced (not least because other means are at work). But neoliberal co-governance is a vision, practice, and project that does not recognize an enduring relationship between the state and peoples with governance vi-sions and logics that do not entirely conform to that of the market.

As a consequence, neoliberal co-governance is a colonial instrument, rather than a recognition or means to achieving enduring partnerships among quite distinctive governing polities and economies. Neoliberal co-governance neither fully recognizes nor accommodates the long history of relational co-governance that animates Cree hunters' visions, practices, and autonomy.

But the history of the James Bay Crees relations to nation-states and markets does not suggest that instrumental neoliberal co-governance mechanisms or legitimations can readily take the place of historical and coexisting co-governance partnerships, however welcome some of the specific arrangements that can be developed under their aegis may be.

Some governments read the recent agreements as leading to an inevit-able transformation of Cree conduct and governance. They therefore replicate many of the governmental visions of the 1975 agreement. Whether the Crees will come to understand themselves only through this "new" market vision is highly uncertain, and given recent Cree struggles it is unlikely. Nevertheless, the effects of this new agreement are not clear.

In the Introduction to this volume, the editors ask how and why communities accept commands directed at them as legitimate in the context of globalization. Part of the answer is that in colonial settings, like transnational arenas, legitimacy is naturalized in the discourses of colonist difference and supra-ordination. But, as is indicated above, legitimacy has different foundations and forms within many indigenous and non-state societies and polities.

For Crees, rather than being founded on contractual, representational, or market relations, legitimacy is founded on consensual processes, kinship relations, and personalized relations that are kinship-like. Questions of legitimacy are, therefore, about how long-term relationships can continue to exist or be created. Like kinship relationships, governance relationships are not primarily about creating, accepting, or rejecting relationships, for one does not choose or contract with one's kin. Kin relations exist and have a history. This is not to say that kin relationships are not also created, distanced, and sometimes denied, but when they are created in non-state societies they tend to involve obligations and expectations that are intended to endure: they are not contracts for specific terms or purposes. When they are distanced or broken, as happens, they do not fully cease to exist, and renewal remains a possibility.

This open-endedness is not supposed to be because kin relationships are biological; rather, it is because they form the social relations and networks necessary for sustaining personal and collective lives. This is so even though kinship relations are, in practice, subject to continuous negotiation, evaluation, and exhortation. They are relations that encourage taking the needs of others fundamentally into account in what one does. Indeed, kinship relations often assume that it is normal, in many circumstances, to be willing to give up one's life for one's close kin. Kin relations are not ideals but practices that are necessary, and they are recognized, ignored, and lived for better or for worse.

As a result, governance modelled on kinship is more about practices of respect for others to whom one is already connected or to whom one can build a relationship modelled on kinship or friendship than about seeking a contractual or normative basis for relationships that have neither historical nor personal connections.

These forms of governance do not ideally or in practice tend to lead to compliance or commensurability with state governance and conduct. These forms of governance are about dealing with or creating enduring relationships. The term that constantly recurs in these discourses is *respect* (see Blacksmith, Saganash, and Awashish above).

An analysis of Cree-state relations over the last three-quarters of a century, thus, indicates why colonial governmentalities cannot be examined without also systematically analyzing coexisting non-modern projects and forms of governance. These non-modern forms of government may give rise to visions, discourses, and practices of co-governance. Colonial governmentality coexists with these regional forms of governance, which do not conform to the modernizing, resisting, accommodating, or self-governing subject visions of colonial discourses and societies. Nor do these regional forms of governance conform to the frameworks for analyzing governmentality per se. Colonial relationships are unequal, subordinating, exploitative, painful, and controlling. But they can, nevertheless, involve a messy mix of contestation, negotiation, and coexisting governance and co-governance. These latter forms of governance require attention and analysis.

chapter 6:   Protecting Our Resources:
               (Re)negotiating the Balance of
               Governance and Local Autonomy
               in Cooperative Natural Resource
               Management in Belize

Tara C. Goetze

IN BELIZE, AS IN many developing areas, coastal communities and governments alike regard natural resources as being crucial to current and future development initiatives. At the same time, the government of Belize,
several conservation and development-oriented organizations, community-
based non-governmental organizations (NGOs), local resource users, and
researchers have pointed to the need to utilize natural resources in a manner that creates opportunities for economic development locally and nationally while protecting their ecosystems' future viability (Azueta 2000;
CZMAI 2000; TASTE 2001; McField 2002; McConney, Mahon, and
Pomeroy 2004). This situation necessarily involves considering multiple
stakeholders' perspectives on coastal and marine resource use as well as
incorporating their social, political, and economic needs and interests in a
management regime.

     In the past decade, the government of Belize has developed a system
of marine protected areas (MPAs) and subsequently pursued their co-
management as the favoured avenue of action to meet these objectives.
Relevant state agencies negotiate co-management arrangements with
local, often community-based, NGOs. Under these agreements, local partners gain state-sanctioned legal authority to undertake daily management
responsibilities for particular mutually identified resources (e.g., species,
habitats, and protected areas). Because state resources and capacities are
limited, both the state and local co-managing NGOs have turned to transnational conservation NGOs (CNGOs) as partners in MPA co-management.

In the Belizean co-management model, then, powerful global actors exert significant leverage in the multi-stakeholder power dynamic.[1]

Accordingly, globalized ideas about conservation and management of resources created friction (Tsing 2005) when these ideas, put forward by CNGOs, came into conflict with the experience, knowledge, and epistemologies of local fishers. Areas in which natural resources, including fish, had long been managed as commercial fisheries were reconceived as sites of biological diversity under threat and reconstructed as conservation targets in need of protection from extractive activities. Although the Belize state secured financial support from the CNGOs that globalized these ideas, it undermined its own authority among the fishers involved and, thus, its legitimacy when it came to natural resources decision making. This conservation discourse also undermined the personal autonomy of fishers in securing a livelihood and the continued autonomy of the communities in which they lived.

At the same time, the emergence of a community-based NGO, Friends of Nature (FON), to jointly implement the policy shift towards co-managing marine resources through a protected areas system afforded an opportunity to balance the legitimacy deficit and reduce the friction in the local community created by the mobilization of CNGO universals in the area. By formally and informally integrating fishers into its decision-making processes and acknowledging their autonomy in relation to marine resource use, FON raised the likelihood of fishers and their supporters accepting their decisions and subsequent conservation activities. Friends of Nature, therefore, has become an intermediary between particular sets of globalized conservation ideas and the resulting pressure to shift to "alternative" non-extractive livelihoods on the one side and secure the livelihood and, thus, autonomy of the local community on the other. In this role, FON has increased the legitimacy of decisions made in response to globalizing ideological and economic processes.

This situation raises questions about the unforeseen impacts of devolution, a process typically assumed to enhance the autonomy of local actors. In keeping with the theme of this volume, the situation demands a consideration of the extent to which local communities can effectively continue to exert control over their lives within state-sanctioned power-sharing arrangements that, somewhat inadvertently, facilitate the extension of global projects into local contexts. Still further, it requires an exploration of the terrain of legitimacy on which various claims to authority take root, are put forward in demands, and are accepted or rejected.

This chapter explores the continually shifting terrain of claims to, and the exercise of, local autonomy by examining the complex relational dynamics among local, national, and global actors involved in the co-management of two MPAs in southern Belize. In particular, it focuses on how globalizing discourses about sustainable development, conservation, and management of the global commons on the one hand and empower-ment on the other contributed to a reconfiguration of power and author-ity relationships among local, national, and global actors. In combination, this disruption simultaneously contributed to the delegitimation of some existing authority relationships by undermining local communities' au-tonomy and obscuring their pre-existing power, while also providing potentially new sources of community power and legitimation for the reconfigured system of governance in MPAs.

Co-Management in Belize

Based in Placenica, in the south of Belize, Friends of Nature is one of several Belizean co-managing NGOs faced with the task of deploying re-source governance responsibilities in a manner that meets various local, national, and global development and conservation needs. In developing and pursuing its daily management responsibilities for Laughing Bird Caye National Park and Gladden Spit Marine Reserve, FON is inevitably pos-itioned at the nexus of powerful global, national, and local actors.

A major component of co-managing NGOs' mandates is the develop-ment and implementation of management plans, a process facilitated by the technical assistance and financial support of myriad CNGOs. Manage-ment plans must be approved by state agencies prior to their implementa-tion and are scrutinized for their compatibility with agencies' priorities concerning resource use. Partnered with CNGOs, which act as donors and advisors in the planning and implementation of MPA management strat-egies, Belizean NGOs are an institutional means through which globalized conservation priorities are realized at the local level, via CNGO-funded pro-jects that are implemented through these local co-management partners. Finally, the management initiatives that are developed as part of this pro-cess should, ideally, engender the voluntary compliance of local users be-cause they wield the power to disobey management regulations, which can be costly, and sometimes fatal, to conservation efforts (Chenier, Sherwood, and Robertson 1999; Berkes et al. 2001). State agencies, CNGOs, and local users assert the legitimacy of their claim to a role in resource governance in the MPAS based on varying sources of authority. State managers point to their statutory authority over natural resources within Belize's borders, while CNGOs lay claim to an epistemological authority as institutions whose policies and activities are based on "sound science." Local users in Placencia, too, point to their epistemological authority, though it is based on the more diachronic, experiential accumulation of what is commonly referred to as traditional ecological knowledge (Berkes 1999; Inglis 1993). In the background, a globalizing discourse of local empowerment, which has become a cornerstone of sustainable development thinking in de-velopment-oriented international governmental and non-governmental institutions, further disrupted existing authority relations.[2]

In negotiating these agendas to establish cooperative management, it would be natural to assume, as much criticism does, that local claims to authority become lost under the regulatory imperatives of national and global actors. Indeed, some researchers have pointed to the ways in which some co-management regimes act as a means to local peoples' co-optation (Kearney 1989; Nadasdy 1999; Neumann 2001; McConney, Mahon, and Pomeroy 2004). In contrast, among the most common benefits cited is the opportunity for local "empowerment" that co-management presents, largely through community members' participation in management deci-sions (Pinkerton 1989; Hoekema 1995; Stevens 1997; Weitzner and Borras 1999; Berkes et al. 2001; McConney, Mahon, and Pomeroy 2003b). Critics have, however, problematized the practice of participation itself. They argue that the ways in which participation is deployed, for example, within development projects may perpetuate or obscure unequal power relations between communities and external actors or within communities them-selves (Rahnema 1992; Menike 1993; Mohan and Stokke 2000).[3] Although these perspectives usefully highlight the debate about the advantages and constraints of co-management, they also mobilize a shared discourse on empowerment that implies a common assumption: local users are, in some way, powerless.[4] Thus, empowerment discourse potentially has the ironic consequence of delegitimizing co-management arrangements. Whether in practice it serves to legitimize or delegitimize governance of natural re-sources depends on the actual construction and implementation of co-management arrangements.

To reveal these dynamics, this chapter examines the power relations that coalesce and shift as a part of FON's implementation of management strat-egies in the MPAs by analyzing the complex global-local power dynamics of CNGO intervention via co-management. It explores the construction of a discourse of local empowerment and the ways in which FON's implementation of CNGO-sponsored MPA management strategies affects fishers' control over resource activities and, in turn, local autonomy in resource governance. I argue that rather than simply "empowering" fishers, thereby enhancing local autonomy, the process both expands and constrains fishers' options along with that of other actors involved. As participants in co-management, fishers engage in a well-established practice of considered decision making that strategically increases or diminishes the control of these local users according to shifting needs and interests. This situation implies that understandings of power, authority, legitimacy, and autonomy must consider the process of discursive construction and the negotiation, (re)prioritization, and deliberation of interests, all of which are bound up in how community members "participate" in state-local joint governance initiatives such as co-management agreements.

FON Co-Management, Participation, and Discourses of Local Empowerment

For the government of Belize, co-management has less to do with promoting participation that empowers local users by giving them a determinative role in resource management decisions and more to do with capitalizing on economic input from CNGO donors in the management of valuable national resources (Azueta 2000; McConney, Mahon, and Pomeroy 2003b). For their part, CNGOs working in Belize broadly endorse the participation of resource users as part of the process of building partnerships with local people to secure their support for conservation projects. The website for Conservation International asserts that "conservation cannot succeed without the support of local people," and The Nature Conservancy site page titled "Our Partners" contends that "effective conservation cannot be achieved unless the people who live and rely on those lands are an integral part of the conservation process." According to the World Wildlife Fund website, community participation is a critical factor to ensure project success. As has been observed elsewhere, this partnering is typically encouraged by CNGOs as a way to better advance their global strategies and implement their conservation activities locally (Stevens 1997; Brockington 2004; Adams 2004; Forsyth 2004). For both the state and these transnational CNGOs, the central purpose of community members' participation is to

133

meet the goal of effective resource management for either economic or ecological purposes. Empowering local users is a secondary objective, if it is mentioned at all.

Nevertheless, the empowerment capacity of participatory resource management regimes has been actively promoted in Belize by some transnational organizations involved in MPA co-management. In a 2001 workshop on co-management held in Belize, a program officer for a US-based CNGO spoke about the importance of co-management. Among four key elements, she noted that, through participation, successful co-management builds a community's capacity to practice good long-term decision making that, in turn, results in community empowerment (TASTE 2001, 26). A Caribbean Conservation Association report on its Coastal Co-Management Guidelines Project defines empowerment as "having the power and responsibility to do something; the ability of a person or a group of people to control or to have an input into decisions that affect their livelihoods" (McConney, Mahon, and Pomeroy 2003b, 52). It connects this decision-making control to "the extent to which stakeholders, other than the government authority, have power to make decisions on their own" (ibid., 26-27). Achieving local empowerment through co-management is also defined in economic as well as legal terms. In its *Good Practice Guide,* the Centre for Development Studies (2000), which supported the guidelines project, links successful co-management to the process of poverty eradication and alleviation through community empowerment, which is associated with giving the poor an opportunity to participate in resource management. In sum, the terms by which empowerment takes place is defined by institutions external to the diverse communities living in the different areas in which co-management will occur, a process that has also been observed within participatory development processes (see Rahnema 1992; Menike 1993; Gardner and Lewis 1996).

Ideas about empowering community members through their participation in co-management are not simply expressed by transnational organizations. According to the FON staff and board members I interviewed, the goal of local empowerment through co-management is highly valued by FON, and they note that this position is implicit in the organization's motto, "Protecting our natural resources through developing our human resources." The organization prides itself, and is hailed by others, on being truly community-based and locally representative and on making consistent use of community consultations to integrate community interests into its work.[5] This discourse suggests that political legitimacy, as is argued in the Introduction to this volume, must be rooted in a political community.

Friends of Nature's interest in promoting local empowerment was clear at the Caribbean Coastal Co-Management Guidelines Project Workshop in May 2003 in Belize City. In discussion of the FON case study, the issue of local empowerment was raised as a key part of the co-management process.[6] It was noted in a general presentation on co-management that among the "forces driving co-management" in the Caribbean was the "empowerment of civil society in governance" (CCA, UWI, and MRAG 2003, 42). During another presentation, which evaluated the status of FON co-management, it was suggested that "the increased empowerment of stakeholders" was among the priority actions for FON to create the conditions for successful co-management (ibid., 37).

The idea of empowering the community was debated at length by facilitators and FON members. It was agreed that the path to empowerment lay in participation, which meant involvement in management decision making and activities and active representation within a co-management regime. Staff from FON agreed with one workshop facilitator that there was a need for "a trickle down of government decision-making power to [community] stakeholders" (CCA, UWI, and MRAG 2003, 38). As the session progressed, the unspoken understanding that framed the discussion was that resource users in the FON areas had limited power; workshop participants unanimously agreed that one of the central benefits of co-management was that it could empower community stakeholders such as fishers.

The concomitant notion that co-management can function to fill this vacuum discursively constructs local stakeholders such as fishers as being powerless and posits co-management as the solution to this problem. Because these discussions of local empowerment do not reference fishers' own expressions of feeling powerless in a particular way, they suggest that this powerlessness is a general state of being. Conceptually, power is discussed as a commodity that people either have or do not have, which creates a space in which external institutions may become the socio-technical means to empower the powerless. Despite the good intentions that inform the discourse, this framework misrepresents the situation and has unforeseen effects. As my interviews with fishers revealed, co-management relates to a pre-existent context of power relations: a dynamic, complex, fluid process in which actors assert and constantly (re)negotiate competing and complementary sets of interests that reflect a diversity of needs.

The rest of this chapter examines historical and more recent ways in which these resource users asserted control prior to FON and how they have accessed new forms of leverage through co-management. It suggests that one outcome, unforeseen by either progenitors or critics of empowerment discourse, is the manner in which fishers feel that their existing level of influence has changed, being simultaneously increased *and* compromised, through their participation in FON co-management. These findings suggest that the result of this change is to increase legitimacy for decisions made on the basis of globalized ideas of conservation and resource management. The implications of this new order, however, as it is legitimated by managing institutions for local community autonomy and power, is more complex than critics or supporters often suggest.

Power Players: Fishers and Their Influence

Prior to the negotiation of FON's co-management agreements, fishers were developing and advancing, largely through a system of nationally linked local cooperatives, their control as active decision makers in the process of accessing the resources upon which their incomes rely. Palacio (2001, 46) describes how the local fishing cooperative has long acted as a mechanism for asserting fishers' interests: "In the South, only the Placencia Producers Co-operative Society Ltd., provides organizational support to community members going back for forty years." Since its inception in 1962, the member-run cooperative has provided a variety of services to fishers, facilitating the purchase of equipment that they could not otherwise afford, providing additional income through profit sharing, and presenting their interests nationally. Key (2002, 9) identifies the creation of the Placencia Producers Co-operative Society as a significant element in fishers' political activity that meant they "were now able to take complete control of fishing in the village ... With the industry in the fishermen's hands, they were able to fight against quotas and extend seasonal limits for the high valued items." Indeed, the cooperative system in Belize also affords significant political leverage to fishers at the national level. Emerging in the 1960s, the Belizean fishing cooperatives

> wrestled lobster processing and exporting rights from foreign monopolists, accused of exploiting the local producers ... Its umbrella organization, the Belize Fishermen Co-operative Association (BFCA ... uses the defense of this privilege-turned right of monopoly over

the processing and exporting of lobsters, and later on, of conch, as a rallying point for unity against any imagined or real threat from both internal and external sources ... This significantly enhances their independence and reduces their dependence on government largesse. The BFCA operates from a position of both political and economic strength, and has been successful in warding off any attempts to deprive the members of their hard won rights ... Through the BFCA, the member co-operatives have the ability of bargaining for concessions from governments, and are able to influence decision-making through dialogue, lobbying, negotiations and effective use of their membership on the National Fisheries Advisory Board. (Brown 2004, 1)

Brown contends that the cooperative system in Belize is an example of power sharing between local and national actors in which local actors are able to assert their interests effectively vis-à-vis those of the state: "This is a classic case of a dynamic partnership between a resource appropriation organization and government functionaries in management relationships, in which the scale of strength and influence seems to weigh in favour of the former" (Brown 2004, 2). Brown is not alone in his observation of the considerable leverage of Belize's fishing cooperatives. In their study of the Fisheries Advisory Board (FAB), McConney, Mahon, and Pomeroy describe the board as "a powerful force in fisheries development since its establishment along with the Fisheries Department in 1965" and note that "fisheries co-operatives exercise considerable power in and through the FAB" (2003a, 6). During their research they observed that "fishing co-operatives had easy access to Ministers" and that representatives of the Belize Fishermen Co-operatives Association (BFCA) met several times with the minister directly to press their perspective on issues currently before the FAB (ibid., 51). This prompted McConney, Mahon, and Pomeroy to conclude that "the power exerted by fishing industry stakeholders and the types of decisions that the body has taken causes [the FAB] to exhibit characteristics of collaborative management on particular issues" (ibid., 56).

Perhaps because of their experience with cooperatives, fishers in Placencia expressed a well-developed sense of control in relation to management activities in the MPAs. They most commonly referred to "an understanding between FON and fishers" that decisions about the restriction of fishers' access by regulations depend on fishers' approval if they are to be successfully implemented. This perspective is echoed in the statements made by two well-respected fishers in the village. In a speech at the Gulf and Caribbean Fisheries Institute's annual conference, which was held at Playa del Carmen, Mexico, in November 2002, Carleton Young Sr., FON's board representative for fishers, asserted that "FON doesn't make the rules for Gladden Spit Marine Reserve, the fishermen do ... We work *together* in the management of Gladden." He later said that at the time that Laughing Bird Caye was put forward for park status he had to voice his opinion because a six-mile boundary was originally proposed: "And I tell them, 'Hell no, man!' ... I said, 'That cannot work, that's too much. You're taking *all* the conch ground from the fishermen, that thing will have to reduce.' And we got to reduce it to one mile" (interview with the author, Placencia Village, Belize, 14 February 2003). On the fishers' relationship with FON, Lennox Leslie said, "They gotta get our views to make them do something, right? They don't do it to fit their own time, their own rules. They can make rules, but they contact the fishermen *before* they make the rules [to see] if it is ok for them to do it or not" (interview with the author, Placencia Village, Belize, 9 February 2003). Voicing a sentiment that was often put forward during informal discussions with other fishers, he commented, "Because fishermen, you get them against you, and that's it" (ibid.).

The leverage fishers hold is based, in part, on the well-established power of the cooperatives and, in part, on the need for their compliance with resource regulations. In contrast to awareness of this leverage, fishers also talked about experiences in which they did feel a sense of powerlessness. For the most part, fishers expressed a sense of being helpless in two key areas that directly affected their needs and interests. First, there was the CNGO-sponsored closure of the area's winter grouper spawning aggregations and the ongoing efforts of CNGO researchers to extend the closure to the spring snapper aggregations, critical fishing grounds for fishers during the waning of the lobster and tourist season. Laurence Leslie talked about "the others who were out there experimenting because they wanted us to come to a full closure ... They tricked us *[laughs]*, all of us. What they told us, right, was that they didn't think to harm us ... And then the thing was turning around the other way, to close it. Recommendations were going in, you know, and it was hurtful to us" (interview with the author, Placencia Village, Belize, 11 February 2003).

Second, fishers suggested that they felt powerless when faced with the government's failure to constrain illegal fishing, which they say significantly endangers the fish stocks that they depend upon for their livelihoods. When asked what they did when they saw boats fishing illegally,

Villa Godfrey, as most others, said that there was nothing to do but report it to authorities: "You can't do nothing. Sometimes you tell them, but they don't listen to you" (interview with the author, Placencia Village, Belize, 3 February 2003). In their experience, those with the authority to act against poaching do not use it effectively. Carlton Young Sr. conveyed this feeling well, exclaiming, "You know it's hard for you to go out there and to see somebody taking maybe lobster during the closed season, and you can't do anything about it! ... They brought in five [offenders] and to our surprise, the government gave them back their boats!" (interview with the author, Placencia Village, Belize, 14 February 2003). In light of such events, veteran fisherman Tony Eiley suggested, "Well, that is Belizean style ... This poor reef has been hammered. It's time for somebody to do something. That's why I say Friends of Nature has to do something" (interview with the author, Placencia Village, Belize, 24 February 2003). Other fishers also pointed to FON as the means to mitigate threats when existing avenues of leverage proved ineffective.

In contrast to the totalizing tendency of empowerment discourses, Placencian fishers situate themselves in their own discourse as being more influential vis-à-vis some actors and less so in other relations. They feel they have the least impact on resource depletion problems that are embedded in relations between national and transnational actors. In these scenarios, fishers suggested that FON was proving to be a useful partner. To the degree that the partnership, in practical terms, acted as a power resource, it increased the legitimacy of decisions. At the same time, it obscured or undermined pre-existing community power. Thus, increased legitimacy may be double-edged from the perspective of local autonomy: on the one side, it facilitated legitimate decision making within the new authority relationships and governance structure of the protected areas; on the other side, it potentially legitimated an order that limited the ability of the local community to exercise direct autonomy (for example, by non-compliance) as it had been able to do prior to the creation of the co-management regime.

Of Giving and Taking: FON and Fishers' Interests

Although fishers' statements did not reflect a generalized sense of being powerless, they point to areas in which they have less leverage over their interests. And they noted that FON co-management provides the means to augment fishers' control in these areas. Most often this shift was observed in relation to illegal fishing and the restriction of fishing in the Gladden

Spit area, matters of key concern over which they themselves have little influence. In other words, fishers benefit from new forms of control that FON's co-management arrangements have introduced for managing protected areas.

During interviews, several fishers suggested that their existing level of control over resources was enhanced through FON. Long-time fisherman Villa Godfrey believes that FON is beneficial for fishers because, he explained, FON "get to us, they get to we, and then they go to government and tell government what they hear from us. So, the three of us are involved, you see? The government, the people and everything" (interview with the author, Placencia Village, Belize, 3 February 2003). He thinks this is a better system for the fishers than before FON, when they had only the cooperative or their local elected representative to deal with protected areas and other issues affecting local fishing activities. With FON, he said, "We tell them what we want and then they tell government ... The area representative is good, too, but we don't see him often [be]cause they have a lot of other villages to take care of, too" (ibid.). Carlton Young Sr. also suggested that FON co-management has been a useful development for area fishers: "It is because you have a *voice* in what will be done in *that* [protected] area, instead of the government coming and telling you, 'Well, you should do *this,* and you should do *that* and shouldn't do *this,*' you know? *We live here.* We are in and out of that area *every* day, so we know what should be done there" (interview with the author, Placencia Village, Belize, 14 February 2003).

Laurence Leslie acknowledged that FON is better situated to assert fishers' interests in certain cases: "They have more power to do certain things for us. Because [our fishing grounds] out here [at Gladden Spit] were to be closed, too, I understand. But they can't close it because it was controlled out here by Friends. So, I'm glad for that because it was destined to be closed" (interview with the author, Placencia Village, Belize, 11 February 2003). His brother Lennox also called attention to the fact that the government has not closed Gladden's spring aggregations as advocated by the Nature Conservancy. He used this restraint as an example of how FON has proved to be a powerful ally to fishers: "They say that they are there to help the fisherman ... and they fight for us to hold [Gladden Spit] still open. As I said, the guy [from the Nature Conservancy] at first wanted to close it down. But [FON] are the ones who really fight to keep it open ... And they pulled through with it. You know it's very good that you can have some fishing there" (interview with the author, Placencia Village, Belize, 9 February 2003).

As a member of the FON board of directors that represents fishers, Carlton Young Sr. explained FON's position on the proposal to permanently ban fishing in Gladden Spit: "The Nature Conservancy wanted to close it entirely! No fishing at all. But we [on the FON board] are saying ... 'You cannot do that right now.' Then what will the fishermen who depend on that for their livelihood, what will they do? ... But you can't do it just like that, say 'You fished there last year and this year you can't fish.' No" (interview with the author, Placencia Village, Belize, 14 February 2003). Being both an active fisher and a board member lends Young a unique perspective on the implications of FON co-management for fishers: "This co-management it helps us have a voice in what is going on in the reserve, you know? ... [FON] will have to take a little away from the fishermen, but ... if we take, we're going to give back something. And I think most of the fishermen understand that ... there has to be some kind of restriction. But they are not up in arms about it because they know that something has to happen" (ibid.).

Not only do they know that restrictions must happen, the hard core fishers who most heavily depend on fishing at Gladden Spit are actively defining what they should be through FON. During a FON consultation on how to control fishing in Gladden Spit to minimize its impact on fishers, fishers themselves made a significant concession by offering to give up fishing the area's aggregations in the winter and during one of three months in the spring. This concession reflects a well-established approach to navigating the power relations of which fishers have long been a part. It demonstrates fishers' strategy for negotiating the powerful interests of CNGOs to maintain their access to the lucrative fishing grounds at Gladden. Fishers realize that the new leverage they gain through FON may necessarily involve restricting the exercise of their existing control in terms of the decisions they make as harvesters. Consequently, they position their partnership with FON as one in which there are trade-offs. In fishers' discourse, participating in FON co-management results in both gains and losses of control: Gladden remains open for spring fishing, but the winter harvest has been given up.

The process of strategically conceding a measure of control in one area to augment it in another also takes place in relation to FON's enforcement activities that aim to reduce illegal fishing in and around its MPAs. Many fishers pointed to the increased presence of FON rangers as a significant deterrent to illegal activities continuing in the area. Carlton Young Sr. said that FON co-management has been a good thing for fishers because of the regularity of patrols it has undertaken: "It kind of takes some of the weight off the fishermen knowing that we have people doing patrolling in the area. That we know for sure now that they will be scared to come back" (interview with the author, Placencia Village, Belize, 14 February 2003).[7] Oftentimes, they added that the patrols' targets included any illegal activities in which local area fishers may engage. Lennox Leslie contends that the benefit of the increased presence of patrols, though they impose a new level of restriction on fishers' own decision-making behaviour, will ultimately wield results that are of greater value to him as a fisher: "They have rangers that say you can't go there and take out what you're not supposed to take ... now they're policing the area so you can't do nothing like that again. So [the fish stock] is coming back in a big abundance" (interview with the author, Placencia Village, Belize, 9 February 2003).

Over time and through more discussion with fishers, it became clear that they understood and had carefully considered the concessions that were involved if FON is to effectively reduce poaching of "their" fishing grounds. Fishers' discourse constructs the process of participating in FON co-management in a manner that highlights both the opportunities and restrictions that FON's conservation activities may present to fishers within the scope of existing power relations and agendas. It suggests that they are aware of their position within this power dynamic, which is strongly influenced by sponsoring CNGOs, and that they operate within it in ways that assert their needs, knowledge, and interests while still recognizing the necessity of restrictions. Instead of defining their engagement with the co-management process as the solution to the problem of their powerlessness, fishers' discourse frames their partnership with FON as one that can both bring control and take it away as local resource users.

The Power Dynamics of Co-Management: Fishers, FON, and Conservation Intervention

The perspectives offered by fishers underscore that empowerment does not singularly come from above: they suggest that what FON actually does to or for fishers is more complex than empowerment discourses tend to imply. It requires that the analysis move past the "who empowers or co-opts" view of participation's power-sharing function to see how co-management engages and transforms the power dynamics in which fishers are involved. This approach focuses on how co-management impacts power relations among local, national, and global actors and explores the shifts that transpire as a result.

Like many local-level resource management institutions, FON is the locus of multiple assertions of control. The key actors and their predominant expressions of power as they relate to the operation of FON co-management include the state (legal power), CNGO donors (economic power), local users (power of non-compliance), and FON (regulatory power). Empowering fishers in this co-management scenario would involve maintaining, as well as enhancing, their existing ability to assert their interests and authority in relation to the state, and also in relation to CNGOs. Both of these have the power to retract the leverage they share with FON (legal authority to manage and economic support for activities) at any time. As per the terms of reference of FON's co-management agreements, the minister may declare that an area is not protected at any time. Similarly, donors may simply refuse to grant funding for project applications. Fishers, likewise, may choose not to comply with management regulations. Even with regular patrols, the area is of sufficient size and the fishers possess enough knowledge and skill to pursue harvesting activities within the protected areas in a manner that would significantly compromise conservation efforts. All are constrained from doing so, however, by the very nature of their interest in FON. Each relies on FON as the means to furthering his or her respective agendas and obligations with regard to the marine resources and their socio-political goals.

Although the state has the ultimate statutory authority to designate and revoke protected area status, it *needs* FON to secure CNGO funding through which the country's MPAs are actually managed. For Belize, protected areas are critical to the government's vision of shifting the national economy from agriculture to tourism, specifically the eco-tourism activities that capitalize on Belize's "pristine" ecology. In addition, Belize's government is bound to promote the protection of its natural resources by virtue of a debt-for-nature swap it negotiated with the US government.[8]

Correspondingly, CNGOs need in-country partners with regulatory powers to mobilize their global environmental vision. Like most aid organizations, the general preference is to transfer skills and financial support to community organizations rather than to governments. In this way, CNGOs need FON to provide them with access to the management of ecological areas that have been identified as in need of protection for the sake of the global good. This involvement is critical to demonstrate to their members and supporters that they are legitimately carrying out their stated agendas. To wit, they are working with local partners to implement sound conservation actions and, consequently, are meeting their conservation objectives successfully.

Like the state and CNGOs, fishers would like a healthy marine environment because it provides the ecological foundation necessary for retaining their livelihoods and providing for their families. A healthy marine environment is also the basis for the continuation of a lifestyle that allows them to be on the sea. Beyond being their preferred lifestyle, it is the means to fulfill various social obligations and to practise and pass on cultural traditions that are directly linked to specific marine activities.[9]

As the local co-managing institution, FON must negotiate the agendas and pressures of all these actors to develop a management regime for the MPAs. Being the site of such interdependent and dynamic power relationships, FON's impact may be described as that of a filter effect: the organization must negotiate local, state, and global actors' competing areas of influence to mobilize its overarching vision of conserving resources for the benefit of local communities. Implementing various MPA management strategies as the new local management authority, thus, results in the process of either limiting or extending the control and interests of these actors. It can affect control in this way because, at its core, FON is a legitimating institution for the new governance order.

Friends of Nature is, therefore, a catalyst for the extension of the regulatory power of the state and the conservation imperatives of CNGOs in the daily lives of fishers. Consequently, co-management has constrained fishers' influence. With government approval of its management plan, FON can enact regulations to create use zones, issue licences, and establish user fees, all of which place new restrictions on fishers. Conservation non-governmental organizations have capitalized on this local authority by citing scientific research findings that necessitate conservation strategies that restrict fishers' access to marine areas and funding training programs that promote "sustainable" marine activities. The institutionalization of a local management regime with a central conservation objective has resulted in the creation of boundaries that define no-take marine areas, along with more patrols. Local fishers, thus, have less choice in where they may harvest and are more likely to be caught if they themselves are fishing illegally. Fishers commonly voiced their sense of being "kept out" of MPAs that were areas in which they were once at liberty to use as they desired.

Friends of Nature staff and board members are aware of the need to show users, particularly fishers, the benefits they can derive from the MPAs and FON's management of these areas. As a locally initiated institution, FON has its own relationship with the people it represents. As its motto suggests, its interest in protecting local resources is connected to a sense of protecting the needs of the community members it represents. Consisting solely of representatives of local stakeholders, including current and former fishers, the composition of FON's board restrains the top-down imposition of state policies and CNGO conservation strategies that may be in direct contradiction to local interests. Thus far, its actions in relation to establishing regulations for Gladden Spit have taken the objections and needs of fishers as determinative directives, while maintaining the need to restrict their harvesting activities in the MPAs.

As fishers' statements suggest, co-management has provided the means to address two key areas in which they felt they lacked control: the CNGO-initiated closure of fishing grounds at Gladden Spit and illegal fishing by non-locals. At the same time, fishers have made and accepted significant concessions that limit their use of marine resources in the reserve because it strategically supported their primary objective to retain some harvesting access to Gladden Spit.

Fishers also pointed to the ways in which FON allows for the extension of their influence in changing circumstances. Fishers have direct personal access to the institution that manages the resources upon which they depend. They may capitalize on the moral suasion of FON's claim to being locally representative and responsive. For additional leverage, fishers have the benefit of sharing with most FON staff and board members a lifestyle, location, and understanding of the value of the resource to themselves and their families. Thus, fishers assert that FON also augments their sense of determinative leverage. It allows them more immediate influence over the creation of legally binding regulations that govern local resources through a local institution whose stated agenda includes protecting the interests of area fishers. Giving fishers increased access and authority over the decision-making process by which regulations are formulated allows them a greater degree of control over the direction of local resource governance.

Fishers are not only aware of this dialectical process in which their leverage is expanded and restrained, they actively engage with it. Their participation in FON activities is strategically based on their understanding of potential benefits and drawbacks. Like membership in the cooperatives, participating in the local co-management institution's activities is the means to particular ends. Fishers may see FON as a form of state- and CNGO-sponsored intervention, but they can also appreciate and support FON for the way it has functioned to reduce illegal fishing and halt the closure of Gladden's fishing grounds. As events occur and circumstances shift, fishers' stated views and interactions with MPA co-management vary accordingly.

Although fishers are cognizant of the authority CNGOs and governments exercise through FON, they do not view FON as having total control. Understanding the need to relate to government and CNGOs, fishers see FON as a means to contest or negotiate these external forms of control while asserting and even enhancing their own sense of control. Fishers can partner with FON and usefully participate in its activities because they see themselves as empowered in the first instance.

Conclusion

In Placencia, fishers' alternative discursive framing of their position within the power relations between local, national, and global co-management stakeholders demonstrates one of the means by which fishers mobilize their ideas and needs. It also highlights that fishers are conscious of the influence they assert and the ways in which participation limits and augments their leverage. This framework functions in opposition to empowerment discourses that imply that fishers are generally powerless. It also reflects fishers' awareness of the choices they are faced with as partners in the co-management and conservation process. They must make strategic decisions by considering how their own priorities relate to the respective agendas of other powerful actors.

Prior to the introduction of FON co-management, the state's imposition of new regulations regarding harvesting activities, transnational conservation agendas, and the increasing intrusion of outside fishers challenged fishers' control over local resources. Local fishers largely exercised their influence through the system of local and national cooperatives in Belize. With the creation of protected areas and the formation of FON as the local managing institution, the dynamics of resource use in Placencia shifted. The influence of state and CNGO agendas became a more immediate, daily experience for fishers in Placencia, and it further limited fishers' access to those local resources now encompassed within protected areas. In contrast, fishers have also capitalized on the presence of FON to resist some restrictive CNGO initiatives and to lobby for enforcement against illegal fishing. Thus, co-management has contributed to processes that have reduced fishers' control of resources and activities while also producing some of their most effective responses to these processes. Co-management expands local actors' influence against efforts that would have otherwise further restricted it.

Fishers' experiences with FON suggest that co-management's power-sharing function is a complex process of discourse, negotiation, contradiction, and transformation. As a site of conservation intervention, FON is the nexus where the ideas and agendas of local, national, and global actors are put forward and come into competition. As a result, FON co-management is a continually shifting, multivalent area of contested interests and understandings, a site of domination and resistance, and a means to limit and augment local control. It is a process of continuous strategizing in which participating actors' influence is constantly negotiated or challenged, allowing it to expand and contract across various issues and events. These contestations have diverse consequences for local users' autonomy over the use of and access to local resources.

As a lens into the broader themes of this volume, the experience of protected areas co-management in Belize addresses the importance of focusing on the political practices and power relations of multiple actors to understand how governance is legitimated under conditions of globalization. In this case study, globalizing discourses created disruptions in existing power and authority relationships. These disruptions had a clear impact on local actors' capacity to exert influence over the management of local resources. The resulting shifts in the pattern of resource governance simultaneously acknowledged the legitimacy of both local and global authority. The new management arrangements established as a result of their influence shored up actors' legitimacy, but within a new configuration of political authority. Ultimately, and perhaps unexpectedly, the situation demanded that the exercise of this authority be negotiated by fishers and CNGOs alike. Critics are indeed correct in pointing to the ways in which devolution, as joint governance, may undermine pre-existing sources of power and authority for local peoples. At the same time, co-managing institutions can act to create new forms of leverage that buttress and even augment local actors' power over local resources. As the dynamic between FON, local fishers, and CNGOs in Belize suggests, these shifts in power relations result in a complex matrix of predictable and unpredictable impacts, including costs and opportunities, for local autonomy. Thus, negotiations and power sharing create considerable potential for sustaining the legitimacy of decisions taken by co-management authorities.

chapter 7

Globalization, European Integration, and the Nationalities Question

Michael Keating, John McGarry, and Margaret Moore

THIS CHAPTER EXAMINES THE dynamic interrelationships between global-ization, legitimacy, and a diverse set of struggles for political autonomy by nationalist movements without states. In particular, it focuses on the rela-tionship between the process of European integration and the nationalities question.

Globalization has several dimensions that are relevant to this subject. First, it involves a process of global economic integration, with increased mobility of capital, goods, services, and, to a lesser extent, labour, as well as the rise of the transnational corporation. Second, there is a normative di-mension: globalization involves changing norms of state sovereignty. There has been a rise of new understandings of human rights, with transgressions being seen as justifications for violations of state sovereignty that lead to, in some cases, armed interventions to protect minorities. Accompanying this development has been the proliferation of international non-governmental organizations such as Amnesty International and Human Rights Watch and the construction of new forms of international jurisprudence, includ-ing the International Criminal Court and the war crimes tribunals for Rwanda, Sierra Leone, and the former Yugoslavia. Third, globalization has a cultural dimension. A revolution in communications technology, includ-ing the Internet, and increased travel has promoted the spread of English as a lingua franca. Various types of global culture have emerged, although they are mainly products of the culture of the United States. Finally, new trans-national institutions have emerged, and many of them, including the World

Trade Organization, have a global reach. Some — including the Association of Southeast Asian Nations (ASEAN), the North American Free Trade Agreement (NAFTA), and the African Union — are regional.

These processes have been most intensely developed in Europe, although it is possible to see European integration as an attempt to limit the impact of globalization by pooling the resources of sovereign states. Europe has taken economic integration further than anywhere else, particularly since the achievement of European monetary union and the Schengen Agreement, which removes border controls among participating countries. Twenty-seven European countries have now pooled their sovereignty within the European Union (EU), and several more stand ready to become members within the next few years. Europe has a plethora of transnational political and institutional structures, most notably the EU, but also the Council of Europe (CE), the Organization for Security and Co-operation in Europe (OSCE), and the North Atlantic Treaty Organization (NATO). There is a European Court of Human Rights, a European Convention on Human Rights (under the CE), and a number of other rights-based documents, to which many European countries are signatories.

The nationalities question is the issue of politically conscious national movements with no states of their own. This phenomenon is global and includes the Québécois in Canada, the Palestinians in Palestine/Israel, the Kurds in several Middle Eastern states, and the Kashmiris in India and Pakistan, but it is most clearly manifest in both eastern and western Europe. A nationality comes in different varieties. It may exist as a minority that is wholly contained within a host state, such as the Scots within the United Kingdom. It may also be a minority in one state (the host state) who have ethnic kin who dominate another state (the kin state). This is a classic configuration throughout central and eastern Europe. Examples include the Hungarians of Slovakia, Romania (see Sunday, this volume), and Serbia; the Serbs and Croats of Bosnia-Herzegovina; the Serbs of Kosovo; and the Turks of Bulgaria (Brubaker 1996). A prominent example in western Europe is Irish nationalists in Northern Ireland. Nationalities may also be minorities in more than one state and majorities in none, such as the Basques in Spain and France. Given that their preferences are shaped by these political-geographic circumstances, nationality movements may seek cultural or territorial autonomy within a state, secession, autonomy combined with cross-border links between them and their ethnic kin, or dual or multiple secessions followed by the unification of what is seen as their national territory.

Nationalities in Europe are usually distinguished from immigrant communities that have recently arrived from distant countries. Unlike immigrants, such as the Turkish and Kurdish minorities in Germany, or the predominantly Arab minorities in France and Spain, members of nationality movements see themselves as living on their ancestral territory and as seeking some form of collective self-government. Some communities, such as the Russians of the Baltic republics, bear features of both nationalities and immigrant communities. Most Russians arrived after 1945, but they were settled in such large numbers that they are now demographically dominant in particular regions.[1] Moreover, they were settled at a time when the Baltic states were seen, however unjustly, as part of their Soviet, previously Tsarist, patrimony. The term *nationalities,* thus, covers what others, and we in earlier works, have called both national minorities and minority nations.[2] Many nationality movements, however, resist being identified as minorities. They see this identification as blurring the distinction between them and immigrants, thereby undermining a claim to equality between them and the given state's dominant national community.

We use the term *nationality movements* to underline that these are political projects rather than primordial categories and to avoid the standard criticisms of constructivists. Not every cultural or ethnic community develops a vibrant nationalist project. There are examples of groups throughout Europe — such as the Sorbs, Wends, and Frisians — that did not develop a nationalist project either in the nineteenth century (Hroch 1985) or more recently. Where nationalist projects develop, not everyone from a particular cultural or ethnic community will automatically consider herself or himself part of it. Even in Northern Ireland, where there is a remarkable degree of coincidence between cultural community and national community, a significant number of Catholics are not Irish nationalists politically.[3] Similarly, nationalist projects, while based predominantly on one cultural community, may have support across these communities. To accept that nationalist movements are socially and politically constructed does not mean, as some think, that they are superficial or unpopular, or that their aspirations do not need to be taken seriously if justice and stability are to prevail.

In this chapter, we argue against the view that globalization and European integration are leading, or will lead, to the disappearance of nationalities and the associated view that this outcome would necessarily be a progressive development. We examine the role that globalization and European integration have played in the mobilization of nationality movements and discuss the potential they generate for accommodating their concerns. The remarkable diversity in these movements and the contextual and historical differences in the formation of the communities involved suggest that conditions for legitimate rule are beyond generalization at this point.

Are Globalization and European Integration Eroding Minority Nationalism?

The view that economic and social forces would secure the triumph of the nation-state and the end of the nationality question has been around since the nineteenth century (see Keating and McGarry 2001, 2-3). Marx and Engels famously distinguished between historical nations and nations without history and dismissed the latter as necessary casualties in the march of progress. Eventually, of course, the triumph of the proletariat would do away with all forms of nationalism (Marx and Engels [1848] 2002). Karl Deutsch (1953), writing a century later and representing a dominant view in US political science, argued that a modernity-induced increase in social communications among diverse communities was bound to erode differences.

The latest phase of globalization has produced another wave of "post-national" thinking. From this perspective, the hegemony of national identities is being eroded and replaced by more complex, multiple identities. Individuals, it is believed, are now forming non-territorial allegiances along lines of function, gender, or sexual orientation and multiple territorial allegiances to the city, the region, the state, and beyond (Kearney 1997). By the end of the 1980s, Marxist historian Eric Hobsbawm was convinced that the new transnational order, which was reducing the functional importance of nation-states, would put an end to all nationalisms. At the very time that the former Yugoslavia and Soviet Union were breaking apart along national lines, Hobsbawm (1990, 182-83) wrote that these events, ironically, confirmed the imminent end of the nationalities question: "The world history of the late twentieth and early twenty-first centuries ... will see 'nation states' and 'nations' absorbed or dislocated by, the new supranational restructuring of the globe ... The very fact that historians are at last beginning to make some progress in the study and analysis of nations and nationalism suggests that, as so often, the phenomenon is past its peak. The owl of Minerva which brings wisdom, said Hegel, flies out at dusk. It is a good sign that it is now circling round nations and nationalism."

Other post-nationalists have focused more narrowly on European integration, arguing that it portends the erosion of nationalism and the creation of new overlapping and multiple forms of identity linked to an overarching

Europeanness (Kearney 1997). From this perspective, the nation-state model, to which nationalists are purported to be wedded, involves assumptions about the congruence of nation and state, centralized notions of power, and absolute notions of sovereignty; these assumptions are seen as becoming increasingly anachronistic in a world of overlapping sovereignties and identities. One version of this argument has been around at least since the inception of the European order with the Treaty of Rome, but the more explicitly postmodernist and postcolonial versions are relatively recent (McKay 1996, 46-49). The original vision underlying the European Economic Community (later the EU) was based on twin economic and political bases. Economically, the community would foster prosperity and prevent a return to the destructive protectionism of the interwar years. Politically, it would resolve the historical problem of the coexistence of German and French nation-states.[4] Some had even broader visions, ones that were inspired by notions of European federalism that dated back as far as the Renaissance period and were taken up again in the face of nineteenth-century nationalisms. These visions were directed against state nationalism, particularly German nationalism, but Europeanist postnationalists and postmodernists also directed them against minority nationalism (Kearney 1997). Whatever was the precise target, the idea was a post-national one: the institutional structures of cooperation would lead to the transcendence of nationalism, which had wreaked such havoc on the European continent, in favour of a genuinely post-national or European identity.[5] These thinkers argued not only that minority nationalism (or nationalism) would die away but also that this was desirable.

Others have resurrected the nineteenth-century distinction between the nationality of large established states (good) and that of stateless nations and minorities (bad) (Dahrendorf 1995). Dahrendorf claims that the large nation is needed to sustain democracy and civic values within the European market. This claim is part of a long tradition in which minority nations are presented as dysfunctional, atavistic, romantic carry-overs of a different and bygone world order. They were regarded as uncivilized, as vessels for ethnocentrism and illiberalism, and as obstacles to social justice and solidarity. Nationalism was not only unattractive and unattainable, it was also dangerous because there are an infinite number of potential nations. It was also unnecessary, because nations are not real but the creation of states or state-aspiring nationalist intellectuals who mobilize the masses behind their projects. Nationalism — not only the expansionist state nationalism of Nazi Germany or Milosevic's Serbia but also the minority nationalisms of the Basque Country, Northern Ireland, and the Balkans — was seen as producing conflict and instability.

These arguments are suspect on both empirical and normative grounds. Predictions that minority nationalism would fade away have run up against observed reality. What we have seen instead throughout the world, including parts of Europe, is the emergence or re-emergence of ethnic and nationalist politics. In western Europe, post-Franco Spain has experienced a number of strong nationalist movements, particularly in Catalonia and the Basque Country; since the late 1960s, the United Kingdom has had vibrant nationalist movements in Scotland and Northern Ireland and an emergent one in Wales; and Belgium has evolved from a polity in which the main division was between the religious and the secular to one that is more focused on communities defined by language. In eastern Europe, three multinational federations — the Soviet Union, Yugoslavia, and Czechoslovakia — fell apart at least partly because of nationalist divisions. The nationalities question also poses continuing difficulties in many of the successor states, including Serbia, Bosnia-Herzegovina, Slovakia, Estonia, Latvia, Moldova, Georgia, Azerbaijan, and Russia. To these cases can be added the question of Turks in Bulgaria, Kurds in Turkey, and the long-standing dispute between Turkish and Greek Cypriots in Cyprus.

These facts suggest that recent predictions that global transformations will wash away minority nationalism are as suspect as their nineteenth-century equivalents. Far from weakening minority nationalism, a number of recent changes can help account for its emergence and re-emergence in various places. First, the process of economic integration — with the increased mobility of capital, goods, services, and labour — and the rise of transnational corporations has weakened the state's capacity to manage its economy through tariffs, taxes, and subsidies. It has shifted power from the state to the marketplace. Minority nationalist movements are sometimes a response to this weakened state and an attempt to forge a new collective response to economic change. Second, the lowering of international tariffs and the construction of regional economic associations, particularly the EU, have helped reduce the risks associated with independence and have heightened the popularity of nationalism in places such as Scotland and Quebec. Even small countries now have easier access to global markets. The development of multilateral defence organizations, particularly NATO, has also made statehood more viable than it once was. Third, the cultural dimension of globalization — with the development of new communications technologies, increased travel, the spread of English as a lingua franca, and increased migration flows — has posed a threat to some minority cultures and facilitated a nationalist response. The new communications technologies — satellite TV, desktop publishing, and the Internet — have also provided tools that facilitate minority mobilization. Finally, the spread of global norms on human rights has made minorities more resistant to a subordinate status than they once were. We now live in a world in which discrimination and alien rule are more difficult to justify. The spread of norms of self-determination, brought about first by decolonization and then by the emergence of multiple new states in eastern Europe, may also have reinforced pro-independence arguments from minority nationalist leaders. Even the EU's enlargement process provides a fillip to minority nationalist leaders in western Europe: every time a small state joins the EU, it provides a reminder to sometimes larger nationalities in western Europe that they do not have direct representation in the Council of Ministers and that their language is not an official language of the EU.

Minority nationalism is not always, as some socialists and liberals have assumed, a conservative reaction against economic change. This change may also give rise to regional forms of cooperation and mutual defence associations that permit and even encourage the flourishing of more local forms of identity. Whereas in the past, for example, the Scots saw the force of the argument that they had to be aligned with the British political project to survive in the imperial age, in the current context it is possible for much smaller units to survive and do well (Keating 1996, 62-54; Colomer 2007). Minority nations are no longer as dependent on their host state, but they are more dependent on international and continental regimes, such as the EU. This shift in dependent relations gives minority nations some autonomy, at least in the sense that they are able to play off these various forms of dependency against one another. Moreover, smaller units might be better positioned in these circumstances than larger units to take advantage of local expertise — to tailor their policies and programs to highlight and reinforce their particular competitive advantage.

Nor are minority nationalist movements necessarily more illiberal and ethnocentric than their state-led counterparts, as some liberals believe (Dahrendorf 1995). Scotland, the Basque Country, Catalonia, and Quebec are societies in which democratic and liberal norms are deeply entrenched, and nationalists in these societies are no less committed to democratic government and justice than the majority national communities of the state in which they are encapsulated.[6] It is not that minority or majority nations are inherently less or more just or democratic: the question of their values is strongly related to their political traditions, not to their minority or majority status in the state as a whole.[7]

In addition, the minority nationalism that has been facilitated in the new transnational context of European integration is not necessarily of the hard-core, uncompromising, secessionist variety. Europeanization has encouraged moderation so that nationalist movements may be accommodating — more willing to be satisfied with forms of autonomy and political input within the state context, as long as there are possibilities to transcend this context across a range of functional and symbolic issues (Keating 1996, 2004).

Finally, nationalities can reasonably claim that the current state system is unfair. Like majority nations, they are politically mobilized, they have a history and homeland, and they seek to exercise political self-government. Increasingly, their demands have been framed in exactly the same language and with the same normative underpinnings as the claims to self-determination made by the states themselves; these demands move from an ethnic particularism to a broader civic nationalism that invokes liberal democratic norms and often embraces the new international order. This normative approximation might be thought to reduce the ideological distance between majorities and minorities, and to some degree it has. Paradoxically, it may make self-determination issues more difficult to resolve because they are competing on the same normative ground, with majorities and minorities invoking the same principles to lay claims to broad powers of social regulation (Keating 2001a). Civic nationalism may represent a form of social and political progress, but it does not in itself resolve the fundamental question of where authority lies: It calls into question the legitimacy of that authority.

Nationalism, then, is not simply going to go away. It cannot simply be demobilized or deconstructed, and minority nationalism is actually more likely to thrive in the new institutional arrangements of Europe. It cannot be dismissed as inherently reactionary and alien to the emerging European value system. Nor is secession and the redrawing of boundaries the answer. States are generally reluctant to abandon territory, and secessionism, particularly if it becomes widespread, is likely to be enormously destabilizing. It is notoriously difficult to draw new state boundaries that satisfy everyone's national preferences. Inevitably, there will be minorities in the new state who would rather remain in the old (rump) state, minorities in the old rump state who would rather be in the new state, and minorities in both areas who would rather have their own new state (McGarry 1998). There are also likely to be people with multiple (nested) identities who identify with both the new state and the rump state. Moreover, because identities that depend on context are more or less fluid and amenable to change in the new state configuration, consensus about independence in the secessionist region may soon be replaced by post-independence dissensus. It is, therefore, important that we examine the ways that the concerns of national minorities can be addressed without breaking the state apart and that can yield structures and justifications for shared rule.

European Integration and the Accommodation of National Minorities

In our view European integration has helped to alter the contours of the nationalities question and to defuse the minority question that is endemic in the nation-state system. It has not removed that question, however, and progress has been uneven, especially on the eastern part of the Continent.

An Erosion of Unitarism

Although Europe has not promoted a post-nationalist politics, it has facilitated a post-sovereigntist politics conducive to the accommodation of minorities, one in which the notions of the unitary nation-state, and of the international order as being one between competing and discrete states, have receded. The EU is based on the idea of shared sovereignty and challenges the doctrinal basis of the traditional state. At the same time, several western European countries have been transformed from unitary states to federal or decentralized ones. Policy areas that are important to minority national communities have been transferred to their jurisdictional authority, a development that goes some way towards meeting the aspirations of minority nationalists for greater control over their collective life (Danspeckgruber 2002). In 1978 Spain established itself as a decentralized state in which the Catalan, Basque, and Galician nationalities were given significant autonomy. Belgium was transformed from a unitary state into a federation of three language communities and three regions in 1992. Italy negotiated autonomy for the South Tyrolese in 1948 and extended it in 1972 and 2001. The United Kingdom created a parliament for Scotland in 1998, as well as assemblies for Northern Ireland and Wales. Even France has been prepared to extend limited autonomy to Corsica and more modest concessions to other regions. Arguably, this preparedness to decentralize has been influenced by European integration. The kind of sovereignty sharing among states that is associated with transnational institutions like the EU may have made states, including regions controlled by minorities, more prepared to devolve power downwards. The European principle of subsidiarity, in which decisions are made at the most decentralized level possible, pushes in the same direction. The demonstration effect of decentralization by other co-members may have been helpful. The context of membership in transnational bodies, such as the EU and NATO, may also have reduced fears about the consequences of granting autonomy to minorities in the form of security threats, irredentism, and the distortion of markets.

While western Europe has been moving towards decentralization, this process has been uneven. France and Greece have largely resisted the trend towards autonomy seen elsewhere and, like many states outside Europe, have sought to avoid creating regional governments that correspond to historical nationalities or minorities. Spanish governments of both parties have resisted special concessions to the nationalities by resisting change and then, when it is inescapable (usually because of the need for the votes of nationalist parties in the central parliament), applying it uniformly across the country. In eastern Europe the ideal of the centralized unitary state remains dominant. This is not surprising given the recent history of the region, which saw three ex-Communist, multinational federations break apart along the lines of their internal administrative boundaries and the constant fear of irredentism fuelled by twentieth-century history. Moreover, the 1992 opinion of the international Badinter Commission on the former Yugoslavia, which declared that its republics could secede but that there could be no secessions from the republics, appeared to confirm that self-governing structures facilitated the prize of international legal recognition for secessionist regions and that unitary structures prevented it.

A Weakening of Borders

European integration is also reducing the significance of borders in ways that may facilitate the accommodation of minorities cut off from their co-nationals by state boundaries. The most obvious sense in which borders are less significant is related to the EU's common market — which has removed restrictions on the flow of capital, goods, and labour — and which, within the Schengen countries, even dispenses with passport controls. Borders are also less significant in the sense that many policy areas that were once matters of sovereign state jurisdiction have been transferred upwards and are now matters to be discussed at the European level or have been transferred downwards, to more local levels, in accordance with the principle of subsidiarity. New functional systems are emerging that no longer respect state boundaries (Keating 2006). These provide minorities in control of their own regions with new opportunities to explore the constitution of cross-border political communities with their co-nationals, without the disruption, chaos, and possible bloodshed associated with re-drawing state boundaries (Miall 1992; Danspeckgruber 2002). The EU directly encourages cross-border initiatives through its INTERREG program, while the CE, through the Madrid Convention, has produced a legal instrument for establishing cross-border partnerships. The European Parliament has also encouraged interstate and cross-border cooperation in a way that has been helpful to national minorities (Haagerup 1984).

European integration processes may also make states less sensitive about cross-border cooperation, including cooperation between kin-states and host-states over national minorities. It has promoted good neighbourly relations and cooperative behaviour among western European states, including previously warring states such as Germany and France, and it has firmly embedded the principle of the territorial integrity of states. Although states previously resisted cross-border cooperation, or even autonomy for minorities, because this was thought to facilitate irredentism, this concern is now, perhaps, diminished. European integration has also made it possible for minorities to sell these ideas to states or to members of the state's dominant community exposed in border regions. The cooperation can be marketed in functional rather than political terms and as the sort of development that is not peculiar to their situation but common throughout the EU (Alcock 2001, 177).

Austria's accession to the EU in 1995 was immediately preceded by a new treaty with Italy and followed by more cooperation in South Tyrol. The most far-reaching example of cross-border and interstate cooperation within the EU is that between the United Kingdom and the Irish Republic with respect to Northern Ireland. In 1985, through the Anglo-Irish Agreement, the British government formally allowed the Irish government to have a role in the governance of Northern Ireland to address the aspirations of its large Irish nationalist minority. In 1998 cross-border (all-Ireland) political institutions were established, including a North-South Ministerial Council (McGarry and O'Leary 2004, 273-76). As part of the agreement, the Irish Republic removed its constitutionally entrenched irredentist claim to Northern Ireland. European integration cannot be the only explanation for these arrangements, because cooperation elsewhere has been less radical. Cooperation between the British and Irish governments over Northern Ireland, although it was facilitated by a supportive European context, was also influenced by the imperatives of managing an intractably violent conflict, by the increasingly interventionist diplomacy of the United States, and, fundamentally, by the fact that London had long wanted to abandon Northern Ireland, if it could do so peacefully (McGarry 2006). These examples suggest that we should not expect this level of cross-border cooperation to develop evenly across the Continent, particularly in settings where irredentist fears remain rife, as is the case in much of eastern and southeastern Europe.

Just as European integration has promoted centralization rather than autonomy in some cases, so too has it erected new barriers between kin-states and related minorities. Although the EU erodes internal boundaries, it has also strengthened boundaries between it and neighbouring states. Hungary's accession to the EU required it to enforce the EU's common visa regime in Romania, Ukraine, and Serbia, all of which contain Hungarian minorities. This step forced Hungary to renege on an obligation it had made to its kin-minorities not to hinder their access to their motherland, and it made it markedly more difficult for Hungarians in these other countries to travel to Hungary. Attempts to get around this difficulty by issuing long-term multiple-entry visas are unlikely to survive Hungary's accession to the Schengen Agreement in 2006 (Batt 2006). As Sunday suggests in her chapter in this volume, these steps may reinforce the determination of a minority to secure autonomy within its given state, which will raise more intensely the question of the legitimacy of state authority. It is also unlikely that the EU will tolerate Croatia's policy of maintaining a dual citizenship agreement with Bosnia-Herzegovina, which is aimed at eroding frontiers between the two states in the interests of the latter's Croatian minority. This policy will likely fall foul of the Schengen acquis (the body of law and practice to which aspirant members must adhere) and perhaps EU anti-discrimination law, which prevents discrimination on the basis of ethnicity. These problems go beyond Hungary and the former Yugoslavia to potentially affect minorities and the basis of legitimate authority elsewhere, including the Turkish minority in Bulgaria, the Kurdish minority in Turkey, and relations between Romania and the ethnic majority in Moldova.

Political Space beyond the State

Transnational organizations, particularly the EU, have the potential to create political space to include non-state actors such as subregions, including those controlled by nationalities. In the nation-state model, the only legitimate voice is that of the central state, which expresses the undifferentiated will of the people. This model has the perverse consequence that it leads nationalities to place a high value on secession or independence as the only effective form of recognition, the only mechanism for having an international personality, and the only way of being accepted as a nation within the global family of nations. Autonomy arrangements by themselves have the drawback of having no external dimension in which the minority community can imprint its public culture on the international community; the prized aspiration for recognition is not satisfied by this sort of institutional arrangement. In a regional association such as the EU, however, there is the potential for more imaginative arrangements in which not only member states are represented and have a voice and institutional recognition of their collective identity but so, too, are regions and minority national communities.[8]

Access to political space beyond the state, however, remains largely the gift of the states themselves, and some have been more open than others. While some, such as Belgium, give their regions input into state policy towards the EU; others, such as Spain until recently, do not. Thus, achieving a role of this sort requires victory at the member-state level, and there has been an understandable reluctance at the European level to develop general approaches to this question. The Committee of the Regions gives regions some direct input into EU policy making, but it has very weak powers, lacks resources, and has been a general disappointment to its members. The Convention on the Future of Europe and the draft constitution were a missed opportunity to address the position of actors beyond the state. Some nationalist political parties, consequently, came away from the convention convinced that, because its agenda was statist, statehood was necessary. Others were prepared to accept it because they continue to value European integration and what it can do for nationalities. The lack of a suitable space in Europe helps to explain the fate of the Ibarretxe Plan for the Basque Country, in which both the Basque government and the Spanish state reverted to the old logic of nation and state (Keating and Bray 2006).

An International Regime of Minority Rights Protections

One shortcoming of the traditional nineteenth-century state order is the presumption that the treatment of minorities is an internal matter for the states concerned. This position leaves minorities open to discrimination or persecution and bereft of external protections, which gives them a strong incentive to seek their own states. As a result of European integration and changing international norms, traditional conceptions of state sovereignty are now being questioned. There are several mechanisms for transferring conceptions of minority rights. One is normative diffusion through European organizations, including the EU, the CE, and the OSCE. In this process, states adopt the logic of appropriateness to adapt their behaviour to what is expected as a member of the club and gradually internalize the new norms. These norms are diffused by European organizations and by imitation of Western states. A second is conditionality, by which states that wish to accede to European organizations are forced to change their laws and behaviour. Another mechanism is the use of international jurisdictions by members of minorities to gain redress. A fourth mechanism is direct intervention in crisis areas such as the Balkans, where European and international organizations have effectively established protectorates and exercise wide control over domestic policies. It is notoriously difficult to assess or distinguish these mechanisms. Normative change is likely to be slow and difficult to measure. Conditionality is easier to record; although it is not easy to assess how far behaviour has changed, and it often goes along with normative pressure (Kelley 2004). Direct intervention is easier still, although the need for this intervention would suggest that normative adaptation has not occurred. Empirical studies have tended to suggest that hard conditionality is the key mechanism (ibid.; Sasse 2006), but this conclusion might be an artifact of a methodology that makes this easier to measure. It is also the case that the EU's use of hard conditionality is informed by ideas that have emerged from softer institutions such as the CE and the OSCE.

There are, moreover, various ways to define minority rights. At a minimum it involves non-discrimination and the application of individual civil rights to members of minorities. Members of the CE are subject to the European Convention on Human Rights and the European Court of Human Rights. These agreements have been used by members of nationality groups to challenge state persecution, such as the British government's treatment of Irish nationalist detainees in Northern Ireland. The

European Convention has the advantage, from the perspective of nationalities, in that it is not connected, as individual states' bills of rights often are, to a nation-building project, and the European Court may be seen as less partisan than state courts.[9]

A stronger form of protection is to refer directly to group rights. In the early 1990s, international organizations started to move in this direction, which included recognizing the rights of national minorities (Kymlicka 2006). The Council of Europe's 1992 European Charter for Regional or Minority Languages and 1995 Framework Convention on the Protection of National Minorities (FCNM) include some positive group rights, including public funding for minority elementary schools and the right to write to public authorities in one's own language. The FCNM is a legally binding document that has now been ratified by thirty-four states and signed by eight more.

Conditionality can be seen at work in several instances. Since 1991, minority rights have been one of the four criteria that states must meet to join the EU. A number of scholars have shown that European pressures have facilitated the accommodation of minorities in eastern Europe, including Russian minorities in the Baltic states (Bernier 2001; Jurado 2006; Kelley 2004). Perhaps unsurprisingly, the rights conceded tend to be the type that are least threatening to states. The rights that are promoted in the FCNM, and by the OSCE, do indeed move beyond those included in earlier documents, such as the UN's 1966 Covenant on Civil and Political Rights, in the direction of group rights. However, they do not deal with the central aspirations of nationalities, which include territorial autonomy, official language status, minority language universities, and consociational-type rights to participate at the level of the central governments. There was a tentative commitment to support territorial autonomy for nationalities in the OSCE's Copenhagen Declaration of 1990 and in recommendation 1201 of the Council of Europe's Parliamentary Assembly in 1993. Since then, there has been a marked movement away from this support as international organizations, such as the High Commissioner on National Minorities, have appeared more interested in supporting less threatening forms of non-territorial autonomy (Kymlicka 2006; McGarry and Moore 2005). Around 2000, EU regional development policy and advice on state restructuring shifted from promoting decentralization to favouring centralization (Hughes, Sasse, and Gordon 2003; Keating 2003). Similarly, in some cases, pre-EU accession steps in southeastern Europe have had the effect of promoting centralization. These moves seem to go against what Keating has described as a growing norm in western Europe, the de-ethnicization of nationality movements and an associated increased emphasis on territory as the criterion of inclusion.[10]

There are also some questions about Europe's commitment to minority rights. There is no western European consensus about these rights. Some states have generous provisions for minorities, while others, such as France, have been much less accommodating. This lack of consensus helps to explain why the thrust of Europe's efforts at minority rights protection has been directed against states in eastern Europe. This outcome, in turn, has given rise to a double standard in which the EU's member states pressure candidates to embrace documents, such as the FCNM, that several of them have not accepted. Western Europe's lack of consensus may also help to explain why the policy of conditionality has been inconsistently applied. Sasse (2006) acknowledges that conditionality has produced positive results, particularly when external pressure coincides with favourable domestic circumstances. She also notes, however, that the minority rights criterion has not been a key determinant in the EU's assessment of applicant countries, and that it declined in importance towards the end of the accession process. She notes that when minority issues were raised by the EU in eastern Europe, it was often the Roma that were of uppermost concern, rather than larger minorities such as the Magyars of Romania and Slovakia or the Turks of Bulgaria. This phenomenon was at least partly because of the association in western European minds between the maltreatment of the Roma and their migration to the West. Self-interest rather than a concern for minorities drove matters. It may also have been because the sorts of rights sought by the Roma were of the non-threatening kind: as a dispersed minority, the Roma do not seek territorial autonomy.[11] The Russian minorities in the Baltic states have also been a focus of attention, which is a result, arguably, of the need for good relations between Russia and the EU.

When the Copenhagen criteria were added to the acquis in 1997, the criterion that minority rights must be protected was left out. Similarly, the draft European Constitution incorporated the Copenhagen criteria minus minority rights. The commitment to generalized minority protections is so weak that some supporters of minority rights have concluded that, having set itself the task of protecting the rights of national minorities, Europe has now lost its nerve. And "the bold experiment of articulating international norms targeted at national minorities, and capable of resolving potentially violent ethnonationalist conflict, is slowly being abandoned"

(Kymlicka 2006). Skovgaard (2007), however, upon reviewing the efforts of the EU, the CE, and the OSCE, has detected an emerging consensus, based less on overarching theory than on practice and mutual learning around forms of consociationalism light and multiculturalism light. This consensus would suggest that there has been some diffusion of norms or what Gurr (2000, 278) has described as a novel and "emergent international regime of minority rights protection."

The will and effectiveness of European support for minority group rights has been context sensitive, and the role of European integration has been a facilitative rather than a sufficient or even a necessary means for minority protection. In Hungary, which in the early 1990s enthusiastically endorsed the new European norms on minority rights protection, the chief motive appears to have been to shame its neighbours into acting to protect their large Hungarian minorities. The same has been true of Austria in recent decades. The fact that Magyars are minorities in several states helps explain why Hungary reacted differently than Slovakia, even though both were presumably open to the influence of European norms and conditionality incentives. Similarly, we can expect those parts of Europe in which memories of nationalist conflict are still raw to be less open, *ceteris paribus,* to new norms on minority rights than areas in which hostilities are a more distant memory. Because the most obvious incentive that has been brought to bear on eastern Europe is membership in prestigious Western organizations such as the EU and NATO, there is a question mark over what will happen to minority rights once membership has been granted. Two distinct scenarios appear possible: optimists anticipate a form of reverse conditionality in which pre-2004 member states come to embrace some of the policies and minority rights documents that have been adopted by the new member states from eastern Europe; pessimists forecast a tacit policy consensus on inaction within an enlarged EU.

European organizations have also been involved, in eastern and southeastern Europe, in direct intervention, which involves conflict prevention, post-conflict mediation, reconstruction, and peacekeeping. Concerned by the violence that accompanied the breakup of the Soviet Union and Yugoslavia, the OSCE established the Office of the High Commissioner on National Minorities (HCNM) in 1993. The HCNM's job has been to monitor the treatment of national minorities and to encourage states to adopt policies conducive to stable majority-minority relations. The OSCE and, to a lesser extent, the EU have also engaged in conflict mediation activities throughout the European periphery, from Moldova to the Caucasus. They have also participated in democratic development and economic reconstruction in Kosovo and Bosnia-Herzegovina, while the EU is currently in charge of peacekeeping in Bosnia-Herzegovina. Most radically, NATO has twice, in Bosnia-Herzegovina in 1995 and in Kosovo in 1999, intervened militarily to bring an end to civil war and human rights abuses. International organizations have played an important role in the design of post-conflict constitutions in both countries, which are now European and international protectorates.

Here, too, the record is mixed. In some failures, the problem has been one of ineptitude. It could be argued that EU diplomacy in Cyprus helped to prevent conflict resolution. The Turkish Cypriots were told that they had to compromise to get into the EU, and they did, by endorsing the Annan Plan in a referendum. Greek Cypriots, on the other side, were told that Cyprus would be accepted into the EU regardless of whether there was an agreement. The incentive structure set by the EU made it possible for Greek Cypriots to plausibly conclude that their negotiating hand would be strengthened if they refused a deal, were admitted into the EU, and acquired veto rights over Turkey's accession. The result was that European diplomacy, instead of contributing to a settlement, increased tensions in the area. The OSCE's mediating activities in a number of conflicts on Europe's eastern periphery — including Moldova, Georgia, and Azerbaijan — have been similarly ineffective.

Although international organizations have endorsed autonomy for nationalities in a number of areas of eastern and southeastern Europe — including Bosnia-Herzegovina, Kosovo, and Macedonia, as well as Georgia, Moldova, Azerbaijan, and Cyprus — this step occurred because the minorities in these cases have been able to win autonomy through military rebellion, sometimes aided by kin-states. Support for autonomy in these cases, then, is not the result of some pan-European norm, but a reaction to *realpolitik* and the threat to regional stability. In Kosovo, where NATO intervention had effectively separated the province from Serbia, Europe was sharply divided on the recognition of independence. Some states argued for an acceptance of the facts on the ground, while others feared the precedent and noted that recognition violated the existing Badinter doctrine, brought in to deal with the breakup of Yugoslavia, whereby only constituent parts of federations could secede. Optimists argue that, in due course, the absorption of the whole of the Balkans into the EU and other European bodies will resolve these problems. This argument implies commitments that Europeans may not be prepared to accept. It also comes up against the problem that Europe cannot resolve all security and ethnic conflict problems at its borders by consistently moving to enlargement. It has not yet found a way to extend its imperial reach (Zielonka 2006; Colomer 2007) to its "near abroad."

Conclusion

European integration offers a historic opportunity to reframe the old nationalities question at the level of norms, institutions, and practices. Norms take a long time to change, but over time ideas of Europeanism have served to inculcate democratic practice in southern and then central and eastern Europe. To some degree, this observation is true of minority rights, although Europe has not evolved as consistent a line on these rights as it has towards individual rights and democratic practice.

Nationalist parties have sought to use the European framework to project their demands, and in the process they have been Europeanized. There has been some institutional innovation, in the form of cross-border partnerships in places like Ireland or the Tyrol in which Europe provides a context and some instruments. Practices are emerging in which nationalities issues are no longer zero-sum matters but questions of normal politics, amenable to negotiation and compromise. Europe of the Fifteen (the EU before 2004) showed a remarkable ability to resolve the problem of state nationalism and interstate war, to the degree that the achievement is hardly noted any longer. The EU has some prospect of spreading this zone of international peace eastwards. Its record on non-state conflict is more difficult to assess in the short run, if only because conflicts that do not take place are not recorded. Compared with the interwar experience, however, the management of nationality issues has been largely successful, with the notable exception of the former Yugoslavia. Even there, the prospect of membership in European institutions is providing some incentives to engage in cooperative behaviour. At the same time, there have been failures, and European institutions have often tried to dodge the difficult issues of minority politics or reduce them to matters of democracy and individual rights. European diplomacy has committed mistakes, as in the case of Cyprus. This issue is not going to go away, and if the European project is to continue to expand and deepen, policy makers will need to address the nationalities question in a more thorough and explicit manner.

Whether these circumstances can be repeated outside Europe, as a result of globalization and the construction of supranational alliances, is a difficult question that is related to the presence of several conditions. One is the preparedness of minority nationalist movements elsewhere to accept the limitations of the doctrine of sovereignty in modern conditions. Some minorities in other parts of the globe appear to accept that they do not need their own state, but this position is far from being the rule. As a consequence, the general tendency outside western Europe is for states to be hostile to the accommodation of minorities through territorial autonomy lest it lead to secession. A second condition for moderation is international security and good neighbourly relations between states. States are much more reluctant to accommodate minorities in times of international tension or when their territorial integrity is challenged by other states. There are few cases outside Europe where this condition exists, although Quebec is one. A third condition is free trade and market access so that new forms of autonomy do not impose economic barriers or costs. Fourth, it will be helpful if an overarching regime of human rights develops, one that will be applicable both to individuals and to cultural minorities to ensure that autonomy for one group will not lead to the oppression of its internal minorities. Finally, a repeat of Europe's experience elsewhere will be facilitated by the development of a common political space and a set of institutions that give reality to these other factors.

chapter 8

Challenging Legitimacy or Legitimate Challenges? Minority Encounters with a State in Transition

Julie Sunday

SINCE THE REVOLUTION TO overthrow Communism in 1989, the Democratic Alliance of Hungarians (DAHR) — a political party that represents the Hungarian minority in Romania — has sought "autonomy" for that community. The Romanian state has largely been resistant to these claims for autonomy, fearing them to be inherently secessionist. Without this autonomy, the minority group suggests that the Romanian state lacks legitimacy. Members of the minority are concerned about accepting shared rule with the majority without more collective autonomy.

The Hungarian minority is the largest minority in Romania at 6.6 percent of the population, followed by the Roma at 2.4 percent. Although there are a number of other minorities in Romania, the Hungarians represent a unique case study for a number of reasons. First, they are regionally concentrated in Transylvania, representing 22 percent of the 7.7 million people in the region and a majority (between 80 and 95 percent) in two counties. Second, they are the only minority in Romania with a political party (the DAHR) that consistently receives between 6.8 percent (2000) and 7.5 percent (1992) of the popular vote. Importantly, the DAHR has made the strategic choice to pursue its goal of autonomy within the Romanian political system. Although other minorities are represented in Parliament, this electoral strength means that the DAHR has been in the unique position of holding power as a member of coalition governments from 1996 to 2000 and from 2004 to the present. Currently, members of the DAHR are in cabinet and responsible for large portfolios. The DAHR's position as part of the state and privy to state power creates a unique tension for a minority that seeks to advance claims and define itself against the state. No other minority in Romania finds itself in a similar strategic paradox.

Transylvania is a diverse region and has, throughout history, changed jurisdictions as part of both Hungary (before the First World War) and Romania (after the war). Given this legacy of border changes, the Romanian state perceives Hungarian claims for autonomy as a potential threat to its sovereignty and the legitimacy of its shared rule over the present Romanian territory. Kymlicka and Straehle (1999, 73) describe the Romanian state's response to the Hungarian minority, and the threat that it is deemed to pose, as an example of a state engaged in nation-destroying activities. Given this negative response from the state, the DAHR has strategically argued for autonomy by aligning its goals with those of the European Union (EU) and its support of regional integration (for further discussion of the EU in this regard, see Keating, McGarry, and Moore, this volume). Since 1996 a formal relationship has developed between the Romanian state and the Hungarian minority in government with the stated impetus on both sides being Romania's ultimately successful inclusion in the EU in 2007.

This relationship brings the claim for autonomy by the minority into more direct connection with globalizing processes. From the point of view of member states, the EU is an arrangement that involves reducing their respective sovereignty as states in exchange for participating in political arrangements that permit them to better influence other member states. As a union of states, the EU is also seen as an arrangement that strengthens the possibility for EU states to engage with globalizing processes and to influence and shape these in ways that would not be possible as individual states. In foregoing sovereignty for influence in these ways, the EU states relax borders *within* the union, making them more porous and fluid, while also working to strengthen some aspects of the borders between the union and other nation-states. Given these developments, cultural minorities' claims for rights and autonomy become less threatening to member states. This change in perspective on minority rights opens the way for cultural minorities such as the Hungarians in Transylvania to make legitimate claims for minority rights.

Romania is proposing to engage with globalization by becoming a member state of the EU. In doing so, it is creating openings for claims for new forms of cultural autonomy within its own territory. The potential, therefore, exists for more collective autonomy for the Hungarian minority and, with it, more personal autonomy for its members. Engaging with globalization as part of the EU creates new avenues to potentially realize autonomy claims. My central argument, then, is that globalization in the form of European enlargement has created an opening for the DAHR to strategically lobby for recognition as a demos — a popular unit or community that exercises political rights and from which political legitimacy is generated — in which some degree of autonomy as a minority group is recognized.

The analysis of bases of legitimacy and illegitimacy of shared rule in this chapter derives from interviews with thirty-seven members of the DAHR that took place during three separate field trips to Romania in the fall of 1999 and 2000 and the spring of 2001. Twenty-seven men and ten women of varying ages were interviewed using an informal format. According to Bernard (1995, 209), these unstructured interviews are not informal in the sense that they are not based on a clear plan. Nonetheless, they are characterized by a minimum of control on the part of the researcher, allowing people to express themselves in their own terms. Most interviews took place in the party offices at the Parliament or the Senate. Interviewees included a variety of individuals who worked for the DAHR in both the executive and elected branches of government: expert councillors, members of Parliament (including former and future ministers), senators, media spokespeople, and youth leaders. These interviews lasted anywhere from forty-five minutes to two hours and led to hundreds of pages of text that I analyzed by coding thematically and looking for relations between different themes. The methods I used can be considered inductive.

Theory within this framework is not conceived in terms of logical deductions but rather through relations between observed phenomena (Eyles 1988, 4). Because of the high rank of some of my informants, the relatively small community of officials, and the potentially inflammatory content of some of these conversations — from the perspective of members of both the DAHR and the Romanian government — anonymity was a crucial factor in getting my informants to speak in greater depth, beyond the party platform.

As the elected representatives of the Hungarian minority, members of the DAHR are focused on redefining the current basis for political legitimacy in Romania — what they interpret as an exclusive form of ethnic nationalism. The exclusive nationalism that the Romanian state has promoted, throughout its history, is well documented in the literature (see Verdery 1991). Although this chapter does not include narratives from members of the Romanian majority per se, it does focus on one concrete expression of the newly democratic Romanian state — the 1991 Constitution — and Hungarian reactions to it. A constitution is a document that outlines the official definition of a society: it delineates how members recognize and cooperate with one another (Tully 2001, 11). Therefore, constitutions can be read not only as legal but also as cultural documents. The Hungarian reaction to the definition of the Romanian state found in the 1991 Constitution is the focus of this chapter. The Constitution, in both theory and effect, represents majority Romanian discourse about *who,* precisely, constitutes the political community.

It is in reaction to the content of the 1991 Constitution that members of the DAHR posit their need for greater autonomy. Rather than discussing autonomy as a normative category, I am interested in tracing the strategic political use of the term *autonomy* on the part of the DAHR. This discourse on autonomy is a means to challenge a highly centralized state, which, according to members of the Hungarian elite, refuses to recognize them.

My conversation with the Hungarians in Romania was with the elite and focused on Romania's political future. I wanted to understand how power is exercised in post-revolutionary Romania and how the DAHR sought to change it to make the exercise of power more legitimate and, in their terms, more democratic. As Williams (this volume) posits, legitimate power need not be democratic, but it must, nevertheless, be accepted as just. It became evident during my research that the DAHR did not perceive the current basis for legitimacy in Romania as just, despite the state's claims (since 1989) to being democratic. From the perspective of the DAHR, a conversation about how power can be legitimately exercised in Romania is concomitantly a conversation about how pluralism can be accommodated and incorporated into the Romanian state. For this reason, democracy, diversity, and legitimacy are inextricably bound within the DAHR's political discourse.

Legitimacy, Nation, and State in Romania

The form that the Romanian state has taken post-1989 — in particular, its democratic credentials — has at times been difficult to establish (see Tismaneanu 1998; Verdery and Kligman 1992). It is, therefore, not surprising that the DAHR directs its struggle towards the state's most concrete and tangible post-Communist expression — the Romanian Constitution adopted in 1991. Specifically, members of the DAHR cite this Constitution and its assertion of a "sovereign, independent, unitary and indivisible National state" as concrete evidence of their exclusion. The DAHR is attempting to redefine the terms of inclusion and exclusion defined by the Romanian Constitution to challenge the "unity of the Romanian people" (article 4[1]) as the founding principle of the Romanian state, a principle that undermines the notion of shared rule when it comes to cultural minorities.

Because democratic legitimacy is based in popular sovereignty, *who* precisely constitutes "the people" is of central importance (see Kraus 2003, 244). I argue that it is precisely the link between democratic consent and legitimacy — normatively conceived as popular sovereignty — that allows the DAHR to mount its challenge for official recognition. Stated alternately, this lack of recognition for the Hungarian minority — the necessary condition for its consent to be governed — places in question the democratic legitimacy of the Romanian state.

Rhoda Howard-Hassmann (this volume) claims that states must be legitimate for people to have autonomy. What the DAHR posits as necessary for legitimate government is, effectively, an inversion of Howard-Hassmann's claim: the people must have autonomy for the state to be legitimate. This claim raises the question: in the case of substate nations, are challenges to the state's legitimacy (garnered through popular sovereignty) legitimate challenges? Arguing that the claims of national minorities are legitimate challenges builds on Murphy's (2001) contention that, rather than being perceived as claims for cultural preservation, minority claims are political claims for legitimate government. I argue in this chapter that although there is a slippage in emphasis depending on how the terms of this debate are ordered, in conceptual terms both the state's legitimacy and the autonomy of its people are inextricably bound. Neither one — the state's claim to legitimacy or the people's claim to autonomy — precedes the other. This argument does not prejudge whether claims to autonomy by the people take the form of recognition of individual rights or collective demands for the right to make rules that affect the culture and the future of a minority group.

The literature on minority rights has effectively problematized the assumption that states (particularly states in transition to democracy) must establish their legitimacy before the claims of substate nations can be contemplated. The maxim applied to the democratizing states of eastern Europe — first democracy and then stability — has proven to be unfounded. Through countless examples (Quebec, Catalonia, Scotland) it is evident that the claims of minority nations do not dissolve once democracy has been established. In contrast, the claims of national minorities in democratic societies, if mounted as "just" claims, problematize the state's own claims to authority and, thus, its legitimacy. The ability of substate nations to place into question the state's claim to legitimacy is, at its essence, a challenge about who is entitled to autonomy and how collective autonomy should be shared. In other words, it is a challenge to define the character of the demos.

Globalization, in the form of European enlargement, has created an opening for the DAHR to strategically lobby for a demos in which some degree of autonomy as a minority group is recognized. Importantly, the DAHR's argument, that the Romanian demos must be constituted in such a way as to recognize some degree of autonomy for the Hungarian minority, links to larger discourses about globalization and sovereignty. An example is the responsibility to protect doctrine, which contends that if the state does not provide adequate protection for certain members of the demos, an opening is created to evaluate the state according to international norms of legitimacy. As Nyers (this volume) emphasizes, sovereignty then becomes contingent on how the term *protection* is defined.

To create this opening for sharing collective autonomy, the Hungarian minority situates its claims within global processes that already impact state sovereignty in Romania and drive it towards EU membership. A discussion of autonomy is, therefore, simultaneously a discussion of the changing relations of power that inflect this "sovereignty." By engaging with international bodies, most importantly the EU, Hungarian politicians have placed pressure on the state to devolve power. By aligning themselves with principles associated with the EU (for example, the principle of subsidiarity), the DAHR has attempted to increase the legitimacy of its claims within a state that is struggling to establish its own legitimacy.

Given the terms established by the Romanian Constitution, the DAHR argues that its members are not recognized as part of the demos and, by extension, not adequately protected by the state. In this particular case, the minority group and the state share common perceptions of international conventions for legitimacy represented in the EU and the desire for Romania to be included. Although the DAHR and the Romanian state are perhaps pursuing "Europe" for different ends (cultural and political versus economic), the road towards Europe is shared and is fuelling a conversation within Romania about how power is legitimately exercised.

To illustrate the contingency of claims to legitimacy on the acceptance of just rule, I will begin by discussing how the DAHR uses the concept of autonomy to mount its claims for official recognition.

Autonomy

According to the DAHR, recognition would be realized through autonomy. Although this condition for legitimacy appears to be straightforward, recognition for the Hungarian community in Romania is difficult because of the role nationalism has played in establishing political lines of inclusion in Romania. Southeastern Europe is "burdened by the historical legacy of competing communal identities, as well as with the consequences of historically unaccommodated diversity" (Salat 2003, 16). Because of this legacy, the transition to democracy in the region has been characterized by political action that ranges from "ethnic voting to ethnic cleansing" (Stein 2002, 1, cited in Salat 2003).

In particular, the use of nationalism to garner legitimacy means that state actions are characterized by ethnic bias. In Romania this bias is reflected in the form that the post-1989 Romanian state has assumed: a semi-presidential system with a highly centralized state administration. This type of system creates opportunities for presidents to increase their influence, particularly when the party system is fragmented (Salat 2003, 17). This influence has been evident in the frequent use of ordinances in Romania — a situation of which the EU has been critical (Linden and Pohlman 2003, 322).

This centralized state structure poses a distinct challenge to the Hungarian minority's quest for recognition and autonomy. Despite these conditions, the Hungarian minority attempts to impact the formal (written) and material (structural) constitutions of the state in Romania and concomitantly, its democratic practices. In particular, Hungarian political action is directed towards expanding definitions of who precisely is entitled to recognition from the state and then politically codifying this recognition in a form of autonomy. Simply stated, the DAHR is challenging current definitions of the demos and, thus, who is included in shared rule by withholding their consent to be governed.

To recast the debate about political legitimacy in Romania, the DAHR has placed the term *autonomy* at the centre of its political discourse. Autonomy is described as an all-encompassing and multi-faceted concept that exists at the level of the individual, community, and territory. In my interviews I found that it was at the outer edges of this discourse — the territorial level — where autonomy became difficult to define. For example, when I asked members of the DAHR if territorial autonomy could be interpreted as an advocation for some form of federalism, I was quickly cautioned about the implications of using the term *federalism*. At this point my respondents would often begin to speak of a Europe of the regions to couch the negative connotations associated with federalism (i.e., separatism and irredentism) within Romania. In this sense, the concept of autonomy that the DAHR presents — individual, collective, and territorial — is purposefully nebulous: it is a flexible and effective political strategy used to counter constitutional assertions by a state from which they find themselves excluded.

Let me begin by relating an anecdote that I was told to illustrate how the political discourse of the DAHR is focused on redefining current perceptions of the Romanian state as a monolithic and unquestioned authority:

> Let me give you one example about how people view the state, in general. There is a guy who has been arrested by the police because they think he has committed a burglary. Legally, that's all. The police crew is filming this guy; they are sticking a microphone in his face and saying, "Tell us what you did, confess in public." Whenever I spoke to my Romanian friends about this, I said, "Come on, that's a gross violation of people's individual rights." I said, "I wouldn't like to see myself on TV with handcuffs." And they say, "Why?" They say, "It's very educational, people should learn that they should not do that." And I said, "Come on, guys, you don't get it." And they say, "What?" "You don't get it," they say, "it's in the 'interest of the state.'" So you see that's the point in many situations — people tend not to think about their rights. But they are very concerned about the state. (Interviewee 25, House of Parliament, 15 March 2001)

My respondent conveys his impression that the state's interest supersedes all other interests, including, in this case, individual rights. He implies that the activities of the state are legitimized not through any kind of legal code but simply by the state seeming to act in its own interest. What this interest is remains vague and indefinable. When pressed to clarify, he continues: "It's 'Oh the country, the country.' There is this idea, this sort of entity that is called 'the interest of the state.' It's not exactly the raison d'état, but it's something so vague that nobody can define what it is. So, basically, everybody says that something must be done in the 'interest of the state'" (ibid.). It is precisely the vagueness that he attributes to this notion of state "interest" that allows the state to assert control in the ideological field. Following Žižek (1989), state interest can be considered a reified concept that masks inconsistencies and contradictions within the ideological field. According to Žižek (ibid., 45) ideology is an illusion or fantasy construction that structures our real social relations. In this case it is the overlap of the state's interest with the interest of the Romanian people that shows precisely how this ideology has taken hold: "An ideology is really 'holding us' only when we do not feel any opposition between it and reality — that is, when the ideology succeeds in determining the mode of our everyday experience of reality itself" (ibid., 49). The same respondent contests the conflation of his interest with that of the state and, consequently, contests what Žižek would describe as the fantasy of unity expressed by his Romanian friends.

My respondents have reacted to the nebulous concept of state interest with the notion of autonomy — a concept that is equally difficult to pin down but that provides the flexibility necessary to respond to the hegemonic forces of the state. They describe autonomy as the desired outcome of Hungarian claims for rights and equality based on the concept of difference. They direct this discussion of autonomy towards expanding the political subject formally identified by the Romanian state to one that includes Hungarians. One respondent elaborates: "In the DAHR there are such diverse opinions that I don't think anyone can define what they mean by *autonomy* perfectly. Everybody means something different by personal, cultural, and territorial autonomy. What is certain, though, is that individual rights are not enough" (Interviewee 11, party headquarters, 10 October 2000). According to my respondent, autonomy exists at a number of different levels — personal, cultural, and territorial — and has a multiplicity of meanings. Each of these levels has a wide range of impacts — on individual freedom, on belonging in community, and on belonging to a concrete place, respectively. Autonomy, therefore, becomes an exercise of freedom and directly challenges constitutional definitions of the relevant political subject — the united Romanian people.

Discussions of autonomy are, therefore, simultaneously discussions of how power is exercised. Another respondent describes this relationship between power and autonomy: "The politicians in Romania, those who rule the country, want to have a centralized power. It is too slow; some steps were done, but not enough. The DAHR is very consistently asking for local autonomy. We say that the people have the right to decide themselves in their problems, at the local level" (Interviewee 13, House of Parliament, 2 November 2000). This respondent defines autonomy as the ability to exert power at a local level. Nonetheless, the consequence of devolving power is not simply pragmatic, according to another respondent it also has ideological implications: "Yes, it's practical. But decentralization is also ideological. I want to be my own boss in my own garden. Of course there is a fear — in part because of the Palestinians: the idea that if they give us autonomy it will lead to something bad. But this is our duty to convince the Romanians that this won't happen. If I had the power or the money I would send all the politicians to study the western European system" (Interviewee 30, House of Parliament, 11 April 2001). Despite the impediments faced, another respondent argues that the Hungarians remain committed to pursuing autonomy through legal channels:

> We don't want to be in a violent situation, to use violence to get into Parliament. We only want our rights respected. This means the right to make decisions over things that affect your life. These are the reasons why we are in Parliament — to gain autonomy over our culture. This means that all people who belong to this community have the right to make decisions in cultural, educational, and other realms. In terms of territorial autonomy, we mean autonomy for the local administration.
>
> But these terms are unacceptable to Romanians — the word *self-government* is not well received. For Romanians, self-government is the most evil thing in the world. So we say "autonomy of the local public administrations." They don't accept that local administrations in a region have a right to make decisions about things that affect them. The Romanians think that all government has to happen from Bucharest. Right now, we can only do things if Bucharest agrees. (Interviewee 28, House of Parliament, 28 March 2001)

This respondent defines autonomy as the freedom to make "decisions over things that affect your life" — a vague yet all-encompassing assertion. He outlines two main categories for autonomy, namely, culture and territory. His argument for autonomy has undeniable political implications — notably, it is directed towards achieving self-government — and uses the less contentious term *autonomy* to advance these claims. Nonetheless, for another respondent even *autonomy* evokes a negative response: "We don't dare mention autonomy much, because it instantly produces a negative response. What we mean is cultural autonomy, personal autonomy, and local autonomy. I think our striving for autonomy would converge with what the European Union advocates. I think these ideas are perfectly compatible in Romania. If we continue decentralization, which is partly imposed by the accession process and a little bit imposed on the ruling party by us as well, if we continue with that, then we have a good chance" (Interviewee 8, Senate, 28 September 2000). My respondent suggests that although *autonomy* evokes a negative response from Romanians, it remains achievable because it converges with the goals of the EU. Specifically, Romania desires membership in the EU; therefore, Romania will have to adopt these same values, despite the negative reaction the word *autonomy* continues to provoke. The Hungarians are hopeful about the decentralization that they feel is imposed by the accession process through the principle of subsidiarity. This process presents a larger web of interest beyond that of state sovereignty and is described by another respondent as a direct challenge to the absolute power exerted by the state over those within its territory: "Yes, we're hopeful, but at the same time I don't think autonomy will be a community thing, it will be more of a territorial thing. So it will not depend upon whether it's for Hungarians or not. It will be territorial. It could be a beginning — inter-ethnic relations are generally good, and so I don't see why it won't work at a territorial level. There are a lot of mixed marriages; the separation between Romanians and Hungarians is not clear" (Interviewee 26, Party Headquarters, 20 March 2001). Nonetheless, it is precisely this coupling of autonomy with territory that causes a negative reaction from the Romanian state. Given this reaction, another respondent attempts to link Hungarian interests to regional interests within Romania. "I think that there is a huge overwhelming majority of Hungarians in Romania that think that it's useless to think about border issues. That's nonsense because, especially in Transylvania, people live together, and the overwhelming majority of people in Transylvania are Romanian" (Interviewee 5, House of Parliament, 18 September 2000). My respondent suggests that Romanians and Hungarians live well together as a strategy to counter the dominant nationalist rhetoric that is focused on social division. She suggests that one need not be Romanian to be part of a united Romania. In contrast, she suggests that there is unity among diverse groups in Romania.

Despite this unity, the notion of difference remains the basis for Hungarian claims for autonomy. Nonetheless, a large part of this difference is described as deriving from the region of Transylvania — a region they also share with Romanians — which allows my respondents to align themselves regionally as well as culturally. The notion of difference, as it underlies their claims for autonomy, is simultaneously cultural and territorial. As a political strategy, arguing for regional autonomy, for both Hungarians and Romanians, is considered less threatening. What is implied, however, is that once territorial decentralization occurs, cultural autonomy will follow naturally.

One respondent describes this process in simple and direct terms: "We want autonomy for us, autonomy for the regions, Romania in NATO and in the EU" (Interviewee 30, House of Parliament, 11 April 2001). For this respondent, culture, territory, and global forces are intertwined in the process of decentralization, which he prioritizes as (1) autonomy for the Hungarian minority, (2) autonomy for the different regions of Romania, and (3) Romania within NATO and the EU. Although his first two assertions are clearly related, given the concentration of the Hungarian community within the region of Transylvania, the link he makes between Hungarian autonomy and Romania being accepted by NATO and the EU is revealing. Specifically, he is recognizing that Romanian state interests are currently impacted by larger global forces. State sovereignty over autonomy is being eroded from above — a process that the Hungarians view as creating an opportunity to advance their own claims against the state. Another respondent describes this approach in greater detail:

> The strong roots of nationalism in this country and the fears and nightmares of Romanians to lose a part of their national territory make progress very difficult. But I think that the special political situation of the country, the basic choice of Romania — basic trend maybe, not choice — basic trend is to go west. We try to use this basic trend to obtain our specific minority cause. Speaking with our Romanian colleagues in Parliament, "Okay, if you want to be part of this distinguished club, let's say Council of Europe or EU or NATO, you must behave — the rule is," and so on and so on. And all the time we use this kind of rhetoric, this kind of political action. In the meantime, we try to elaborate a special, specific Hungarian program inside of the country. Because it's not true that there is in Europe or somewhere in this whole earth a unitary accepted minority policy.

It's a joke only. There's no such kind of policy. There are some minimal levels, but for us the minimal level is not enough and never was.
Because all the time we make references to international regulation,
to this minimal level accepted by Helsinki, etc. ... But all the time we
declare, there is a community who has special needs. The main field
of battles is this notion of autonomy: local autonomy, cultural autonomy, personal autonomy. These were the main battlefields in these
eleven years after the so-called revolution.[1] (Interviewee 22, Senate, 5
March 2001)

This respondent directly identifies the discourse on autonomy as the
battlefield on which the Hungarian struggle for recognition is being fought.
By alluding to Helsinki and the minimal rights afforded by it, he emphasizes that individual human rights are not adequate to provide the autonomy that he desires. This is an important point: the DAHR is not engaged in
a conversation about individual human rights. Rather, it is pursuing a conversation about the character of the political community and the exercise
of just rule within its bounds. As the respondent emphasizes, this is a conversation that is not yet reflected within international norms (despite references to self-determination in the Charter of the United Nations (Chapter
11) and the UN Covenant on Civil and Political Rights). This is an important distinction because the adequate protection of the "human rights" of
the Hungarians in Romania (since 1989) is often used as a rationale to
dismiss their claims. To dismiss the claims of the Hungarians by arguing
that their human rights have been met misreads the content of their claims:
through a discourse on autonomy, the DAHR removes itself from a generalized discussion of the application of basic human rights to individuals to
engage in a larger and more political conversation about how power is
legitimately exercised by a defined group within a democracy.

Although my participants attempt to moderate the perceived threat that
this discourse poses by framing their goals within those of a united Europe,
they nonetheless encounter resistances. One participant elaborates:
"Important issues cannot be discussed. There are many taboos in Romanian
public opinion. This is not a normal society in these terms. We cannot
discuss important issues connected with modernization of the society, the
future of the society. We cannot discuss, for example, questions connected
to regionalism, federalism, autonomy, or other historical taboos. Those actors who have tried to put these issues on the table of public opinion, they
were strongly sanctioned against" (Interviewee 33, House of Parliament,

19 April 2001). Despite this reaction, another respondent argues that autonomy need not be perceived negatively:

> The perception in Romania, actually, is that these problems could be resolved by a single law, and we would resolve them indefinitely. Or that by inviting the Hungarians' alliance to government in 1996, between 1997 and 2000 ... we resolved the minority problem because the Hungarians are in the government. This is an absolutely wrong and pathological perception because this kind of relationship can only be changed in many years, with many measures, by changing mentalities and having a package of laws. In my country, we are lucky because no minority group wants to fight violently for freedom. But the majority of the Hungarians accept that our situation could be consolidated by different forms of autonomy. Unfortunately, the issue of autonomy cannot be discussed with our Romanian partners. We can discuss on different laws, on different topics, but autonomy is taboo. (Interviewee 23, House of Parliament, 8 March 2001)

This participant highlights the danger inherent in solving minority issues with simplistic answers. His assertion resonates with Tully (2001, 6): "Struggles over recognition do not admit of a definitive solution." The unstated intention of creating a law to deal definitively with minority issues would be that these claims, and by extension these groups, would disappear. Through this approach, who deserves recognition by the Romanian state would remain unchanged: the law would simply become a more sophisticated means to negate the existence of minority groups through a generalized human rights discourse. It is precisely this negation that places into question the state's own claims to legitimacy. Following Mouffe (2000), this perspective, that minority issues can be resolved definitively and singularly, would involve closing down the democratic space itself by resolving the antagonisms that are integral to democracy.

Constitutions

The lack of official state recognition for the Hungarian minority is most clearly emphasized in debates about the Constitution. Hungarian responses to the Constitution reveal contested notions of citizenship and belonging in Romania. There is an inherent tension between (1) a Hungarian identity predicated on the concept of difference and, by definition, excluded from the state and (2) the Hungarian minority's desire to be recognized by the state and achieve equality in terms of rights, citizenship, and belonging. Hungarian responses to the state and its "constitution" highlight how their claims for autonomy *within* Romania are directed towards changing the state's current basis for legitimacy.

According to Tully (2001, 5), the primary goal of these constitutional struggles is not recognition but rather freedom: "the freedom of the members of an open society to change the constitutional rules of mutual recognition and association." Changing these rules, however, requires that the state expand the terms of inclusion and exclusion and relinquish its monopoly on definitions of the political subject deserving recognition. Relinquishing this monopoly is necessary to end a structure of domination and permit the exercise of freedom (ibid., 6). According to Lane (1996, 11), in an ideal world the formal or written constitution is in agreement with the substantive constitution.

The Romanian Constitution defines statehood in ethnic and national terms rather than in civic-territorial language and reflects a form of ethnic bias (Salat 2003, 17).[2] Specifically, the Constitution reflects the exclusion of national minorities from the state. This exclusion has been a constant feature of constitutions in Romania (1923 and 1965) and is historically consistent with a state policy that "held that national minorities did not really exist" (Nedeva 1993, 141).

Article 1(1), which describes the Romanian state, most clearly conveys this bias: "Romania is a sovereign, independent, unitary and indivisible National state." The emphasis on the national and unitary character of the Romanian state, in the first article, clearly draws lines of inclusion and exclusion. These lines of exclusion are further expressed in the definition of the foundation of the state: "The state foundation is laid on the unity of the Romanian people" (article 4[1]). Thus, rather than being defined in terms of territory or citizenship, the state derives its legitimacy from the "unity of the Romanian people." Because of the definition of the state proposed in article 1, the message given is that "the people" are also defined in national and ethnic terms. Recently (2003), article 4 was revised to read: "The state foundation is laid on the unity of the Romanian people and the solidarity of its citizens." Simply stated, the state foundation remains the unity of the Romanian people, although other citizens are now included as constitutive elements of the state. Nonetheless, what is required of these other citizens is that they be in solidarity with the Romanian people. To be included as constitutive of the state precludes citizenship based on the concept of difference. The notion of difference is considered antithetical to the definitions of the united Romanian state outlined in the Constitution. Although there are certain articles pertaining to the "right" of citizens to equality and identity (article 4[2] and article 6), the underlying text is that minority groups are to be tolerated rather than included as constitutive elements of the state.

My participants directly address the implications of this Constitution for how they experience belonging. Specifically, they highlight the contradictions between belonging based on nationality versus how citizenship is set out in the Constitution. According to one participant, the implication is that some citizens belong more than others:

> Romania is defined in the first article of the Constitution as a national state and a unitary state. We didn't agree that Romania is a national state. And that is why, in 1991, the representatives of the Hungarians' alliance voted against the Constitution. We never accepted it. And now, also, we are asking to modify this article because it does not reflect the truth. In Romania there are fourteen national minorities represented in the Parliament. How can a nation be pure if it has so many minorities in the Parliament? (Interviewee 35, Party Headquarters, 2 May 2001)

This participant suggests that the main issue is revising the description of Romania as a pure national state to one that reflects that there are fourteen national minorities represented in the Parliament. He elaborates on this problem of nationalism as a precondition for inclusion: "The problem is that, from our perspective, in the second year of the twenty-first century, it is not important (bearing in mind that we want to become members of the European Union) if a country is national or not. What matters is that we strengthen the important principles of a democratic country — principles of democracy, pluralism, and human rights. These should be in the first article of the Constitution, not that Romania is a national state" (ibid.). Nationalism, he suggests, is becoming increasingly unimportant because of these integrating global processes. This dismissal of nationalism, however, is only half the story. His declared interest in modifying the Constitution suggests that the national character of the state remains an important question. What his assertion does highlight is the hope that European enlargement and the democratic principles it brings with it will liberate him from the implications of living within the borders of a nationally defined

Romanian state. The symbolic content of the Constitution remains important and is reflected in his stated desire to have it changed. Another participant describes the practical necessity of these modifications:

> We issued in 1991 a proposal — a special proposal — about who is a constitutive element of the state. Actually, there is a formula in the Constitution, that the unity of the Romanian nation is the basic element of the state. And we said that maybe this is a sentimental article, without any judicial consequences. Unfortunately, we have realized that there are judicial consequences, because many laws, especially in 1993-94, used this formula: Because Romania is ... we propose that ...
>
> We proposed at that time that the unity of the Romanian nation and other minorities should be the base. We wanted to declare that we were constitutive elements of the state. It was not accepted at that time, in 1991, not to define the country as having more than only Romanians. (Interviewee 14, House of Parliament, 3 November 2000)

According to this participant, current definitions of the state, based on an exclusive form of nationalism, have legitimized state actions against the Hungarian minority.

The first article of the Constitution defines the conditions for belonging and exclusion, and, therefore, it was repeatedly mentioned in my interviews: "The first article of the Constitution has no validity anymore — Romania is not a 'national organic and unitary state'" (Interviewee 19, House of Parliament, 1 March 2001). To counter this constitutional claim, my participants frequently spoke of Romania's inherent diversity. This assertion of diversity was directed towards gaining official recognition by the state. According to my participants, this official recognition would then be formalized through concrete changes to the Constitution: "The problem in the Constitution is with the idea of 'nations.' Hungarians want to change the Constitution in Romania. But Romania is still a national country, which is not fair because there are many minorities in Romania. Romania is the last country in Europe, not speaking of the Ukraine and Russia, to have this type of constitution. Everybody else has changed theirs to a popular one, a republic maybe, but not an organic nation. But according to the Constitution here, Romania is only for Romanians" (Interviewee 27, House of Parliament, 27 March 2001). By describing Romanian resistance to changing the Constitution, my participants paint a picture of

Romania being behind other countries in the region. Another participant suggests that who is identified as constitutive of the state denigrates those citizens who are not ethnically Romanian. "At that time, in 1991, when the Constitution was passed, during the discussions in Parliament, we asked to eliminate the 'nation' because we define ourselves as Hungarians. Although we accept that we are Romanian citizens, judicially, we pay taxes, we obey the laws, we respect the Constitution and everything, but we have the right — as persons, and as community, among ourselves — to be Hungarians." As citizens, he argues, they should be included in definitions of the state: "Now that we're discussing the possibility to modify the Constitution, one of our basic objectives is to modify that provision of the Constitution that says that Romania is a national, organic state. We are not discussing the unity of Romania — that is out of the question — we're discussing the national character of Romania." (Interviewee 12, House of Parliament, 12 October 2000, 10:00 a.m.). Importantly, this participant distinguishes a desire to modify the Constitution to include the Hungarian minority from a discussion about the unity of Romania. This distinction is clearly made to counter the perception that changing the definition of the Romanian state concomitantly threatens the territorial integrity (read unity) of Romania.

The political subject represented in the Romanian Constitution is one that the Hungarians actively seek to change. One participant outlines the great difficulties experienced in attempting to amend the Constitution: "The 1991 Constitution was written by a bunch of old Communists. It's very difficult to amend this Constitution. For example, article 148 states that as long as there exists a Romanian state it is forbidden to modify the Constitution. That sounds like Hitler wrote it. From what I've heard, they're planning to remove that part of it. But the point is that there have been no amendments to the Constitution since 1998" (Interviewee 29, House of Parliament, 4 April 2001). The Constitution is cited as evidence that Romania is "behind" Europe — a condition that this participant suggests will have to change if Romania intends to be integrated.

My participants frequently present these distinctions between Romania and Europe as a rationale for change. One participant outlines this relationship between Europe and change: "Romanian political practice is very different from the European one. Here, the government will just abolish a law. That makes it difficult to amend the Constitution. Both NATO and the EU demand constitutional change, and this is a good thing" (Interviewee 31, Senate, 16 April 2001). For this participant it is the centralized and authoritarian political culture in Romania that distinguishes it from the West.

Although I would argue that constitutions are necessarily difficult to amend, my participant reveals his perception of the state as being both authoritarian and exclusionary. In particular, it is a state that is considered to be hostile to minority groups because of insecurity about its borders.

Contested notions of history are, therefore, central to efforts to amend the Constitution. One participant alludes to history's legacy: "History makes Romanians nervous because they know the borders are unfair. We will never accept the borders as fair, but we do accept them. In a united Europe, we should think about regions and not countries. But right now we are in a Romania whose Constitution doesn't even recognize us. We are not even accepted as a fact" (Interviewee 16, House of Parliament, 15 November 2000). Despite his perception that Hungarian claims to autonomy in Transylvania are legitimate, the participant stresses the Romanian state's reluctance to divide or share its sovereignty. Given this reluctance, the Hungarian minority is looking to engage alternate forces that impact state sovereignty. In particular, its members are hopeful that the pressures associated with European integration will be a catalyst to changing the political subject currently defined by the Constitution. One participant addresses the importance of Europe: "We did not vote on the Constitution. We want to change it. And if there really exists a political intention of trying to become a European member, then we have to harmonize our Constitution with the rest of Europe" (Interviewee 21, House of Parliament, 1 March 2001). This participant suggests that changing the Constitution to include the Hungarian minority is contingent on Romania's inclusion in the EU. Another participant elaborates on the impact that Europe will have:

Well, first of all, in the first Constitution, we never accepted this Constitution because of the first article where Romania is defined as a "national" state. Our first demand was to remove this article. Anyway, it's a very archaic idea. No European state would have such a definition. If you want to be in Europe — I say this again and again — you have to be at the same level, in a constitutional point of view, as other member states. My view is that we should be working towards an entirely new Constitution — not modify the old one. We want a new Constitution. We want a reformed Constitution — not a modification. The whole thing must be changed. The best thing would be a new Constitution without such tribal ideas. (Interviewee 18, Senate, 17 November 2000)

Tellingly, the participant describes the mindset behind Romania's Constitution as being tribal and requiring modification if Romania is to be
included in Europe. The implication is that being in Europe means recognizing the autonomy of national minorities. Nonetheless, another participant acknowledges that this is an argument that does not necessarily hold
sway in Romania: "When we said that the Constitution is an old-fashioned
one and Europe and the whole modern world ask us to change it and
throw away the terminology of 'national state,' many Romanian politicians
immediately took a stance against this. These politicians simply threw back
the idea because they saw it as coming from the Hungarians. They keep
telling us to be good Romanians" (Interviewee 13, House of Parliament, 16
October 2000). My participant suggests that Romanians interpret the
Hungarian minority's desire to change the nationalistic language of the
Romanian Constitution as evidence of their lack of loyalty to the state. To
counter this perception of disloyalty, he suggests that changing this language will improve Romania's chance of being included in Europe — a
goal held by both Romanians and Hungarians.

By accessing an international body, the Hungarian minority attempts to
increase its legitimacy within a state that refuses to recognize it. Despite
initial resistance to constitutional change, one participant is optimistic
about the future: "Our Constitution states that in Romania there are only
Romanians. I think this will change, though nobody really wants to change
it right now. I mean no Romanian wants to change it. The political elite
have to prepare themselves for this debate. They fear it because it would be
something different. The national myth is so strong here" (Interviewee 4,
House of Parliament, 15 September 2000). Fuelling this optimism are the
limitations on state sovereignty that EU integration will entail. One participant elaborates: "But sooner or later we'll need to make some changes. For
example, the definition of state sovereignty will have to change if we are a
part of Europe — you must give some of that up, I think" (Interviewee 20,
House of Parliament, 1 March 2001). What my participant highlights —
and what I would suggest is at the heart of these debates about the
Constitution — is that Hungarian claims for recognition are perceived as a
direct challenge to state sovereignty. To temper this perception, my participants couch their claims within the discourse of an expanded Europe — a
goal that is shared by Hungarian and Romanian politicians alike. Rather
than challenge the state — which would surely generate a negative reaction — they engage the international and global pressures that are already

impacting state sovereignty. They recognize that, in engaging with globalization, the EU has already set up arrangements to pool sovereignty.

By accessing the possibilities associated with EU integration, my participants reveal sovereignty as being constructed and contested. It is within this rupture that the political strategy of the DAHR — to increase autonomy for the Hungarian community — becomes most evident. According to my participants, the reality of Romania's diversity is masked by the illusion of unity represented in the Constitution. Importantly, this illusion structures concrete power relations. Whether the Constitution is a true representation of Romanian beliefs is inconsequential — what is important here is how my participants encounter the ideology of the state and the power relations that support it.

Constructing the Hungarians as a threat gives credence to this ideological fantasy of Romanian state unity. Taussig (1992, 2) uses the metaphor of a nervous system to describe the fetish power of the state — "might not the whole point of the nervous system be it's always being a jump ahead, tempting us through its very nervousness towards the tranquil pastures of its fictive harmony?" Consequently, the Hungarian minority has had to develop a concrete strategy to respond to the state and avoid being subsumed by this fictive harmony. One participant addresses this fear directly:

> I do suspect that, being given the opportunity, they would subsume us. You see that, from an exclusively political point of view, I cannot condemn them. I mean, eventually, when you've got these national minorities within your countries, it means a whole lot of countries are interested in what you do internally. Now, if you've got a minority of two million people, which is about 10 percent, then it means that the whole of bloody Europe is quite interested in what you do internally. So for them it would be easier to know that there are no Hungarians. (Interviewee 34, Senate, 25 April 2001)

For this respondent, it is precisely this fear that drives the Hungarian minority to maintain a separation between itself and the state as a constitutive feature of its "distinctive" identity. She is also aware that this separation allows nationalists to convincingly portray the minority as a threat.

The historically centralized Romanian state, defined constitutionally in national terms, is one that the Hungarian minority encounters directly in its quest for inclusion. My respondents embrace their identity as being different from that of the nationally defined state, yet they make subtle attempts to mitigate the potential accusations (of threat) generated by this difference. Tellingly, members of the DAHR consider themselves political outsiders, despite their presence in Parliament. I would argue, though, that my respondents are not so much arguing for *inclusion* into the state per se as they are arguing for *access* to the power that legitimizes the state. Sharing in that power and in ruling through autonomy is a prerequisite for legitimacy. A degree of antagonism is, therefore, central to advancing their claims and, also, central to maintaining a strategically necessary distinction between themselves and the state.

This antagonism is a reality of the democratic game (Mouffe 2000) — yet it is considered distinctly threatening to a state founded on the "unity" of the Romanian people. The goal of the DAHR is for its members to be partners with the state rather than a part of the state. To do so requires that the state relinquish its monopoly on sovereignty; consequently, Hungarian narratives about the state focus on its centralized character. One respondent comments:

> It's difficult to say what my relationship is with the state. But I think that if the state would realize that decentralization and human rights, minority rights, are important, not because [the Hungarians] are asking for it but because if [the state] wants to belong to a democratic world — western Europe say — then it's a necessity for it to recognize our rights. If two million Hungarians decided that they were Irish suddenly and demanded Irish schools, the state should provide them. It isn't up to the state to decide my identity — that is up to me. If the Romanian state would realize this, they would realize they should change — not just because Europe wants them to. (Interviewee 36, House of Parliament, 3 May 2001)

In sum, the argument made by my respondents in favour of recognition for the Hungarian minority fits all the claims outlined by Tully (2001, 15). First, they suggest that the present form of constitutional recognition of their identity is non-recognition. Second, they argue that this is an injustice. Third, they suggest that the proposed new form of recognition, framed in terms of autonomy, is just. Finally, by linking the goal of autonomy to a democratic future within Europe, they further imply that providing recognition would allow the overall constitutional identity of Romanian society to be more just and more stable. In other words, Hungarian autonomy is required if the state is to have legitimacy.

Legitimacy and Autonomy

The perceived foundation of the state, as being based on absolute sovereignty, gives the illusion of fixedness. The conceptual link between sovereignty and territory is strong, yet territorial sovereignty has been fluid in eastern Europe because of the legacy of changing borders. More generally, economic and political globalizing processes have added a measure of porousness to territorial boundaries. Despite the fluidity (or, rather, in spite of it), my respondents describe great resistance on the part of the state to re-imagining political authority. Despite this resistance, sovereignty and the principle of mutual non-intervention can no longer shield states from responding to internal minority claims (Bishai 1998, 178). Nonetheless, uncoupling the territory–nation-state nexus requires acknowledging that sovereignty is itself contingent and flexible.

The norm of sovereignty is now arguably changing in international law to a commitment to democratic governance (Crawford and Marks 1998, 85). According to Connolly (1991, 202): "The State receives its highest contemporary legitimation when it presents a democratic appearance." Linklater (1998b, 117) suggests that the recognition of sovereignty should be contingent on constitutional guarantees for minority rights. Importantly, there is an emerging consensus that democratic governance also requires that the state engage in dialogue with those groups that exist within its territory yet are excluded from political power. This phenomenon of internal exclusion, and the frustration it generates, I would argue, is best viewed as the central risk to democracy rather than the possibility that minority groups will attempt to secede from the state. Throughout my research, members of the DAHR emphatically stated that they were against secession. The demographic situation also makes secession unlikely in the Romanian case — put very simply, the Hungarians are not a majority, even in Transylvania. Violent responses are more likely in the desperate conditions generated by a lack of recognition by the state.

Minority nationalisms, like that of the Hungarian minority in Romania, are most often directed towards democratic and political ends rather than founded on the definition of a thick identity (MacLure 2003, 46). Therefore, minority nations are not attempting to protect their identity from globalization; rather, they are engaging global forces to further their claims for autonomy within democratic structures. In the case of states that are democratizing, this claim is particularly important because it suggests that the relationship between minority groups and the state is central to the democratic content of the emerging political system. According to MacLure (ibid., 45), we need to conceptualize how difference is woven into the fabric of the nation-state. Furthermore, he suggests (ibid., 48) that stability and cohesion within nation-states must "in the end rest on something thinner than the sharing of 'national identity.'" Within this framework, belonging to the state is transformed into the ability to express democratic freedom. In contrast, centralist state nationalism has directly contributed to secessionist aspirations of minority groups, threatening the conditions of stability in multinational democracies (see Gagnon, Guibernau, and Rocher 2003).

The persistence of minority claims suggests that multinational democracies must move beyond the "sterile politics of mutual negation" (McRoberts 2003, v). Autonomy for the Hungarian minority would represent a partnership with the state — it therefore requires that the state relinquish its monopoly on sovereignty. "The devolution of sovereignty *within* states would allow for improved autonomy: Personal and political autonomy is in some real sense the right to be different and to be left alone; to preserve, protect, and promote values which are beyond the legitimate reach of the rest of society" (Hannum 1990, 4). Importantly, Hannum (ibid.) suggests that an independent state is not necessary to achieve this autonomy; rather, the devolution of meaningful power is adequate.[3]

If there was any remaining question that the Hungarian minority locates its hopes for devolution and autonomy within Europe's borders, this was clarified during the 2004 Romanian election, the last before accession to the EU. This focus on Europe, and the Hungarian minority's place in steering the Romanian ship in this direction, was evident throughout the minority's campaign. Marko Béla (its presidential candidate) tellingly entitled his electoral statement "Together in Europe: Integration, Autonomy, Welfare." In it, he proposed a regional framework and autonomy to correspond to Romania's future in the EU. Importantly, he linked this cultural autonomy for communities (or sometimes regions) to democracy. He, in turn, defined democracy as the devolution of power to the regions. Despite his view that each region should determine its own destiny, one region's destiny in particular was described as somewhat more urgent for Romania's democratic future. According to Béla, Romania needs what he terms *Transylvanian thinking* to democratize.

That the Hungarians are sophisticated politicians is not in question. The question is, however, whether the Hungarians seek something that is actually attainable or whether they simply idealize a political arrangement that has not been realized even in the context from which they seek it (witness Europe and its recent constitutional struggles). Béla finishes his statement tellingly: "Our slogan is: globalization plus localization equalizes glocalization" — a cumbersome word but an interesting example of the global imagination at work. According to Michael Keating (2001b), this narrative of glocalization holds within it two possibilities: it can be dismissed as wishful thinking or, alternately, it can be viewed as thoughtful wishing.

Conclusion

The flexibility between these conceptual inversions reflects the generative power of "Europe" — imprecisely defined — for those who remain outside its borders. The remaining question is whether Europe really holds such promise. As Ian Cooper (this volume) claims, functionally legitimate multi-level governance has not yet been realized. Furthermore, he argues, it is not clear what the conceptual foundations of this governance arrangement might be. This uncertainty, however, does not stop the DAHR from acting as though it does. Thus, wishful thinking, or thoughtful wishing about the possibilities generated by Europe by those outside its borders, might be best perceived as a concrete political strategy. The remaining question for national minorities is the extent to which such a strategy will be effective at advancing *both* the state's legitimacy and the autonomy of its people.

To conclude, I err on the side of thoughtful wishing. This conversation between the Hungarian minority and the Romanian state, I believe, has had an increasingly positive impact on the state of democracy in Romania. The conversation — of who is in and who is out, which is directed towards modifying the terms of inclusion — is an example of the democratic game in play. Just as important, it is a necessary conversation for a state in transition away from an authoritarian legacy that is attempting to establish the necessary legitimacy for democratic government. It also illustrates how globalizing processes, by redefining understandings of territoriality — economically, politically, and culturally — can create openings for conversations about minorities that might not take place otherwise. This relationship between the Hungarian minority and the Romanian state, though perhaps motivated by nothing more than the inevitability of their shared fates (and shared border), seems to hold within it the promise of democracy. What this democracy will look like, in the face of European integration and evolving globalization, is perhaps the remaining question.

Part 3
Legitimacy, Autonomy, and Violence

chapter 9

Sovereignty Redux?
Autonomy and Protection
in Military Interventions

Peter Nyers

To raise the topic of international military interventions is to enter a
contentious debate about the legitimate use of violence in a global context. Is it ever legitimate to forcefully transgress the autonomy of another
state? Can the autonomy of states be defied in the name of protecting the
autonomy of individuals whose lives are at risk? Who can legitimately
authorize such an intervention? These questions have been answered in an
innovative — yet, as I argue, ultimately problematic — way by the International Commission on Intervention and State Sovereignty (ICISS). The
commission's report, *The Responsibility to Protect* (ICISS 2001), makes a
major intervention into the debate on international intervention. It does
so by sidestepping the traditional debate about whether states have a right
to intervene and, instead, argues that interventions are a legitimate performance of sovereignty when an international responsibility to protect
exists. Soon after the publication of the report, then UN secretary-general
Kofi Annan expressed his admiration of the commission's "diplomatic skill
in redirecting the debate" on intervention (quoted in Roberts 2003, 144).
Human rights scholar Jack Donnelly (2003, 251) predicted that the commission's report would come to be seen as "a watershed event in international discussions of humanitarian intervention." Although the attacks of
11 September 2001 and subsequent interventions in Afghanistan and Iraq
initially muted the reception of the commission's findings, Donnelly's pre-
diction seemed to come true when, at the 2005 World Summit in New

York City, the 192 UN member states unanimously approved responsibility to protect as the new international doctrine for legitimating military interventions.

This chapter presents the argument that the production of new knowledge about intervention and sovereignty cannot be separated from the regimes of power that structure our understanding of political autonomy and legitimacy. In its theorization of the responsibility to protect, the commission presents a new way to understand the relationship between state autonomy (sovereignty), individual autonomy (human beings at risk), and the legitimacy of certain global practices (military intervention). At the core of the new doctrine is an innovative rethinking of the nature and scope of sovereign power, including the power to act "responsibly" in a global context. The commission's formulation of sovereignty comes at a time when there has been a great deal of interest in academic and policy circles in reflecting on the meaning of sovereignty. Central to this rethinking is an engagement with the dimension of sovereign power known as the state of exception — that is, the capacity for authorizing exceptions to the norm. This theme was first made famous by Carl Schmitt (1985) and has been revived and recast in the recent writings of Giorgio Agamben (1998). If sovereign power is the capacity to authoritatively decide upon the exception (Schmitt 1985; Agamben 1998), then the commission is concerned with the conditions under which this exceptionalism can exist in a global context.

The commission seeks to determine the conditions that would allow the autonomy of a sovereign state to be violently transgressed in the name of protecting the autonomy of the at-risk sovereign individuals within. What is so innovative about the commission's answer to this puzzle is the way it takes a victim-centred perspective. The primary source of legitimacy for any act of intervention motivated by a responsibility to protect is the abject victim who desperately needs protection from what the commission calls "conscience shocking situations crying out for action" (ICISS 2001, xiii, 55, 74). According to the commission, the debate should no longer be about the right of states to intervene but the right of victims to be protected.

There are real challenges in assessing the impact of the responsibility to protect because the doctrine has not been tested in practice. There has yet to be a successful argument made to mount an international intervention in the name of this principle. This is not to say that such a move has not been attempted. For example, the International Crisis Group, led by ICISS co-chair Gareth Evans, has directly invoked the idea of responsibility to protect in the context of Sudan, Uganda, and Zimbabwe. Indeed, immediately following the 2005 World Summit, the conflict in Darfur came to be seen as a test case for the new doctrine, but one that most observers have concluded has been a failure. Similarly, the Burmese government's intransigence regarding accepting emergency relief aid in the wake of Cyclone Nargis in 2008 provoked the invocation of the responsibility to protect by a number of international figures. Lloyd Axworthy (2008) argued with reference to the humanitarian crisis in Burma that "there is no moral difference between an innocent person being killed by machete or AK-47, and starving to death or dying in a cholera epidemic that could have been avoided by proper international response." The French foreign minister, Bernard Kouchner, invoked the responsibility to protect when he formally called for a UN Security Council resolution to force Burma (Union of Myanmar) to accept international humanitarian aid. This call was immediately rejected by China — already an opponent to the doctrine — on the basis that while the 2005 World Summit agreed that there is an international responsibility to protect, it limited the scope of the doctrine to cases of "genocide, war crimes, ethnic cleansing and crimes against humanity" (ibid.).

In each of these cases, however, the responsibility to protect was invoked as part of a larger argument to intervene to protect human life at risk. None of the arguments was successful in mobilizing the UN Security Council to authorize a military intervention. In the language of securitization studies, a securitizing move was made in an attempt to protect human lives at risk, but there was no successful act of securitization (Buzan, Waever, and de Wilde 1998).

Clearly, the relationship between human insecurity, protection, and the desire for autonomy by at-risk individuals and groups is a deeply contested one. It is not the intention of this chapter to engage in detailed case studies of successful and unsuccessful moves to invoke the responsibility to protect. Instead, the aim is to critically reflect on the foundational assumptions of the doctrine. After all, military interventions are always very interesting in the sense that they may, or may not, be reshaping the meaning and practice of state sovereignty in a way that shifts our understanding of political autonomy in a global context. Consequently, questions about the meaning, desirability, and legitimacy of military interventions have come to the forefront of debates about the future of the world order. For example, some scholars have argued that international interventions to protect human life can contribute to a cosmopolitan world order (Archibugi 2004). The question remains, however, whether cosmopolitan interventions provide a novel framework for ethical and political practice in the twenty-first century or whether they reproduce rather conventional categories and practices much like new wine in old bottles.

In this vein, it is relevant to note that the commission considers its major problem to be determining who has the responsibility to protect the victims of genocide, state collapse, and "supreme humanitarian emergencies" as well as how to mobilize an effective international response. Much of the debate about the commission's findings has focused on the contentious question of what, exactly, is implied by *responsibility*. By contrast, the matter of protection has been considered to be relatively uncontroversial. It is taken for granted as an uncontroversial fact that victims exist and that they need protection. Protection, however, is not the straightforward and unproblematic concept it is often taken to be. Acts of protection are never disinterested or impartial and always involve a complicated politics. Central to the politics of protection are claims about the legitimacy of sovereign power and the relationship between the protector and the protected (Huysmans, Dobson, and Prokhovnik 2006). The commission argues that sovereignty involves an international responsibility to protect. But what does it mean to protect? Who can legitimately claim a need for protection? Who can legitimately provide protection? What is the relationship between the protector and the protected? Does the responsibility to protect bridge or deepen the divide between us (the interveners) and them (the intervened)? Finally, are outside interventions always necessary, or can vulnerable groups organize autonomously to protect themselves?

Human Security, Sovereignty, and Intervention

The debate over intervention is by no means a new one: it gained a certain prominence in discussions about world politics over the course of the 1990s and into the new millennium (Annan 1999; Weiss and Collins 2000; Wheeler 2000; Holzgrefe and Keohane 2003). With the conclusion of the Cold War, the relative certainties of a bipolar international politics were replaced by a variety of complex challenges to world order. The proliferation of internal wars, the disruptive effects of economic globalization, and the multiplying forms and instances of forced displacement and failed states are among a host of developments that conjoined to transform both the theory and practice of international security. At the same time, the expansion of a global human rights network created enormous pressure for the international community to respond to global human suffering. It is in this context, for example, that a human-security agenda in foreign policy emerged, with the campaign to ban landmines being one of its early and most notable achievements (Axworthy and Taylor 1998).

The human-security agenda challenges many of the conventional assumptions that are made about security. For example, realist approaches to international politics have traditionally interpreted security largely in terms of the military capabilities of states. The advocates of human security, by contrast, argue that putting people first is the necessary precondition for any meaningful and lasting national, regional, and international security (Axworthy 2003). The concerns of human security, therefore, exceed the narrow focus of state military security. Human security takes a universalizing trajectory, encouraging a vision of rights and duties that goes beyond the state's concern for military preparedness and border security. In this sense, the supporters of human security share a similar goal with the proponents of international human rights, cosmopolitan citizenship, global civil society, or a post-sovereign world order. They all want to highlight a shared human identity to avoid the degree of violence associated with carving out the world's territories and cultivating moral sympathies along strict sovereign lines (Archibugi, Held, and Köhler 1998).

Despite its moral and potentially emancipatory appeal, the human-security agenda faces considerable challenges, most notably, the difficult political question of military intervention. Military intervention marks the limit of the human-security agenda, making it "the single most controversial unresolved foreign policy issue of the 1990s" (Evans and Sahnoun 2001). In the academic discipline of international relations, intervention is understood almost exclusively in military terms. Most studies assume an understanding of intervention similar to R.J. Vincent's (1974, 3) famous definition of intervention as a "discrete event" in which a state, a group of states, or an international organization "interferes coercively in the domestic affairs of another state." Although non-military forms of international intervention can challenge a state's autonomy (e.g., economic penetration by multinational corporations with global reach), armed intervention is so controversial because it transgresses the constitutive principle of international order: the territorial sovereignty of the state (Jackson 2000, 251). Sovereignty claims to be the principal way of achieving collective political autonomy in the world-system. Acts of intervention represent an extreme violation of this claim to collective autonomy. As a consequence, the stakes of intervention are such that there is near unanimity that it should be the exception and not the norm of international affairs. In a classic international relations text, for example, Wight (1966, 28) reserves intervention for situations where there are "gross violations of human dignity." Similarly, Vincent (1986, 126-27) asserts that intervention is "reserved for extraordinary oppression, not the day-to-day." More recently, Archibugi (2004, 6) has argued that "military humanitarian intervention is straightforwardly necessary when, and only when, blatant collective violations of human rights are being perpetrated."

Another reason why violations of sovereignty are so controversial is because the provision of security is one that is very dear to states and their claims to political legitimacy. The capacity to provide protection has historically been a key element of sovereign power. Modern states claim to protect their populations from both internal and external threats. Citizens are protected from one another (through laws and police) and from the external aggression of other states (through military force and border policing). This claim to having a monopoly over matters of security — what Max Weber (1994, 38) specifically identified as the "monopoly of the legitimate use of violence within a given territory," or what Tilly (1985) has more evocatively called the protection racket of the state — is a crucial source of legitimacy for sovereign power. But security is not only about securing the autonomy of the state. States have long argued that state security is the condition of possibility for individual autonomy — understood as the capacity to shape the conditions under which one lives (Held 1995). Individual autonomy is, arguably, only possible once the problem of (in)security has been solved. The provision of security can, therefore, be described as a precondition for citizens to pursue lives that are autonomous, self-determining, and possessive of individual sovereignty (Walker 1993). The provision of security also, and this point is crucial for the responsibility to protect doctrine, allows for the constitution of the responsible subject. The responsible subject requires a secure space for responsibility, a place where responsibility can be temporalized, enacted, and put into practice.

For these reasons it should not be surprising to find that sovereignty and intervention are typically cast as mutually exclusive concepts. On the one hand, the principle of state sovereignty is marked by its power to exclude, to make exceptions, to authoritatively distinguish friends from enemies, citizens from foreigners, insiders from outsiders. An intervention for human protection purposes, on the other hand, can claim notoriety for its inclusiveness, for its willingness to go beyond the narrow focus of state military security to address security as part of a broader process of emancipation and social justice. An intervention for human protection purposes meets not only the basic needs but also the fundamental social, political, and human rights of all people. And whereas sovereignty serves as the foundation and ordering principle of a world order composed of autonomous nation-states, the concept of humanitarian intervention supposes that there are conditions in which the negation of territorial sovereignty is necessary to protect fundamental human rights. Sovereignty, therefore, is conventionally cast as a problem to be overcome, usually by the coordinated actions of some supranational political body (e.g., the UN or NATO).

Rethinking Autonomy: The Responsibility to Protect

The expressed goal of the commission is to overcome the impasse in the sovereignty-intervention debate to actualize the autonomy rights of individuals (Evans and Sahnoun 2001). Although the governments of both the Netherlands and Denmark conducted inquiries into the legal and political status of intervention (AIV and CAVV 2000; DUPI 1999), the Canadian-initiated commission has proved to be the most ambitious attempt to achieve a political consensus on the issue of international intervention. The commission was initiated in direct response to the challenge posed by UN Secretary-General Kofi Annan in his Millennium Report, *We, the Peoples*: "If humanitarian intervention is, indeed, an unacceptable assault on sovereignty, how should we respond to a Rwanda, to a Srebenica — to gross and systematic violations of human rights that affect every precept of our common humanity?" (quoted in ICISS 2001, 2). In response to this challenge, Canadian Prime Minister Jean Chrétien announced the creation of the commission at the UN Millennium Summit in September 2000. The twelve international members of the commission had former Australian foreign minister Gareth Evans and special advisor to the UN secretary-general Mohamed Sahnoun as their co-chairs.[1] As well, an international advisory board and research team were established to assist the commission in its work. Together, they claim to have reached "new common ground" (ibid., vii) on the legal, moral, operational, and political dilemmas associated with international military interventions.

From the outset, the commission was concerned about the legitimacy of its findings and how the international community would receive them. Much of the work of the commission centred on the question of legitimacy. To address this question, the commission took a three-fold approach:

(1) it held consultations that were global in scope; (2) it produced an innovative alternative in the doctrine of the responsibility to protect; and (3) it emphasized a victim-centred human rights framework for authorizing interventions. First, to promote an aura of global legitimacy, the commission organized its central work around eleven national and regional consultations. These were held in major centres in North America, Europe, Africa, Asia, and the Middle East between January and July 2001. The consultations brought together academics, government officials, and representatives from non-governmental organizations and civil society to reflect on the various dimensions of the intervention-sovereignty relationship.[2] A common theme running through each of these consultation meetings was the desire for new terms and concepts to capture the changing dynamics that mark an increasingly complex and interconnected world politics. The consultations allowed the commission to claim to have reached a global consensus on the issue of intervention. While impressive, clearly there have been definite limits on who and what gets included in the dialogue. For example, no representative from China was included on the commission, its advisory board, or its international research team. China is well known for giving very little support to the idea of intervention, not least because of how threshold criteria might impact its human rights record in places like Tibet or Xinjiang. Therefore, when the commission held its final consultation meeting in Beijing, the idea of an international responsibility to protect was pointedly, if politely, dismissed, as this telling quote from the minutes of that consultation meeting demonstrates: "Humanitarianism is an admirable virtue, but intervention is a red herring and widely condemned in the world; grafting humanitarian considerations onto intervention adds no lustre to the idea of meddling but will, contrarily, smear the lofty cause with dirt" (ICISS Beijing Consultation 2001, 2). Although the commission claimed to be engaging in a dialogue that was global in scope, it is clear that arguing *against* the idea of outside military intervention marked the limit of acceptable discourse.[3]

The second source of legitimacy came through the production of new knowledge about military interventions. For those invited to the consultation table — almost all of whom could be described as elite members of their respective societies — one of their lasting contributions was to impress upon the commission the importance of replacing the traditional language on military interventions. For example, the commission bans the adjective *humanitarian* from being applied to the noun *intervention*. This was a direct response to the oft-repeated complaint by international humanitarian agencies about the growing militarization of humanitarianism (ICISS 2001, 6). Their attempt to be seen as neutral and impartial actors is seriously undermined when militaries label their actions "humanitarian," as in NATO's "humanitarian bombing" campaign in Kosovo. It is, therefore, in the name of the right to humanitarian intervention that the terms *humanitarian* and *right* are banned from the discourse on intervention (Downes 2004). Instead of "humanitarian intervention," the commission employs the much more specific, if somewhat awkward, language of "interventions for human protection purposes." Instead of the "right to intervene," the commission speaks of the "responsibility to protect."

According to the idea of the responsibility to protect, the relationship between sovereignty and intervention is not the mutually exclusive one found in traditional debates on the topic. The relationship between sovereignty and intervention, the commission asserts, is consistent, complementary, and not at all contradictory. Sovereignty is typically understood as a political relation that involves authority, territory, and population. The commission adds responsibility to this list and argues that the primary responsibility of states is to provide protection to the population on its sovereign territory. In this sense, sovereignty is not an absolute, it is a conditional right dependent upon a state providing adequate protection to its citizens. This protection serves as a key source of legitimacy for sovereign power, both from the population it protects and from other sovereign states. Protection, the commission argues, is one of the most basic of human rights: "Everyone is entitled to basic protection for their lives and property" (ICISS 2001, 41). The key conceptual move of the responsibility to protect position is its insistence that in cases where a state abdicates, abandons, or otherwise fails to protect its citizens, it then becomes the responsibility of the international community of states to provide protection. Therefore, for a state to be truly legitimate and truly sovereign, fulfilling its internal obligation to protect its citizenry is not sufficient. Sovereignty implies an international responsibility to protect human life wherever it exists. Consequently, the responsibility to protect is linked to membership in the international community of states (Evans and Sahnoun 2001). As the commission states in its report: "Sovereignty as responsibility has become the minimum content of good international citizenship" (ibid., 8).

This position brings us to the third source of legitimacy, which itself addresses the matter of who can legitimately authorize an intervention.

According to the commission, legitimate international interventions are those that are made for "human protection purposes" (ICISS 2001, 32). These interventions are qualitatively different from conventional acts of war in that their purpose is not to eliminate or subjugate the sovereign state that is being attacked. This point is explained by one of the commission's members, Ramesh Thakur (2003, 163): "The substance of the responsibility to protect is the provision of life-supporting protection and assistance to populations at risk. The goal of intervention for human protection purposes is not to wage war on a state in order to destroy it and eliminate its statehood, but to protect victims of atrocities inside the state, to embed the protection in reconstituted institutions after the intervention, and then to withdraw all foreign troops. Thus military intervention for human protection purposes takes away the rights flowing from the status of sovereignty, but does not in itself challenge the status as such." The consequence of this position is that the commission can claim that state autonomy "still does matter" (ICISS 2001, 7). Sovereignty is described as the "best line of defence" (ibid.) for maintaining autonomy in a complex and dangerous world. To be sovereign is to be recognized as holding "equal worth and dignity" (ibid.) in the international system. The interrelationship of the two subjects of sovereignty — state and individual — is revealed in these kinds of claims. Faced with the pressures of globalizing forces, sovereignty serves as an important condition of possibility for realizing freedom, autonomy, and self-determination.

Protection, Autonomy, Agency

The responsibility to protect implies a new way of understanding the relationship between sovereignty and intervention. But what exactly does it means to protect? What is the relationship between the protector and the protected? Do the protected have a say in the terms of their protection? To begin answering these questions, it is useful to inquire into the meaning of protection. Didier Bigo (2006) has provided a useful etymology of the word *protection*. His aim is to understand "the social practices of surveillance and control which are embedded in labelling an action one of 'protection'" (ibid., 84). Bigo's analysis reveals that there is not one but several origins of the term. Each of these terms carries a different connotation and structures the meaning of protection in a unique fashion. I argue that the three Latin terms for protection that Bigo identifies in his etymology

— *tegere, praesidere,* and *tutore* — are of particular significance for understanding what the international responsibility to protect might mean for sovereign power.

Tegere, Bigo explains, is the oldest Latin word for protection and is itself of Greek origin; it means "to cover," "to hide," and "to shelter." *Protegere* (to cover up front) means to provide shelter against an oncoming danger, with a shield, for example. A related word is *tegmen,* which refers to the armour one uses to protect oneself. This latter term is important because protection, as it is defined here, involves an active role for the protected, which can in fact be the same person or entity as the protector.

The Latin word *praesidere* also means to protect and defend. However, it has the additional meaning of "to supervise" or "to preside over" (from its etymology, "to be placed in front of, ahead"). To protect, in this sense, is an elevated activity that involves a hierarchy of roles. It can be used to describe military escorts or a secured place such as a camp or garrison. It can also be employed to designate a chair or headperson, as well as to indicate precedence. As a form of protection it involves a clear distinction between the protector, the enemy, and the protected. In terms of the dangers posed by an enemy, the protector alone has the capacity to face them, to act, and to speak in the name of protection. The protected, by contrast, are reduced to speechless subjects without agency.

Finally, the term *tutela* also means "to protect" and, like *praesidere,* involves a hierarchy of positions. Protection here is a type of a guardianship, as in the protection and defence of someone in the protector's charge. It is related to the word *tutore* (to look at, to have eyes upon). *Tutela,* therefore, emphasizes the monitoring of the protected to secure their obedience to the protector. Here, the enemy is virtually forgotten and largely disappears from the scene. Instead, the matter of monitoring and surveillance of the protected comes to the forefront. The strength of the enemy is less important than the capacity of the protector to react quickly to dangers and, indeed, to pre-empt their emergence.

What Bigo's analysis makes clear is that each of the terms varies considerably in terms of how the relationship between the protector, the protected, and the enemy or danger is framed. With use of the terms *praesidere* and *tutela,* for example, the issue of tutelage and patronage is introduced into the politics of protection. Here, the relationship between protector and protected involves an asymmetrical power relation, which can have important consequences for making claims to political agency and autonomy. The protected is either rendered as a passive and neutral object of protection or as a subjugated person that requires obedience. In both conceptions, as Bigo argues, the agency and autonomy of the protected is undermined or otherwise effaced: "The protected is considered as passive. He has no right to speak but only to obey in the name of his own safety. He does not know what the protector knows. The protector by interposing itself in the relation is winning the claim to have the right to be the spokesperson of the protected" (Bigo 2006, 88). The term *tegere,* by contrast, allows the autonomy of the protected to be considered as an important factor in the politics of protection. Bigo credits this meaning of the term with providing an escape from the triangular relation between the enemy, the protector, and the protected. Instead, the protected has an active role: "He has a voice but is obliged to hide, to withdraw" (ibid., 90).

Protector or Protected: Who Is the Legitimate Agent?

How, then, does responsibility for protection get determined in the international context? In his ongoing work on this topic, Daniel Warner (1991, 1999, 2003) argues that the first step in resolving this question involves determining that there has been a generating fact. A generating fact is a triggering condition or spike test that asks if there has been a spike in the level of human suffering, mortality, forced displacement, and other abuses of human rights. The generating fact, Warner argues, plays a key role in identifying the agent or subject who is responsible. Determining responsibility, more so than determining causality, follows a line of imputation. Causality, Warner explains, involves a simple connection between an action and what has caused the action. Imputation makes a normative connection between an act and agent and includes a judgment about whether the agent should be praised or punished. The implication of this argument is that the responsible subject is never predetermined but is, instead, an effect of a highly contextualized (and politicized) generating fact. Imputing responsibility is, therefore, a backward process, with the process beginning "with the consequences in order to define the subject" (Warner 1991, 12).

For much of the commission's report, the subject of responsibility is left undetermined. The urgency of the responsibility to protect lies with the generating fact identified by Kofi Annan — that is, the "gross and systematic violations of human rights that affect every precept of our common humanity" (ICISS 2001, vii). However, the subject of responsibility is not fated to be the human victims, the intervening states, or even multilateral institutions. At first blush, therefore, the commission's use of protection oscillates between tegere and praesidere — that is, between a form of protection that emphasizes respect, dialogue, and cooperation between the protector and protected and a form of protection that is more concerned with securing people and an abstract space and defending them from a clearly defined enemy. As I demonstrate below, although the commission considers tegere when it comes to resolving the question of legitimacy, it ultimately settles upon praesidere. In the next section, we see how the commission ultimately includes tutela as an important dimension of the responsibility to protect. In this case the enemy disappears and the monitoring of the protected comes to dominate the responsibility to protect.

The commission's report has been called a revolutionary document because of the way it shifts "the onus from the rights of the intervener to the rights of the victim" (Axworthy 2003, 193). For example, when the commission underscores the importance of right intention for making an intervention legitimate (discussed below), it also establishes a number of conditions for assessing whether this key requirement has been met. Included among them is that the intervention be "clearly supported by ... the victims concerned" (ICISS 2001, xii). Giving the victim a voice, however, is not just a practical problem of providing opportunities, especially when the hierarchies of giver and receiver, helper and victim, and listener and crier are left untouched. The problem is fundamentally a political one, and it cuts to the core of who counts as an authentic political subject. By taking the perspective of the victim, and not the intervener, the meaning of *protection* in the responsibility to protect is not unlike *tegere*. The victims in need of protection are not rendered without agency and passive in the face of danger: they still have a potentially active role in securing the terms and conditions of any intervention for human protection purposes. Warner (2003, 111) credits the commission on this point: "By emphasizing the generating fact of the violation of the human rights of individuals — that which drives the process of imputation [of responsibility] — the Report begins with neither a static, reified state nor non-situated human rights." If the responsibility to protect is like tegere, it can act like a shield to protect a people from a failed or abusive state. The act of protection, however, does not necessarily efface the subjectivity of the protected, nor does it deny outright that the victims can, at least in part, be agents of their own self-protection.

Despite its claim to radically transform the debate on military intervention, the commission provides a remarkably conventional — some have argued conservative — framework for determining what generating fact makes a military intervention legitimate.[4] Basically, the commission adopts a just war framework: military intervention for human protection purposes is legitimate only if it is intended to halt or avert "serious and irreparable harm occurring to human beings" (ICISS 2001, xii). The commission sets a high, conscience-shocking threshold to be met to justify a military intervention, such as a large-scale loss of life or ethnic cleansing. The commission insists further that these interventions should be only an extreme and exceptional measure and recommends a series of precautionary principles to temper the deployment of intervening forces. Foremost among these is right intention: the primary purpose of any military action must be to prevent or end the suffering of vulnerable human populations. The use of military force as a last resort and the scale, duration, and intensity of the intervention being of proportional means are also included as precautionary principles. Finally, the intervention must also have reasonable prospects for attaining success (ibid., 31-33). On this last point the commission has come up with clever terms, such as *prudential consequentialism* (Thakur 2002, 333), to describe why no intervention into a major military power will occur. This kind of intervention is not legitimate because the human suffering caused by an intervention would likely be greater than taking no action at all. Consequently, the responsibility to protect the population of the Russian province of Chechnya from the ongoing violence and abuses there would not be considered a legitimate intervention according to the commission's criteria. Score one for *realpolitik*.

Nicholas Wheeler (2000, 38) argues that the problem with relying on a right intention when making interventions "is that it takes the intervening state as the referent object for analysis rather than the victims who are rescued as a consequence of the use of force." The commission claims to bypass this problem with its victim-centred doctrine of the responsibility to protect. The problem is reintroduced, however, once the question of authority is raised. Who can legitimately exercise authority in the context of international interventions? The commission answers this question by defining legitimacy as "the connecting link between the exercise of authority and the recourse to power" (ICISS 2001, 48). For an intervention to be legitimate, the commission argues that the right authority should sanction the act. The commission comes close to establishing the people in need — the vulnerable human — as the legitimizing agent, but it stops short of doing so. Instead, the UN Security Council was chosen as the most important legitimizing body. The commission does recommend that the

Security Council make internal changes, most notably having the permanent five members refrain from using their veto powers "in matters where their vital state interests are not involved" (ibid., 75). Given the inconsistency, however, in which post-Cold War interventions have been made (and not made), having the UN Security Council legitimate interventions is hardly an uncontroversial choice. In doing so, the sovereignty of the states system — if not each and every individual state — is reaffirmed. Faced with the opportunity to think about international authority and legitimacy in a way that is not centred on the sovereign power of the state, the commission, in Warner's words, "blinked because it looked into an abyss" (Warner 2003, 113).

The emphasis on right intentions is also problematic because it overlooks how easily the argument for an international responsibility to protect can be utilized for a whole host of intervening acts. For example, Feinstein and Slaughter (2004) have utilized the commission's doctrine of the responsibility to protect to develop an argument that there is an international duty to prevent states from acquiring weapons of mass destruction. Buchanan and Keohane (2004) have similarly drawn upon the commission's work in their arguments for a "cosmopolitan" use of preventive military force. Defenders of the commission argue that a rigorous application (Weiss 2004, 144) of the principles of the responsibility to protect would not allow for its usurpation for neo-imperialist military adventures. Nevertheless, the United States turned to a human protection argument to justify its intervention and occupation of Iraq once it became clear that no weapons of mass destruction or credible al Qaeda links would be found. This step is a disturbing reminder of how easily the discourse of protection can become politicized and employed in contexts radically different from those envisaged by the report's authors.

Protection at a Distance

Although international interventions may be said to be acts in defiance of sovereignty, the international responsibility to protect suggests that such acts are, in fact, legitimate projections of sovereign power. A certain unevenness characterizes the commission's understanding of sovereignty: a rigid conception of state sovereignty is weakened in favour of the rights of sovereign individuals, but only in those states likely to be subject to military intervention. These states cannot be responsible because they are seemingly incapable of responding to the needs of their populations

(Warner 2003, 113). The sovereignty of the intervener, by contrast, is actually reinforced and legitimated in cases of interventions for human protection purposes. Utilizing sovereignty as responsibility as a way to determine membership in international society involves a globalization of sovereign power, the globalization of the autonomy of some states in the name of protecting the autonomy of individuals in others.

But whose sovereign power can be legitimately globalized? This question raises the critical matter of the geopolitics that is assumed by the responsibility to protect. The problems of state failure, dictatorial abuse of power, ethnic cleansing, and forced expulsion all occur "over there," outside the sphere of allegedly fully sovereign states that are capable of making interventions. Much of the critical debate about the commission has focused on how sovereignty as responsibility may effectively serve to carve the world into so-called civilized and uncivilized zones. The threshold of intervention, according to these critics (e.g., Ayoob 2002), is also a threshold of civilization, a dividing line between fully sovereign states that are members of an enlightened international community and so-called failed states that are incapable of adequately protecting their citizens. Does this observation make the commission nothing more than a moral compass for empire? Is the flip side of the commission's report that there exists in practice an international responsibility to protect Western states and their citizens from international disorder?

These are difficult questions with potentially unsettling answers. To better understand what is at stake with them, it is important to recognize how the commission envisages the responsibility of protection as a spectrum of responsibilities: the responsibility to protect actually implies a three-fold responsibility to prevent, to react, and to rebuild. Each of these responsibilities involves a unique spatio-temporal frame. The responsibility to react, for example, occupies a space-time that is identical to traditional understandings of military intervention. It is a discrete event with a definite beginning (the start of the crisis) and ending (the cessation of hostilities). As we saw above, as a form of protection, the doctrine is most like praesidere in that it involves a militaristic defence of humans facing insecure and dangerous conditions. Given the supreme humanitarian emergency of such situations, this form of protection is consistent with sovereign power to decide to make an intervention into the autonomy of another state. Here, the responsibility to protect means to preside (praesidere) over the protected and ensure their safety.

By contrast, the dimensions of the responsibility to protect that involve prevention and rebuilding invoke another conception of protection. The connotations of *tutela* come to be important for understanding these responsibilities. Both the responsibilities to prevent and to rebuild involve a relationship of guardianship and obedience, and they both utilize surveillance and monitoring to ensure compliance from the protected. Where they differ is on the time frame associated with these responsibilities. Bellamy (2003, 334) warns of the spectre of liberal neocolonialism emerging whenever there are calls for more conflict prevention and post-conflict rebuilding. The commission attempts to displace this criticism by rejecting the idea of a long-term form of trusteeship (ICISS 2001, 43). Instead, the commission argues that the responsibility to rebuild "must be directed towards returning the society in question to those who live in it, and who, in the last instance, must take responsibility together for its future destiny" (ibid., 45). A statist understanding of autonomy is at work with this dimension of the responsibility to protect: "The responsibility to protect is fundamentally a principle designed to respond to threats to human life, and not a tool for achieving political goals such as greater political autonomy, self-determination, or independence for particular groups within the country" (ibid., 43).

Consequently, the commission reaffirms once again its constitutive assumption that autonomous sovereign states are to serve as the basic units of world order. It assumes, however, that a responsible state will naturally follow a failed state. As the recent experiences with trying to "rebuild" Bosnia, Kosovo, East Timor, Afghanistan, and Iraq indicate, however, post-intervention reconstruction is a much more difficult and messy process than the commission seems to want to admit. Warner (2003, 114) argues that the international community wants to quickly remove itself from this kind of protection because it is incapable of protecting the human rights of individuals (*tegere*) over the long term: "It is an admission of a lack of competence rather than objectives to return sovereignty to the people."

The responsibility to prevent, by contrast, involves a near continual form of intervention into states that are at risk of failing to protect their citizens. If traditional inventions claim to be the exception to the norm, preventative strategies ensure that the exception becomes the norm. As the commission sees it, the "single most important" (ICISS 2001, xi) element of the responsibility to protect is addressing the root causes of global human insecurity in the first place. The development of preventative strategies under the banner of "good governance" and "sustainable development" is hardly uncontroversial, however. Sidaway (2003), for example, suggests that the "weakness" of certain African states may not be the result of a lack of domestic political authority and international political relations, but rather an excess of them. Like tutore, this form of protection places an emphasis on collecting information, filtering it according to threshold criteria, and analyzing the data to assess if threshold criteria have been met. Protection, in this case, is not concerned with the strength of the enemy but rather with the capacity of the protector. The space-time of protection has changed. Protection takes place at a distance and involves a kind of policing the future (Bigo 2006) through surveillance and profiling states that are at risk of experiencing a crisis in human protection.

The responsibility to protect recognizes that sovereignty is a practice that can be performed at the level of the international community as well as at the domestic level. But if the primary responsibility of sovereignty is to protect one's own population, then some powerful states can presumably globalize this responsibility to better protect their populations from global sources of disorder. For example, in cases where the commission's threshold criteria of large-scale killings or ethnic cleansing are met, it is likely that refugee flows will be one of the major consequences. Although the international responsibility to protect humans "over there" from insecurity is considered a viable policy option, humans "over here" who are asking for protective asylum from the same sources of persecution are facing more and more restrictions.

Protection as monitoring implies a power-knowledge nexus with the protector as its sole interlocutor. Protection, in this case, involves a monitoring dimension whereby would-be victims are provided with preventive protection to pre-empt the conditions that cause people to leave as refugees and asylum seekers in the first place. Since the end of the Cold War, major international policy developments with regard to forced displacement have included voluntary repatriation, preventive protection, the right to remain, in-country protection, safe havens, and so on. On the one hand, these are humanitarian measures designed to quickly and efficiently bring much needed aid and protection to forcibly displaced persons who need assistance, even if they have not crossed an international border. On the other hand, the spatial politics of these forms of protection are such that the policies are also clearly source control measures designed to contain forced migration in their country or region of origin (Hyndman 2000). To be sure, these measures were developed at the same time as an attack on the domestic cultures and institutions of asylum occurred in Western states. Increasingly restrictive immigration and asylum policies have drastically reduced the number of asylum applications, curtailed avenues for appeal, increased powers of detention, and allocated more resources for deportation and removal efforts. Although most of the measures were well developed in the 1990s, the attacks of 11 September 2001 only expanded the reach of these policies and exacerbated their effects.

Conclusion

The commission wants sovereignty *and* intervention. In doing so, however, it ends up reaffirming the state as the only possible source of legitimacy in the politics of protection. To the question of how individuals and communities influence and control global decisions that affect them, the responsibility to protect doctrine gives very little room for any form of local political agency. The matter of legitimacy is accorded to sovereign authorities, not to the subjects of intervention themselves. Protection is less about the autonomy-respecting tegere and more about reaffirming sovereign power as praesidere or reconfiguring it globally as tutela.

It is never a straightforward or a particularly easy task to silence the protected, displace the enemy, or transform a forceful trespass into a compassionate embrace. The ambiguities in the terminology of protection are very important to understand the complexities of the commission's doctrine of the responsibility to protect. The asymmetries of the terminology of protection underscore the asymmetrical way that the politics of protection gets enacted in the case of international interventions. Consequently, when one speaks of the responsibility to protect, we must ask what kind of protection is being envisaged? When we assess the politics of protection, are we referring to the politics of the protector or of the protected as the object of our analysis? Does the legitimacy of the responsibility to protect depend on the manner in which protection gets enacted?

chapter 10

From Ethnic Civil War to Global War: (De)legitimizing Narratives of Global Warfare and the Longing for Civility in Sri Lankan Fiction

Heike Härting

IF GLOBALIZATION REFERS TO uneven and contradictory processes of restructuring social space within and beyond the space of the nation, then it is fundamentally disruptive. From Kosovo, Bosnia, and Chechnya to Rwanda, Sudan, Afghanistan, and Iraq, the violent disintegration, fragmentation, and invasion of former nation-states are accompanied by genocidal forms of extreme violence, which seem to be symptomatic of the various political, cultural, and social pathologies of what some theorists call neoliberal globalization (Amin 2003, 77). In fact, global violence and warfare have become quotidian phenomena for millions of people, and they are apparently ineluctable and intrinsic to the reordering of global relationships of power and institutions following the end of the Cold War. Frequently, metaphorical constructions of globalization as a steamrolling juggernaut and machine gone out of human control that works by means of immeasurable speed invoke violence as a fully naturalized aspect of globalization, rendering it a moral and presentist phenomenon rather than a political and historical relationship. What seems crucial here is an understanding of globalization as an unfinished process produced and shaped by contesting cultural and political narratives that negotiate and seek to secure claims to sites of global power. As Peter Nyers suggests in this volume, narratives of responsibility and military protection in the context of an international UN-politics of intervention serve not the autonomy of those seeking protection but current power configurations and the autonomy of those states overriding the sovereignty of targeted countries.

Similarly, global warfare cannot be easily defined beyond its most general sense: a form of warfare that is fought on one steadily expanding territory not demarcated by conventional national boundaries. Although global war may not function bilaterally, it can certainly operate, as the current US-led "war on terror" demonstrates, on a multilateral plane, which returns the question of global war to the political and theoretical arena of the nation-state. This chapter, however, discusses global war neither as a current phenomenon that emerged in the wake of 9/11 nor as a term that is designed to cloud the unilateral interests of the United States in the war on terror. Rather, I am interested in exploring the imperial dimensions of contemporary warfare and their effects across multiple localities. In particular, I am interested in the ways in which the exercise of extreme violence intersects with the cultural logic of global wars — that is, their mobilization of identity politics and reliance on the production of competing imaginaries of perceived cultural differences. More specifically, from a cultural point of view the notion of global war as it is understood by Michael Hardt and Antonio Negri, for instance, can frequently be misleading because it tends to obscure the transnational dimensions of what we previously saw as highly localized forms of ethnic civil war. Thus, although Sri Lanka's war might not be as global a war as the one fought in Iraq or Afghanistan, it is what we might call a localized transnational war. In other words, Sri Lanka's war, as I discuss later, certainly anticipates the violent biopolitics and the global privatization of the means of warfare also characteristic of contemporary forms of global conflict. It also remains grounded in the country's colonial history and post-independence transnational alliance with India. What Sri Lanka's war also projects is a fierce battle over the normative narratives of identity and cultural purity that underlie and drive the articulation of political claims to collective autonomy. Thus, in terms of this volume's understanding of legitimacy — the acceptance and justification of shared rule by a community — I am referring to the cultivation of acceptance of the reconstructing of shared rule by violent means in communities outside one's own. It is perhaps in the pursuit of this acceptance that such euphemisms and oxymorons as "humane wars" (Coker 2001) and "the new military humanism" (Beck 2002) have gained critical and popular currency.

In this chapter, I examine the ways in which literary accounts of war help us rethink and delegitimize dominant narratives of global war and violence. Let me take a few moments here to discuss the critical and, in my view, productively deconstructive and inextricable relationship between literature and politics. At the outset I wish to emphasize that the literary texts I consider in this chapter neither constitute a source of empirical truths nor promise to produce such truths. Nor are they necessarily to be read as a symptom or allegory of the postcolonial nation-state (Jameson 1986; Szeman 2003). Instead, as Benedict Anderson and Homi Bhabha have famously argued, literature — "textual strategies, metaphoric displacements, sub-texts and figurative stratagems" (Bhabha 1990, 2) — affects the ways we address, imagine, and construct political, national, and transnational communities. Literature, then, is instrumental in the production of localized and global imaginaries — that is, in the formation of images and narratives that project idealized as well as alternative visions of what it means to be human or a social subject under conditions of globalization. What literary texts share with non-literary texts, as the historian Hayden White argues, is their reliance on modes of emplotment, namely, on a narrative and discursive construction of social and historical realities. A. Sivanandan's monumental novel on the political and historical origins of Sri Lanka's war, *When Memory Dies* (1997), provides an excellent example of the narrative construction or emplotment of Sri Lanka's violent conflict.

To bring the critical value of literary texts to bear on the interdisciplinary study of globalization and autonomy requires us to follow at least two trajectories. First, if, as Edward Chamberlin (2004, 2) insists, stories not only "tell people where they came from, and why they are here; how to live, and sometimes how to die," they also legitimize claims to land and identity. The descriptive and legitimizing function of literary texts extends equally into ways to address the effects of globalization and modernity on the individual and his or her various communities. In fact, literary texts imagine and track how violent conflict and globalization restructure the quotidian life of people and put under pressure and disarticulate localized notions of belonging and subjectivity.

Second, literary texts are valuable ideological and cultural commodities on the global marketplace. For instance, novels on Sri Lanka's war such as Romesh Gunesekera's *Reef,* Michael Ondaatje's *Anil's Ghost,* and Shyam Selvadurai's *Funny Boy* have contributed to *and* unsettled the production of legitimizing narratives and discourses of global humanitarian intervention. They, thus, have shaped the global imaginary in the North through stories from the global South. Both of these trajectories suggest that literary texts have an important epistemological and political role to play. On the one hand, the literary, to adapt Gayatri Spivak's terminology (2004, 83), ideally functions as an "interruption of the epistemological" given that endows political empiricism and historical linearity with a high truth coefficient to construct "the Other as object of knowledge." In contrast, the literary aims to "listen to the Other as if it were a self, neither to punish nor to acquit" (ibid.) and, thus, rethinks the conditions of identity and subjectivity to be legitimized and legislated, managed and reified in political policies.

On the other hand, in the particular context of literary narrativizations of Sri Lanka's war, the war's international dimension (e.g., India's and Norway's interventions in the peace process) is reflected in the fact that, as Chelva Kanaganayagam argues, "very few contemporary [Sri Lankan] writers would adopt a straightforward binarism to characterize the present context in Sri Lanka. In such situations, one almost feels the need for a new vocabulary, a new grammar of sorts, to address the new political reality" (2003, 45). Indeed, in countries that continue to struggle with extreme forms of violence caused by localized transnational warfare, "authority, legitimacy, subjectivity, and affiliation have become contested sites" (ibid.). It is precisely the creative imagination, the literary text or image, that holds an arbitrating function, if not power, in the dramatization of new political realities and the rearticulation of collective and individual forms of authority and legitimacy.

In this chapter my understanding of the theoretical and methodological relationship between literature and globalization is, first, attuned to what Spivak (1994) calls worlding: the cultural, narrative, and political reconfiguration of colonial space as imperial or global space. Second, culture and literature, as the writer and journalist Arundhati Roy insists, have a translational relationship that makes legible globalization's affect on people's everyday life psychological constitution. "What is happening to the world," she writes in *Power Politics*, "lies, at the moment, just outside the realm of common human understanding. It is the writers, the poets, the artists, the singers, the filmmakers who can make the connections, who can find ways of bringing it into the realm of common understanding ... who can translate cash-flow charts ... into real stories about people with real lives" (Roy 2001, 32). As Arundhati's fiction and non-fiction suggest, literature not only represents the dislocating effects of globalization, it actively generates what I call delegitimizing narratives of localized transnational warfare. In this way, literature does not merely illustrate and explain global social transformations, it offers legitimizing cultural narratives of globalization (Spivak 1994, 340). These narratives counter the legitimation of violence.

In this respect, literature has the potential to intervene in the normative politics of the representation of globalization and its effects, including the naturalization of structural and military violence, and to enable a critical practice of transnational literacy (ibid., 315). This chapter explores how the literary text allows us to question and shift the loci of power from which to narrate, imagine, and rearticulate the most pervasive practices of localized transnational warfare.

Thus, my reading of three short stories of Sri Lanka's ethnic civil war — set during the conflict's most violent phase in the 1990s — suggests that although Sri Lanka's war does not usually appear on the global radar of conflict management, epistemologically and politically it constitutes a localized transnational war *avant la lettre*. In fact, although Sri Lanka's war neither interferes with nor contributes to the global order of power, it helps us rethink the historical dimensions of global warfare. The central argument of this chapter critically builds on Michael Hardt and Antonio Negri's understanding of global warfare as a regime of biopower (2004, 13). Employing a postcolonial reading — rather than discourse analysis — of global warfare, I argue for the need to conceptualize global war in the history of imperial and colonial modernity. This approach enables a tentative redefinition of global war as localized transnational warfare. To expand my earlier definition, and in contrast to Hardt and Negri's concept of global war, localized transnational warfare cannot be reduced to exceptional forms of violence enacted in disconnected theatres of war. Instead, it denotes the most extreme, and often local, manifestations of an unequal distribution of global risks (Beck 2002). Second, and most importantly, it operates through the long-term militarization and brutalization of former colonial societies and relies on the instrumentalization and institutionalization of race and racial violence, or what Achille Mbembe calls the necropolitics of global imperialism. The term *necropolitics* emphasizes the phenomenology of colonial violence and theoretically disallows a purely discursive or Foucauldian approach to reading and understanding the cultural logic of localized transnational warfare.

Third, localized transnational warfare reflects and perpetuates the functioning of predatory global capitalism, including the making of "superfluous human beings" (Razack 2004, 160). Historicizing a predominantly ahistorical and universalist notion of global war, I suggest, moves our understanding of contemporary warfare beyond a pragmatic analysis of military strategy and organization towards a clearer comprehension of its cultural and necropolitical logic and rationale. This logic has purchase on a local and global plane and helps legitimize the denial of collective autonomy in many instances and horrific attacks on personal autonomy in others.

Through a reading of Jean Arasanayagam's collection of short stories *All Is Burning*, this chapter critically reads the biopolitics of war in the context of Mbembe's necropolitics of imperial war while examining the routinization and racialization of violence as it conditions Sri Lanka's conflict in the global present. Moreover, I read Arasanayagam's short stories against Étienne Balibar's (2004, 115) concept of civility and analyze different configurations of what I call the "quotidian representation of localized transnational warfare": the ways in which global and local violence interact, become legitimized, and reshape collective and personal autonomies. The longing for civility as a political and cultural ideal crucial to an understanding of autonomy first and foremost entails historicizing the global dimensions of extreme violence or the necropolitics of global war. Applied to Sri Lanka's war, Balibar's notion of civility mediates what Lorraine Code calls the "perversion of autonomy" (2000, 180) and gestures towards the undesirability and impossibility of collective autonomy and, thus, its legitimacy, if the latter is understood as a claim rather than as a process of mutual recognition, in the context of global and national conflict resolution.

Global War and Sri Lanka

Rather than an ancient tribal battle, Sri Lanka's war constitutes a relatively recent conflict. Stanley Tambiah (1996, 7) considers the war a "truly twentieth-century phenomenon ... exhibiting over the last three decades ... an increasing 'ethnic' mobilization and polarization previously unknown." This trend "owes more to the politics of nation making and election winning" (ibid.) than to perceived ethnic and cultural differences between Sri Lanka's majority population, the Buddhist Sinhalese, and its largest minority group, the Hindu Tamils. In some ways, as David Scott (1999) suggests, the conflict is in part a colonial legacy because Britain's divide-and-rule politics privileged Sri Lankan Tamils as civil servants but introduced a constitution that emphasized the rule of the majority. The cultural nationalism of Sri Lanka's anti-colonial period emerged through the revival of Buddhism and its normalizing narratives of Sinhalese identity, culture, and modernity and narratives of Tamils as colonial collaborators.

Sinhalese rule quickly led to a politics of ethnic exclusion that was expressed in the denial of citizenship to estate Tamils, restrictions for Tamils to get access to education and administrative positions, and, in 1956, in the Sinhala Only Act, which made Sinhala the only official language and elevated Buddhism to a state religion. Thus, Buddhism was increasingly politicized and spurred on the ethnic divide, while the Tamils were pushed into the northern and eastern parts of the country. Since the 1950s the country has experienced continuous revolts; the demand for an independent Tamil nation-state, Tamil Eelam; and the rise of the Liberation Tigers of Tamil Eelam (LTTE) in 1976. It was only in the wake of the Sinhalese legislation of the Prevention of Terrorism Act (1979) and the infamous Black July (1983), which saw what amounted to a state-sanctioned slaughter of thousands of Tamils, that full-fledged civil war broke out between the LTTE and the government. Although the controversial Indo–Sri Lankan Peace Accord internationalized the war in 1987, its global dimension has come into focus at the same pace as the legitimacy of the Sri Lankan government (specifically its monopoly over state violence) has deteriorated. In fact, the 1990s saw an especially violent period of the war as the government used paramilitary troops and mercenaries to fight the LTTE without being held accountable for torture, disappearances, and killings. The LTTE resorted to equally illegitimate forms of violence and systems of fear to control the Tamil population. For this reason, as Jayadeva Uyangoda (1999) suggests, the escalated and still escalating war has produced a culture of conflict in which fear of a settlement determines its intractability. This war is ultimately fought over political power, and its national dimensions have long since been privatized and globalized through a prolonged confrontation between state and particularist terrorism.

Arasanayagam's collection of short stories was published at a critical historical juncture in Sri Lanka's civil war, namely, at the moment of the war's entanglement in the global politics of the South and the rise of the Sri Lankan nation-state as one of its principal and most corrupted actors. This kind of violence has given rise to several narratives. For example, Mary Kaldor (2001) acknowledges the asymmetry of violence that is characteristic of what she calls the new wars of globalization. These wars rely on mercenaries, an illegal weapons trade, and the criminalization of so-called rogue or failed nation-states. They aim at population control, are fought over questions of identity, and are best regulated through cosmopolitan democracy. In this narrative, the new wars are symptomatic of the historical rupture of national forms of political organization brought about through globalization. Another common narrative stresses the culturalist origins of global wars. More specifically, as Samuel Huntington (1996) and Arjun Appadurai (1996) argue from two radically different political perspectives, global — or as I think it is more apt to say, localized transnational wars — signal the incommensurablity and clash of cultures and "mobilize cultural differences in the service of a larger national or transnational politics" (Appadurai 1996, 15).

Trying to define global war raises the question, as Edward Said (1993) reminds us, of who has the power to narrate. Indeed, the "power to narrate, or to block other narratives from forming and emerging," Said explains, "constitutes one of the main connections between culture and imperialism" (ibid., xiii) and, as I propose, between legitimacy and localized transnational warfare. To establish the relationship between the two, I draw from Hardt and Negri's biopolitical notion of contemporary warfare without necessarily endorsing their system-immanent construction of globalization and warfare.

Not unlike Hardt and Negri's notion of global war, Sri Lanka's war "tends towards the *absolute*" (Hardt and Negri 2004, 18) in that it polices civil society through elaborate security and surveillance systems; negates the rule of law; militarizes quotidian space; diminishes civil rights to such a degree that it increases torture, illegal incarceration, disappearances, and emergency regulations; and fosters a culture of fear, intolerance, and violent discrimination. In this sense, Sri Lanka's war constitutes "a *permanent social relation*" (ibid., 12) and does not function anarchically or without purpose and reason. Rather, it "becomes a *regime of biopower* ... aimed not only at controlling the population but producing ... social life" (ibid., 13). Furthermore, a biopolitical definition of war changes war's entire legal framework, for "whereas war previously was *regulated* through legal structures, war has become *regulating* by constructing and imposing its own legal framework" (ibid., 22). Although Hardt and Negri consider this dimension to be a new and absolute feature of global warfare, in Sri Lanka warfare has been a biopolitical means and permanent, everyday reality at least since the country's Sinhala Only Movement in 1956 and President Jayawardene's election campaign for a referendum in 1982.

In contrast to Hardt and Negri's notion of global war, I suggest that localized transnational wars frequently manifest themselves as extremely violent civil wars fought across the boundaries of the nation-state. Historically and politically, they are rooted in both colonial administrative practices of ethnicizing or racializing the colonized population and the legacies of anti-colonial liberation struggles. Moreover, the question of the use of legitimate violence becomes increasingly cynical and obsolete because the nation-state is often a corrupt and aggressive agent in the conflict. More importantly, the Sri Lankan government's use of extreme violence with impunity and the war's historical structure and logic of an anti-colonial liberation war define it a priori as a localized transnational war. Thus, while Hardt and Negri's tendency to underscore the ubiquity of violence attends primarily to the ways in which global war absolutizes social relationships in biopolitical terms, it also universalizes and obscures the different genealogies and effects of global violence.

For this reason, it is useful to follow Jean-Luc Nancy, who suggests that the global dimension of wars such as Sri Lanka's is twofold. First, it consists in "the global role — economic, technical, and symbolic — of certain states whose sovereignty is involved in the war" (2000, 102). Second, it lies in the fact that the crises of sovereignty and legitimacy of particular nation-states are deeply rooted in global histories of the present. The term *global,* however, is a misnomer because it denotes the imperial, colonial, and neocolonial history of Europe and its former colonies. In this regard, Arasanayagam's texts raise two crucial questions: When do representations of particular cultural and political crises become manifest in the exercise of habitual violence and turn into legitimizing narratives of localized transnational war? What are the effects of this legitimization?

A preliminary answer would have to consider the following: while legitimizing narratives of localized transnational warfare come in the various guises of humanitarianism, responsibility, protection, retributive justice, and human security, most tend, as Drucilla Cornell (2004, 87) observes with reference to Étienne Balibar, to put "under erasure" the necessity to mediate, adjudicate, and historicize violence. Recent treatments of these issues, specifically the critique of humanitarianism and the politics of protection, have become, as Peter Nyers demonstrates in this volume, increasingly controversial and hinder rather than promote social justice. For example, Michael Ondaatje's novel *Anil's Ghost* illustrates that normalizing violence entails the transformation of violence into a construct of history that universalizes violence and positions it outside the realm of public, symbolic, and political discourse (Härting 2006). It requires the disavowal of the historicity of violence itself.[1]

Civility, the Necropolitics of Global Warfare, and the "Perversion" of Autonomy in Jean Arasanayagam's *All Is Burning*

Arasanayagam's short stories interrogate the relationship between identity, violence, and communal space. Although she testifies to the ubiquitous presence of violence and fear in both Sinhalese and Tamil communities, Arasanayagam chronicles the strangeness or perversion of the ordinary in a world governed by prolonged civil war (Lawrence 2003, 102). For example, one of her stories, "The Buddha's Fire Sermon," documents the slaughter of a village's entire male population at the hands of paramilitaries and, thus, the monstrous transformation of communal space into a mass grave. The title of the story ironically reflects how the ordinarily peaceful teachings of Buddhism have been taken into the service of ethnocide to literally set the "country on fire" (Arasanayagam 1995, 169). *All Is Burning* examines the politicization of extreme violence — indeed, the substitution of extreme violence for politics — and its effects on quotidian life. More specifically, two of Arasanayagam's stories, "I Am an Innocent Man" and "Man without a Mask," conceptualize the privatization of Sri Lanka's war as a localized transnational war while questioning the viability of the demand for national and cultural autonomy under conditions of extreme and routinized political violence. A third story, "The Journey," contemplates ways to unhinge identity from the violence of political claims.

All of Arasanayagam's stories, however, present an early articulation of what Balibar identifies as a global topography of cruelty (2004, 115). Balibar's understanding of cruelty represents the enormous increase and visibility of extreme forms of violence as an experiment of globalization "in which the very possibility of politics is at stake" (ibid.), as an experiment of globalization that reflects the "totalitarian aspect of globalization" (ibid., 130). In the global era, cruelty, according to Balibar, is best conceptualized in spatial or topographical terms. The notion of topography implies both a concrete geopolitical perspective and an abstract cultural dimension. For "the causes and effects of extreme violence," Balibar explains, "are not produced on one and the same stage, but on different 'scenes' or 'stages,' which can be pictured as either 'real,' 'virtual,' or 'imaginary'" (ibid., 116). In this sense, Balibar's notion refuses to diminish cruelty to a mere by-product of globalization. Instead, he conceptualizes extreme violence as a central site of global power and as a product of globalization. Extreme violence produces human beings without subjectivity, and while it occurs in seemingly disconnected contexts for heterogeneous reasons, its effects are cumulative and tend towards exterminism (ibid., 126). What links extreme forms of violence are both their globalized methods of inflicting death and their radical politics of racial exclusion and antipolitics (ibid., 130). For these reasons, Balibar's notion of cruelty contests an understanding of the production of global violence in which all human beings come "into one fate" (Ondaatje 2000, 203). Rather, as a human experiment, the employment and globalization of extreme forms of violence divides the world, in Balibar's words, into "*life zones and death zones*" (2004, 126) and, thus, denotes the necropolitical logic of localized transnational war. The life zones, however, create the death zones by perpetuating uneven relationships of economic and political power, which are the legacy of colonization, by implementing elaborate security, immigration, and refugee laws of exclusion and by protecting received Western standards of wealth and cultural comfort. Although Balibar primarily addresses the construction of a new and global Europe and foregrounds a spatial conceptualization of cruelty, I read his conception of cruelty as an apposite critique of the ways in which localized transnational warfare has been conducted over the last three decades in Sri Lanka. Read in this light, Arasanayagam's stories may be understood as narratives of cruelty from the death zones of the Global South that originally emphasize the temporal dimensions, namely, the historical continuities of the production and globalization of extreme forms of violence and conflict.

Mercenaries and Necropolitics

In the story "I Am an Innocent Man" (Arasanayagam 1995), a schoolteacher witnesses a shootout between guerilla fighters and government-paid mercenaries. Armed to the teeth, the mercenaries slaughter an entire village. The schoolteacher recognizes the countries the mercenaries belong to but keeps silent because "identity does not count for a mercenary" (ibid., 42). As the primary combat forces of postmodern warfare (Hardt and Negri 2004, 47), the mercenaries signify a practical and an ethical dimension of global warfare. For, as Hardt and Negri point out, they have to be "biopolitical soldiers who must master a variety of technical, legal, cultural and political capabilities" (ibid., 49), and they constitute an army of corruption, unhampered by political ideals, identities, and loyalties. The observation is crucial because it immediately questions the often-presumed intrinsic link between violence and identity, thereby disrupting primordialist accounts of contemporary transnational warfare. In Arasanayagam's story neither violence nor identity figures as a natural or anarchistic phenomenon but as concepts with particular political and economic investments designed to gain absolute control over the population. Being for hire by the government and the insurgents alike, the mercenaries, as Tambiah (1996, 6) observes in his study *Leveling Crowds,* also reflect the sinister significance reached by the "'privatization of war' — that is, the ability of governments ... [to] farm out contracts for subversive military and political action to private professional groups willing to be hired or capable of being mobilized." The mercenaries, thus, denote the reign of a global free market economy, through which the state privatizes its institutions and services, including the army. The state profits from the unrestricted trade in war technologies and from foreign and local mercenaries through what Arundhati Roy in *War Talk* calls corporate globalization (2003, 41). The privatization of politics and war, then, contributes to the globalization of extreme violence, which, represented through the presence of an international crew of mercenaries in Sri Lanka, creates global zones of large-scale extermination and death. The mercenaries, however, denote not only the global configuration of death zones but also, and now I am slightly shifting Balibar's understanding of the term, the restructuring of local communities or collective autonomies into death zones.

What goes unnoticed, then, is that the presence of the mercenaries affects the militarization and brutalization of communal space. For example, as a passive observer of the massacre, the schoolteacher no longer feels confident to see himself as an innocent or objective bystander of the war's atrocities. When the soldiers take him away for interrogation, and presumably torture, he reverts to silence, for he knows that the truth can easily become his and his neighbours' death sentence, a lesson also suffered by Sarath and ignored by Anil in Ondaatje's novel (Härting 2006). The silencing of the schoolteacher is a common reaction of those who live under conditions of severe political oppression and structural violence, witness "disappearances and extrajudicial executions," and who, in order to survive, must "learn not to speak and to know what not to know" (Lawrence 2003, 105). In the Sri Lankan war, the privatization of violence poses a tremendous threat to "dignity and life" (ibid.) and, as the schoolteacher comes to understand, violates the safety of communal space. Upon his return to his school, he "place[s] his fingers on the bullet holes that pit the walls" of the school (Arasanayagam 1995, 42), as if to learn new ways to understand and orient himself in a communal environment that has become, as Arasanayagam puts it in another story, a "territory of fear" (ibid., 391). The schoolteacher's gesture also suggests that extreme violence and identity entertain an intimate relationship, so that violence — rather than ethnicity or history — functions as both a condition and point of departure for the rearticulation of identity. The militarization of communal space — that is, the construction of local extermination zones — transforms everyday spaces of life into death and encompasses the violent unmaking and remaking of individual and communal identities.

Similarly, the story "Man without a Mask" contemplates the politicization of violence but is told from the perspective of an elite mercenary who clandestinely works for the ruling members of the government and leads a group of highly trained state assassins. Possibly a member of the ex-SAS (British Special Air Service), veterans the Sri Lankan government hired after the failure of the Indo-Lankan Accord, the narrator represents the tenuous link between Sri Lanka's violent present and its imperial past. The story follows the narrator's thoughts while he, together with his death squad, is en route to a political assassination. Like a craftsman, he finds satisfaction in the precision and methodical cleanliness of his work, in being, as he says, "a hunter. Not a predator" and his ability to leave morality out of "this business" (Arasanayagam 1995, 98). He embodies Hardt and Negri's biopolitical soldier (2004, 49) and is an extreme and perverted version of what Martin Shaw describes as the soldier-scholar, "the archetype of the new [global] officer" (1999, 9). As a self-proclaimed scholar or scribe (Arasanayagam 1995, 100), the mercenary plots maps of death. Shortly before he reaches his victim (a politician who underestimated the political ambition of his enemy), he comments that bullet holes in a human body constitute a new kind of language: "The machine gun splutters. The body is pitted, pricked out with an indecipherable message. They are the braille marks of the new fictions. People are still so slow to comprehend their meaning" (ibid.). These new maps or fictions, I suggest, constitute what, unbeknownst to each other, Balibar and Mbembe term the *topography of cruelty* (Mbembe 2003, 40). More specifically, they simultaneously hint at the ways in which the systematic use of what Balibar calls ultra-objective and ultra-subjective violence replaces politics and enacts the necropolitical dimensions of Sri Lanka's localized transnational war.

According to Balibar, ultra-objective violence suggests the systematic "naturalization of asymmetrical relations of power" (2002, 27). For example,

the Sri Lankan government brings this process into being with the prolonged abuse of the Prevention of Terrorism Act. In the past, its use
plunged the country into a permanent state of emergency, facilitated the
random arrest of and almost absolute rule over citizens, and, thus, created a
culture of fear and a reversal of moral and social values. As the story clari-
fies, under conditions of systematic or ultra-objective violence, corruption
becomes virtue and "the most vile" man wears the mask of the sage and
"innocent householder" (Arasanayagam 1995, 102). In this milieu, the mercenary has no need for a mask because he bears a face of ordinary violence
that is "perfectly safe" (ibid.) in a society structured by habitual and systemic violence. But the logic of the new fictions of political violence is
also ultra-subjective because it is intentional and has a determinate goal
(Balibar 2002, 25), namely, the making and elimination of what Balibar
calls "disposable people" to generate and maintain a profitable global economy of violence. The logic of ultra-subjective violence presents itself
through the fictions of ethnicity and identity as they are advanced and in-
strumentalized in the name of national sovereignty. The mercenary perfectly symbolizes what Balibar means when he writes, "We have entered a
world of the banality of objective cruelty" (ibid.). For if the fictions of
global violence are scratched into the tortured bodies of war victims, the
mercenary's detached behaviour dramatizes a "will to 'de-corporation,'"
namely, "to force disaffiliation from the other and from oneself — not just
from belonging to the community and the political unity, but from the
human condition" (ibid.). In other words, while transnational localized war
becomes embodied in those whom it negates as social subjects — and
thereby reduces to mere flesh, in Giorgio Agamben's sense — it remains a
disembodied enterprise for those who manage and instrumentalize the
politics of death of such a war. It is through the dialectics of the embodiment and disembodiment of global violence that the dehumanization of
the majority of the globe's population takes on a normative and naturalized state of existence beyond any hope for individual or collective
self-determination.

   Arasanayagam's short story also casts light on the limitations of Hardt
and Negri's understanding of the biopolitics of global war. The latter can
account neither for the new fictions and political realities of violence in
former colonial spaces nor for what Mbembe calls the necropolitics (2003,
11) of late modernity. Mbembe's term, *necropolitics,* refers to his analysis of
global warfare as the continuation of earlier and the development of new
"forms of subjugation of life to the power of death" and its attendant

reconfiguration of "the relationship between resistance, sacrifice, and terror" (ibid., 39).[2] Mbembe's notion of necropolitics, then, sees contemporary warfare as a species of such historically — rather than spatially — rooted topographies of cruelty (ibid., 40) as the plantation system and the colony. Thus, following Foucault rather than Hardt and Negri, Mbembe argues that the ways in which global violence and warfare produce subjectivities cannot be dissociated from the ways in which race serves as a means of deciding over both life and death. Race also legitimizes and makes killing without impunity a customary practice of imperial population control.

If localized transnational warfare is a continuation of imperial forms of warfare, as the presence of the British SAS mercenaries in Arasanayagam's story suggests, war must rely on strategies of embodiment. These strategies involve the politicizing and racializing of the colonized and now "disposable" body for purposes of self-legitimization, specifically when making decisions about the value of human life. It is precisely for this reason that images of the body pitted and inscribed with bullet holes abound in Arasanayagam's stories. After all, on a global level, race underlies the ideological and physical division of the world into zones of life and death, a division that, in some cases, must be guarded by means of war. On the local plane, race serves to orchestrate the brutalization and polarization of the domestic population, reinforcing and enacting patterns of racist exclusion and violence on the non-white body.

But the mercenary also fosters a pragmatic and populist knowledge of the necropolitics and the criminalization of localized transnational warfare. He knows well that he lives "in a country rent apart by forces of violence, ethnicity, subversive elements, violations of every right under the sun ... [where] it's never clear who the real enemy is ... [and] the huge drug cartels, the arms dealers, those who bag the biggest tenders, manipulate the small man. The powerful remain inviolable for a long, long time" (Arasanayagam 1995, 102). The mercenary's assessment echoes a dominant understanding of global warfare, suggesting that the new wars are based on the fragmentation of older state formations. As Jonathan Friedman suggests, the integration of "new fragments into regional and global circuits of control and finance by both state and non-state actors" (2003, xiv) is also part of this understanding. Moreover, Friedman remarks that the increasing privatization of wars and the globalization of the means and technologies of extermination "is not chaos by any reckoning [but points to] the systematic nature of the global as it configures what might appear as chaotic" (ibid., ix). Here, Friedman unwittingly articulates the ways in which the necropolitics of global war engage, in Balibar's terms, in a systematic anti-politics designed to perpetuate a teleology of violence without end and accountability (Balibar 2004, 130).

More specifically, the necropolitical logic of war denotes the abolishment or, more often, mutation of politics into violence and the acceptance of violence as a normal state of social existence. In this context, Stanley Tambiah (1996, 221) suggests that under conditions of chronic civil war it is possible to speak of the routinization of violence that derives from violations of political and moral norms as they are staged, for example, during election campaigns and public rallies. For instance, the mercenary's memory of the "the provocative and aggressive body language of ... election candidates whose voices blast through the grating loudspeakers with all their shrieking distortions" (Arasanayagam 1995, 101) recalls the violent and coercive methods of political campaigning that accompanied President Jayawardene's election campaign for a referendum in 1982. This campaign was based on the racialization of politics and took place only a few months before the state-endorsed anti-Tamil pogrom in 1983, the event that sparked the country's civil war. Thus, political violence fosters a political culture of normalized violence in which the government compensates its loss of sovereignty and autonomy. The necropolitics of war, then, mobilizes ethnic divides and essentialist concepts of identity to maintain and conceal the conditions of the new wars. As Michael Wieviorka argues, these wars are always globalized and localized, general and molecular and, thus, contribute to "the reduction of these [binary] concepts" (2003, 125). Under conditions of necropolitical transnational warfare, then, the disintegrating nation-state claims autonomy not through a pluralist discourse of national or cultural identity but through a particularistic and violent identity politics (Kaldor 2001, 6). This politics, as my reading of Arasanayagam's stories exemplifies, is persistently unsettled through the cultural and literary production of counter-narratives of identity and violence.

Civility and the Perversion of Autonomy

The mercenary's ultra-subjective violence cannot be resolved dialectically or converted into a narrative of eventual liberation. In contrast, Arasanayagam's short story "The Journey" dramatizes the enforced negation of identity not as a loss but as a possible gain. Indeed, "The Journey" suggests delegitimizing the claims of identity politics and countering the necropolitics of localized transnational warfare with a discourse of civility and

Heike Härting

connectivity. Both of these terms, *civility* and *connectivity*, challenge those notions of autonomy that have their roots in the Kantian traditions of the European Enlightenment and that, without acknowledging the racialized and uneven formation of discourses of the self and the nation, posit autonomy as the chief condition of national and individual sovereignty. Indeed, as theorists such as David Theo Goldberg and Lorraine Code point out, the Enlightenment concept of autonomy is contingent on the concept of heteronomy and governed by an unacknowledged process of racialization that determines who is worthy of national and individual autonomy and who "should be directed" (Goldberg 1993, 148). Understood through its Kantian origins, the concept of autonomy first and foremost signifies the identity and dominance of a unified, self-knowing, and transparent subject over heteronomously defined configurations of individual and collective agency. By the same token, autonomy functions as a moral narrative that legitimizes the "guidance" of others into a state of maturity, reason, and progress. This narrative of autonomy and progress lies at the heart of the colonial and imperial project and, according to Code, accounts for the perversion of autonomy as an Enlightenment ideal in socially disadvantaged or colonial spaces. Consequently, autonomy is "prescriptively coercive" and "a locally specific value and ideal that is prone to exceed its reach" (Code 2000, 184). If autonomy is constructed as a claim in the context of exclusionary identity politics — as in the Sri Lankan conflict — or as a derivative of its racialized Enlightenment legacy, this claim can easily be taken into the service of the necropolitics of transnational warfare.

To dismiss claims for autonomy as atavistic, however, not only denies self-determination and particular historical experiences to different individuals and social collectivities, it also aborts the possibility of thinking about autonomy as an empowering and dynamic project that mediates and recreates the ways in which, to follow the original meaning of collective autonomy, a social group gives itself its own laws. In fact, Cornelius Castoriadis suggests that autonomy primarily consists of the people's faculty of self-reflection. Autonomy, he argues, "emerges when explicit and unlimited interrogation explodes on the scene — an interrogation that has bearing not on 'facts' but on the social imaginary significations and their possible grounding" (Castoriadis 1991, 163). In this sense, autonomy constitutes and conditions what Castoriadis calls society's radical imaginary (ibid., 143) — that is, the way that people imagine their society (i.e., its political forms of government and its social and cultural forms of organization). To Castoriadis, autonomy denotes an integral component of the transformative functions of the social imagination, and it is constitutive of state-governed and global social relationships. Admittedly, with its emphasis on the self-knowing and knowable individual and social subject, Castoriadis's notion of autonomy remains, in part, rooted in its Enlightenment tradition. Rather than taking his understanding of the self-reflexive and transparent subject as the conceptual foundation of the radical social imaginary, I suggest, via Balibar and Arasanayagam's story, that we should think of autonomy as a practice of civility based on the political and cultural negotiation of extreme and racialized violence, in both its global and local configurations. These negotiations, in turn, counter the legitimization of violence in global wars.

To take the notion of civility into an emancipatory project appears to be as fraught with danger as reclaiming autonomy for non-essentialist discourses of belonging. In fact, the term *civility* seems to be as mired in the legitimizing narratives of imperialism and the rise of the European nation-state as the term *autonomy*. A reappropriation of the term *civility*, however, has, at least in my mind, two advantages. First, with its connotations of race and the history of racism, the notion of civility can serve as a means to critique the racial dimensions of extreme violence exercised in global and local contexts of war and displacement. It foregrounds that extreme violence is not a new phenomenon born of a presentist understanding of globalization. Second, the notion of civility evokes questions of citizenship and rights and, in Balibar's view, entails the demand for the democratization of borders (2004, 117) — that is, for a politics of inclusion instead of exclusion. This understanding of civility opposes itself to the philosophical and political preponderance of identity and identity politics. In particular, Balibar argues that the condition and status of *homo sacer*, to use Agamben's popular term, is defined by a lack of civil rights, a lack that not only posits homo sacer as the object of humanitarian aid, rather than making him or her the subject of human and political rights (see also Nyers, this volume), but also translates his or her very existence into racialized categories of the human and the subhuman. The construction of homo sacer through a discourse of given or withheld rights circumvents the possibility of seeing resistance against such a conditioning of perpetual unbelonging and marginalization. For it is frequently the condition of marginalization that also enables the articulation of new communities and "process[es] of creation of rights" (Balibar 2004, 118). In other words, as a means and practice of political critique, the notion of civility narrates a radically democratic imaginary. It rethinks the very conditions and legitimizing strategies on which a global process of democratization may be based. Arasanayagam's story, then, helps us conceptualize autonomy as a practice of civility among those who are most severely affected by extreme violence and, deprived of political subjectivity, might be assigned the status of homo sacer.

Narrated through the eyes of the only Sinhalese refugee among a group of sixteen illegal Tamil refugees, the story recounts the group's perilous journey from the north of Sri Lanka to Berlin. Initially, the narrator presents the journey as a quest for political and moral enlightenment, one that is modelled on the "several lives of the Bodhisattvas" (Arasanayagam 1995, 2). While the quest may be undertaken in the name of the Buddha, it first of all requires the narrator to acknowledge the loss of his Sinhalese Buddhist majority status and to assume a minority position within the group. In fact, the opening of the story subtly criticizes received legitimizing narratives of democracy and suggests that the experience of complete displacement decentres the significance of politically and ethnically constructed majorities and minorities. The narrator, thus, observes: "TWO ... THREE ... FIVE ... eight ... twelve ... sixteen ... Always the counting. Numbers. Under the breath. In soft, sibilant whispers. There must be no slip in their precise numbering. But we had names. Must we forget them now? Names that were known among friends. Parents. Loved ones. In which country?" (ibid., 1). The emphasis on the relationship between numbers, identity, and politics provides the story's symbolic organization and recalls the British imperial influence on Sri Lanka's path to independence. As David Scott argues, the British initiated a political process that equated majoritarianism with democratization when "the Donoughmore commissioners in 1928 introduced the majoritarian principle into colonial Ceylon politics" (1999, 163). More specifically, the commissioners sought to modernize the constitutional process by introducing the universal franchise, abolishing the "atavism" of communal politics, and "institutionally inscribing the liberal-democratic project into the political domain in colonial Sri Lanka" (ibid., 164-66). The introduction of majoritarianism was legitimized through quantitative demographic data; it propelled the rise of the colonial elite; and, thus, it laid the foundation for the country's ethnic and racial conflict and guaranteed British political and economic influence through Sinhalese rule. While seeking to escape the violent logic of dehumanization and racial divide implied in the symbolic and historical prevalence of numbers, the refugees must begin their journey by becoming "numbers" (Arasanayagam 1995, 4) to be inserted into the illegal global economy of human trade. As the narrator remarks, "We are not human beings to them [the guides] ...We are dollars ...We provide employment to them" (ibid.). It is this kind of war profiteering and traffic in poverty and human loss that constitutes what Balibar (2004, 128-29) calls the "economy of global violence," which produces for both elimination and perpetual insecurity. The latter is of particular significance if we consider that the refugees' "claims of rights and citizenship are perceived as a threat for 'civilization'" (ibid., 129), an aspect poignantly dramatized through the incarceration of the illegal refugees in Arasanayagam's story.

To reach their destination and survive the brutality of the human smugglers, then, the refugees must destroy all documents that link them to their former names and identities. Indeed, identity is a liability — on the journey, as well as in the country of their past and their future. As the narrator well knows, it is the literally "burning question ... in [his] part of the world; [it] separates and divides" (Arasanayagam 1995, 3). Shedding it lightens the load of the refugees, ensures their survival, and symbolically forces them to "use signs" and gestures "to communicate with each other" (ibid.) — that is, to search for a language or resistance beyond the homogenizing fictions of ethnicity imposed on them by the nation-state, imperial history, and prolonged war. This language of civility, the story suggests, both entails balancing the uneven historical relations of power and changing those border politics that foster "ethnic cleansing" (ibid., 5) and racialized restrictions of entry. It challenges, as Spivak (1994, 86) puts it, Europe's deliberate "sanctioned ignorance" of the histories of the global South and Europe's own participation in the imperial and contemporary politics of race. This kind of sanctioned ignorance confers and claims autonomy by relinquishing historical and political accountability. For, as the narrator contemplates, while "we know the histories of all these worlds [the changed worlds of Europe]," "our wars, our revolutions, our conflicts, our displacements, are important only to ourselves. We become refugees, asylum seekers. Their laws restrict our entry into their countries" (Arasanayagam 1995, 5). In the story Europe's immigration laws figure as laws of exclusion that embody the denial of intersecting imperial histories and that, in the narrator's words, "we opened our doors to the invader ... adopted the colonizers' way of life ... changed our language, our religion, our culture" (ibid.). Here, autonomy becomes a historical chimera designed to legitimize the former invaders' claim to national sovereignty.

By relinquishing their personal and social identities, the refugees not only experience "a new kind of freedom" (Arasanayagam 1995, 12), they also suffer a complete lack of legal and political protection and are subjected to acts of random violence. In Agamben's words (1998, 114), their existence is reduced to "bare life" — that is, life without rights and defined by its "capacity to be killed" with impunity. On the one hand, "The Journey" compares the refugees' condition of bare life with that of Jewish survivors of the Holocaust. When the narrator contemplates Berlin's fascist history, he remains haunted by the presence of numbers tattooed into the skin of Holocaust victims that are now indicative of the refugees' dehumanized status (Arasanayagam 1995, 18). Given, however, that the narrator understands his hazardous journey to Germany as being parallel to the experience of the south Indian indentured "plantation workers who were brought to [Sri Lanka] two hundred years ago ... in ships" (ibid., 4), "The Journey," in contrast to Agamben's *Homo Sacer*, considers slavery and colonial displacement and violence as the paradigmatic conditions of modernity and its racialized history of the presence. Indeed, according to the narrator, colonialism, the Holocaust, the burning of Turkish people in Germany, Sri Lanka's war, and the business of human smuggling, while rooted in different historical contexts, share the logic of racist exclusion and extreme violence as an experiment in creating global and localized zones of apartheid (Balibar 2004, 120). Thus, the narrator foregrounds the various connections — rather than autonomous relations — between racial violence and the "new racism" (ibid., 122), which serves to legitimize and structure national and supranational institutions and their political relationships. In this sense, then, under conditions of globalization, the various stages and histories of racial violence do not come into comparison, they "produce cumulative effects" (ibid., 126).

The journey, as the narrator learns, also creates new bonds of survival and care among formerly divided people. Indeed, it creates a tender relationship between the narrator and a Tamil boy, whom the narrator eventually considers his little brother. Thus, formerly filiative relationships — that is, those based on blood and ethnic ties of exclusion — are slowly transforming into affiliative relationships of choice and cultural inclusion. Moreover, what the journey entails for the narrator is an unlearning of identity and ethnic privilege. It is precisely in this Deleuzean process of becoming minoritarian, of privileging disidentification over a normative model of identity, that Balibar locates the politics of civility (Balibar 2002, 34). Civility denotes a critical analysis of the global topography of cruelty, understood in both Balibar's and Mbembe's sense of the concept. As a critique of the history of racial violence, then, the notion of civility "is certainly not a politics which suppresses all violence; but it excludes extremes of violence, so as to ... enable violence itself to be historicized" (ibid., 29-30). As a discourse of subjectivity, however, civility "regulates the conflict [between totalizing and relativizing forms of] identification" (ibid., 30). What is at stake in the making of a "radical social imaginary" is the way we conceptualize the "autonomous practices of the self" that are enacted by those who lack social and political subjectivity. In other words, the discourse of civility questions how we understand a practice of the self *before* the constitution of the political and social subject. It then extends the notion of autonomy — of giving oneself laws and shaping the radical imaginary of the society one lives in, but is not necessarily born into — to those without civil, political, and human rights. Thus, the practice of civility destabilizes dominant notions of autonomy. Instead of positing the Kantian sovereign subject as its conceptual foundation, the practice of civility imagines a different kind of non-subject as the legitimizing and ethical ground of autonomy. For, conceptualized as a non-subject, the illegal refugee, as the narrator of "The Journey" knows, transgresses the restrictions of movement enforced by global and national border politics but remains criminalized as a threat to civilization and is forced to confront anonymity, invisibility, illegal labour, social rejection, and racialized violence (Balibar 2004, 129).

Conclusion

In this chapter I examine the ways that literary narratives of Sri Lanka's war generate legitimizing cultural and political discourses of extreme violence and autonomy. This chapter's reading of Sri Lanka's civil war as a localized transnational war begins with a challenge to those concepts of global war that tend to see contemporary warfare as a presentist occurrence rather than as a highly amorphous phenomenon. In fact, as I suggest, localized transnational wars are often wars with imperial roots or prolonged wars of anti-colonial liberation that are susceptible to change under the pressures of national disintegration and global politics and economics. My reading of Arasanayagam's short stories underscores that these wars are not an innately human and universal phenomenon; rather, the stories map the cumulative effects of war as a part of a larger global topography of cruelty (Balibar 2004; Mbembe 2003) and develop a critique of the history of racial violence that underpins both localized transnational warfare and the cultural logic of globalization. The stories foreground the ways that the routinization and privatization of military violence create new fictions and legitimizing narratives of extreme violence and replace the possibility of politics with a radical global anti-politics. Moreover, by exploring the ways in which people are most affected by extreme violence, on both a quotidian and global level, Arasanayagam's stories rethink autonomy as a practice of civility. The latter, as I argue along with Balibar, foregrounds the common logic and linkages between various histories of modernity and racial violence, and it constitutes homo sacer, or the non-subject, as the ethical and social foundation on which to develop legitimizing discourses of global citizenship and belonging.

Part 4
**Legitimacy and Autonomy on Global
and Regional Scales**

chapter 11

An Airborne Disease: Globalization through African Eyes

Rhoda E. Howard-Hassmann

AFRICA IS THE CONTINENT that is the least globalized and the continent that benefits the least from globalization (Collier 2007). It is missing from global capitalism, global institutions (in a substantive, if not formal, sense), and global rule making. It is, at best, a passive recipient of globalization, not an active forger of global processes. It seems that Africa can do little or nothing to control the whims of the outsiders who control its economies. There is no continental autonomy for Africa as a region or as an economy. This characterization applies especially to sub-Saharan Africa, the area with which this chapter is concerned.

The way to control a globalization that is seemingly imposed from outside is not by asserting an autonomy divorced from the world economy or from world political and institutional standards. The African actors who control their continent politically can only assert economic control through the creation of legitimate institutions at the national, regional, and continental levels. Legitimate, well-organized, and competently run institutions might be able to control the forces of globalization within Africa and their leaders might be able to negotiate with other actors on the international stage.

These legitimate institutions must be national as well as continental. Continental autonomy is not possible without national legitimacy. National legitimacy in Africa, as elsewhere, rests on the capacity to create efficient, rule-bound, law-abiding democratic governments that can fairly deliver needed goods to their citizens. This capacity is crucial to Africa's ability to negotiate as a regional body on the global scene.

In this chapter, then, I refer simultaneously to continental, national, and individual autonomy and legitimacy. My analysis of how individuals respond to globalization rests on interviews with seventy-four elite Africans. These individuals displayed loyalties to their families, clans, and ethnic groups; their local regions; and their nations. But they were also loyal to and identified with their continent. It appeared to them that they lived in a continental community of *shared fate,* to use a term explored by Melissa Williams in this volume. That fate was one of misery, poverty, exploitation, and powerlessness.

Africa is by far the world's poorest continent. In 2002, 44 percent of sub-Saharan Africans lived on less than $1.00 per day, and 75 percent lived on less than $2.00 per day (World Bank 2007). In 2003, 7.5 to 8.5 percent of adults in sub-Saharan Africa were living with AIDS (UNAIDS and WHO 2003, 5), and according to the AVERT (2005) website, 2.2 million Africans died of AIDS in 2003 alone. This terrible disease has undermined much of the capacity of Africans to control their own fate. Moreover, Africa in the 1990s and early twenty-first century was plagued by civil wars, genocide, and state-induced famines in areas such as Sierra Leone, Liberia, Angola, Rwanda, Congo, Sudan, and Zimbabwe (Ali and Matthews 1999, 2004). Very few African states were functioning democracies without internal unrest.

What does globalization mean, then, to a continent still so economically underdeveloped, politically disorganized, and plagued by disease and war? And what does globalization mean to individual Africans? William Coleman, co-editor of this volume and editor of the entire series in which it appears, suggests the following definition of globalization:"Globalization is the growth of supraterritorial relations among people creating a complex series of connections that tie together what people do, what they experience, and how they live across the globe. In participating and acting in these connections, individuals and communities see the world increasingly as one place and imagine new activities and roles for themselves in this world" (Coleman 2005, 77). This definition correctly stresses the aspect of supraterritoriality, which was pointed out earlier by Jan Aart Scholte (2002, 44). But such a short definition cannot make clear the inequalities of the connections among people. Globalization is driven by capitalist expansion, and it is a class-biased phenomenon (Howard-Hassmann 2005). "People" do not connect as equals but as individuals constrained by region, economy, and politics. Africans are the least able of any group of people to interact as equals in the new supraterritorial world. They have the least capacity to travel, the least access to the Internet, and the least capacity to influence others. For them, the globalized world is not a space without borders but a space that locks them in, forcing many to risk their lives in illegal migration to more prosperous regions.

Given these severe constraints, is *autonomy* a meaningful term for Africa or Africans? One classic reference to autonomy in the Western philosophical literature is Immanuel Kant's insistence on the necessity for moral autonomy as a form of self-legislation. Man (as Kant put it at the time) is an end in himself, and all men must respect all others as ends, not means. Man regulates himself by autonomously deriving laws that follow the rule: "Act only according to that maxim whereby you can at the same time will that it should become a universal law" (Kant 1999, 496). Thus, man is subject to autonomy, or self-rule, not heteronomy, or rule by others. Autonomy is also the grounds for human dignity. When the maxim of universality is upheld, we "ascribe a certain dignity and sublimity to the person who fulfils all his duties" to uphold the law (ibid., 502). When we act on our own will to fulfill these duties, we ourselves become "the proper object of respect" (ibid.).

Kant's eighteenth-century Enlightenment view makes sociological sense in the twenty-first century, for Africans even more than for those fortunate enough to live prosperous lives in the West. All human beings deserve dignity; indeed, the founding human rights document of the modern era, the 1948 United Nations' Universal Declaration of Human Rights, declares in its Preamble, "Recognition of the inherent dignity and of the equal and inalienable rights of all members of the human family is the foundation of freedom, justice and peace in the world." In my own work on human dignity, I have concluded that "dignity requires personal autonomy, societal concern and respect, and treatment by others in society as an equal" (Howard 1995, 16). To have personal autonomy means "to have the freedom to act on one's decisions and to have one's decisions respected by the state and other citizens" (ibid., 17). In modern society, I believe, everyone must be treated with respect. An individual who does not enjoy respect, who feels stigmatized or inferior, will not be able to make autonomous decisions and act on them.

Both Kant's philosophical reading and the reading I propose as a political sociologist suggest that autonomy is a property of the individual. Many communitarians reject this reading and assert that individual autonomy removes the individual from his family and community (Etzioni 1993). In Africa especially, one might argue that this removal is more harmful than beneficial. The community — the extended family, the village, the ethnic group — is what protects individuals from the harmful effects of non-autonomous integration into the world capitalist economy. However, as Africa enters the integrated globalized world, its citizens increasingly move from their villages and communities to cities, mines, or industrial centres; they are increasingly mobile, and they have more and more contact with outsiders. Thus, like the citizens of Kant's eighteenth-century Europe, the citizens of Africa are becoming independent beings desirous of the capacity to make autonomous choices (Howard 1995, 86-91).

One might also move this concept of autonomy up several levels to that of the nation or the continent. Perhaps self-legislation also pertains to the continent as a whole. Perhaps only through generating a capacity for continental self-regulation will Africans enjoy, on the world stage, that dignity that Kant also considers essential for individuals. In a world in which racist perceptions of Africans are still common, perhaps only a strong continental presence can protect individual Africans from negative stereotypes that undermine their individual dignity. Without a sense of personal efficacy, Africans cannot take part either as individuals or as members of collectivities in the globalized world. Globalization is, for them, an imposed change. They do not participate as equals in the larger world, nor do they view it as a place that offers them new roles and activities.

A young Tanzanian man we interviewed referred to globalization as an "airborne disease" (Interviewee 19, Sainte-Anne-de-Bellevue, Quebec, 18 June 2003). This phrase encapsulates what the supraterritoriality implied by globalization means to many Africans, as I show below.

"Sitting on Gold and Digging for Food": Africans Discuss Globalization

Between 1 June 2002 and 31 March 2004, two graduate assistants and I interviewed seventy-one elite Africans and obtained the opinions of another three via email. The major focus of our interviews was the general question of whether the Western world owed reparations to Africa. One specific aspect of this question was whether the West owed Africa reparations for neocolonialism, postcolonial interactions, and/or globalization. We posed this question loosely (we used a semi-structured questionnaire) and then listened as our respondents elaborated on their answers. From this research, I draw the African opinions of globalization discussed in this chapter. In keeping with this volume's stress on autonomy, as well as with standard qualitative methodology, I do not evaluate this material. Rather, I leave these Africans to speak for themselves, even when my own analysis differs from theirs.

Twenty-two of the interviews were in French, and fifty-two were in English. The interviews took place in various locales in North America and Europe, where our respondents were living or where they were attending academic conferences or short courses on human rights. Our sample consisted of eight ambassadors to the United States, twenty-four academics, and forty-two human rights activists and policy makers (many of the academics were also activists) from twenty-six countries. Of the fifty-eight who gave us their age, the range was from twenty-six to sixty. Fifty-four were men, and twenty were women. We defined "African" as anyone who was a citizen of an African country, regardless of "race." All but seven of the people we spoke to were either permanent residents of Africa (including the eight ambassadors) or had moved to North America within the preceding three years. I refer to these Africans as "elite" because all of those for whom we had information on educational attainment had at least one university degree. Although elite, they were still close to members of their extended families, many of whom were still farmers in rural villages. Many had parents with little or no education. Despite their education and the professional positions many of them held, our respondents were, tragically, all too familiar with economic decline, civil war, and life-threatening illnesses.

Thus, we interviewed a purposive, focused sample (Patton 1990, 169). We looked for individuals who were familiar with the debate on Western-African relations. Our sample is not statistically representative of all Africans, but there was a remarkably high degree of consensus among the people with whom we talked. The consensus was based on perceptions of the massive material harm perpetrated on Africa by the West and on Africa's urgent need for material assistance. It was also based on the perception that Africa was a powerless victim of globalization. Indeed, to some respondents, globalization was almost a deliberate conspiracy. This conspiracy was concocted by Western powers and institutions to extract the maximum profit from Africa while treating African nations, societies, and individuals with massive disrespect.

Much analysis of globalization regards it as a new, disruptive set of political, economic, and social relations. In this analysis, previously self-sufficient communities and nations are undermined by global relations that force their dependence on more powerful (Western) global actors. The Africans with whom we spoke, however, did not regard globalization as something new. Rather, they regarded it as another episode in five centuries of disruption and dislocation forced upon them by Western powers.

Africans, in their view, completely lacked autonomy; they were subject to the capricious, rapacious, and vicious rule of others. In their conversations with us, our respondents frequently evinced a sense of despair and abandonment. The era of globalization was to them merely one more epoch of Western exploitation of Africans, like the earlier eras of the transatlantic slave trade and European colonialism. The West, it seemed, was incapable of treating Africa as if its inhabitants were real people. A Togolese activist said, "I ask myself if they ever take account of the human aspect of Africa. Because with globalization, with structural adjustment programs, all that, they cry, 'No, it's for your benefit.' But at the end of the day ... the people suffer a lot from those programs" (Interviewee no. 53, Sainte-Anne-de-Bellevue, Quebec, 23 June 2003).[1]

Several of our respondents specifically referred to globalization as a continuation of the slave trade and colonialism. An older, professional woman from Tanzania said, "Really, globalization is another way of colonialism. They're coming in another fashion" (Interviewee no. 23, Sainte-Anne-de-Bellevue, Quebec, 18 June 2003). A Cameroonian said, "Globalization, okay, it's simply another form of colonization ... of the South by the North, simply ... a modern colonization" (Interviewee no. 61, Sainte-Anne-de-Bellevue, Quebec, 22 June 2003). Even an ambassador asserted, "With the globalization we can see ... the very same logic of colonization" (Interviewee no. 7, Washington, DC, 8 April 2003). While conceding that both colonialism and globalization might have some positive effects, a young Kenyan activist seemed to view its effects mostly as negative: "Globalization ... like colonialism, it has its advantages and also disadvantages ... People are able to move freely, probably will get employed somewhere else ... from African countries where the main problem is unemployment. People are also able to ... advance in terms of technology, because the West is ahead of Africa. But then there's also several disadvantages ... one is unfair competition ... we do not tread on a equal footing: somehow we ... [are] on the losing side ... When you look at industrialization, the products from the West, when they are brought to Africa they kill the local industries" (Interviewee no. 14, Sainte-Anne-de-Bellevue, Quebec, 17 June 2003).

In this colonial enterprise, African economies were once again being marginalized. One Togolese activist said, "Africa has been particularly marginalized in globalization. Only 1 percent of external investment [is] in Africa, and output of Africa in world trade is less than 1 percent. But at the same time, African resources are crucial for ... the global economy. So, as somebody put it ... we are sitting on gold and digging for food" (Interviewee no. 17, Washington, DC, 28 March 2003).[2] All of Africa's resources, it seemed, were being appropriated by those with superior power, leaving Africans themselves to starve. Nor was globalization something that Africa could escape. According to a middle-aged Congolese scholar, "Globalization is a totalitarian phenomenon ... globalization is a whole ... Africa should fight for a new international order, because the one we're in now ... its rules were made without us" (Interviewee no. 59, Quebec City, 18 November 2003).

Our respondents frequently referred to globalization as merely a continuation of nineteenth-century colonialism. As a very angry Kenyan man said, "There is still the scramble ... Now we are being colonized by more than one power" (Interviewee no. 26, Sainte-Anne-de-Bellevue, Quebec, 26 June 2002).[3] In this colonial enterprise, international institutions loomed large. An older man from the Democratic Republic of Congo said: "The restructuring required by the International Monetary Fund ... and all those international financial authorities, require that a country have a definite, sound management ... But are the measures that accompany [the demands] beneficial for the majority of the recipients? ... I don't think so, at all." He continued by stressing how much Africans had lost since the implementation of structural adjustment programs by the World Bank. "We hear, 'Don't hire people, don't raise their salaries.' They stop our services ... But the IMF doesn't help our governments solve inflation ... with the consequence that our currency loses its value, no employment is created in the country ... and there is unemployment. So, these measures are imposed, perhaps to help states function better, but in reality it's the people who suffer. This entire history, it's suffering, from the colonial period ... to independence. It's the same history of suffering, of all this suffering, that continues" (Interviewee no. 50, Quebec City, 9 December 2003).

The economic strictures imposed by international institutions had no legitimacy in the eyes of most of our respondents. If there were any economic justifications for them, they were completely outweighed by their highly detrimental human impact. Globalization has brought poverty and unemployment to Africa. A Rwandan woman with whom we spoke was still deeply traumatized by the 1994 genocide. She viewed the international community as one that was deepening her country's suffering. "Now,

what's in fashion is globalization. After colonization, there's globalization
... Maybe it's a good idea, but it damages life in general, for Africans.
Because they privatize ... despite the people's low purchasing power. It's
caused ... a lot of unemployment ... And lots of poverty, it's all over Africa."
She continued, "Globalization ... if it's the World Bank ... if it's the
International Monetary Fund ... at the level of Africa, they haven't con-
sidered social life, or even life itself" (Interviewee no. 63, Sainte-Anne-de-
Bellevue, Quebec, 17 June 2003).

Colonialism, neocolonialism, international institutions, globalization: all
were one for most members of the African elite with whom we spoke. In
their view, there was one undifferentiated, unmediated, deliberately exploitative relationship between the West and Africa. Private multinational
corporations were also part of this relationship. In our respondents' eyes,
multinational corporations worked hand-in-glove with international institutions to impoverish Africans. A Kenyan woman abruptly defined globalization as "a lot of multinationals coming in and just exploiting a lot of
resources and going away" (Interviewee no. 31, Sainte-Anne-de-Bellevue,
Quebec, 24 June 2002). Similarly, a young Tanzanian man said, "I see it as a
process whereby poor economy is impoverished ... by the rich economies.
I don't see it as a process where the poor economies are integrated for
their benefit" (Interviewee no. 62, Lund, Sweden, 15 March 2004). Another
Kenyan believed that multinationals were merely looking for cheap labour.
"There is a rush for ... corporations to up their production in Africa not
because they're interested in ... the economy for this country but because
... [the] position that Africa has in international affairs makes it easier to
exploit cheap labour in Africa, it makes it possible to get raw materials
cheaply in Africa" (Interviewee no. 32, Sainte-Anne-de-Bellevue, Quebec,
16 June 2003). A few respondents referred particularly to the principle of
privatization of formerly state-owned resources, a common demand in the
structural adjustment programs accepted by many African countries since
the mid-1980s. An activist from Togo said:

Globalization has enormous effects ... I just take the case of multinationals ... In my country, today, there is what we call the "new"
[English in original] industrial force, where industries come from the
West and establish themselves. They don't pay taxes ... But you should
see the conditions my compatriots work in in these industries. The
conditions are atrocious. They don't respect workers' rights at all ...
And you should see the privatizations of our state industries. Water,

for example ... it's privatized. Electricity, privatized ... I take the case of water ... because it is a natural treasure that God has given us. But these corporations invade us and privatize our resources ... Those are some of the effects of globalization. (Interviewee no. 45, Sainte-Anne-de-Bellevue, Quebec, 28 June 2002)

Not one individual with whom we spoke considered globalization to have had more positive than negative effects on Africa. Our respondents clearly saw globalization as principally an economic phenomenon, one in which the West dominated and in which Africa could not possibly compete. A very angry Malawian woman said: "As a nation, we are being forced, we are being plunge[d] into this globalization situation, where we cannot actually move out. And there is no way we can say, 'We should not join the force.' Because it stays. It's coming to stay ... So the Western countries are moving at ... five kilometres to catch up with the globalization issue. In fact, they are the one[s] starting it. But for us, that is perhaps two thousand kilometres to catch up" (Interviewee no. 20, Sainte-Anne-de-Bellevue, Quebec, 25 June 2002).

The speed of change also made it impossible to catch up, as a young man from Burundi put it. "[Globalization] can ruin Africa. We must go gently" (Interviewee no. 69, Lund, Sweden, 17 March 2004). The angry Kenyan man quoted earlier said: "Globalization ... comes with such momentum that no other group has been able to stand in its way ... We need to ... construct appropriate *speed governors* of globalization ... In Kenya ... thirty-four local industries have closed shop because the markets are flooded by cheap good[s] coming from the West or brought by multi-national[s] who have the benefits of economies of scale, who can exploit cheap labour in Asia and bring their products in Africa. I think it is ... fulfilling the last aspect of neocolonialism in Africa" (Interviewee no. 26, Sainte-Anne-de-Bellevue, Quebec, 26 June 2002). These comments echo those made by Joseph Stiglitz (2002, 180-81) and others, warning against the "shock therapy" style of globalization. The shock our African respondents experienced was real and often overwhelming.

Global Pillage and Missing Africans

For many of our respondents, globalization was, in effect, theft. It was a way to continue the theft perpetrated on Africa by the transatlantic slave trade and by colonial exploitation of labour and resources. And this stripping of resources often means death. The world's neglect of Africa is an important cause of AIDS, as the traumatized Rwandan woman with whom we spoke reminded us. "The existence of AIDS is a consequence ... of all these problems [of globalization] ... Women prostitute themselves ... it's a consequence of poverty, of unemployment ... Because when they privatize ... they reduce the number of employees" (Interviewee no. 63, Sainte-Anne-de-Bellevue, Quebec, 17 June 2002).

Some of our respondents' comments might have sprung in part from the education about the world economy that they had received in African, Western, or indeed Soviet (in at least one instance) universities. Few, if any, of the potential economic benefits of globalization were mentioned in their discussions with us.[4] But their comments also arose from their lived experiences. They, or members of their families or colleagues or friends, had lost their jobs because of the retrenchment imposed by structural adjustment programs. A Tanzanian respondent told us his mother, a nurse, had been laid off from her job in a clinic because of the retrenchments necessitated by Tanzania's structural adjustment program (Interviewee no. 62, Lund, Sweden, 15 March 2004): yet no one would argue that Africa has enough qualified health care professionals. The Africans we spoke with had witnessed the rise in the price of water that followed the privatization of government services. They saw foreign companies exploiting the products of their soil. A Nigerian lawyer pointed out that structural adjustment was not only a national economic policy; rather, each individual literally had to restructure himself by tightening his belt. "We are the ones who are going to tighten our belts and structurally adjust ourself to help them pay for what they have stolen" (Interviewee no. 54, Lund, Sweden, 11 March 2004).

A small minority of our respondents viewed globalization as carrying mixed benefits. Those who most favoured economic globalization were several ambassadors who were fairly conversant with international trade or banking. One ambassador did not object to globalization as long as everyone followed the same rules. He supported moves to reduce tariffs and subsidies to permit freer trade among countries that renounced protectionist measures. If this liberalization occurred, his own country could sell more fruit and vegetables to Europe (Interviewee no. 25, Washington, DC, 25 March 2003). Another ambassador said, "I think Africa and [the ambassador's country] ... want to be part of the world ... It should be [done] in such a way that it does not profit only one side of the world" (Interviewee no. 1, Washington, DC, 15 April 2003). Like his colleague, he was suggesting not that the rules of the international game were wrong but that they should be implemented fairly. This was not a perspective that most of our respondents shared, perhaps for lack of knowledge of the actual working of the world trading system.

Among the vast majority of our respondents, who were not ambassadors or otherwise embedded in the international political or economic elite, only a few mentioned the benefits of globalization. A young man from Cameroon thought globalization meant that Africans could have more contact with the rest of the world. "Africans can have an opportunity, those who have not travelled abroad, to use the same machines ... It is possible ... to import products from Europe without actually travelling to Europe" (Interviewee no. 49, Lund, Sweden, 18 March 2004). An Eritrean thought that foreign investment would create opportunities for Africans, who would also benefit from "knowledge, interaction, experience, exchanges" (Interviewee no. 75, Waterloo, Ontario, 3 February 2004). Two spoke of the global human rights movement. An activist from Malawi said, "Because of globalization ... our leaders have been able to interact at large with ... their counterparts and they have learned quite a lot in terms of ... respect for human rights" (Interviewee no. 65, Lund, Sweden, 15 March 2004). This was an unusual comment about how globalization favours the flow of ideas.

According to the account of globalization given to us by the seventy-four Africans with whom we had our discussions, Africans are missing from the globalized world. They are missing from the global stage, from global institutions like the World Trade Organization, and from international financial institutions. Our respondents, who were educated people, for the most part would have understood that, formally speaking, their governments are represented in these institutions. But they would have argued that, in practice, this representation was meaningless. They would not be surprised, for example, to learn that the director of the International Monetary Fund who represented the United States in 2005 controlled 17 percent of the total voting power at the organization, whereas the two directors who represented almost all of sub-Saharan Africa controlled just under 4.5 percent (IMF 2005). Nor would they be surprised by Sylvia Ostry's account elsewhere in this volume of the many institutional obstacles to equitable participation by Southern countries in the World Trade Organization. In the opinion of these Africans, the West cares little, or not at all, about African views of African affairs. There is no respect in the West for the principle of continental autonomy. Africa is missing from international governance.

The people we spoke with did not feel that they were part of the community that makes the rules under which they live. And, indeed, this feeling may be accurate. If a community is a group of individuals or entities that feel a sense of obligation to one another, then it is not clear how strong the international community's sense of obligation is to Africa (Howard 1995, 5). As the young Nigerian lawyer explained, "I have a problem with understanding what globalization exactly means ... maybe trying to make a village where everybody will have access to everything ... If that is what it is, then it's a positive move. So you make the community ... more habitable for everyone" (Interviewee no. 54, Lund, Sweden, 11 March 2004). But no one among the people we spoke with thought that globalization was indeed creating a village "where everybody will have access to everything." Rather, as our angry Kenyan stated, "There is a lot of pillage that also goes on in that village" (Interviewee no. 26, Sainte-Anne-de-Bellevue, Quebec, 26 June 2002).

Most of the Africans with whom we spoke had little trust in international organizations. To them, global governance was not a legitimate enterprise. Many felt abandoned by the international community. Whatever the international laws might ostensibly be, our respondents felt they were actually subject to the capricious and self-serving power of the West and the ostensibly international organizations that were actually controlled by the West.

Even more, our respondents mistrusted the international economy. It appeared to many of them that this economy was deliberately designed to misappropriate their resources and leave them with nothing. A West African graduate student studying in Canada said: "[My] understanding of globalization is to have what's called equal partnership, equal relationship, but I realize that the relationship has been two thirds in favour of the developed world, and, therefore, the developed world continues to suppress the developing world ... African countries cannot begin to trade some of their own commodities ... the price of commodities are determined by the developed world ... They [African countries] don't even get the benefit, or even enough money to even use to develop their countries, because they sell based on what the buyer determines" (Interviewee no. 35, Hamilton, Ontario, 23 October 2003).

A middle-aged academic from Tanzania said the following about world trade: "When the seller is from the developed country, it's the developed country that fixes the prices. When the seller is from the developing countries, it's the developed country that fixes the prices ... In Tanzania, in my home ... last year, 2001, the price of coffee, before June, it was around three hundred Tanzanian shillings. August, the price fell down from three hundred Tanzanian shillings to eighty. By November it was at eight. And the prices would not go up. Why? The WTO can address why" (Interviewee no. 13, Sainte-Anne-de-Bellevue, Quebec, 27 June 2002). Both of these quotations imply that globalization is a plot, a conspiracy by the West to defraud Africa. World prices are set by self-interested Westerners, not by neutral market forces.

It seemed to our respondents that there is no real room for Africans to participate in the global market. An older activist from Guinea said: "Yes, globalization. We are subjected to it but we do not participate. Globalization should mean the participation of each state with its economic, political, and cultural values. But we are subjected to it, because we have very little ... We have cultural goods to sell, but economic goods, in relation to Western progress, we have very little ... We don't play an equal part with our partners who have their multinationals, which exploit [our] resources. So ... we submit, but we don't participate" (Interviewee no. 52, Sainte-Anne-de-Bellevue, Quebec, 18 June 2003).

Legitimacy, Governance, and Autonomy

How, then, can Africa emerge from this subordinate role in globalization? The opinions of elite Africans discussed above suggest that international governance enjoys almost no legitimacy in African eyes. A concerned Westerner, cognizant of the exploitation of Africa during the slave-trading and colonial eras, might well agree that these opinions warrant a restructuring of international relations. Africa, it is clear, needs help. It needs massive assistance to combat HIV/AIDS and other diseases. Perhaps the key to progress in Africa comes from outside that continent. Without reform of the global economy and all global institutions, no progress can be made within Africa.

Timothy Besley and Robin Burgess (2003) are two economists interested in poverty reduction. They do not agree with the account of globalization presented above by our respondents, nor do they agree that the key to progress lies only in the external global economy and institutions. In their view, poor countries need economic growth more than internal or global redistribution of wealth. This economic growth requires increased foreign investment. Increased foreign investment follows institutional improvements, especially the establishment of more transparent, accountable governments and the rule of law. These improvements would also benefit individuals. Improved security of tenure in land and property is necessary, as is better access to small-scale credit for individuals. A better-qualified, more educated labour force is more likely to draw investment. And, finally, narrower income inequalities correlate with a better capacity to fight poverty.

Besley and Burgess's argument accords with my own view. I believe that globalization may have significant positive effects in the long term for all human rights, including economic rights. Africans need more globalization, not less. But they need it within a context of democracy, workers' rights, the rule of law, and citizens' active involvement in the decisions their governments make. The institutional reliability that might attract foreign investors ought not to be implemented at the price of the individual rights of the citizens of African states. This interpretation is not merely a moral one that considers Africans' needs, nor is it a cultural imposition of Western norms on Africa. It is a pragmatic evaluation of how societies actually progress that is based on a reading of how Western, industrialized states evolved in the nineteenth and twentieth centuries and how the more de-veloped non-Western societies changed during the last half of the twenti-eth century (Howard-Hassmann 2005; Sen 1999). Although I cannot present a full account in this short chapter of my own theory of how soci-eties develop, it is clear that Africans need governments with greater organ-izational and institutional capacities than most now possess. They also need leaders who are responsive to their populations and who are not corrupt.

The starting point for external legitimacy is internal legitimacy. Unless there is serious, autonomously driven, and conscientious reform in sub-Saharan Africa, the conditions to have some independent influence over globalization will not emerge. This reform must be internally driven; if it is not, it will merely be seen as another example of Africans' having to conform to alien norms. Indeed, according to a young woman from Burundi, democratization was yet another aspect of nefarious globaliza-tion. "For me, really, globalization ... I consider it like the law of the jungle ... It's the law of the strongest ... 'You come with me into democracy, or you don't come; if you don't follow, you go to the side, and at the side, you know what that means.' That's the threat that hovers over you" (Inter-viewee no. 57, Sainte-Anne-de-Bellevue, Quebec, 27 June 2002). Although she herself had been a victim of political violence, this young woman did not view democracy as something Burundi needed but as something imposed by outsiders. To her, political reform, like economic reform, was part of the supraterritorial airborne disease of globalization.

To ground this airborne disease and turn it from an evil to a benefit requires institutional changes that only Africans can guide. Good governance, the rule of law, democracy, and human rights are not simply aspects of life that protect individuals from arbitrary rule: they also create the stable, reliable conditions that attract long-term investment. And, conversely, they create the conditions that will permit Africans to speak out and organize politically when — as often happens — foreign investors want to exploit their labour and resources without any responsibilities to the continent. As the editors of this volume state in the Introduction, "there is a need to take far more seriously twentieth-century liberal values, especially ... [the] rule of law, democracy, and other expressions of empowerment and self-rule." These are essential underlying conditions for the deliberative democracy that Williams and the editors discuss in this volume.

Recognizing this position, heads of state in Africa in 2002 established a new African Union (AU), which is a successor to the Organization of African Unity (OAU). The OAU had been preoccupied above all with anti-colonialism, anti-apartheid agitation, and the preservation of state sovereignty. By contrast, the AU promotes the universal values of democracy and human rights that earlier postcolonial generations of African leaders often rejected as Western impositions. Article 4(m) of the union's Constitutive Act specifies that the union shall function in accordance with "respect for democratic principles, human rights, the rule of law and good governance."

It is not feasible, then, for Africans to "autonomously" derive a set of rules for governance that differ from international standards. They cannot be independent authors of law in an already globalized world. Rather, Africa must become a stronger player in the international system, with a greater capacity to exercise continental agency. It must become an active part of the community that justifies and accepts the shared rule of international law and international economic regulation. Legitimacy of both the world economic system and African governments will result only from an autonomous, continent-driven decision to enter the world markets and adhere to world norms of good governance, human rights, and the rule of law. To resist heteronomy — rule by others — requires adherence to standards that others adopted earlier but that African individuals and states realize will also benefit them. The African leaders who have established the new AU have come to the independent decision that democracy is the best form of governance and that individual human rights — the basis for individual autonomy — are worth promoting.

Among our respondents there was some sense that democratization was occurring in their various states. Many were human rights activists in countries where, even ten years earlier, activism would have meant torture, prison, or death. In these countries there was some room for independent civil society and non-governmental organizations by 2002. In the early twenty-first century, many African governments were gaining internal legitimacy. But — at least in the eyes of our respondents — that legitimacy was not yet so extensive as to generate a sense of confidence that African leaders could productively represent their citizens in international forums. International institutions and the international economy appeared to be still stacked against sub-Saharan Africa.

Steven Bernstein (2004, 13), the co-editor of this volume, states, "Critical scholarship ... attacks the new focus on global governance for obfuscating a history of domination by Western states and powerful economic classes, acting at times through international institutions to further legitimate their interests." Most of the African individuals we interviewed would agree with this critical scholarship. The notion of African autonomy, in particular, seems a dream in the era of globalization. There is little space for individual autonomy in societies so buffeted by AIDS as many African countries are today. Orphaned children raising their younger siblings, great-grandmothers raising great-grandchildren are not exercising autonomy (Bicego, Rutstein, and Johnson 2003; Jacques 1999). AIDS is not merely a natural phenomenon: it spreads as rapidly as it does because of the social conditions in which Africans live, and those conditions are a consequence of past history and current politics and economics. Nor are the women forced into prostitution, the men forced underground into mines, or those hiding in containers on ships bound for Europe exercising their individual autonomy. Autonomy is exercised freely: to choose between starvation and prostitution or starvation and suffocation in a cargo container is not autonomy.

If Kant's (1999, 496) categorical imperative is "Act only according to that maxim whereby you can at the same time will that it should become a universal law," then it would seem that the West does not adhere to Kantian principles. In the view of most of our respondents, the West exploits others:

256

it does not expect others to exploit it in return. Although the West enjoys autonomy, it expects others to be content with heteronomy. The West expects Africa to fulfill its duties, but it does not fulfill its own. In this world of exploitation, respect goes to the strong not to the moral. Dignity is ascribed to Africans who suffer in silence, while Westerners, devoid of any concept of duties to others, enjoy the perquisites of wealth and power. Kant's eighteenth-century discussion of morality remains merely a philosophical conceit, one that is irrelevant to the relentless exploitation caused by global political and economic relations.

Is there, then, any room for continental African autonomy? Can continental autonomy result in some degree of national control over economics and politics? Do the other continental, regional, and national actors engaged in global governance listen to African voices? Are they capable of empathic reactions to Africans? Our interviews suggest that there is very little, if any, common life world (Bernstein 2004, in reference to Habermas's concept) between even elite Africans and the Westerners who run the international show on which empathic social relations could be built. Some of the people we interviewed asked, in effect, "Am I not human?" This was Shylock's question four centuries ago in Europe (Shakespeare 2003, 122). Then, the Jews were the merely tolerated, often excluded, and frequently murdered Other. Now, it seems, the West barely tolerates Africans, systematically excludes them from international governance, and leaves them without a thought to murder one another.

The Africans we spoke with saw themselves as outsiders in a global process controlled by the West. As individuals, nations, or a continent, they had no autonomous effect on globalization or on globalization's effects on them. They did not enjoy respect or dignity in the world community. Indeed, if such a global community existed at all, it systematically, if not intentionally, excluded Africa and Africans from its realm of concern.

A Kenyan told us, "We feel that there is a moral responsibility that should rest on the West to pursue more equitable, more humane ... economic policies than those that tend to dominate the economies of the Third World ... where in the final analysis you find that all the benefit comes to the West and very little ... goes to African countries" (Interviewee no. 32, Sainte-Anne-de-Bellevue, Quebec, 16 June 2003). Many Western philosophers and ethicists would agree with him (Pogge 2002), as would many Western activists. Yet Africans remain "sitting on gold and digging for food." While Africans starve, their resources, it appears, are exploited by the West. Globalization does not open up possibilities for Africans. It is an airborne disease. Knowing no boundaries, this disease, our respondents believed, causes deep harm in Africa. That the reality might be quite different, and globalization might have the potential to contribute to economic growth in Africa, seemed too overwhelmingly unlikely to be imagined.

chapter 12   **The World Trade Organization: System under Stress**

Sylvia Ostry

IN THE POSTWAR GOLDEN decades, the 1950s and 1960s, trade issues hardly made headlines. The GATT (the General Agreement on Tariffs and Trade) was described even by policy wonks as "a better soporific than hot milk" and was known as "the General Agreement to Talk and Talk." By the end of the 1990s, the World Trade Organization (WTO), the institution created by the Uruguay Round negotiations, had become a magnet for dissent. The street theatre of the Seattle ministerial meeting in 1999 was not only big news on television, the debacle that emerged as the meeting collapsed fed newspapers around the world (Blackhurst 2001).

There are many reasons for the transformative change in the ambience of trade policy. Certainly, economic globalization — the deepening integration of countries through trade, financial flows, investment, and the revolution in information and communications technology (ICT) — has had and continues to have an ongoing effect on government policy space and on individuals' perception of government. The role of the mass media and the Internet in penetrating public awareness is of increasing importance. Because of the perceived role of intergovernmental organizations (IGOs) in global policy making, issues such as legitimacy and governance are now debated vigorously. There are no agreed upon definitions of *legitimacy* for IGOs, and there are seemingly endless proposals for good governance (or goo-goo, as it was called by the activist movement in the nineteenth century). When it comes to the WTO, however, a number of reform proposals have been made that have both procedural and substantive aspects

(Coicaud and Heiskanen 2001; Petersmann 2003; McGivern 2004; Narlikar 2006; Power et al. 2001; Woods 1999). Rather than entering into the definitional and theoretical morass, this chapter focuses on reform proposals to enhance both the substantive and procedural legitimacy of the WTO.

To place this approach in context, I begin with a brief account of the radical systemic change that resulted from the Uruguay Round. This new global trading system was the catalyst for a good deal of the outcry over legitimacy and transparency. The question of fairness, as a distributive dimension of legitimacy, is also explored. On the procedural side, the question of transparency has been insistently proposed as an important requirement to reduce the legitimacy deficit of the trade institution. Reform proposals are suggested for both of these features of the WTO. Finally, the conclusion presents a brief tour d'horizon of the challenges confronting the system in a shifting and changing global landscape.

The Uruguay Round Legacy

The Uruguay Round was the eighth negotiation held in the context of the GATT, which came into force on 1 January 1948 as part of the postwar international economic architecture. The primary mission of the GATT was to reduce or eliminate the border barriers to trade that had been erected in the 1930s and contributed to the Great Depression and its disastrous consequences. The GATT worked very well through the concept of reciprocity (denounced as mercantilist by trade purists) and because of rules and other arrangements to buffer or create an interface between the international objective of sustained liberalization and the objectives of domestic policy stability. This effective paradigm, termed *embedded liberalism* (Ruggie 1982), was also aided by the Cold War and the virtual exclusion of agriculture (by a US waiver and the near-sacrosanct European Common Agricultural Policy). From the 1960s on, the successive negotiating rounds were essentially managed by the European Community (EC) and the United States, with a little help from industrialized friends. The developing countries were largely ignored as players (although this began to change in the 1970s, largely as a consequence of the Organization of Petroleum Export Countries [OPEC] oil shock).

The Uruguay Round was a watershed in the evolution of the system. Agriculture was at the centre of negotiations as US exports to the EC diminished and the EC's heavily subsidized exports flourished and even penetrated the US market. A US call for negotiations started in 1981 but was stalled by the endless foot dragging of the EC, which was aided by a small group of developing countries, led by Brazil and India, that was strongly opposed to the so-called new issues of services, intellectual property, and investment demanded by the United States. The Uruguay Round was finally launched in September 1986 at Punte del Este, Uruguay. It concluded in December 1994, four years beyond the target date agreed on at the launch.

The negotiations were almost as tortuous as the launch. The grand bargain, as I have termed it, was completely different from old-time GATT reciprocity (Ostry 1990, 1997, 2002). It was essentially an implicit deal: the opening of Organisation for Economic Co-operation and Development (OECD) markets to agriculture and labour-intensive manufactured goods, especially textiles and clothing, in exchange for inclusion in the trading system of services, intellectual property, and (albeit to a lesser extent than originally demanded) investment. The deal also entailed, at virtually the last minute, the creation of a new institution, the WTO, which had the strongest dispute settlement mechanism in the history of international law and virtually no executive or legislative authority.

The grand bargain turned out to be a bum deal. There was far less opening in agriculture than expected, and the reduction of restrictions on textiles and clothing was backloaded and more than offset by the impact of China. The South side of the deal would require a major institutional upgrading and change in the infrastructure of most Southern countries, changes that took time and cost money. The new issues did not involve border barriers but domestic regulatory and legal systems. The barriers to access for service providers stemmed from laws, administrative action, or regulations. The intellectual property inclusion covered comprehensive standards for domestic laws and detailed provisions for enforcing corporate property rights. Social regulation that covers product standards and health and safety involves sophisticated administrative procedures law as well as highly trained scientific human resources. Implementation, thus, involves considerable investment on the part of developing countries with uncertain medium-term results. In effect, the trading system was transformed from the negative regulation of the GATT (what governments must not do) to positive regulation (what governments must do).

It is important to note that the inclusion of the new issues in the Uruguay Round was a US initiative, and this policy agenda was largely driven by US multinational enterprises (MNEs). These corporations made it clear to the government that without a fundamental rebalancing of the

GATT they would not continue to support a multilateral policy but would prefer a bilateral or regional track. But they did not simply talk the talk; they also walked the walk, organizing business coalitions in support of services and intellectual property in Europe and Japan as well as some smaller OECD countries. The activism paid off, and it is fair to say that MNEs in the United States played a key — perhaps even *the* key — role in establishing the new global trading system. This conclusion merits a brief digression (Drahos and Braithwaite 2004).

In the United States, the private-sector advisory process established in the 1970s for the Tokyo Round of multilateral trade negotiations was designed to cope with or broker interest-group pressures acting on Congress. But in the Uruguay Round, its impact spread well beyond its original objective. The US service sectors were world leaders, and the same was true in investment and technology. American MNEs controlled 40 percent of the world's stock of foreign investment at the outset of the 1980s, and the US technology balance of payments was well over $6 billion, while every other OECD country was in deficit. This was high-stakes poker, and the MNEs launched the game. The US Advisory Committee for Trade Policy and Negotiations, in cooperation with other US business groups, undertook the task of convincing European and Japanese corporations to lobby for the new issues. In the services sector, US activism extended well beyond these two trading powers. Nine country service coalitions were organized and met regularly with the GATT Secretariat. In the case of intellectual property, the US group, called the Intellectual Property Rights Committee — working through the principal corporate interest groups, the Union of Industries of the European Community and the Keidanren in Japan — persuaded their counterparts to table, in Geneva in 1988, a detailed trilateral proposal for an intellectual property agreement drafted by US legal experts. This proposal bore a remarkable resemblance to what eventually came out of the Uruguay Round. The strategic skills of the US MNEs were aided by the role of the US government. A multi-track policy, including NAFTA, helped by locking in high standards and undermining Latin American cohesion in opposition to the anticipated Agreement on Trade-Related Aspects of Intellectual Property Rights (TRIPS). Even more effective was the use of unilateralism in the form of a new special section 301 of the 1988 Trade and Competitiveness Act, which was targeted at developing countries with "inadequate" intellectual property standards and enforcement procedures. In Brazil the section 301 gambit worked, and so India was left isolated.

The Uruguay Round consisted of a single undertaking because of some clever legalistic juggling by the United States and the EC in the end game.[1] There were no "escape hatches" for the Southern countries: it was a take it or leave it deal. So they took it. But it is safe to say now that they did so without a full comprehension of the profoundly transformative nature of the new system, to say nothing about the bum deal. As one of the Southern participants was reported to have said, "TRIPS was part of a package in which we got agriculture" (Drahos and Braithwaite 2004, 1).

There were two significant unintended consequences of the Uruguay Round. The rise in profile of the MNEs because of their crucial role in securing inclusion of the new issues served as a catalyst for activist non-governmental organizations (NGOs) that launched the anti-corporate globalization movement. Equally important and not unrelated, the Uruguay Round left a serious North-South divide in the WTO. Although the South is hardly homogeneous, there is a broad consensus that the outcome was seriously unbalanced. A key feature of this aspect of the systemic transformation is asymmetry.

Asymmetry

The definition of *fairness* in the literature on international institutions remains contested (Coicaud and Heiskanen 2001; Petersmann 2003; Franck 1995; McGivern 2004; Narlikar 2006; Power et al. 2001; Woods 1999). Most analysts would probably agree that the distributive aspects of outcomes should be included in a concept of substantive legitimacy. Although the idea of equity (insofar as it is included in WTO rules, it relates to special and differential treatment for developing countries) is both weak and ambiguous, the concept of systemic asymmetry has been completely ignored. Perhaps even more to the point, could the incomprehension of many negotiators (not just Southern) of the full implications of the negotiating outcome perhaps be considered as somewhat a lack of legitimacy? But that notion is a bit sweeping, so let us consider asymmetry per se. Two aspects are worth considering.

Complexity

The member countries of the WTO vary widely in power. Power is linked to autonomy, which in this volume is understood to combine the availability of choice with the capacity to act. The power of the United States was unique in the postwar years when the GATT was created, so the autonomy of the other members of the "club" that managed the system was, for the most part, deferred to the US hegemon, and all went well accordingly. In contrast, the WTO houses a very different system that can be described in many different ways, but the word *complexity* is quite appropriate. The need for advanced and sophisticated knowledge is essential. Complexity requires knowledge, and knowledge enhances power and, therefore, autonomy. Already strong states become stronger in the WTO because of their store of knowledge; the weak become even weaker because of their poverty of knowledge. The weak lack autonomy in any system, but in the WTO system complexity reinforces asymmetry and, thus, diminishes autonomy. Maybe the concept of the poverty trap should be replaced with that of the knowledge trap.

A number of case studies by the World Bank demonstrate both the capacity deficit in poor countries and the heavy costs of implementation (Finger and Schuler 2000; Hoekman 2002). There was very little participation by the African countries in the Uruguay Round because of the lack of secretariats in Geneva delegations and the lack of coordination and expertise at home. The situation in Geneva has not improved very much, as Table 12.1 demonstrates. It has been estimated that the WTO councils, committees, working parties, and so on involve over twenty-eight hundred meetings per year — an impossible number for the poorer countries to attend. Worse, the WTO delegates of poorer states in Geneva often have to cover the United Nations organizations as well as the WTO. In addition, there is still serious weakness in domestic coordination mechanisms among a number of ministries, and this institutional deficiency is not confined to the poorest countries but affects many developing and transition economies (Shaffer 2006; Ablin and Bouzas 2002). Finally, there is little if any coordination between Geneva officials and home country governments. The lack of resources and capabilities in poor countries virtually eliminates policy choice and participation.

Because the poorest countries are primarily dependent on agriculture, and often on only a few commodities, the disappointing results of the Uruguay Round in agriculture have ensured that the form of the Agreement on Agriculture remains at the centre of the Doha agenda. But what is equally important and far less studied is the impact of the Agreement on Sanitary and Phytosanitary Measures (the SPS Agreement). Case studies from the World Bank provide incredible examples of the imposition of

Table 12.1: African countries with permanent missions at the UN office in Geneva, as of April 2005

Country	WTO delegates	WTO delegates not in UN directory
Angola	4	–
Benin	8	–
Botswana	8	–
Burkina Faso	4	–
Burundi	2	–
Cameroon	7	1
Chad*	4	4
Central African Republic	–	–
Congo	4	–
Côte d'Ivoire	5	–
Democratic Republic of Congo	4	2
Djibouti*	1	1
Gabon	5	–
Gambia	–	–
Ghana	3	–
Guinea	3	–
Guinea-Bissau	–	–
Kenya	4	–
Lesotho	4	1
Madagascar	3	–
Malawi	–	–
Mali	3	–
Mauritania	3	–
Mauritius	7	–
Mozambique	2	–
Namibia	1	–
Niger	–	–
Nigeria	7	7
Rwanda	2	–
Senegal	5	–
Sierra Leone	–	–
South Africa	9	–
Swaziland	–	–
Tanzania	9	–
Togo	–	–
Uganda	4	–
Zambia	8	–
Zimbabwe	8	–

* No UN delegation list was found for these countries.
Sources: WTO directory (circa May 2005) and "Missions Permanentes auprès des Nations Unies à Genève," no. 96, Nations-Unies, Genève, avril 2005.

new standards for alleged (minor) health reasons that cut African exports of nuts and grains by 60 percent (UN Millennium Project 2005, 146-65; Zarrilli 1999).[2] The poor countries play no role in the setting of international standards, which takes place at the Codex Alimentarius Commission, because, lacking both monetary and human resources, they cannot participate. So standards developed by a limited number of countries can get the status of international standards.

The situation is likely to worsen as developed countries increase regulation for high valued-added products and as large multinational buyers increasingly dominate the retail market. "Wal-martization" of standards may be the new wave, and the small and medium enterprises in poor countries, lacking information about export markets, are unable to compete. The gap between domestic and international regulation is widening. The need to reform agriculture by moving up the value-added scale would require major changes in the institutional infrastructures of many countries. The cost would be high, and the poor countries do not have the resources. Similar problems exist in the Technical Barriers to Trade Agreement (TBT), which covers trade in goods. Although both the TBT and the SPS Agreement were supposed to provide technical assistance, this help has been inadequate, and, in any case, significant infrastructure investment is required. Once again, however, some case studies demonstrate that in places where investment in technology and institutional building were undertaken, successful export-driven growth is feasible (UN Millennium Project 2005, chap. 10; Anderson, Martin, and van der Mensbrugghe 2005).

These are but a few examples of how the complexity of the global trading system requires more than trade policy if the poor countries are to be integrated fully into it. Although the Uruguay Round agreements included some recognition of the need for technical assistance, and the Doha Development Agenda is littered with references to technical assistance and capacity building, it has been repeatedly emphasized that the true jewel in the crown was the creation of the WTO and the Dispute Settlement Understanding. For the first time in international law, a truly effective institutional constraint on the powerful has been achieved. But is the increased legalization a welcome offset to asymmetry? Not exactly.

Legalization

The WTO was not part of the Uruguay Round agenda. The Canadian proposal was not put forward until April 1990. It was soon endorsed by the

European Union (which had opposed stronger dispute settlement in the Tokyo Round) because of growing concern about US unilateralism. It was deemed a useful device for the constraint of power. The United States, dubious about the quality of legal expertise in the GATT Secretariat, insisted on the creation of an appellate body (to review the legal aspects of panel reports). So a paradigm shift took place, which Professor Weiler calls "the juridification of the process, including not only the rule of law but the rule of lawyers" (Weiler 2000). And since it is said that although the United States has only 4 percent of the world's population, it has 50 percent of the world's lawyers, the legal culture of the WTO is, by and large, American. One could argue that the most important export of the United States has been its legal system: transparent, contentious, and litigious. And, of course, it is based on the common law, which often differs from European systems. It is no coincidence — however amusing — that after the Multilateral Agreement on Investment was killed at the OECD, a memorandum from the French negotiators pointed out that it would be very important for the French universities to begin teaching experts in "le droit économique international qui est encore très largement anglo-saxon" (Lalumière, Landua, and Glimet 1998).

Be that as it may, the main focus of concern in the context of asymmetry is whether the paradigm shift of juridification benefits the poorest countries. It is not possible to get data on the number of legal experts in the Geneva missions or domestic ministries. But one can safely assume that the numbers are very small or even non-existent when it comes to these countries. And, as may be seen from Table 12.2, there is no participation as complainant or respondent by any of the poor African countries. This is asymmetry writ large. Further analysis as to the reasons for this opt-out is worthy of a brief review.

There have been a number of studies on dispute settlement and the poorest countries in the WTO, many of which were sponsored by the World Bank (Bagwell, Mavroidis, and Staigler 2004; Bown and Hoekman 2005a; Hoekman and Mavroidis 1999; Horn and Mavroidis 1999; Shaffer 2006). Although much more remains to be done, the research clearly documents the absence of African countries in this essential crown jewel of the trading system. What accounts for the mystery of the missing cases (Bown and Hoekman 2005a, 2005b)?[3]

One clear reason is very simple and straightforward — lack of money. The absence of government legal services either at home or in Geneva would require hiring private lawyers, which is far too expensive. A

Table 12.2: Participation in WTO dispute settlement cases (1995-2005)

Appearances as complainant		Appearances as respondent	
Complainant	Number of disputes	Respondent	Number of disputes
United States	79	United States	89
European Community	69	European Community	55
Canada	26	Argentina	17
Brazil	21	India	17
India	16	Japan	14
Mexico	15	Korea·	13
Korea	12	Canada	12
Thailand	11	Mexico	12
Japan	11	Brazil	12
Chile	10	Chile	10
Argentina	9	Australia	9
Australia	7	Turkey	7
Honduras	6	Egypt	4
New Zealand	6	Peru	4
Guatemala	5	Philippines	4
Hungary	5	Ecuador	3
Philippines	4	Belgium	3
Switzerland	4	Ireland	3
Colombia	4	Belgium	3
Poland	3	Venezuela	2
Indonesia	3	South Africa	2
Costa Rica	3	Romania	2
Pakistan	3	Pakistan	2
Turkey	2	Slovak Republic	2
Ecuador	2	Dominican Republic	2
Peru	2	France	2
Pakistan	2	Czech Republic	2
Norway	2	Trinidad and Tobago	2
China	1	Nicaragua	2
Separate Customs Territory of Taiwan, Penghu, Kinmen & Matsu	1	Malaysia	1
Antigua and Barbuda	1	Croatia	1
Bangladesh	1	Slovakia	1
Nicaragua	1	Uruguay	1
Chinese Taipei	1	Greece	1
Czech Republic	1	Netherlands	1
Sri Lanka	1	Panama	1
Hong Kong	1	Thailand	1
Uruguay	1	China	1
Venezuela	1	Sweden	1
Singapore	1	Denmark	1
		United Kingdom	1
		Portugal	1
		Poland	1

Source: World Trade Organization, Dispute Settlement Gateway, "Disputes, chronologically," World Trade Organization, http://www.wto.org/english/tratop_e/dispu_e/dispu_e.htm.

conservative estimate of attorney fees in trade litigation runs from around $90,000 to $250,000, depending on the complexity of the case, plus another $100,000 to $200,000 for data collection, economic analysis, travel, administrative assistance, and so on (Bown and Hoekman 2005a). An Advisory Centre on WTO Law (ACWL) was established in December 1999 and entered into force in July 2001 to provide some legal assistance for poor countries. It requires a membership fee based on per capita income and share of world trade. It is funded mainly by European governments and the Canadian government. The United States refused to join or to provide funding. While the ACWL is certainly a welcome initiative, it will require further funding and coordination with enterprises and governments in developing countries and the further development of capabilities in economic research (Shaffer 2006). The role of sophisticated econometric research and economic evidence in WTO dispute settlement is another example of the reinforcement of power by complexity in the mechanism designed to constrain power.[4] And it does not end there. For example, a prominent Washington-based law firm states on its website that its specialty involves advising "numerous governments and companies in over 175 WTO disputes on intellectual property, government procurement, subsidy, trade, remedy, environment, taxation, telecommunication, and investment matters." It is great for business since the dispute settlement mechanism of the WTO is the supreme court of international tribunals (Bown and Hoekman 2005a).

But the cost side of the cost-benefit model for dispute participation often includes more than money or legal service subsidies. Political costs — threats by richer countries to reduce development aid or remove trade preferences — may also be very powerful deterrents to initiating a WTO dispute. An example of political deterrence is provided by a former US trade official who argued in an African capital that "the US might withdraw food aid were the country's Geneva representatives to press a WTO complaint" (Shaffer 2006).

Another clue to solving the missing cases issue concerns the WTO's institutional arrangements. The WTO rules are self-enforcing. Retaliation (imposition of countermeasures) is, in theory, a means to induce implementation of obligations. The threat of retaliation by a poor or small country, however, means nothing to most OECD countries. So, it is argued, poor countries are increasingly skeptical about "assured" market access or other rights. Various ideas are being floated concerning this conundrum, but one proposed recently by Mexico suggests that countermeasures should be allowed to be auctioned (Bagwell, Mavroidis, and Staigler 2004). This proposal is not likely to be accepted by WTO members, but it certainly highlights the problem that small and poor developing countries have in countervailing fundamental asymmetry. And, one hopes, it will stimulate more research on a multilateral approach to enforcement for poor countries.

It is not only reform of the dispute settlement arrangements that will be required. The missing cases mystery is one part of what Rhoda E. Howard-Hassmann (this volume) rightly calls "missing Africa." Rhetoric about Millennium Development Goals is hardly the end of the story. The issue of asymmetry — or "inequity" in street parlance — must receive increasing attention. I shall return to the question of reform options to begin to tackle asymmetry, but I first want to consider another feature of the WTO's legitimacy — the demand by increasing numbers of NGOs and others for greater transparency. Transparency can be viewed as one key aspect of procedural legitimacy.

Transparency

The impact of global civil society on the WTO is a matter of ongoing debate. But there is little question that, with the ICT revolution, the NGOs have made the market for policy ideas and agendas contestable. Their influence goes well beyond the mobilization of protests at meetings or the capture of the moral high ground on disease. Less visible, but over the longer run very significant, is their repeated and insistent demand for more transparency.

In WTOese there are two kinds of transparency: internal and external. On the internal front, the main and increasingly contentious issue involves negotiating arrangements for ministerial meetings that involve the exclusion of many member countries (the importance of the so-called Green Room). But the NGOs have been most active with respect to external transparency, which comprises three main requests: more access to WTO documents, more participation in WTO activities such as committee and ministerial meetings, and the right to observer status and to present *amicus curiae* briefs before dispute panels and the appellate body.

The WTO has made considerable progress in providing information speedily and effectively on its website and through informal briefings. It has allowed NGO representatives to attend parts of ministerial meetings, has sponsored public symposia on trade and environment issues, and, in the case of the Committee on Trade and Environment, has engaged civil society in discussions (Shaffer 2001). But all these incremental developments have been opposed by many developing countries. The de-restriction of documents took four years of gridlocked negotiations, and the policy passed with restrictions. And far more contentious has been the request to open up the dispute settlements to amicus curiae briefs. But a dispute panel recently decided to allow closed-circuit television cameras into the courtroom. The three parties — Europe, the United States, and Canada — agreed to try it as an experiment, perhaps in the hope of establishing a precedent (Esserman and Howse 2005).

As noted earlier, there have been a number of proposals for WTO reform in the years since the Seattle conference.[5] The issue of transparency and participation at the national level has only been raised by a coalition of NGOs once, just before Doha, in October 2001. There was no response, and a similar silence greeted a US proposal after Seattle (Ostry 2004). A review of recent developments in other international institutions such as the OECD, the World Bank, and the United Nations Economic Commission for Europe all stress the importance of engaging citizens in policy making or what is often called the ownership of policy (ibid.). Furthermore, a recent UN report of the Panel of Eminent Persons on United Nations Civil Society Relations underlines the need to "emphasize and highlight the country level" (United Nations, General Assembly 2005, 41). Indeed, an entire school of international law based on interactional theory points out that "law is persuasive when it is perceived as legitimate by most actors and legitimacy rests on inclusive processes [that] reinforce the commitments of participants in the system" (Burnnée and Toope 2000, 53). In a report to the Trilateral Commission called *The "Democracy Deficit" in the Global Economy: Enhancing the Legitimacy and Accountability of Global Institutions,* one of the authors, Joseph Nye Jr., suggests it might be a good idea to start at the national level (Nye et al. 2003). The interlinking of the national and the global is an ongoing process, and policy spillover is hardly surprising, although it has not yet reached the WTO. So maybe a small push could help.

Some Proposals for WTO Reform to Enhance Legitimacy

Transparency and Participation

The OECD's pioneering work was, in part, a response to a general decline in trust in government in all OECD countries since the 1970s (Ostry 2003;

Inglehart 1999). The data for this assertion stem mainly from the World Values Survey of the University of Michigan. There are many different views on the reasons for this worrisome phenomenon, and no doubt different factors are operative in different countries. But one response, as noted above, has been to foster ownership of the policy process by increasing information, consultation, and active participation by a wide range of stakeholders. A set of guiding principles was enunciated, and, while not binding (being a form of "soft law"), it was hoped that they would encourage a more open and participatory form of governance (OECD 2001). It is most intriguing (and not coincidental) that the current ruling party in Brazil pioneered participatory policy making in the province of Porto Allegro — the host for the newest innovation in global civil society, the Global Social Forum (Baiocchi 2004).

While it was endorsed enthusiastically by many WTO members, there is one mechanism in the WTO that lends itself to external transparency. This is the Trade Policy Review Mechanism (TPRM).

One of the original negotiating groups in the Uruguay Round was the Functioning of the GATT System. It was designed to enhance the effectiveness of the domestic policy-making process through informed public understanding (i.e., transparency). Section B spells it out: "Members recognize the inherent value of domestic transparency of government decision-making on trade policy matters for both Members' economies and the multilateral trading system, and agree to encourage and promote greater transparency within their own systems, acknowledging that the implementation of domestic transparency must be on a voluntary basis and take account of each Member's legal and political systems" (GATT 2004, 434).

To underline that the TPRM is voluntary and flexible in subject matter, the declaration of objectives states in section A that "it is not intended to serve as a basis for the enforcement of specific obligations under the Agreements or for dispute settlement procedures, or to impose new policy commitments on Members" (GATT 2004, 434).

The TPRM's origins and objectives clearly embrace the policy-making process. The WTO Secretariat is already seriously overburdened, so it might be necessary for the early volunteers in the process to ante up some funding. If a number of developing countries became involved, the issue of more permanent funding would have to be faced since there would be capacity-building and technical-assistance requirements. But these latter costs should clearly come under the arrangements agreed to at Doha on capacity building. Enhancing capacity to improve and sustain a more transparent trade policy process sounds like a good investment. It is hardly a new idea. In the 1970s, during the Tokyo Round, a US official remarked to an academic researcher that the advisory committees established under the 1974 Trade Act were working extremely well because "when you let a dog piss all over a fire hydrant he thinks he owns it" (Winham 1986). That's a rather less felicitous version of today's concept of ownership. So why not give it a try? The TPRM reports could be published, and a feedback mechanism would begin to operate. Transparency at the domestic level would create pressure for more information from Geneva. And information about one country could encourage stakeholders (especially NGOs) to pressure their governments to participate.

Moreover, by sharing information on national processes, stakeholders in many countries without adequate technical or financial resources — like small and medium enterprises — could gain useful information on market opportunities. The policy process should be evolutionary, reflecting systemic changes and changes in the policy environment. And, of course, although benefits will accrue from a more participatory process, there are also costs. There are costs for governments in terms of time, expertise, and financial resources, and there are significant differences in resources among stakeholders. This is another facet of asymmetry that is ignored. The launch of this pilot project could serve as a catalyst for a very useful discussion about basic policy issues, including capacity building and other aspects of asymmetry.

Asymmetry and International Coherence

One of the intentions of the Uruguay Round was to improve cooperation and coordination among the main international economic institutions. Driven largely by the experience of the wide exchange misalignment of the 1980s and its impact on trade, the euphemism *international coherence* was devised. But little emerged from the objective apart from worthy rhetoric and some subsequent agreements as to who should attend what meetings and when (Ostry 1999, 2001, 374-75).

However, in 1997 a specific project was launched to coordinate trade and poverty reduction in the least developed countries. It was called the Integrated Framework for Trade-Related Technical Assistance (IF) and involved the WTO, the World Bank, the IMF, the United Nations Conference on Trade and Development, the United Nations Development Programme, and the International Trade Commission, as well as a number of bilateral donors. An evaluation of the program in June 2000 was not very encouraging. Lack of clear priorities, an ill-defined governance structure, and low levels of funding were among the problems cited. The heads of the six agencies then decided to revamp the IF. A new evaluation was undertaken in 2004 by the World Bank's Operations Evaluation Department (OED). The results of the very thorough OED analysis, as presented in the executive summary, are worth quoting:

> Despite the restructuring, some of the weaknesses of the original program remain, including insufficient focus on improved trade outcomes rather than on the process alone, and the shortage of resources to meet the mounting demands for technical assistance in developing countries. IF may have contributed to placing trade back on the developing agenda of LDCs [least developed countries] through the joint work of the international agencies. But the objective of fully mainstreaming trade ... calls for holistic, results-based program management processes to achieve improved trade outcomes for developing countries. These need to be combined with on-the-ground action, well-defined roles of partners, and minimum transaction costs, supported by the necessary financial and administrative resources for a program that has now created too many expectations on which it is unable to deliver. (Agarwal and Cutura 2004)

The OED study goes into considerable detail about the problem of the IF, and the message is quite clear: it is a good start, but a great deal more needs to be done. Reading this material can be depressing, but it should not be. As must be underlined again, this is new territory, and policy innovation involves learning by doing, doing well, and often doing not very well. Case studies are data, and the task of absorbing and contextualizing will not yield to a minimalist mathematics model.

One policy option could be based on the IF idea — the project as process. The promotion of international coherence by a specific project for Africa — one that involved the WTO, the World Bank, and the new African institution, the New Partnership for Africa's Development (NEPAD) — that seeks to integrate trade and development fits well into a "redefined" concept of technical assistance and capacity building (especially since the precise meaning of both is rather fuzzy and flexible). Country "ownership" would be paramount, and this project would require funding for both the WTO Secretariat and the physical and intellectual infrastructure of the countries. And some of the problems — governance, for example — may prove to be insurmountable. But whatever the outcome of the Doha Development Agenda, it would be feasible and desirable to launch a genuine (not rhetorical) project to reduce poverty and stimulate development.

But tackling asymmetry is a formidable challenge, and the IF is but one step on a long journey. The construction of the WTO is asymmetrical — it is judicialized, but, with a very small secretariat and a very limited budget (equal to the travel budget of the International Monetary Fund), there is no real executive or legislative power. This comparison with the Bretton Woods twins could be described as lack of coherence writ large. These structural deficiencies greatly exacerbate the rich-poor asymmetries. Not only do the OECD countries have a wide array of research resources, they also have their own well-endowed think tank — the OECD. The substantive scope of the OECD is very broad, and its Secretariat is part of a government network with access to soft power — "the power of information, socialization, persuasion and discussion" (Slaughter 2004a, 27). So the OECD is very effective in securing adherence to rules, fostering changes in rules, and achieving agreement on policies.

There is no policy forum in the WTO. There had been one, the Consultative Group of Eighteen, which was established in 1975 on the recommendation of the Committee of Twenty Finance Ministers following the breakdown of Bretton Woods. The composition of the membership was based on a combination of economic weight, regional representation, and regular rotation. The forum involved senior officials from capitals. The Consultative Group of Eighteen was never officially terminated, but meetings ceased at the end of the 1980s.

Establishing a WTO policy forum would be a great step forward. But it is unlikely to function effectively without an increase in the WTO's research capability. Analytical papers on key issues are needed to launch serious discussions in Geneva and to improve the diffusion of knowledge in national capitals. The basic issues of trade and development need country-specific case studies. There is no agreed upon model — indeed, there is growing dissent. A top priority for the forum should be to undertake a thorough analysis of the unsolved issue of special and differential treatment. The WTO research secretariat would form part of a research or knowledge network linked to other institutions, including, of course, the World Bank as well as academics, NGOs, and business and labour organizations.

The Sutherland Consultative Board has recommended that there be more political involvement of ministers and senior policy makers from capitals in WTO activities and puts forward a number of suggestions, including the establishment of a senior level consultative body — Consultative Group of Eighteen redux (Consultative Board 2004). Obviously, there will be opposition from some countries to these proposals. But the dissenters should be encouraged to consider the alternative — an ongoing erosion and decline of the multilateral, rules-based system.

Finally, the membership of the policy forum will be the most contentious aspect of the proposal. This aspect, of course, is the same issue as the conflict between legitimacy and efficiency in the negotiating modalities — the Green Room syndrome. Although, in theory, the consensus principle that governs the WTO should require that all 152 members (soon to be close to 170) be present in every negotiating group, paralysis by consensus is guaranteed. The reality of the GATT/WTO decision-making rules has been aptly described as "organized hypocrisy in the procedural context" (Steinberg 2002, 342), with the Big Two (the United States and the European Community) running the shop. Green Rooms are essential, regardless of whether they are informal or formal. But maybe the organized hypocrisy worked in the past because of the transatlantic alliances. What happens with the ongoing shift in the balance of power — the new geography?

Conclusion

The consensus on the postwar paradigm of embedded liberalism was, in fact, not really much of a consensus. The British (and, later, most Europeans) were committed to Keynesianism: the creation of full employment and the welfare state. The United States was far less committed. There was no government-constructed "social contract," as in the UK's Beveridge Plan. Although an Employment Act was passed in 1946 in the United States, the Republican-dominated Congress ensured that the role of the Council of Economic Advisers was limited. The European social compact involved an expanded role for the state, which was alien to the historical and deeply held conception of the government's role in the United States. (American support for the GATT stemmed largely from the United States' investment abroad and its leading position in the world economy [Ostry 1997;

Ball and Bellamy 2003].) These transatlantic differences have not disappeared; in fact, they may have widened because they reflect deep-seated historical and cultural legacies. In many European countries, a renegotiation of the social contract is ongoing and promises to be a long and difficult process — most prominently in France and Germany, which are hardly marginal players in trade issues.

But of equal if not greater significance is the ongoing shift in the balance of power engendered by the rise of China and India. The new geography, as it has been called, first became visible in a striking fashion at the WTO ministerial meeting in Cancun in September 2003. The two new coalitions of Southern countries — the G20 (led by Brazil, India, and China and including a number of Latin American countries and South Africa) and the G90 (a coalition of the poorest countries, mainly from Africa) — have continued to play a role in the ongoing Doha negotiations. The G20 has been a major player in agriculture, and both coalitions have managed to withstand strong threats and pressure from the United States and Europe. There have been Southern coalitions before, of course, most notably the G77 during the 1970s. But the demand for a New International Economic Order (NIEO) failed, and the 1980s debt crisis ushered in the infamous Decade of Despair. The comparison between these new coalitions (especially the G20) and the G77 is not very compelling. The demand for a NIEO reflected the commodity power of OPEC. The new geography involves a genuine transfer of power within the international system. The comparison is often made with the rise of Germany in nineteenth-century Europe. As Henry Kissinger has argued in a recent article, however, "the rise of China as a potential superpower is of even greater historical significance, marking as it does a shift in the centre of gravity of world affairs from the Atlantic to the Pacific" (Kissinger 2004, 32). Compare Kissinger's statement with the executive summary statement of the National Intelligence Council's report, *Mapping the Global Future:* "The likely emergence of China and India, as well as others, as new major global players — similar to the advent of a united Germany in the nineteenth century and a powerful United States in the early twentieth century — will transform the geopolitical landscape, with impacts potentially as dramatic as those in the previous two centuries" (National Intelligence Council 2004, 9).

But the impact of the new geography on the trading system will require careful study. The Doha meeting in Hong Kong at the end of December 2005 avoided another failure, and there was even a press conference of the

G110 (the G90 and G20). But it is not easy to discern any fundamental impact on the shape of the system. It is too early to tell.

Finally, we should not ignore the other actors in the trade policy arena, the NGOs. As mentioned earlier, the 1990s anti-corporate globalization movement was sparked by the WTO, and the enemy that bound the disparate groups together was neoliberalism (usually undefined). And the best (or worst) symbol of neoliberalism was the WTO.

Even before the WTO was established, rulings by the GATT concerning environmental issues in the early 1990s shook mainstream environmental NGOs, and the streets of Geneva and Washington were plastered with posters of a monster Gattzilla. The new slogan was "GATT: Guaranteeing a Toxic Tomorrow." But the concerted attacks on the WTO involved what I call "mobilization networks" whose chief objective is to rally support for dissent at a specific event — a WTO ministerial meeting, for example. There is, of course, no homogeneous set of institutions that constitute global civil society, but the impact of the mobilization of dissent plays an important role in heightening public awareness in our media-centred world. These loose and diverse mobilization coalitions are largely a product of the Internet revolution and, more recently, the spread of mobile phones. Mobilization coalitions are very skilled in dealing with the media, and, indeed, "independent media" have been established as part of the movement. Policy entrepreneurs are springing up everywhere. As is the case for all entrepreneurs who create innovations, there are important feedback loops. An NGO network established at the Rio Summit in 1992 was used by American, Canadian, and Mexican anti-NAFTA advocacy groups, and this experience was vital in mobilizing the fight against the Multilateral Agreement on Investment (MAI) at the OECD. The lessons learned were put to use in preparing for Seattle, and so on. Although the dominant NGOs are from the North because of their ability to raise money and their influence with government, media, and business, links have been built with some Southern NGOs, especially in Latin America and parts of Asia, particularly Korea and India. The Third World Network headquartered in Malaysia and Focus on the Global South in the Philippines are important in fostering the radical wing of the movement, but it is not known what links they have with other NGOs in other countries. And, as was seen in Hong Kong, the Korean peasant movement is now very prominent and is part of a growing worldwide movement (e.g., Via Campesina). Indeed, the expansion of NGOs in low-income countries during the 1990s was greater than in the OECD. It should be stressed, however, that much more research is required to understand or evaluate the civil society movement (see Smith, this volume, for one recent attempt). And this type of research is enormously difficult and time-consuming. So what I am presenting here should be regarded as preliminary and treated with caution.

Coordinating and organizing the demonstrations is the main function of the mobilization networks. Since the members are so diverse, no coherent substantive message has emerged; instead, there is a coherent diagnostic framework (neoliberalism is bad) but no prognostic framework (What is the new global system going to look like?). This absence deserves some exploration.

Global civil society has been described as acephalous or headless. This property is praised by some as an outstanding virtue because it ensures that there can be no hierarchy — that is, everyone is equal. If this sounds like an echo of nineteenth-century anarchism, that's because it is. And it also accounts for the role of the Black Bloc in demonstrations at Prague, Genoa, and Quebec City. But most importantly, it generates a built-in incapacity to generate ideological consensus. And with the increasing violence that culminated in the killing of a protester in Genoa, and with the impact of 9/11, dissent as a brand is seriously tarnished, except, perhaps, in the case of the vigorous anti-war movement. While protests and demonstrations continue, there is now more interest by many mainstream NGOs in dialogue and debate.[6] The World Social Forum that began in Porto Allegre, Brazil, to counter the Davos World Economic Forum has attracted a large and diverse collection of NGOs. It is not a dissent platform, and the event is self-selecting. It may be a forum for seeking consensus — that is, getting a head for the movement — but there has been no sign of success so far. Conflicts remain rife among the diverse groups, and the yearning for a new utopia seems to be alive and well. There is an irresistible desire for romantic journeys, even if the destination cannot be reached. Incremental reform is not very exciting. But it could certainly shore up a system under severe stress.

chapter 13

Governing the Electronic Commons: Globalization, Legitimacy, Autonomy, and the Internet

Leslie A. Pal

THE INTERNET IS ONE of history's great transformative technologies, paralleling and perhaps even eclipsing the impact of radio and TV (see Gorman 2009). No discussion of globalization can ignore the impact of information and communications technology (ICT) as a pre-eminent driver, and the Internet is one of the most important components of these ICTs. If modern globalization is distinguished by simultaneity (e.g., much of the world watching the Beijing Olympics at the same time) and decentralized coordination (e.g., global value chains), it depends almost completely on the computerized codification of information and computerized communications. Here again, the Internet is a key feature. Understanding economic globalization in terms of international currency flows, global outsourcing, or 24/7 global production also relies on the ubiquity of ICTs and the Internet. Even a more culturally oriented definition of globalization as the sledgehammer of the present or the past, of rooted identities in the face of modernity and cosmopolitanism (Archibugi and Held 1995) assumes that a key force is a new communications technology that shatters the barriers of culture and mind.

The Internet is equally important for the evolution of autonomy, both at the individual and the community or state level. For the individual, ICTs and the Internet enhance capacities and increase the space for critical self-reflexivity. They do so in various ways, none of which is new but which in combination define a politically transformative technology. A good example is the surge in popularity of social networking through sites such as

Facebook and the application of social-networking technology (wikis, blogs, and the designation of friends or colleagues in private-sector informational management tools such as Microsoft's SharePoint server). The ability to communicate globally allows a wider exchange of views and ideas. The capacity to easily access limitless amounts of information enhances effectiveness. The ability to collaborate instantly with many others in different places multiplies the functional and the political capacity of individuals. Obviously, access to ICTs is unequal in developed countries and between the North and the South, and some governments restrict access. Nonetheless, the rate of increase in the penetration of Internet and ICT technologies in developing countries is nothing short of astonishing (Internet World Stats 2009).

The autonomy-enhancing effects of the Internet on state and community are more ambiguous. Although it is usually argued that there is a connection between individual autonomy and collective autonomy, when it comes to the Internet and ICTs this connection is unclear. More autonomous citizens do not necessarily mean more compliant ones. As the Introduction to this volume suggests, a more autonomous global civil society may also feel more disenfranchised and frustrated. Indeed, analyses of the Internet's impact on citizenship generally argue that it undermines a sense of territorial loyalty and that by empowering citizens (through their enhanced autonomy) it threatens the conventional legitimacy of government. Another problem is deterritorialization. Globalization, in every era but particularly now, undermines or reorganizes politically charged spatial boundaries and permits their supersession in some instances. Things and symbols (information, currencies) and even people flow more fluidly across borders now than ever before (even if after 9/11 states have tried to move to tighten the security of their borders). But the international system of states assumes defined territories, over which states exercise their sovereignty and secure the community's collective autonomy. With globalization, an increasing number of important issues lie beyond the state, cannot be controlled by it alone, and are not answerable to it. International organizations such as the United Nations, the Organisation for Economic Co-operation and Development (OECD), and the World Trade Organization (WTO) help fill the void as states cooperate at a global level to deal with problems that they cannot deal with alone (see Ostry, this volume). But at the level of citizen identity, the problem has a more brutal impact. Cultural globalization through ICTs may enhance individual autonomy, but it may weaken loyalty to a single political community. This weakening becomes a problem for individual autonomy, since it depends on the autonomy of the political community to make laws for itself, in particular for those services that enable individuals to live and act autonomously (e.g., health care, economic self-sufficiency, education, and civic freedoms). So the same technology that enhances individual autonomy may, in the end, undermine collective autonomy.

Speculation could be endless. Fortunately, this chapter will not address the Internet or ICTs per se. Instead, it focuses on the governance issues surrounding the Internet. While the system seems uncomplicated from a user's perspective, it requires significant regulation and coordination to work. There are technical issues that deal specifically with system operability but also others more clearly political in nature, such as the designation of domain names (e.g., .com or .ca or .cn) and the adjudication of copyright disputes over trademarks (e.g., www.gmsucks.net). Two other factors make Internet governance interesting. The Internet has become so important for communication and for economic development that all governments, as well as international organizations, want a say in how it evolves and functions. The other factor is that unlike telephone technology, which because of early government oversight resolved its governance issues at the start, the Internet initially developed with little government oversight and suddenly exploded globally with the World Wide Web. It became a global common property resource without any international regulator, and its core governance institution was a non-profit corporation named the Internet Corporation for Assigned Names and Numbers (ICANN). ICANN is an unusual experiment in global governance, one that sheds light on globalization and autonomy as well as legitimacy.[1]

A key governance question in the last half-century, when the latest form of globalization has evolved, is how to develop legitimate global institutions (on legitimacy, see especially the chapters by Bernstein and Coleman and by Cooper in this volume). Legitimacy from this perspective cascades upwards — the people of a political community (state) legitimately elect or support their state, which then represents them in global institutions. Although imperfect, this system of representation has traditionally reflected Castoriadis's sense of collective autonomy, in which members of a political community engage in their mutual destiny. But Internet governance faces two key problems. First, the Internet is a common property resource that emerged without state control and became a global medium. Second, because it facilitates one-to-one, one-to-many, and many-to-one communication, the Internet short-circuits the traditional legitimizing mechanisms of institutional autonomy in favour of individual autonomy.

This chapter explores the ruptures, contestations, and conflict over autonomy, legitimacy, and democracy with respect to Internet governance through an analysis of ICANN and the 2005 World Summit on the Information Society (WSIS). Rather than trying to determine whether there is more or less autonomy, I examine the dynamic interplay of institutions, mechanisms, and legitimacy that are framed within the larger global autonomy project. I argue that the story of ICANN and the WSIS illustrates three things about globalization and autonomy.[2] First, the autonomy project for individuals is going global — this conclusion is consistent with analyses of global social movements and networks (Friedman, Hochsteller, and Clark 2005; Bandy and Smith 2005; see Smith in this volume). People are connected, and they wish to exercise their personal sovereignty on a global level. Global institutions and organizations do not necessarily welcome this development, and the clash over participation is a central theme in their quest for legitimacy and democracy. Second, globalization's erosion of state influence and power is not left unchallenged — community autonomy is expressed in the clamour of states to be engaged in Internet governance. As Held and colleagues (1999, 86) point out, "While the concept of sovereignty has by no means been rendered redundant, state sovereignty today jostles for recognition alongside novel forms of political power and sites of authority."

Finally, the saga of Internet governance demonstrates that globalization is stimulating experimental concepts in legitimacy and democracy: should Internet users be considered Internet citizens with the right to vote on its regulations? Can a non-profit corporation take the place of an international organization that represents states? Should interests be represented functionally within a global organization and still be involved in a more traditional democratic process of one person, one vote? ICANN is not a crucible of democracy. Because of its nature, and the properties of the Internet and its evolution, however, it reveals dynamics of globalization and autonomy that are sometimes obscured elsewhere.

As I illustrate with the WSIS, the Internet's nature engages it deeply in globalization and autonomy. Information and communications technologies are the obvious technological foundation for globalization, but the deeper connection is globalization's potential impact on autonomy. Access to knowledge, information, and the consequent enhanced capacity for self-reflexivity is acknowledged as a key element of autonomy. Nussbaum, for example, lists senses, imagination, and thought; practical reason; and affiliation as central human functional capabilities (Nussbaum 2000, 78-80). Castoriadis (1991, 162-63) also highlights self-reflection and critical thought in the dynamic process of achieving heteronomy. Doyal and Gough (1991) similarly define autonomy in terms of flows of information: autonomy is a key human need that depends in part on understanding, cognitive skills, intellectual capacity, and free agency. Increasingly, ICTs are seen as the tools to develop all these capabilities and, thus, are seen as being central to the notion of active, autonomous citizenship as well as to the material bases (the information economy and society) that are required for these capabilities to be actualized. Evidence for this conclusion is that after the 2005 WSIS, which itself linked ICTs to development, the UN established the Global Alliance for Information and Communication Technologies and Development (GAID) to better harness ICTs to the Millennium Development Goals.

A Brief History of Internet Governance

It is important to remember that the Internet as we know it grew to its present state without a conscious design or master plan, even while each incremental step naturally had objectives and rationales.[3]

The four key phases were the original design of a packet-switching mode of data transfer through distributed networks of computers (1960s); the development of TCP/IP as a protocol that allowed different computer networks, whatever their underlying language, to communicate with one another (1970s); the growing use of email as a major form of communication through the nascent Internet (1970s-80s); and, finally, the advent of the World Wide Web (early 1990s).[4]

The only technical point relevant to this chapter is the Domain Name System (DNS). It consists of the usual web addresses that people type into their browsers. The text addresses are unreadable to computers, and so they correspond with unique numeric addresses that computers (or routers, as they are known) can read. The system is hierarchical, with a root directory at the top and subdirectories. Routers move through the hierarchy, beginning in the root with top-level domains, from which subaddresses sprout. This system has to be maintained, especially since new addresses get added every day. It is as though every telephone book in the world had to be dynamically interactive with all others, second by second. Computers can do a lot of this work, but a framework or system — the DNS — has to be designed, maintained, and regulated for it to work.

Starting in the 1960s, the US Department of Defense (Defense Advanced Research Projects Agency) supported the development of a network of networks, which later became known as the Internet. The network was owned largely by the government and managed voluntarily. By the early 1990s, however, the National Science Foundation moved to privatize the management of the network. The foundation contracted AT&T and Network Solutions to provide a single network information centre and to administer the "A" root server. As the Internet became a more popular and commercial medium, various disputes arose over trademarks, Internet architecture, and fees. By 1996 there were symptoms of institutional crisis, and various proposals came forward from international agencies, particularly the International Telecommunications Union (ITU) and the European Union (EU), that effectively sought to wrest control of the root from the United States (Mueller 2002).

The US government intervened and, in 1997, set in motion a process that resulted in a white paper in June 1998 that turned over administration of Internet domain names to a private, non-profit corporation that became ICANN in November 1998. This paper was an official US policy that established private-sector governance as opposed to government control.

It was clear that the creation of ICANN was controversial, but it nonetheless established a vehicle that could be more efficient and representative than the ad hoc mechanisms built in the early years. ICANN has faced growing pains since its establishment, many of them technical. But the core of ICANN's difficulties centred on issues of legitimacy, democracy, and autonomy. One problem of democratic legitimacy was ICANN's relationship with the US government (ICANN is incorporated in the United States, and the root is still "owned" by the United States). This relationship still bothered the EU and the ITU: a global common property resource was being managed by a hybrid global organization accountable to only one government. In addition, there was the balance between commercial and non-commercial interests to consider. The initial ICANN Memorandum of Understanding stated that ICANN would be a participatory organization with global representation. The trick was in designing a governance architecture that would accomplish this goal. ICANN did actually attempt to hold global elections for its at-large members, but that was the last time it attempted to experiment with democratic representation in this way. Finally, ICANN also faced a legitimacy deficit with governments — although there was government representation in ICANN, it was not determinative. This property was unlike the governance of any other international organization that wielded real power over a global resource or asset. In a sense, ICANN was being squeezed by the twin pressures of autonomy — from individuals and civil society organizations who saw themselves as global netizens and who wanted to engage directly in decision making (what Castoriadis refers to as making laws for oneself) and from governments who wanted to more fully exercise the same function but wanted to do so collectively, on behalf of their citizens and communities. It is not surprising that states wanted to enhance their autonomy. That individuals desire participation in a global forum is somewhat more surprising. Nonetheless, it is hard to conceive of an organizational initiative like ICANN, launched when it was, without strong pressures for both types of autonomy.

Coincidentally, with the establishment of ICANN, an international movement was launched through the UN system to deal globally with the information society. Governments by the late 1990s were belatedly aware of the importance of the Internet and ICTs more broadly for both communication and economic development. On the one hand, the pressure came from developing countries (the first proposal for a World Summit on the Information Society, for example, came from Tunisia) that feared that ICTs might add a digital divide to other global inequalities. On the other hand, pressure also came from developed countries that were dissatisfied with the uncoordinated nature of global Internet governance and policy making. Accordingly, at the ITU's Plenipotentiary Conference in Minneapolis in 1998, the government of Tunisia sponsored a resolution that a proposal for a world summit on the information society be submitted to the UN. In 1999 the proposal was accepted, and the ITU was given the lead responsibility for organizing the summit.

Global summits are complicated affairs (Cooper 2004, chap. 1), but the WSIS became especially so once the ITU decided to conduct the summit in two phases, the first being in Geneva on 10-12 December 2003 and the second in Tunis on 16-18 November 2005. (The reason was the intransigence of Switzerland and Tunisia, who both wanted to be hosts.) The WSIS was also explicitly harnessed to the UN's Millennium Development Goals.[5] Internet governance was clearly going beyond simple technical network issues. Information and communications technologies and the Internet were being linked to the loftiest aspirations of the global community. Indeed, the Millennium Development Goals may be viewed as a statement on the pursuit of autonomy on the global level.

The 2003 Geneva meeting yielded the usual statement of principles and plan of action, but it also contained some specific language on Internet and ICT governance that would lead to a fundamental review of ICANN and its role. The action plan stated that the "Internet has evolved into a global facility available to the public and its governance should constitute a core issue of the Information Society agenda. The international management of the Internet should be multilateral, transparent and democratic, with the full involvement of governments, the private sector, civil society and inter- national organizations. It should ensure an equitable distribution of resour- ces, facilitate access for all and ensure a stable and secure functioning of the Internet, taking into account multilingualism" (WSIS 2003, para. 48). It stated that policy authority over Internet-related public policy issues is the "sovereign right of states" but that other stakeholders were responsible for technical standards and economic and community development. It also recommended the establishment of a Working Group on Internet Govern- ance (WGIG).

The WGIG was formally established on 11 November 2004, with forty members from governments, the private sector, and civil society. Although drawn from these sectors, the members participated as individuals and were not designated as representatives of their sectors. The WGIG had four meetings in Geneva in 2004 and 2005, and it submitted a preliminary re- port on 21 February 2005 and its final report in June 2005 in support of the Tunis meeting of the WSIS in November of that year. The WGIG was given the task of reporting on (1) a definition of Internet governance, (2) key Internet governance policy issues, and (3) the respective roles of stake- holders in developed and developing societies (WGIG 2005).

The WGIG undertook several open-ended consultations to comple- ment its private meetings. Online processes were used to allow for more observers and interventions. Regional and subregional meetings were held throughout Southeast Asia, Africa, and the Arab world, which dem- onstrated a strong emphasis on input from the developing world in Internet governance. In addition, WGIG members wrote several working papers as a basis for discussion. In its preliminary report, the WGIG identi- fied a number of key policy areas for further examination. It is interesting to see how the question of Internet resources and addresses, which had been the main focus of ICANN in the 1990s, was now nested in policy

issues that combined concerns about globalization and autonomy. Along
with issues of technical infrastructure management and Internet use (e.g.,
spam, cyber crime), the WGIG identified the following issues:

   iii Issues which are relevant to the Internet, but with impact much
wider than the Internet, where there are existing organisations
responsible for these issues, such as Intellectual Property Rights
or international trade. The WGIG started examining the extent to
which these matters are being handled consistently with the
Declaration of Principles; and

   iv Issues relating to developmental aspects of Internet governance,
in particular capacity building in developing countries. (WSIS
2005a, para. 34)

The WGIG's final report and the results of the WSIS in Tunis are discussed in greater detail below. But clearly, Internet governance is now an
important fulcrum of contemporary globalization; consequently, it has
much to reveal about the dynamics of autonomy and globalization. The
story of the path from ICANN to the WSIS is essentially one of the autonomy project going global — of individuals and communities seeking
participation in a key component of social, economic, and political development. States asserted autonomy, sometimes collectively through
international institutions, against the prevailing system in which the United
States and ICANN dominated Internet governance. Various state and non-
state actors searched for new forms of legitimate governance on the global
stage, forms that would necessarily differ from the nation-state system of
the past 350 years (see Hedetoft 2008).

The Quest for Autonomy: Individuals and Citizens

ICANN's origins reflected a tension between an early Internet culture of
somewhat insular and consensus-based decision making by a tight technical group and the new reality in the 1990s of a wider variety of stakeholders with an interest in transparency and democratic processes. ICANN's
original mission statement, thus, emphasized bottom-up, participatory decision making by highlighting the following principles:

   c To the extent feasible, delegate coordination functions to responsible entities that reflect the interests of affected parties.

d Promote international participation at all levels of decision-making and policy-making.

e Seek broad, informed participation reflecting the functional and geographic diversity of the Internet. (ICANN 2002b)

Nonetheless, the US government continued to play a dominant role: ICANN was incorporated under the laws of California, and the US Department of Commerce prohibited any changes or amendments to the root file of the DNS without written consent by a US government official (Weinberg 2000, 212). In this way, the US government retained ultimate authority over the root. Other governments played a role in supporting the ICANN experiment and providing funding (ICANN 2002a), but the ICANN structure was designed to be decentralized, with key policy decisions being made at lower levels and ratified by those above. Governments were grouped in a Government Advisory Committee, and no member of a government could sit on the board. In addition to the representation of different technical constituencies, ICANN was to have an at-large membership composed of individuals.

In its first few years, ICANN was marked by acrimony and debate over a series of issues too lengthy to catalogue here. But it was evident by late 2001 that the organization would have to reform and reorganize itself. The key problem was the growing burden of policy issues that were crowding out ICANN's technical responsibilities. Also, ICANN had failed to forge the necessary links to governments (ICANN 2002a). On 15 December 2002, ICANN adopted new bylaws to alter the organization significantly (ICANN 2003). It is also instructive to note what happened to the idea of at-large membership. ICANN had been forced in 2000 to have global elections for five seats. The Civil Society Internet Forum was organized, and thirty-four thousand ballots were cast around the globe (Klein 2001). Four of the five seats went to Internet activists who demanded the greater democratization of ICANN. Their terms ended in 2002, and ICANN once again restructured itself so that regional organizations would be the forum for individual participation. Those organizations would elect members to an At-Large Advisory Group that would have only nominal influence over ICANN (ICANN 2005a).

This struggle over how to inject participation into a global organization formally devoted to technical regulation soon overshadowed the rest of the WSIS agenda, which had been designed to focus on the broad theme of the information society. In terms of the argument made in the

Introduction to this volume, this development reflected different definitions by different audiences of what constitutes legitimacy. Governance became a sticking point in the first phase of the WSIS and created the need for the WGIG to address the issue. The WSIS was animated by a strong (if only rhetorical) emphasis on participation by all stakeholders, particularly civil society actors. This emphasis reflected themes that had marked ICANN and the wider discussion of global Internet governance. The WGIG had the opportunity to probe this area more deeply, and the appetite for autonomy — even in the absence of a clear institutional formula to reflect it — is there. In what follows I focus first on individual autonomy and then deal with the issue of state or community autonomy.

The WGIG began its final report with a list of thirteen key public policy issues relevant to Internet governance (WGIG 2005). A number of them were primarily technical: for example, spam (there is no global definition of what constitutes spam or how it should be dealt with); Internet stability, security, and cyber crime; administration of the domain name space (this was a clear criticism of ICANN); and intellectual property rights. The rest, however, touched on aspects of autonomy and problems in Internet governance that reduced or truncated that autonomy. Two issues highlight this aspect clearly:

1 Administration of the root zone files and system
   • For historical reasons, the existing system involves only one government in the authorization of changes to the root zone file.
2 Meaningful participation in global policy development
   • There are significant barriers to multi-stakeholder participation in governance mechanisms.
   • There is often a lack of transparency, openness, and participatory processes.
   • Participation in some intergovernmental organizations and other international organizations is often limited and expensive, especially for developing countries, indigenous peoples, civil society organizations, and small- and medium-sized enterprises.
   • The content produced by some intergovernmental organizations and other international organizations is often restricted to members or is available at a prohibitive cost.
   • The frequency and location of venues for global policy meetings causes some stakeholders from more remote areas to limit their participation.

- There is a lack of a global mechanism for participation by governments, especially of developing countries, to address multi-sectoral issues related to global Internet policy development.

The WGIG (2005, 9) noted that the bulk of civil society contributions have to do with what we would call autonomy-enhancing activities, such as promoting various public interest objectives; facilitating network building; mobilizing citizens in democratic processes; bringing to light the perspective of marginalized groups, including excluded communities and grassroots activists; contributing to policy processes and policies that are more bottom-up, people-centred, and inclusive; "helping to ensure that political and market forces are accountable to the needs of all members of society"; "advocating for the developing of social projects and activities that are critical but may not be 'fashionable' or profitable"; and "contributing to shaping visions of human-centred information societies based on human rights, sustainable development, social justice and empowerment."

And yet there was "a vacuum within the context of existing structures, since there is no global multi-stakeholder forum to address Internet-related policy issues" (WGIG 2005, 10). Coupled to this was the priority of "ensuring the effective and meaningful participation of all stakeholders from developing countries in Internet governance arrangements" (ibid., 11). The WGIG recommended a forum linked to the United Nations for dialogue on crosscutting issues. The forum would be open to all stakeholders from all countries and would be supported by regional, subregional, and national initiatives. The recommendation resonates with concerns about enhancing autonomy: "Such a space or forum for dialogue (hereafter referred to as 'the forum') should allow for the participation of all stakeholders from developing and developed countries on an equal footing. Gender balance should be considered a fundamental principle with the aim of achieving an equal representation of women and men at all levels. Special care should be taken to ensure diversity of participation as regards, inter alia, language, culture, professional background, involvement of indigenous peoples, people with disabilities and other vulnerable groups" (ibid.).

The first phase of the WSIS in Geneva almost foundered on the question of Internet governance, and the WGIG was a stalling mechanism that would facilitate movement towards the Tunis phase in November 2005. The WGIG was to make proposals regarding the nature of Internet governance, the policy issues that would fall under that rubric, and an institutional mechanism for Internet governance. The Internet Governance Project noted that, on the fundamental issue of roles and responsibilities, "the report seems to have been guided by a consensus that 'public policy' is the exclusive domain of governments" (Internet Governance Project 2005, 2). It also noted that "it is clear that there is unfinished business with respect to ICANN's supervision that must be addressed. The unilateralism of the US government in contracting with ICANN and monitoring changes in the DNS root zone file is not consistent with WSIS principles and is correctly criticized in the WGIG Report" (ibid., 3). Unlike the WGIG report, however, which leaned towards a fairly soft form of governance, this group argued that effective governance would require a more robust set of agreements and mechanisms at the international level, especially treaties (ibid.).

Clearly, the WGIG had made some progress on key issues, especially on the notion of multi-stakeholder consultations on Internet governance. In this respect, the dynamic of autonomy in the form of civil society and individual stakeholders participating in self-legislation was confirmed. While the WGIG report did not go as far as the Civil Society Internet Governance Caucus (2003) did in urging grassroots democracy and respect for human rights, it did echo its sentiments. The more intractable problem was the role of governments, and, as the Internet Governance Project noted, the WGIG report leaned towards a government-centric model of governance. Of course, the key issue was the role of the United States. It did not help that, roughly one month before the release of the WGIG report, the US government issued a statement that it would not relinquish its oversight and monitoring role with respect to the Internet in general and ICANN in particular. The key clause in its short statement of principles was as follows:

The United States Government intends to preserve the security and stability of the Internet's Domain Name and Addressing System (DNS). Given the Internet's importance to the world's economy, it is essential that the underlying DNS of the Internet remain stable and secure. As such, the United States is committed to taking no action that would have the potential to adversely impact the effective and efficient operation of the DNS and will therefore maintain its historic[al] role in authorizing changes or modifications to the authoritative root zone file ... The United States will continue to provide oversight so that ICANN maintains its focus and meets its core technical mission. (NTIA 2005, para. 1)

The Quest for Autonomy: Communities and States

The quest for autonomy by states and communities needs to be judged carefully. Robert Mugabe's Zimbabwe expresses a chilling autonomy that is, in fact, tyranny. Autonomy is an expression of human will and self-legislation at the individual and the community or state level. States are, to the say the least, imperfect vessels for individual autonomy. At worst they are its oppressors. But autonomy, properly understood as the process of collective expression and self-legislation, cannot be divorced from the state — true autonomy requires the collective ability to impose agreements.

The story of ICANN and the WSIS is an attempt to define the role of sovereign states in Internet governance. It is also a story of legitimacy, models of governance, and, ultimately, an emergent global democracy. We have already touched on the issue of individuals and civil society as partners in that enterprise. The WSIS and the WGIG also had to grapple with the role of states. The key issue, as noted above, was the United States' role in overseeing the DNS root system. The first phase of the WSIS almost broke down because of disagreements over this issue. The US government deliberately distanced itself from the WGIG in order to be able to more easily dismiss the report on its release. Its statement of principles (see above) was a grenade tossed into the marsh of intergovernmental negotiations. The irony is that most of the root servers physically exist outside of the United States. As Nweke (2005, para. 5) notes: "Currently, there are 12 entities managing the 13 root name servers, specifically: A – VeriSign Global Registry Services; B – Information Sciences Institute; C – Cogent Communications; D – University of Maryland; E – NASA Ames Research Center; F – Internet Systems Consortium, Inc.; G – US DOD Network Information Center; H – US Army Research Lab; I – Autonomica/NORDUnet; J – VeriSign Global Registry Services; K – RIPE NCC; L – ICANN; and M – WIDE Project. Out of these numbers, five servers namely the C, F, I, J and K, exist in multiple locations on different continents of the world."

As noted above, US dominance of the Internet through its Memorandum of Understanding with ICANN was always contentious. The WSIS can be seen as a UN effort to bring governments into Internet governance more directly than ICANN had through its Government Advisory Committee. A way out was suggested in the WGIG's recommendations for four alternative

models of Internet governance. The guiding principles behind the recommendations were unambiguous: "No single Government should have
a pre-eminent role in relation to international Internet governance. The
organizational form for the governance function will be multilateral,
transparent and democratic, with the full involvement of Governments,
the private sector, civil society and international organizations" (WGIG
2005, 12).

Model 1 proposed a global Internet council that would represent governments and key stakeholders. The council would assume functions performed by the US Department of Commerce and ICANN's Government
Advisory Committee. ICANN would report to the council, and governments would give direction. Model 2 suggested that there was no need for
an oversight organization and that the proposed council or forum should
allow input from various stakeholders. However, the WGIG did note that it
might be necessary to "enhance the role of ICANN's Governmental
Advisory Committee (GAC) in order to meet the concerns of some
Governments on specific issues" (WGIG 2005, 14). Model 3 focused on
policy issues that directly affected national interests and proposed an international Internet council that would work on policy issues in tandem with
ICANN.

Model 4 was the most complex proposal. It suggested a three-tiered
governance mechanism. The first tier would consist of a Global Internet
Policy Council, which would be responsible "for international Internet-
related public policy issues, and contribute public policy perspectives to
Internet-related technical standard-setting" (WGIG 2005, 15). The private
sector and civil society would participate, but only with observer status.
The second tier would consist of a World Internet Corporation for
Assigned Names and Numbers. It would be responsible for technical and
economic issues and would be largely led by private-sector interests but
linked — and possibly reporting to — the United Nations. Instead of reporting to the US Department of Commerce, this new body would report
to an oversight committee appointed by and reporting to the Global
Internet Policy Council. In this body, governments and civil society would
be observers. The third tier would be the Global Internet Governance
Forum, which would be responsible for the facilitation and coordination
of Internet-related public policy issues. Participation would be equal
among governments, the private sector, and civil society.

While the WGIG report dealt with many other issues (e.g., spam and
interconnectivity), it was, in fact, devoted primarily to democracy and

legitimacy. For example, it recommended better international coordination founded on a multi-stakeholder approach. Global policy coordination would be grounded in regional and subregional governance mechanisms. The WGIG (2005, 16) explicitly addressed the issue of legitimacy and Internet governance by referring to the "effective and meaningful participation of all stakeholders, especially from developing countries" and the "building of sufficient capacity in developing countries, in terms of knowledge and of human, financial and technical resources." Even issues such as the administration of the root zone files and root server system were linked to the importance of clarifying institutional arrangements. The Internet Protocol addressing issue was discussed briefly in terms of providing equitable access to resources. On interconnection costs, the WGIG called on observers to "take note of the WSIS Declaration of Principles — i.e., to be multilateral, transparent and democratic and to have the capacity to address Internet governance in a coordinated manner, based on a multi-stakeholder approach" (ibid., 17). Most tellingly, it recommended meaningful participation in global policy development, as is detailed above.

The WGIG was effectively addressing the Achilles heel of global Internet governance: ICANN had been established with a promise that the oversight role of the United States would be relinquished eventually. As it renewed the Memorandum of Understanding over the years, the US government repeatedly stated that it would step aside once ICANN met its obligations. The June 2005 statement was, therefore, a complete reversal of this policy and set the stage for a possible major conflict between the United States and the rest of the world at the WSIS in Tunisia in November 2005.

The Tunisia WSIS: Global Governance of the Internet

The WGIG report fed into the third meeting of the Preparatory Committee meetings that took place in Geneva from 19 to 30 September 2005. Meetings of this sort develop the script and a good deal of the resulting text for a UN World Summit, and that was the intent of this PrepCom (as they are known). However, the PrepCom could not come to an agreement on the issue of Internet governance and, in an unusual move, suspended itself to meet again just before the commencement of the WSIS in Tunis (WSIS 2005b). The battle was not only between the status quo group led by the United States (which desired to leave Internet governance in the hands of ICANN rather than transfer it to the United Nations) and developing countries, it also involved a rift between the EU and the United

States as the EU began to shift its point of view closer to the anti-status quo group. The PrepCom was reconvened on 13 November, only one day before the beginning of the WSIS. Under Canadian leadership, a compromise text was developed that essentially protected the status quo while recommending the establishment of a global forum on Internet governance issues that would embrace both governments and civil society actors (Edwards 2005).

This proposal was reflected in some of the key passages in the Tunis Agenda, which was ratified by the WSIS (2005c). The agenda presented the argument that the "international management of the Internet should be multilateral, transparent and democratic, with the full involvement of governments, the private sector, civil society and international Organizations" (ibid., para. 29). It highlighted the "requisite legitimacy of its governance, based on the full participation of all stakeholders, from both developed and developing countries, within their respective roles and responsibilities" (ibid., para. 31). However, as part of the PrepCom compromise, it also — without mentioning ICANN by name — accepted the current Internet governance structure: "We recognize that the existing arrangements for Internet governance have worked effectively to make the Internet the highly robust, dynamic and geographically diverse medium that it is today, with the private sector taking the lead in day-to-day operations, and with innovation and value creation at the edges" (ibid., para. 55).

While ICANN was preserved, the WSIS also called for a new international policy organ, the Internet Governance Forum, which would provide a forum for the discussion of public policy issues by bringing together governments, international organizations, and other stakeholders. This, and other paragraphs in the document, clearly signalled that the United Nations had grudgingly accepted ICANN for the time being but that it strongly believed that ICANN should focus exclusively on technical matters and that policy issues were a matter for all governments, not just the United States. Eventually, in 2006, the Global Alliance for Information and Communication Technologies and Development (GAID) was launched by the UN. As a multi-stakeholder organization, GAID focuses, as was anticipated, on policy issues, but only those linked to development (Klein 2005). As a UN body, it reports to governments and, therefore, brings the international community of states into the Internet governance arena in a way that they cannot accomplish through the Government Advisory Committee in ICANN. But even with the creation of GAID, the results of the Tunis WSIS still did not overturn the basic architecture of ICANN. US Ambassador David Gross, when asked about his reaction to the summit results, said: "It is a document that I think everyone can be very, very proud of. We are thrilled with the document. It does everything we hoped it would do and more. It reaffirms the importance of technology and particularly the Internet to the world. It preserves the unique role of the United States Government in assuring the reliability and stability of the Internet. It took no action with regard to existing institutions including ICANN and others" (Washington File 2005). When asked if the US government had given anything up, Mr. Gross replied: "Nothing, nothing, nothing." The United States did succeed in holding back the international community's desire for a greater policy role, but it now faced GAID as a new instrument for opening up the global community of practice around Internet governance. In 2006 the United States and ICANN signed a new three-year agreement (the Joint Project Agreement) that retained the US government's pre-eminent role with respect to ICANN.

Conclusion

The story of ICANN and Internet governance resonates unusually with the themes of globalization and autonomy. The world in which we live today has been transformed by communications technology, and it is difficult to conceive of contemporary globalization without ICTs. Although the connection between the Internet and globalization seems obvious, the connection with autonomy is more nuanced. It is as though autonomy were an invisible code etched into every dimension and aspect of the Internet — its history, its underlying technical infrastructure, and its governance. Even the technological infrastructure of the Internet is decentralized and deliberately non-hierarchical, and the autonomy-enhancing effects of instantaneous, and sometimes collaborative, access to limitless information are clear.

It is also important to address the counter-autonomy argument. Information and communications technologies, on the one hand, can be limited and controlled by governments and, on the other, can be used by governments for the minute surveillance of citizens. But the argument of this chapter has been that we need to view autonomy not as a condition of being but as a dynamic process of contestation. The state's evident attempts to constrain the autonomy of its citizens, particularly the contemporary security state system, will continue to be resisted.

This chapter has addressed the issue of autonomy from the perspective of governance, democracy, and legitimacy. In the Introduction, Bernstein and Coleman point out that this volume is organized around two key questions: "How do individuals and communities retain or gain influence and control over local and non-local decisions that affect them?" and "Under globalization, how or why do individuals and communities accept commands directed at them, or that affect them, as legitimate?" The experience of ICANN and the WSIS illustrates answers to both. With the creation of ICANN, issues of legitimacy and participation were at the centre of the original Memorandum of Understanding with the US government. We saw that ICANN was not enthusiastic about a democratic and participatory decision-making process. The global elections were held reluctantly, and the at-large membership was restructured to diminish direct influence by netizens in the organization. ICANN has been regularly criticized for being too close to business interests and unresponsive to the wider Internet community. But it is precisely this type of criticism that underscores the importance of autonomy. The notion of stakeholder input in ICANN was crucial to the idea that the organization could legitimately regulate the DNS. The lack of input over the years has compromised ICANN's struggle for legitimacy. Moreover, the Internet has specific characteristics that make autonomy a governance priority. First, it is a global communications medium that allows people around the world to connect directly and to perceive themselves as "stakeholders" in a shared global resource. Second, the early history of the Internet was marked by a sense of radical democratic possibilities (Barlow 1996; Pal 1998). Universal communication and limitless information would undermine hierarchies everywhere. If the Internet has a culture, it is a counterculture suspicious of concentrations of power. The answer to Bernstein and Coleman's first question is that significant numbers of people around the world feel that they have a right to participate in the development of the Internet. The WSIS reflected this demand in its documents and processes, and it had to respond to pressures to be inclusive. And beyond participation, this global community insists that ICANN be accountable in some way to it; consequently, the organization in 2006 began work on a new accountability and transparency framework.

The answer to the second question is related to the first. It is clear that the Internet has created conditions and demands for its own governance that are radically autonomous. Few would think that they should have a direct role in global environmental governance simply because they are humans who share the planet. The nature of the Internet as distributed and decentralized communications does encourage that sensibility, and the history of the Internet is as much about a social movement as it is about a disembodied technology. But that is only one part of the story. The entire history of ICANN, through to the WSIS experience and after, is one of trying to develop an appropriate role for states in a governance system that emerged from below when the technology was not considered crucial. By the time governments woke up it was too late — the United States had control of the root and had established a domestic, non-profit corporation to manage the system, albeit with hopes for some broad global participation later.

The Tunis Agenda, as we saw above, maintained the ICANN status quo, with the addition of a proposal for a global forum and the introduction of a dynamic of review and discussion within ICANN itself. (For example, at its twenty-fourth international meeting in Vancouver, which was held from 30 November to 3 December 2005, there was discussion of the Government Advisory Committee's role in light of the WSIS process, and a joint working group was established to improve coordination between the advisory committee, the ICANN board, and other constituencies [ICANN 2005b].) The dynamics of autonomy were complex in this instance: the United States could plausibly argue that it was defending a model of Internet governance that, while accountable to one government, was relatively flexible, open, and accessible (Cukier 2005). The governments leading the charge against ICANN were headed by China and the Arab world, hardly paragons of community autonomy — indeed, they and members of the EU were animated by a desire to regulate and control the Internet, thereby possibly diminishing the scope of potential autonomy. And yet, even these governments had a point in arguing that, as representatives (however flawed) of the global community, they were being shut out of Internet governance and key policy decisions that affected their communities and societies.[6] Meanwhile, as a backdrop to the WSIS, the Tunisian government suppressed civil society protests that demanded freedom of communication.

The debate is not over, as is illustrated by the creation of GAID, nor is the dynamic interplay of globalization and autonomy on the virtual terrain of cyberspace and the real battleground of Internet governance.

chapter 14   **Contested Globalizations:**
                    Social Movements and the
                    Struggle for Global Democracy

                    Jackie Smith

As is evident from the works in this volume and in much academic literature, the concept of globalization is highly contested. But at its core is the idea that the world is becoming highly interconnected along a number of important and distinct dimensions. Many contemporary political movements reflect conflicts over the nature and emphasis of global integration, even if the proponents involved do not consciously connect their grievances to global processes. As global economic and political institutions come to influence an ever-greater scope of social life, this conflict over the nature and direction of globalization has escalated and come into sharper focus. Following analysts writing in the *Global Civil Society Yearbook,* we identify four major responses to globalizing processes. Predominant among them are the neoliberal globalizers, who emphasize the economic dimension of global integration. These are pure free traders who favour global integration, especially economic ties, without qualification (Glasius and Kaldor 2002; Kaldor 2003). Neoliberals might also be called market fundamentalists, since they generally prefer policies that prioritize market dynamics over public policy making in decisions about the distribution and allocation of resources (Stiglitz 2002). A key element of neoliberal ideology is scaling back the state to enable the free operation of market forces.[1] This vision is captured in Barber's (1995) term *McWorld.*

Neoliberals, however, are not alone in articulating a vision of world order, and we see groups articulating distinctive non-market visions for how the world might be governed. In addition, some groups articulate anti-global visions that have emerged at least partly from their critiques of neoliberalism. Many people and groups support some forms of global integration, but they emphasize forms of international cooperation that protect human rights and enhance the capacity of people to live healthy, fulfilling, and dignified lives. Although their vision of globalization is less homogeneous and, therefore, less clearly defined than that of neoliberal globalizers, what these actors share is a commitment to democratic forms of global integration: they actively seek transborder cooperation that enhances democracy and human rights. I refer to these actors as "democratic globalizers." Democratic globalizers approve of global integration that leads to greater equity and fosters the development of international law. Democratic globalizers constitute a very loosely connected network of groups and individuals that consciously seeks ways to create global level structures to maximize democratic values; the network also includes actors working at more local levels who may not have a fully articulated vision of how their local work relates to a global struggle for democratic governance.[2]

Alongside these two pro-integration or cosmopolitan visions, we find two anti-globalist visions. Proponents of one of these anti-global visions may be called "selective globalizers," since they favour global integration only when it suits their own particular interest (or the interests of their clients) and remain indifferent to any negative consequences for others. They pursue a regressive or exclusionary vision of globalization that seeks to maximize globalization's benefits for privileged groups (through, for instance, selective trade protectionism), often at the expense of the needs or preferences of others. Selective globalizers are anti-global in the sense that although they might like to see other global actors abiding by some set of international rules, they seek to be freed from any constraints that might hinder the pursuit of their own interests.

The other anti-global perspective is represented by rejectionists, those who oppose all forms of globalization as infringements on national or local autonomy. They are involved in both right-wing nationalist and religious struggles, such as those fuelled by groups like al Qaeda, as well as among other groups on the left or right that reject all global agreements and other forms of international cooperation. These are the equivalent of what Benjamin Barber calls the "jihadists" — people of any cultural, religious, or philosophical tradition who seek to defend or protect their autonomy by mobilizing against all forms of global integration. Their approach is exclusive and inward-looking, as opposed to the inclusive and outward-looking outlook of the democratic globalizers. Examples of this strain of anti-globalism include ethnocentric nationalists in right-wing US opposition to international organizations who deny global interdependence and frame international cooperation in zero-sum terms.

Glasius and Kaldor (2002) argue that the global "war on terror" has helped shift the struggle over these diverse visions of globalization from a conflict between neoliberal and democratic visions of globalization to a struggle between the anti-global tendencies of the selective globalizers and the rejectionists. This struggle can only generate greater polarization and violence, since both anti-global visions are exclusionary and intolerant and, therefore, present serious threats to democracy (for discussions of nationalist and other rejectionist responses to economic globalization and their significance, see Rupert 2000). Figure 14.1 draws from the work of Kaldor to summarize these four responses to global economic change and their key elements.

These categories present a rough picture of the key debates surrounding globalization. As pro-global visions fail to capture the support and imagination of more of the world's peoples, anti-global visions will become more attractive to more groups who feel that their basic needs and interests are threatened by expanding globalization. If growing numbers of the world's people see global integration (especially economic globalization) and interdependence as threatening, we are likely to face rising levels of violence in response to globalization, as many — including the US Central Intelligence Agency and Kofi Annan — have argued (see, for example, US Central Intelligence Agency [2000] and Annan [2005]).

Given the finite resources of the planet and the unavoidable and complex interdependence of contemporary human society, only a global vision of world order can provide a desirable and sustainable future for most of the world's people. Therefore, this chapter focuses on the competition between the two globalizing visions to consider how democratic globalizers can offer an appealing alternative to the neoliberal vision, thereby gaining the support of people who might otherwise espouse selective or rejectionist anti-global visions.

Neoliberal Globalization versus Democracy

As Boswell and Chase-Dunn argue, we live in a "single world economy with an emerging global polity" (2000, 16). Neoliberal globalizers have advanced a single global economy that has generated a wide array of protests from those who seek more participatory and accountable forms of

Figure 14.1: Contested globalizations

	Neoliberals	Democratic globalizers	Selective globalizers	Rejectionists
Main arguments or claims	Support all forms of economic integration	Support forms of integration that maximize democracy and equity	Seek integration that favours powerful groups	Oppose most forms of integration, especially institutions and markets
Key proponents	Some transnational corporations, currency speculators, financial and media outlets, the IMF; the World Bank; and the WTO	Some states, some civil society activists, and national and transnational social movement organizations	Some states; some TNCs; national business elites; some financial and media outlets	Fundamentalist religious groups and some political activist groups
Principal goals and values	Economic growth and profit accumulation	Equity in access to resources and political participation and ecological sustainability	Profit accumulation and access to resources for select groups	Group autonomy and national or local identity
Role of government	Should be minimized, but seek global system of rules and backing of developed governments	Should be used to manage equitable distribution of goods and resources and to protect natural environment; should be subject to democratic control	Used to advance interests of select group(s)	Some reject all forms of government; others seek control of state to advance the cultural values and aims of specific cultural groups
Basis of legitimacy claims	Economic growth will eventually benefit all	Global interdependence and notions of shared humanity and democracy	Maximize elite interests amid resource scarcity	Defense of group rights and cultures

Source: Adapted from Kaldor (2003).

global governance as well as from those who simply resist global integration of all kinds. At the core of this struggle is a tension between economic globalization and local autonomy, the capacity of people to influence the decisions that affect their everyday lives. This tension between a need for some sort of global coordination or framework for cooperation and the desire to maintain some group autonomy or control over the nature of integration demands that we find ways to support more inclusive and accountable forms of global integration from those that predominate today. In the absence of finding these forms, the legitimacy of decision making at all levels of authority is compromised.

Abundant evidence suggests that many governments and international institutions are finding their legitimacy in crisis, and this is likely related to the expansion of neoliberal globalization. In this volume, Sylvia Ostry discusses the World Trade Organization's (WTO) weaknesses in regard to substantive (distributive) and procedural legitimacy, and these weaknesses are arguably present in other global institutions. Within countries, more people are refusing to participate in the formal institutions of politics. We see consistent and substantial declines in voter participation across the West as membership in traditional political parties declines (Norris 1999; Verba, Schlozman, and Brady 1995). A parallel development is the emergence of militant groups, such as al Qaeda, that claim that the global system is corrupt and fundamentally incapable of addressing people's needs and interests. These groups are finding a more receptive hearing among those who increasingly feel marginalized by the existing system. They reject the fundamental democratic premises of non-violent conflict resolution and tolerance of diverse positions. When people are asked to participate in a system that is responsive to their input, they feel they have a stake in the survival of the system and are more willing to accept democratic norms. They accept decisions made by that system as legitimate. But as economic globalization exacerbates economic inequalities and denies more and more people an effective voice in the decisions that affect them, more people will support groups that advocate non-traditional forms of political action — including violence — as tools for change. Both trends signal a serious crisis for democracy and, thus, legitimacy.

The crisis of democratic legitimacy is not one that only affects states, it also has an impact on international institutions. In his address at the opening of the 2003 United Nations General Assembly, Kofi Annan urged governments to make progress in their effort to restructure the UN Security Council. His argument highlighted the vast discrepancy between the impact of the Security Council's decisions on member states and the scope of the input that members have on those decisions. Between 1945 and 2003, the United Nations grew by 140 members, while the Security Council gained only 4 additional members. The structure of the Security Council gives the five victors of the Second World War permanent veto-wielding status, which allows them effectively to control all major decisions about how the world will be governed. Annan warned that the 186 member nations that are excluded from the selective club of the "Permanent 5" will be unlikely to continue supporting the global institution if it does not reflect their interests better (Penketh 2003). Because the UN depends on the voluntary cooperation of its members, it cannot survive without a widespread perception that all of its members have a voice. At the same time, the global trade regime remains threatened by a standoff between governments of the Global South, who want a fair system of multilateral trading rules, and the leading rich countries — especially the United States and Europe.[3] As Ostry shows, these states are refusing to abandon the biases that are in their favour in the WTO system, biases that foster their own economic interests at the expense of "free" trade.

The crisis of legitimacy creates openings or vulnerabilities that encourage the kind of surges in popular mobilization (both non-violent and violent) that we have seen in recent years (see, for example, Tarrow 1996, 1998). Groups that have been excluded from decision making are demanding representation in a system that is defined by a growing democratic deficit (Markoff 2004).[4] Transnational activists have long worked to advance a more democratic and inclusive vision of global order than that preferred by either the neoliberal globalizers or those who propose anti-global alternatives. But many activists work on particular issues or campaigns — such as human rights, debt relief, and environmental protection — without developing a comprehensive picture of how their struggle fits into a broader understanding of how the world might be organized. In many cases, these groups are working within the framework of the United Nations and its many agencies and treaty bodies. They operate under a well-established set of democratic norms and principles that encourage equity, participation, tolerance, and a commitment to non-violent cooperation. If we understand the broad array of groups mobilized to promote various progressive change agendas as part of a diverse and loosely connected grouping of democratic globalizers, we can gain some insights into how this network might strengthen the prospects for a global system that is more inclusive and democratic than its neoliberal alternative.[5]

In this chapter I provide a brief overview of the long history of collective efforts to define a democratic vision of globalization that protects popular autonomy and supports multilateral cooperation. I then identify how the authorities' responses to transnational movements are likely to affect broader contests between globalizing and anti-globalist world visions, contests that, in turn, are crucial to the legitimacy of the emerging global system.

The Historical Roots of Transnational Activism for Democratic Globalization

Like other aspects of globalization, political activism has a long history of transcending national borders (see, for example, Boswell and Chase-Dunn 2000; Chatfield 1997; Hanagan 2002; Keck and Sikkink 1998; Nimtz 2002). Throughout modern times, the world has seen a variety of attempts by people working across national borders to affect change at the national and interstate level. They have shared ideas and analyses and cultivated solidarity networks to support their respective struggles, and increasingly they have built more formal and sustained structures for transnational exchange and cooperation. They have promoted goals such as the abolition of slavery, the expansion of worker rights and other international human rights, the elimination of war and colonialism, and the promotion of Socialism and democracy (see, for example, Broad and Hecksher 2003).

In a variety of ways, transnational activists have sought to reorient the distribution of economic and political power in the global system. Although the issues on which they focus have varied, there is a common theme in that they all have somehow sought to limit the capacity of states to wage war, to promote human rights as a protection against the arbitrary use of state power, and to expand access to political and economic resources by marginalized groups. Occasionally, they have adopted explicitly multilateralist aims by seeking to build formal interstate institutions that could check the activities of individual governments. Over time the major emphases of transnational activism have shifted, building upon the lessons of prior activism. Figure 14.2 summarizes four major historical streams of activism and their transnational elements.

Anti-Colonialism, Socialism, and Liberal Internationalism

The earliest forms of transnational activism centred on resisting colonialism and slavery. The nineteenth century saw the rise of more formally

Figure 14.2: Historical shifts in transnational social change activism

Period	Key themes	Central emphases and developments
Pre-1960	Anti-colonialism, socialism, and liberal internationalism	• Anti-colonial • Anti-slavery • Anti-capitalist or Socialist • Pacifist • World federalist or multilateralist
1960s-70s	Altruism to interdependence	• National independence movements • Third World solidarity • Rise of Amnesty International, Greenpeace
1980s-90s	Exploring interdependence and seeking solutions	• Peace movements • IMF/World Bank protests • UN Global Conferences • Emphasis on alliances and networking
2000s	Global justice	• Greater militancy (esp. in North) • More explicit opposition to capitalism or corporate globalization • Reduced focus on or confidence in UN • World Social Forums and proactive organizing

Note: This is not a comprehensive list. Rather, it seeks to capture the most influential streams of social change activism that involved some element of transnational communication, exchange, or cooperation. Certainly much more can be said of these early transnational campaigns, I merely use this temporal scheme to show the traditions on which contemporary activism has been built, particularly in recent decades.

organized networks that sought to build an international Socialist movement, oppose war, and promote international law and institutions.[6] In this era, transnational ties were being mobilized to help define relationships between states, capitalists, and citizens, and, by going outside the state, activists could find ideas, legitimacy, allies, and other sources of leverage to advance their causes. They also aimed to define an interstate system with rules that would help protect people from war and its consequences. This era saw the achievement of major advances for workers. Movements such as women's suffrage grew out of international labour, anti-slavery, and anti-war efforts, and the global justice movement built upon the principles of those earlier campaigns to extend notions of citizenship (Ferree and Mueller 2004; Rosenthal et al. 1985). Some of the organizations of this period — such as the International Anti-Slavery Society, the War Resisters League, and the Women's International League for Peace and Freedom — remain active today.

Altruism to Interdependence

A second era of transnational activism came with the rise of national independence movements and corresponding Third World solidarity movements. Transnational ties helped mobilize opposition to colonial practices
(see, for example, Hochschild 1998), convey messages about revolutionary
and anti-colonial struggles, and cultivate transnational networks for financial and other support (Rucht 2000). The era was marked by transnational
efforts to keep opposition to apartheid on the international agenda, even as
Cold War rivalries and the Vietnam War dampened hope for multilateral
cooperation in the United Nations. The spread of information about conflicts and suffering in different parts of the world, and the connections
these had to colonialism or superpower intervention, helped foster greater
understandings of global interdependence. The experiences of activists
working to change the policies of governments, promote national liberation, or mitigate the suffering of people in the Global South helped lay
the intellectual groundwork for future activism. The contacts between
Northern and Southern activists helped transform (though they could not
eliminate) the paternalistic visions of some Northern activists into more
complex understandings of how the policies of Western states were implicated in wars and human rights violations around the world (Livezey 1989).
Amnesty International was formed in this era, followed a decade later by
Greenpeace, and its formation marked the beginning of a new phase of
rapidly expanding transnational mobilization.

Exploring Interdependence and Seeking Solutions

The 1980s and 1990s saw the pace of transnational communications
quicken as peace movements expanded transnational ties and as opposition to global economic policies mounted around the world, especially
in the Global South. Although there was not necessarily much transnational collective action, the mobilization of similar movements around
common issues generated transnational contacts and analyses that further
enhanced understandings of global interdependence and helped sharpen
activists' analyses of problems and their solutions. Struggles in national
contexts were more likely to be framed in transnational terms, and they
more frequently focused on international targets. Popular protests in the
Global South against the policies of the International Monetary Fund
(Walton and Seddon 1994) coincided with environmental and human

rights mobilizations against the World Bank in Europe and North America (Gerhards and Rucht 1992; Rucht 2003). At the same time, more people were focusing on the United Nations as a potential target for social change activism. The United Nations hosted a series of global conferences aimed at addressing major global problems. The conferences proved to be fruitful settings for transnational exchanges of all kinds; they aided in the development of new understandings of global problems and encouraged transnational networking among those who sought to address them (Friedman, Clark, and Hochstetler 2005; Willetts 1989 and 1996b). They also encouraged citizens' groups to promote multilateral institutions as tools for addressing a variety of problems, including poverty, environmental degradation, and human rights violations. This mobilization paralleled the early efforts of peace activists to promote international law and organization as a means to curb state violence.

Addressing themes such as the environment and development (1992), human rights (1993), population (1994), social development (1995), women's issues (1995), and housing (1997), UN conferences created spaces for individual activists and public officials to discuss shared problems and possible solutions. The rather short time frames between conferences, coupled with the preparatory and follow-up meetings associated with each conference, allowed for sustained discussions of the issues and provided spaces for activists to learn from one another and adapt their views as they gained new information. Moreover, the conferences institutionalized routine review meetings that encouraged activists to monitor government compliance with their promises. They, thus, provided a focal point for geographically dispersed activists and stimulated more systematic efforts to enhance the willingness and capacity of governments to uphold international agreements.

Governments encouraged citizens' participation at the United Nations in part because they recognized that the organization would not succeed without the popular support and legitimacy that social groups bring to it. Broad popular support had been lacking in the case of the League of Nations, which led to the failure of the United States administration to win congressional ratification of its decision to join the organization it had helped to establish. Thus, when President Roosevelt initiated international dialogue on a United Nations Organization, he sought to incorporate citizens' associations into the process. Analysts have identified direct links between the activities of these civil society organizations and the wording of the United Nations Charter, which recognizes human rights and grants formal consultative status to non-governmental organizations (NGOs) at

the UN (Charnovitz 1997; Kriesberg 1997; Willetts 1996a). A similar logic
drove UN officials such as Maurice Strong, the secretary-general of the
1992 UN Conference on Environment and Development, to press for broad
recognition of citizens' associations at global conferences sponsored by the
UN. From the perspective of international officials, the most powerful governments are unlikely to take dramatic action to promote environmental
or social goals without public pressure and support. Encouraging ties between civil society and UN conferences was, therefore, a way to cultivate
the political will to support multilateralism in the UN.

UN conferences were also important training grounds for activists, many
of whom lacked basic knowledge about the politics of interstate institutions and had little experience working in transnational alliances. Most
observers argue that the past few decades of transnational activism within
the UN system have generated new skills and organizational capacities for
mobilization around global issues among a wide array of activists from an
increasingly diverse range of countries and locales (see, for example, Foster
1999; Friedman, Clark, and Hochstetler 2005; Snyder 2003; Riles 2001).
Moreover, the transnational dialogues generated by global conferences
contributed to analyses of global problems and potential solutions that inform contemporary transnational activism.

Certainly, as a result of the UN conferences, the 1980s and 1990s saw
important gains in formal transnational social movement organizing.[7]
Besides developing skills and the capacity to participate in global conferences and monitor international agreements, transnational networks grew
broader and deeper. The number of formal transnational social movement
organizations grew by nearly 200 percent, and participation from the
Global South increased (Smith 2004). Transnational social movement organizations also developed substantially more ties to international agencies
and other NGOs. The networking and dialogue fostered by participation in
UN processes altered the ways transnational organizers framed their struggles. More groups adopted more complex approaches to problems than
they had in the past. During conferences, substantial energy went into efforts to promote common interpretations of priorities and strategies because civil society groups had a limited amount of time to make their
presentations to the formal gatherings of government delegations. Activists
with widely varying backgrounds had to work together to maximize their
joint impact, and this created incentives for activists to be open to radically
rethinking their ideas about the causes and solutions to the problems on
which they were working. Moreover, they often found that working on a

single issue such as the environment became complicated when efforts to protect the environment impinged on the human rights or development possibilities of populations in endangered areas (Brysk 1996; Rothman and Oliver 2002). Social movement networks provided some of the few transnational spaces in which activists could learn the consensus-building and interest-aggregation skills that are essential to democratic governance (Bandy and Smith 2005). The more activists needed to work with other groups to have a political voice, the more likely they were to alter the way they framed problems to accommodate the interests of other allies (Staggenborg 1986).

Global Justice

The most recent period of transnational activism, the global justice era, is characterized by heightened confrontation between civil society actors in the North and international institutions.[8] The era is also marked by the emergence of the Internet and digital technologies as important tools for mobilization, network building, and the nurturing of transnational networks. A greater militancy developed during the 1990s at the meetings of the Bretton Woods institutions (the World Bank, the IMF, and the WTO) and Group of Eight (G8), and it gained widespread attention in the United States after police riots at the WTO protests in Seattle in 1999.

The aims of protesters have also become more explicitly anti-capitalist than they had been in the past, and more diverse groups are focusing on transnational corporations as a major source of their grievances. This shift in focus can most certainly be linked to the years of sustained transnational dialogue enabled by the UN Conferences. Friedman, Clark, and Hochstetler (2005) noted important attempts during the 1995 World Summit for Social Development in Copenhagen to highlight how the global financial institutions undermined commitments to human rights and development that governments had made in the UN. Krut (1997) also reports increased discussion about and tensions over the incompatibilities between the UN treaty system and global financial institutions.

This era also witnessed a much greater diversity in the structures and tactics used by activists in transnational campaigns. Advancements in technology have allowed for more decentralized organizing structures, and it is now more possible than ever for local individuals and groups to have direct contact with their activist counterparts around the world. Organizers have used the Internet to instantly and effectively communicate details of protests to supporters around the world. These technologies have helped amplify the voices of those seeking to promote policy change, and they have dramatized the similarities in experiences — in terms of both grievances and government reactions to protest — of diverse activist groups. Whereas prior to Seattle most transnational activism was limited to lobbying and symbolic protests at formal international meetings, after Seattle mass public demonstrations are more frequently used to target global institutions.

The other shift between this period and the previous one is that activists seem to be devoting less energy and attention to the UN. In part this change is related to the absence of large-scale UN Conferences and the popular mobilizations that surrounded them. Another reason for the shift, however, is the sense that global financial institutions have in many ways eclipsed the UN and undermined its importance. Many activists found that the treaties on which they had focused their energies during the 1980s and 1990s were being trumped by international trade agreements that allow trade law to supersede other international agreements.[9] Many in the activist community have also grown wary of growing corporate influence in the UN, which began during the mid-1990s. The International Forum on Globalization articulated this fear directly when it hosted a meeting to parallel the UN Millennium Forum that was entitled "Can the UN Be Salvaged?"

A final important characteristic of this latest phase of transnational activism is that there is more autonomy from UN and other multilateral agendas than there had been in the 1980s and 1990s. Instead of mobilizing according to the conference schedules of global institutions, activists have advocated a more proactive, decentralized, and grassroots-oriented approach than in previous eras, an approach made more possible by digital technologies. Following criticisms that the global justice protests were only against something and lacked a coherent vision of an alternative to economic globalization, activists in Brazil and France came together to launch the World Social Forum process in 2001. Under the slogan "another world is possible," around ten thousand participants attended the first forum in Porto Alegre, Brazil, and the numbers swelled to more than a hundred thousand in 2005 and 2006. The forum is an "open space" for activists to gather, exchange experiences, support one another's struggles, build transnational alliances, and plan coordinated strategies and actions. It also reflects efforts to define new relationships between movements, parties, and other civic actors (see, for example, Baiocchi 2004). Although its form reflects the NGO conferences that ran parallel to UN global conferences in many ways, the World Social Forum also signals and represents an autonomous civil society approach to defining a global agenda.

The World Social Forum process, although still quite young, holds tremendous promise for expanding transnational activism and for deepening connections between global and local political processes. The forum inspired the proliferation of regional and local social forums that enable activists working at the local level to interact with activists from within their region, as well as with organizers who work at national and global levels. This process can significantly enhance what Sidney Tarrow (2006) has called the domestication of transnational protest, or the articulation of global conflicts within nationally defined political contexts. For instance, the meeting of the Boston Social Forum on the eve of the 2004 Democratic National Convention brought together local groups working on housing and health issues and delegations from Brazil's Landless Workers Movement (Movimento dos Trabalhadores Rurais Sem Terra) and other activists working at national and global levels. The plenary sessions of this meeting framed struggles in global terms and explicitly linked the work being done in Boston to the broader World Social Forum process. Activists — mostly from around the Massachusetts area — were reminded of the global repercussions of the US elections and were exposed to some international perspectives on a variety of US and global policies.

This look at the history of transnational social movement mobilization leads to two key observations. First, social movement efforts to promote more democratic visions of global governance began long before the contemporary global justice movement emerged in force at the WTO meeting in Seattle. In fact, its organizational and intellectual origins can be traced back much further than most people might think. Second, the interactions between activists from different countries over the course of many different campaigns to influence global practices or UN processes had a significant impact on the knowledge, skills, and capacities of activists to build transnational coalitions to advance their social change agendas. Southern struggles against colonialism, apartheid, and the global financial system fostered transnational linkages and helped sensitize Northern activists to issues of interdependence and the broader structural sources of economic inequality. And in the current era, it is the Southern unions, political parties, and movements that are playing central roles as the drivers of innovation (Baiocchi 2004; Chase-Dunn 2002; Kitchelt 2003; Moody 1997). The experience of struggle has informed and nurtured new skills and structures for transnational organizing, and these lessons have developed over time (cf. Polletta 2002).

Although their scope and scale has increased in more recent times, transnational ties have always helped activists generate better understandings of how to build alliances that cross national boundaries and best organize those ties. Transnational ties have also challenged people to think globally in ways that national action alone cannot. These ties have helped cultivate imagined communities beyond nation-states and have fostered collective identities that emphasize transcendent values and goals. They have helped cultivate organizing techniques and leaders who can help bridge the differences between different cultural and sectoral groups. Thus, social movements with transnational ties have been crucial to the advancement of innovations in multilateral governance, thereby contributing to their legitimacy. By expanding the range of participants involved in discussions about global policy and the knowledge and skills that people have, social movements are vital to efforts to democratize the global polity and legitimize the growing number of world institutions.

Neoliberal Responses to Democratic Pressures

Authorities have responded to social movement pressures in a number of ways. Some of the key government proponents of neoliberal globalization — most notably the United States — have sought to curb the role of civil society groups in the UN. Simultaneously, they have also worked to marginalize the UN relative to global financial institutions, which are less accessible to civil society groups. In addition, they have stepped up police repression against those groups that protest neoliberal globalization. Analysts of the policing of protests have argued that Western democratic states are shifting away from established models of negotiated protest management towards more coercive and repressive forms of policing (della Porta and Reiter 2006). Corporate actors have also intervened in the struggle to increase their influence within the UN and to legitimate the role of businesses in governance through partnership mechanisms in the UN and other intergovernmental forums (Bendell 2004; Bruno and Karliner 2002; Paine 2000; Smith 2008; World Health Organization 2000). And as they have sought to limit the space for public intervention in global institutional processes, governments have also moved to make intergovernmental meetings less accessible by meeting in remote locations that are more readily defended by police and military forces (della Porta and Reiter

2006). They have also engaged in what Ferree (2005) calls soft repression, which involves efforts to stigmatize and otherwise marginalize critical voices in public discourse.

In short, we see an anti-democratic backlash against democratic globalizers that seeks to insulate decision makers from their constituents and severely restrict public deliberation about global policy, even as global decisions have increasingly important implications for local practices. By excluding the vast majority of people, neoliberal globalizers are fanning the flames of anti-globalism. They are encouraging support for those selective globalizers who seek to exploit the weaknesses of others to advance their own interests and for the rejectionists who resist global integration of all kinds. Neoliberal globalizers are also further undermining the legitimacy of the very institutions that support global economic integration. The inherent tension between globalization and autonomy will, under these circumstances, generate violent responses — just as authorities have chosen to use violence against those who want to challenge neoliberal dominance in global policy arenas.

Conclusion

Globalization processes have generated and been shaped by diverse networks of actors who promote particular visions of global integration. The neoliberal model of market-dominated globalization emphasizes economic forms of global cooperation largely to the exclusion of others. The key challenger to the neoliberal version of globalization is a more multi-faceted and democratic notion of globalization, one that preserves local autonomy while encouraging international cooperation. In the words of Zapatista activists, this vision is for "one world where many worlds fit." This notion, which is anchored in novel forms of community building on a global scale, creates the possibility for legitimate decision making at global and other sites of authority. Social movement actors have a long history of promoting and shaping multilateral institutions around this vision. Because neoliberalism promotes growing levels of social exclusion among large segments of the world's populations, however, proponents of anti-globalism threaten attempts to manage global interdependence in cooperative ways. As the chapter by Ostry in this volume and chapters by Pauly, Coleman, and Hedetoft in the *Global Ordering* volume in this series suggest (Pauly and Coleman 2008), the effectiveness of global institutions requires greater legitimacy, and this legitimacy demands that greater attention be paid to demands for equity, inclusion, and transparency in international institutions. If governments and other authorities really hope to limit the possibilities for violent conflicts, they should step up efforts to enhance the formal organization of public participation in global policy debates.

A long history of involvement in multilateral institutions and debates has nurtured activists' skills and their organizational capacity to practise global democracy. Activists should embrace and learn from this history and resist the trap of engaging in endless debates between radical and moderate strategies. One can maintain a radical vision of democratic globalization and still identify the practical steps necessary to construct global institutions to realize that vision. The history of transnational activism suggests several avenues for creating institutions that will expand public participation in global policy debates. But building upon these lessons will require a more conscious effort by activists to cultivate in many sectors allies who will help them promote democratic and inclusive multilateral institutions. It will also require more systematic efforts to enhance democracy within social movement organizations themselves, even as activists seek to expand the diversity and inclusiveness of their associations. Many groups are already trying to do this, but they face important resource constraints, among other obstacles.

Governments, for their part, will need to reclaim some of their authority to govern capitalist markets so that democracy can flourish. They must recognize the fundamental weakness of global institutions that deny citizens a meaningful role, even though their legitimacy ultimately depends upon popular acceptance and accountability. Identifying the main incompatibilities between neoliberal and democratic visions of globalization is a first step. And governments must also explore possibilities for democratizing global policy arenas in ways that allow for the more equitable participation of all the world's people. Governments cannot simply criticize a lack of representativeness among civil society groups; they must try to work with these groups to generate new forms of political inclusion — including providing resources and structured spaces that enable participation from resource-poor groups — at the global level. Without these efforts, anti-global responses to neoliberalism will gain wider support among those who feel excluded from full participation in the global economic and political order.

chapter 15   Conclusion

Steven Bernstein

THE CONTRIBUTIONS TO THIS volume have borne out its premise that globalization has unsettled and disrupted legitimacy. It has done so by complicating relationships between individual and collective autonomy on the one hand and forcing renegotiations within political communities over systems of rule that individuals and collectivities inhabit on the other. However, globalization's effects on those relationships are neither linear nor generalizable. These findings militate against definitive conclusions about how globalization affects, or ought to affect, these relationships and, thus, legitimacy. Reflecting this indeterminacy, the theoretical chapters by Melissa Williams, Ian Cooper, and Nisha Shah explored how legitimate authority might be reconstituted in new ways following these disruptions and illustrated the different forms of political community and citizenship that could play out as globalization unfolds. Subsequent chapters showed that individuals and communities have reacted in varying ways to that disruption, with their sense of control over new or reconstituted relationships of autonomy and political authority varying widely.

In some cases, contributors found individuals and communities attempting to reclaim and reconstitute legitimate practices of the past as a way to regain control over their political destinies. A clear example is Harvey Feit's account of the James Bay Crees' attempt to reclaim practices of co-governance to reconstitute their relationship to political authorities. Even in these circumstances, contributors found that globalization forced a reconfiguration and, occasionally, a reconceptualization of how those older legitimate orders could be achieved in contemporary conditions. And these actions sometimes led to unintended or ironic consequences. The most striking example is illustrated in Julie Sunday's and Michael Keating, John McGarry, and Margaret Moore's chapters on minority nationalisms in Europe. Both chapters show how the shifting terrain of sovereignty and discourses of human rights and democracy in Europe have provided fertile ground for the rise of nationalism, the very project European integration arguably set out to delegitimatize. Unlike nineteenth- and early twentieth-century nationalism, however, the claims being made now are much more likely to be for inclusion, not secession. While these struggles, at least in Europe, are less likely to lead to the violent readjustment of borders — the conflict in the former Yugoslavia being the exception that proves the rule — they are proving nearly as difficult for Europe and European states to accommodate as older irredentist and secessionist movements. In other cases, new forms of political order may require new bases of legitimacy. In particular, the chapters on Internet governance, the responsibility to protect (R2P) doctrine, and the World Trade Organization (WTO) suggest that no ready model of legitimacy exists to mediate the relationship between collective autonomy and political authority under globalization.

Although these non-linearities, ironies, or disjunctures may frustrate those expecting a clear causal arrow to run from globalization to particular political outcomes, some general conclusions and observations can still be drawn from these studies. One overarching conclusion is that globalization is a permissive environment for different configurations of rule and ruled. This permissiveness does not mean that contributors found that political agents operate unencumbered or are able to arrive easily at new configurations of a legitimate order of their choice. Indeed, political agency and autonomy have always been highly constrained, mediated by power relationships as well as by the levels of resources and capabilities individuals and communities can bring to bear to assert their autonomy. Under globalization those constraints have manifested themselves in challenges to the legitimacy of new configurations of political power — such as through the global justice movement documented by Jackie Smith — with no signs of easy resolution. At the same time, the experience of those constraints suggests the ways that productive, institutional, and structural power potentially underpin legitimating discourses that leave a more limited scope for autonomy under globalization than a liberal understanding of the modern individual or citizen asserts.

Although contributors disagreed about, or put different emphases on, the way power operated to enable, produce, or constrain autonomy and political legitimacy, a fairly consistent view emerged on what political legitimacy under globalization *ought to* rest: justifications for new or reconfigured relationships of political legitimacy under globalization ought to, and indeed increasingly do, rest on a global form of liberal internationalism. As we described it in the volume's Introduction, global liberal internationalism has three main requirements. First, state authority is needed to secure individual and collective autonomy. At the same time, this necessity is balanced by the need to renegotiate how that authority is manifested as sovereignty is reconfigured. Second, there is a need to seriously engage the growing, increasingly autonomous, yet often disenfranchised and fractured global civil society. Third, it requires that relationships of rule and ruled at all levels of organization reflect that the resonance of twentieth-century liberal values not only persists in this century, but also increases. These values especially include human rights and citizenship, expansive notions of the rule of law, democracy, and other expressions of empowerment and self-rule. The realization of these values can no longer be achieved solely at the level of the nation-state; they are being demanded at local, regional, international (e.g., through international institutions), and transnational levels.

Our contributors did not begin from this premise. Indeed, they were very careful not to assume that democratic theory or practice was the source of legitimate rule, and they did not assume that global liberal internationalism needed to be realized via a particular notion of democracy. Moreover, they arrived at this understanding of legitimacy — albeit with significant nuanced differences and some variance — through an analysis of legitimating practices.

The remainder of this conclusion delineates these practices further and unpacks the general findings through a discussion of how the contributions answered the two core questions of the volume: First, under globalization, how or why do individuals and communities accept commands directed at them, or that affect them, as legitimate? Second, from the vantage point of autonomy, how do individuals and communities retain or gain influence and control over the local and non-local decisions that affect them?

Steven Bernstein

Accepting Commands and Decisions as Legitimate

As is described in our Introduction in reference to Habermas, the conventional liberal understanding of legitimate commands might be seen as follows:

> "The idea of self-legislation *by citizens* ... requires that those subject to law as its addressees can at the same time understand themselves as authors of law" ... This co-originality [of collective and individual autonomy], however, rests on certain conditions. The decisions are located in "a geographically delimited legal territory and to a socially delimitable collectivity of legal consociates, and consequently to particular jurisdictional boundaries. These limitations in historical time and social space result simply from the fact that legal subjects cede their authorizations to use coercion to a legal authority that monopolizes the means of legitimate coercion and if necessary employs these means on their behalf."

We noted that this understanding of legitimacy was subject to a variety of critiques outside the body of democratic theory — for example, by some feminist, postmodern, and communitarian scholars. It nonetheless serves as a useful point of departure for our findings because it captures the paradigmatic or ideal-type liberal understanding of legitimate relationships between rulers or rules and the ruled.

We noted that globalization unsettled these paradigmatic relationships in at least three ways:

1 Those subject to a law have increased difficulty understanding themselves as authors of law, particularly when law originates outside the nation-state (perceived as a loss of individual autonomy).
2 Crucial decisions are no longer confined in many instances to a geographically limited territory and particular jurisdictional boundaries (perceived as a loss of collective autonomy).
3 Citizens find it difficult to understand how they might have ceded the authorization to use coercion to a legal authority that monopolizes the means of legitimate coercion (the co-originality of individual and collective autonomy has fallen apart).

We also noted that these trends had implications for understandings of legitimacy that questioned Habermas's co-originality thesis. In this context, it is worth emphasizing again, as we stated in the Introduction, that the contributors collectively adopted an initial position that they would not pre-judge the appropriateness of a democratic basis of legitimacy or necessarily begin from a normative position rooted in Habermas's co-originality thesis. Indeed, some sections of the volume, most notably the two chapters on legitimacy and violence, question democratic theory as it has been conventionally applied to justify legitimacy.

Nonetheless, from the vantage point of the volume's conclusion, which reflects back on the authors' findings, it turns out that the co-originality thesis provided a useful point of departure for many authors not only normatively but also in terms of observed practices of legitimation. Many of the authors found a democratic impulse, underpinned by something like the co-originality thesis, when they observed practices of legitimation and the demands of political communities as they attempted to construct, negotiate, or react to new configurations or reconfigurations of legitimate political authority.

Although no contributor argued that the ideal of co-originality was always maintained, even in non-globalized periods or geographical spaces, nearly all addressed how these relationships can be put together again in the face of these disruptions. In many cases, their answers also reflect that globalization spurred a deeper questioning of the appropriateness of the paradigmatic liberal thesis in the first place. Contributors' responses to the prospects of constructing or reconstituting legitimate relationships of political authority can be roughly organized along a pessimism-optimism continuum.

Pessimists

Rhoda Howard-Hassmann's chapter on the African perspective can be located closest to the pessimist end of the spectrum. From the standpoint of African elites — that is, those who exercise collective autonomy on behalf of citizens — collective autonomy at global levels provides no power to author laws. Thus, collective autonomy does not exist. To gain power, Africans need to reconstitute themselves on a continental level, and this task is also next to impossible. Hence, those subject to laws (individual citizens but, in the context of international law, also governments) have no reason to understand global decisions as being legitimate. Moreover, globalization increases the degree to which local, national, and continental autonomies are interdependent, which only adds to the challenges already facing many sub-Saharan African states in creating and sustaining legitimate institutions.

Peter Nyers' chapter shows how the R2P doctrine breaks the notion of citizens as authors of laws through their constitution by defining them as weak and in need of protection. Under the doctrine, decisions on their fate are made outside of any collectivity of which they are a part; hence, it is difficult to see decisions about their fate as being legitimate. This negative reconstitution undermines a fundamental premise of the liberal understanding of autonomy: that security of rights entails self-protection or active citizenship. By undermining active citizenship, the R2P doctrine may, in practice, contradict its own principled premise.

Reinforcing both Howard-Hassmann's and Nyers' pessimism in the case of weaker states, Heike Härting argues that elites and citizens who were involved in transnational local wars, or who observed those wars, face a narrative that is focused on the local and the present and "reads out" historical power relationships. These relationships prevented those subject to laws from being authors of the law because the laws originated outside the nation-state in imperial centres. This reading out leads to a potential misunderstanding of how global power relations continue to deny autonomy to citizens living in weaker states, particularly the many states that are faced with communal conflict. Härting suggests that these relations continue to be produced, at least in the Sri Lankan case, through contemporary discourse and practices that justify, or deny, violent attacks on personal autonomy.

Sylvia Ostry backs up Härting's concern about the reading out of historical power relationships by demonstrating how these relationships shaped a key global institution, the WTO. The WTO appears, to many, to increasingly make crucial decisions that affect the lives of rich and poor alike, especially as it moves into areas that require behind-the-border regulatory reforms instead of reduced tariffs or other barriers to trade at the border. For peoples and states that are missing in negotiations, those who are rule takers and have a limited capacity to participate in the new legal dispute mechanisms, there is no co-originality of individual and collective autonomy and, thus, little legitimacy for a global legal authority.

Optimists

On the optimistic end of the spectrum, Melissa Williams sees the possibility of new forms of disaggregated citizenship under conditions of unbundling territoriality and sovereignty (Ruggie 1993). Although Williams fully acknowledges the power relationships under globalization identified by other authors, her project is a reconstructive one. She sees the potential for citizenship beyond the nation-state to operate in a decentred world of disaggregated political authority. However, citizenship can only do so to the degree that its core functions, which Williams identifies as common to modern (i.e., state-based) *and* global forms of citizenship, can be achieved. Thus, while she agrees with Nyers on the need for a secure space for the constitution of a responsible subject, Williams is much more sanguine that such spaces can be created that transcend the state. Her chapter is full of hope in that it imagines the possibilities and expressions of human freedom in citizenships of globalization.

Although more tempered in her optimism, Jackie Smith similarly demonstrates how civil society actors act out global citizenship. Moreover, she shows confidence in some UN institutions and processes, noting especially the more inclusive spirit, and opportunities for engagement provided by, UN global summits. Furthermore, she argues that there is potential for increased legitimacy if international institutions take seriously the need for democratic reform. For her, governments also have a positive role to play in reversing the trend to relinquish their responsibility or authority over, for example, international capital markets. Smith concludes that only under conditions in which states actively assert their authority to govern markets can co-originality be realized. This conclusion echoes Karl Polanyi's (1944) classic thesis on the double movement — that is, the expectation of popular reaction against unfettered or socially disembedded markets. In this view, democracy and socially embedded markets go hand in hand. Under these conditions, Smith sees the possibility of rebuilding relationships so that those subject to law can be authors of law by finding co-originality in global institutions. Her optimism is, therefore, mixed with a warning: failure to reform those institutions will magnify disenfranchisement from without and rejectionism from some elements within civil society, with potentially grave consequences.

From a more local vantage point, Harvey Feit and Tara Goetze also see room for some optimism in reconstituting legitimate relationships of rule under globalization, though that reconstitution is often coupled with loss of older modes of control. Both emphasize that the complex relationships between global, national, and local sites of authority can create openings for disadvantaged groups to build alliances beyond the national level, on the one side, and to exploit global discourses on development and conservation on the other to make a claim for reinforced local authority. In realizing this claim, they build the co-originality of individual and collective autonomy back into some of the most important decisions affecting the lives of people in the communities they study.

Agnostic

The chapters on Europe and Les Pal's chapter on Internet governance present reasons to be both pessimistic and optimistic, which places them somewhere in the middle of our spectrum. For Pal, the problem with attempts to reconstitute or create more legitimate Internet governance is that there is a fundamental tension between the material bases of the Internet — which make it ungovernable by states alone and, therefore, in need of a global authority — and the interests of the historically dominant powers who refuse to relinquish control. If a global authority could be set up to make key decisions related to the Internet, then those subject to laws by that authority would be better placed to be authors of those laws through the actions of their own states or alternative mechanisms that reach directly to communities of Internet users alongside governments. However, the situation in this case is similar to the WTO in that historically dominant powers, the United States in particular, refuse to allow conditions that would permit those subject to laws to see themselves as authors of law. Pal's analysis, consequently, identifies the same problem highlighted by Ostry, Howard-Hassmann, and Härting. Still, as Pal points out, there is progress. Unlike the cases explored in this volume in which countries are "missing" or historical relationships have been "read out," power relations are in the forefront of active debates on Internet governance, and the United States has shown itself to be more responsive.

The two chapters on Europe by Sunday and Keating, McGarry, and Moore address a situation in which crucial decisions in one particular area — the rights of cultural minorities — are increasingly backed up by a legal corpus in a more expansive territorial jurisdiction, the European Union. This situation is one in which minorities see possibilities for increasing the likelihood of being both subjects and authors of political decisions that most affect their cultural concerns. However, both chapters are not sanguine, since they note a variety of tensions, obstacles, and contradictions in the European polity and legal regime. They also throw into tension a more fundamental premise of the liberal ideal of co-originality by further complicating the dichotomy of the individual and the collective as bases for autonomy that Ian Cooper identified in his ideal-type formulation.

As Keating, McGarry, and Moore point out, the remarkable diversity in claims to minority nationalism in Europe does not easily lend itself to generalizations about the conditions for legitimate rule. Both of these chapters, in their own way, put the challenge of accommodating the drive for collective autonomy into tension not only with individual autonomy — as in the classic liberal-communitarian debate — but also with nested and overlapping impulses for collective autonomy at the nation-state and European levels.

However, the two chapters come to starkly different conclusions on the fundamental point of whether a human rights regime, no matter how sympathetic it is to including an accommodation of minorities, can be compatible with minority nationalism. For Keating, McGarry, and Moore, creating space for collective autonomy has the most chance to succeed under a more robust overarching regime of human rights that is rooted in both individual autonomy and collective and minority rights. Conversely, in the case of Hungarian minority nationalism in Romania, Sunday's research revealed deep skepticism about human rights regimes on the part of the Democratic Alliance of Hungarians (DAHR), which perceives the Romanian state as using the discourse of international human rights to dismiss its claims. The DAHR, thus, rejects engagement with human rights discourse. Rather, it views its quest for autonomy as largely a struggle of power that no law or institutional arrangement can solve.

Juxtaposing these positions will not satisfy those looking for clear conclusions on how regionalization in Europe and enmeshment in European and international norms will mediate struggles for collective autonomy and, ultimately, political legitimacy. But this ambiguous conclusion, as Sunday points out, is quite consistent with Tully's (2001, 6) argument that "struggles over recognition do not admit of a definitive solution." There is no magic bullet of human rights law or institutional arrangements that will make the problem of minority nationalism — or the challenge it poses to political legitimacy — disappear. Recognition of collective autonomy is still frequently perceived to be in tension with both individual rights and the collective autonomy of states, both of which often mask the domination of majority national groups.

The special case of globalization as manifested in European regional integration adds a further complicating dimension to this struggle. The overarching economic and political goal of being part of Europe, with its political and economic benefits, has created conditions of alliance between minorities and states, including the Hungarians in Romania. This alliance, documented by Sunday, suggests that although it does not solve the legitimacy problem, pragmatic politics has shifted the terrain of the debate to a discussion of how to be recognized within existing institutions (at the state and European level), rather than how to overthrow them or secede if the struggle for power internally fails. Taken together, these two chapters suggest that it is in the problem of minority nationalisms that the European project runs up against the limits of liberalism. Notwithstanding Sunday's hopeful conclusion that the answer may yet be found in a more inclusive democracy, finding institutional arrangements that can make democracy work under these circumstances continues to be a challenge.

To sum up, in reference to the issue of accepting commands and decisions as legitimate, the pessimistic chapters in the volume have outlined the obstacles to legitimacy; the optimistic chapters have pointed to situations where legitimate decisions can occur under globalizing circumstances; and the agnostic chapters have raised questions about the limits of these possibilities. Together, they reinforce our point that globalization is a permissive set of processes; these processes, however, operate in an environment of ongoing power relations and constraints.

Autonomy, Influence, and Control under Globalization

The volume's second question concerns how the possibilities of political legitimacy — as pessimistic or optimistic as one might be of achieving it — might be put into practice and the limits and possibilities of doing so. It focuses on the mechanisms of achieving legitimate rule and exercising political agency and the limits of both under globalization. A hopeful reading of the volume's contributions suggests that globalization opens up a very wide range of avenues for individuals and collectivities to seek, create anew, or reassert control over decisions that affect them. This reading can even be applied to contributors who saw power — especially productive power — as defining and "redescribing" justifications for rule and, thus, those who might initially appear to deny agency. Even those authors, however, identified exploitable contradictions in the organization or operation of political authorities that have, in practice, undermined individual and collective autonomy. For example, Shah's metaphor of empire invoked its antithesis, multitude. In sum, globalization's permissive environment provides a setting for experimentation in community building, in redefining sites of political authority, and in reconfiguring relationships of political authority. The contributions, with few exceptions, suggest, however, that no experiment can be legitimate without commitments that are at least minimally consistent with the global liberal internationalism described above. Moreover, no arrangement has proved able to respond fully to the toughest dilemmas outlined by the pessimists and agnostics.

One notable general finding is that many of these experiments are attempts to reclaim or reconfigure state sovereignty, a finding that contradicts the expectations of a fuller retreat or transcendence of the state found in some early literature on globalization. Perhaps the best example is Feit's rich and complex account of the James Bay Crees' ongoing attempts to reclaim notions of co-governance under much more globally integrated and intensive economic connections than when the idea of co-governance originated, when it was designed to manage the conservation of beavers to supply European clothing markets. Feit's chapter reminds us that globalizing connections and processes still occur in complex societies that have long histories forging such connections. In each period he investigates — the 1930s and 1940s, the 1970s, and the contemporary period — the Crees responded with attempts to conserve collective cultural and economic autonomy through co-governance arrangements that would permit negotiations with dominant governmentalities: first colonialism, then modernization, and finally neoliberal globalization.

In a snapshot of a similar process, Goetze's chapter finds in co-management an attempt by local communities (fishers in this case) to regain some lost control over natural resources central to their economy and culture. Fishers needed to form a new non-governmental organization to mediate the influence of international conservation initiatives and the interests of the national government on their community autonomy. Like in Feit's example, state activity is not removed; it instead enters into new relationships with international NGOs, foreign tourist companies, and local fishers that change decision-making processes. Globalization has added a new dynamic in which the state is in greater need of mutual legitimation, from global and local community bodies, given new globalizing forces (neoliberal

327

development in the case of the James Bay Crees and global environmental norms in the communities of southern Belize). In both cases, agency and assertions of autonomy are at work, while avenues for empowerment narrow under revised governmentalities that incorporate global norms and practices. Something may be gained, but there is also loss. Collective autonomy remains secured while communities find parts of their ways of living reconstituted as "natural resources" to be exploited or controlled by those outside their communities and their countries.

Several chapters identify and examine attempts to build or invigorate new institutional arrangements internationally. Examples include Ostry's suggestion for a reinvigoration of the Trade Policy Review Mechanism in the WTO, Pal's identification of the new Global Alliance for Information and Communication Technologies and Development in the face of US dominance of ICAAN, and Howard-Hassmann's argument for a continental presence for Africa in arenas of globalized interactions. What connects them all is that these efforts depend on building the capacity to act autonomously at national and regional scales. As Howard-Hassmann argues, national legitimacy in Africa, as elsewhere, rests on the capacity to create efficient, rule-bound, law-abiding democratic governments that can fairly deliver needed goods to their citizens. These institutions and norms are crucial if African states are to be able to negotiate collectively and with credibility at the regional and global scales.

The bad news for autonomy is that none of these contributors is particularly optimistic about success. The room for creativity opened up by globalization does not easily or necessarily translate into actual expressions of autonomy. In almost all cases, the institutional initiatives still depended on adequate resources and capacities being transferred from wealthy countries to poor ones. Autonomy involves a capacity to act, not simply a will to act. Those, like the Crees, who can find resources, traditions, as well as new avenues of agency under globalization are more likely to succeed in empowering these new institutional arrangements. Those who must interact under conditions of unequal power or institutional arrangements that reflect path dependencies or normative or structural foundations built on inequalities are in a fight from the start, one they are likely to lose.

The examples of ICANN, the R2P doctrine, and the global justice movement in particular illustrate that there is an ongoing and percolating legitimacy challenge (if not crisis) as various sets of actors uneasily negotiate the tension between cosmopolitan ideals and the incomplete transformation of sovereignty. In each case, engagement with, and the inclusion of, the state is inescapable, despite the apparent supraterritorial nature of the enterprise in question (governance of the Internet, protection of threatened peoples anywhere, or the achievement of global commitments to fairness in decision rules and outcomes). Sadly, the major powers implicated seem ill-prepared, unwilling, or simply confounded by these new pressures. They often evince little sign of being open to the serious negotiations or renegotiations that are necessary to reconfigure relationships of political community, autonomy, and power to ensure that decisions are accepted as legitimate across the world.

A Final Word

It is tempting to end on a prescriptive note. We might, for example, focus on the overlapping consensus among our contributors that local, state, regional, and global autonomy are interdependent and, thus, the practices that enable co-originality — deliberative and democratic — need to be promoted simultaneously, and institutionalized widely, at multiple levels. This conclusion resonates with much of the cosmopolitan literature and is hardly controversial. Our formulation of global liberal internationalism is certainly consistent with this vision, though it perhaps puts greater stress on the role of the state in promoting and enabling autonomy. It also stresses the need for renegotiations of sovereignty, permissiveness for new sites of authority and regulation alongside the state, and the need for at least minimal universal standards of law and rights.

From this set of premises, the politics of the early twenty-first century leave us rather pessimistic about the future. The interdependence of democracy at multiple levels suggests that reform of international institutions will require a greater commitment to democratic practices in states throughout the world. There are worrisome trends in the opposite direction. In some existing "democratic" states, including the United States and Canada, there has arguably been a regression in democracy, at least as it involves traditional democratic institutions, in favour of executive-centred, less responsible government. Even more worrisome, there are some who see the promotion of democracy and the promise of globalization's benefits by major Western powers as a contradictory and morally hollow legitimation of violence, and even torture, in support of that vision (Brennan 2005). These contradictory moral tendencies are especially evident since the attacks of 11 September 2001. Although our outline of a global form of liberal internationalism was designed to guard against the legitimation of a permanent state of exceptionalism that justifies a suspension of rights, many of our contributors, given the practices of legitimation they see unfolding in their name, were justifiably cautious about accepting the claims of ideal liberal theories of legitimacy.

Beyond the established democracies, the picture is equally bleak. In other key states such as Russia and China, the Gulf states, and many African states, meaningful democracy seems improbable in the medium to long term. If the growth of democracy in states is stagnant, if not declining on a global scale, then the prospects for resolving the problems arising from the unsettling of legitimacy described in this book are dim, to say the least.

Fortunately, the focus on practices of political legitimacy in this volume suggests another way to conclude that departs from ideal theory and prescription. From the perspective of practice, looking back, political legitimacy has always been an aspiration, not a fully reachable destination. That conclusion has not changed under globalization. Similarly, it is a misreading of history to assume that the solutions of the past came into being smoothly, coherently, or fully formed. The United Nations and its affiliated organizations have evolved significantly since their emergence from the cataclysms of the Depression and the Second World War. Even the coalescence of a core set of international economic, security, and democratic policies and ideas, which finally appeared to form a coherent whole in the late twentieth century, was the result of a long period of adaptation and muddling through (Pauly 2007, 93). Globalization has again reopened fundamental questions about a way forward that may have seemed, at least to some, to be settled by the institutional, legal, and normative arrangements of that period and by the apparent triumph of the state and liberal democracy — at least as an aspiration. Recognizing the messy past suggests a bumpy road ahead is to be expected. The hope is that open-mindedness to alternative governing arrangements, alongside a continuing drive for some minimal global standards, will mark the way forward.

Our conclusion is, thus, both cautionary and optimistic. It warns against forgetting or reading out of history the power relations that drove legitimating practices in the past. At the same time, it points to ways in which foundations of legitimate polities and expressions of autonomy and citizenship can be brought forward in new and creative configurations as globalization unfolds. Our hope is that we have opened up a discussion on these possibilities and provided a set of conceptual and analytic lenses and tools with which to investigate them as they emerge and evolve.

Abbreviations

ASEAN	Association of Southeast Asian Nations
BFCA	Belize Fishermen Co-operatives Association
CE	Council of Europe
CNGO	conservation non-governmental organization
DAHR	Democratic Alliance of Hungarians
DNS	Domain Name System
EC	European Community
EU	European Union
FAB	Fisheries Advisory Board
FCNM	Framework Convention on the Protection of National Minorities
FON	Friends of Nature
GAID	Global Alliance for Information and Communication Technologies and Development
GATT	General Agreement on Tariffs and Trade
ICANN	Internet Corporation for Assigned Names and Numbers
ICC	International Criminal Court
ICISS	International Commission on Intervention and State Sovereignty
ICT	information and communications technology
IF	Integrated Framework for Trade-Related Technical Assistance
IGO	intergovernmental organizations

IMF	International Monetary Fund
ITU	International Telecommunications Union
LTTE	Liberation Tigers of Tamil Eelam
MNE	multinational enterprise
MPA	marine protected area
NAFTA	North American Free Trade Agreement
NATO	North Atlantic Treaty Organization
NGO	non-governmental organization
OECD	Organisation for Economic Co-operation and Development
OSCE	Organization for Security and Co-operation in Europe
R2P	responsibility to protect
TPRM	Trade Policy Review Mechanism
TRIPS	Agreement on Trade-Related Aspects of Intellectual Property Rights
WGIG	Working Group on Internet Governance
WSIS	World Summit on the Information Society
WTO	World Trade Organization

Notes and Acknowledgments

Chapter 1: Introduction

The authors thank the contributors to this volume and other members of the Globalization and Autonomy team for their ideas and discussions as this volume evolved. Many of the ideas in this Introduction grew out of those discussions.

1 No social contract theory in political philosophy recognizes the legitimacy of a process whereby states give over their authority in a way that is comparable to the legitimacy of individuals entering into a social contract to give up (authorize) sovereignty to a ruler (Hobbes [1651] 1968, 187).

2 In her chapter, Williams works with the concepts of public and private autonomy as outlined by Habermas (1996). *Public autonomy* refers to the governance of a democratic polity through popular sovereignty. Drawing from German understandings of the difference between public and private law, *private autonomy* refers to the rights of the individual. These concepts are analogous to the terms *collective* and *individual autonomy* used in this Introduction, in some other chapters in this book, and in the series more generally. We use the latter terms more commonly because they permit us to speak across disciplines and levels of analysis more easily than might be possible with the public autonomy–private autonomy distinction.

3 John Weaver, a member of our project team and historian who commented on a draft of this book, brought this reading to our attention.

Chapter 2: Citizenship as Agency within Communities of Shared Fate

1 In the nineteenth century, the idea of the nation emerged as an addendum to the theory of popular sovereignty: to act as sovereign, the people must be unitary. Shared language, culture, and history provided the pretext for the claim to unity within the state, distinctiveness in the international system of states, and, one should add, the colonization of

societies deemed to lack the degree of culture and civilization necessary to support a state of their own. In the twentieth century, the principles of one nation, one state, and the self-determination of peoples emerged as the gold standard for the legitimacy of international boundaries following the Second World War (MacMillan 2001), even as tensions between the state and nation have since continued to wax and wane. Despite the failure of the League of Nations, the principle of self-determination was again expressed in the creation of the United Nations following the Second World War. It also informed the decolonization movement, even as the territorial integrity of the colonial boundaries of the "state" trumped the "nation" in that process. Democracy and the claim to peoplehood were often decoupled as the number of states multiplied rapidly.

2 For a discussion of the implications of the neoliberal globalization variant as a threat to the possibility of justice, see Devetak and Higgott (1999, 487). They write instructively: "A purpose of the sovereign state in modern political life was to stabilize the social bond ... Outside of a settled social bond justice was thought to be unlikely if not impossible. The sovereign state was thus a precondition for justice ... The boundaries of justice were thought to be coextensive with the legal-territorial jurisdiction and economic reach of the sovereign polity."

3 Thus, we can see them as seeking freedom in the form of non-domination, to use Philip Pettit's (1997, 21-26) terms.

4 See Dewey (1927, 3):

> We take then our point of departure from the objective fact that human acts have consequences upon others, that some of these consequences are perceived, and that their perception leads to subsequent effort to control action so as to secure some consequences and avoid others. Following this clew, we are led to remark that the consequences are of two kinds, those which affect other persons directly engaged in a transaction and those which affect others beyond those immediately concerned. In this distinction we find the germ of the distinction between the private and the public. When indirect consequences are recognized and there is effort to regulate them, something having the traits of a state comes into existence.

5 For an account of these bodies' reactions and (limited but non-negligible) responsiveness to social movement organizations, see O'Brien et al. (2000).

6 For descriptions of the Global Compact, see Ruggie (2003b) and Fussler, Cramer, and van der Veght (2004).

7 The above discussion of modern citizenship, I should note, elides the distinction between the republican and liberal strands of citizenship I wish to draw out here because the two strands, while analytically distinct, have been blended in the theory and practice of modern citizenship.

8 Thus, in general, I accept Habermas's arguments about the co-originality of public and private autonomy in *Between Facts and Norms* (1996, 104 and section 3.1 generally). However, to the extent that Habermas's argument presupposes that all forms of public and private autonomy depend upon the existence of a territorially bounded constitutional order, I wish to resist or problematize it. See also the introductory chapter to this volume on this point.

9 In defense treaties such as NATO, for example, the boundaries of security are more inclusive than the boundaries of citizenship. Yet a country need not be wholly self-sufficient in the provision of security to possess the conditions for citizenship as self-rule or self-protection. Beyond a certain limit, dependence on others for security may compromise

political autonomy within state boundaries. To explore these limits, however, would take me far beyond my present purposes.

Chapter 3: Autonomy, Democracy, and Legitimacy

1 I use the term *Westphalian* to refer to the convention in international relations scholarship to date the modern system of sovereign states from the Treaty of Westphalia (1648), while recognizing that the practices and meanings of sovereignty have evolved considerably. The premise of this system is that states enjoy the right to rule, or political authority, within their borders (internal sovereignty) and the recognition of this right by other states (external sovereignty, the idea that there is no authority over states). Both aspects of sovereignty become open to question under globalization.

2 Indeed, it might be discovered that some existing boundaries are a poor fit for either communities of identity or communities of interest. This might be said of rather arbitrary national boundaries in Africa or even of provinces or states within many federal systems.

Chapter 4: Cosmopolis or Empire?

Sections of this chapter are adapted from Shah (2006).

1 This tension between hope and fear as drivers of political life, and their motivating force under globalization, emerged in early discussions of this volume. See the volume Introduction for the original framing.

2 For a conceptualization of globalization along these lines, see Appadurai (1996), Giddens (2000), Harvey (1990), Held et al. (1999), Robertson (1992), Scholte (2002), Szeman (2001a), and Waters (1995).

3 Whether Rorty's reading and application of Davidson's philosophy of language is true to Davidson's purposes and objectives is a matter of debate. However, in so far as Rorty develops his own theory of metaphor, his theory can be evaluated (and criticized) independently of its association with Davidson.

4 The novelty and unprecedented scope of contemporary globalization remains a highly debated question in discussions of globalization. In this study, I point to the ways in which the terminology of globalization pervades our discussions of politics, economics, and culture and works to justify specific policies, practices, and institutions (for instance, the World Trade Organization and the discourse of neoliberal globalization). For this reason, while previous periods in history were marked by transnational flows, I contend that globalization must be a new development in political governance and theory. I contend that the common tendency to point to practices of extraterritoriality as evidence of the relative banality of the recent interest in globalization is misguided (see, especially, Rosenberg 2000). Extraterritoriality was deployed and justified in the language of sovereignty and as a way to bolster state power. Globalization, by contrast, as many scholars have noted, uses extraterritorial practices to delegitimate sovereignty and complicate the legitimacy accorded to state power. For this reason, I consider it to be a unique and potentially transformative moment for established systems of political thought and practice.

5 I thank the editors of this volume for helping to draw out this point.

6 See also Ringmar (1996) and Jackson (2004) for a demonstration of the pervasiveness of this assumption in political analysis.

7   Hobbes does argue that hostility between states is less severe than hostility between individuals in the state of nature. There is a qualitative difference between the two. Hobbes, therefore, does not advocate the creation of an international Leviathan, which absorbs the autonomy of states (Hobbes [1651] 1996, 90).

8   This is not to say that states once had full regulatory capacity over transborder activities but rather that their ability to exert such control through borders, tariffs, and exchange controls has been relatively diminished (Pease 2000).

9   Nyers' chapter in this volume also implicitly demonstrates how cosmopolis, as reflected in cosmopolitan principles, has become a prevailing interpretation of globalization.

10 For an extended analysis and survey of the intellectual debate surrounding Hardt and Negri's *Empire,* see Balakrishnan (2003), Barkawi and Laffey (2002), Brown and Szeman (2002, 2005), and Passavant and Dean (2004).

Chapter 5: Governmental Rationalities and Indigenous Co-Governance

The co-editors and anonymous reviewers of this volume have provided incisive and challenging insights and advice that have greatly improved the chapter. I also want to acknowledge my debt for unexpected ideas over the course of the research to Philip Awashish, Mario Blaser, Jasmin Habib, Colin Scott, and members of the Relational Autonomy Collective. And I want to thank Brian Craik, Sam C. Gull, Peter Hutchins, Monica Mulrennan, Brian Noble, Eva and the late Joe Ottereyes, Alan Penn, Susan Preston, Alan Saganash Jr., and many others who go unlisted but not forgotten. This research was supported by the MCRI grant to William Coleman and a Standard Research Grant to the author, both from the Social Sciences and Humanities Research Council of Canada.

1   Charles Trevelyan (1807-86) was a British civil servant active in Delhi and Calcutta in the 1830s. He is attributed with being the founder of the modern civil service because of an 1853 report he co-authored to modify recruitment practices in the British civil service. Later in his life, he was the governor of Madras.

2   The affidavits were made orally in Cree in the presence of a translator and a lawyer, and they were recorded in English. They were submitted as evidence in *Mario Lord et al. v. The Attorney General of Québec et al.*, S.C.M. 500-05-043203-981, but the case was settled out of court in 2002. Copies of the affidavits are in the possession of the author.

3   Simon Metabie was Charlie's brother-in-law, from whom Charlie inherited the position of *Ndoho Ouchimau.*

4   The institution was compared to land ownership by early twentieth-century ethnographers; however, as a result of more extensive ethnography, it was shown by the 1970s to have no precisely comparable "Western" equivalent, although Crees commonly express it as being translatable to "ownership" for many purposes.

5   I call these forms *mercantilist governance* because, like the later forms of disciplinary governmental rationalities, they continue to be employed after liberal forms of governance develop and become, in the context of liberal discourses, dominant institutions and societies.

6   Given the changes in historical contexts between 1975 and 2002, Awashish notes how the issues are now seen differently. He notes that the agreement "provided a means for achieving, to some extent, their [Cree] vision for the enhancement and advancement of *Eeyou* [Cree] governance but [it was] constrained by the existing political and legal environment of the 1970s. ([It] did not recognize Aboriginal rights ... [nor] the inherent

right of Aboriginal self-government)" (2002, 155, see also 157). See pages 155-59 for Awashish's review of the provisions of the agreement from a contemporary governance perspective.

7 Some of these characteristics of the implementation of the agreement were the effects of the early phases of the adoption of neoliberal governance. By adopting corporate models and delegating authority and functions, governments reduced their accountability and undermined the rational, legal precepts and protections of the agreement.

8 The exact processes by which these decisions were made are not clear from the available records. But it is clear that the Crees' campaign kept the Great Whale project from being started quickly. Crees, therefore, created the opportunity for changes in various arenas to have their effects, including energy market prices and demand, support raised by indigenous individuals working in transnational financial institutions, the development of oppositional alliances and public support, political unease during elections in the United States, and consideration of the effect of the project difficulties on the upcoming referendum about sovereignty in Quebec.

9 Because of the closeness of the referendum vote, this was a claim that Crees share with many others who were active in other aspects of the campaign.

10 Unlike the 1975 agreement, this was a bilateral accord between the Crees and Quebec. A separate agreement with the federal government was negotiated in 2008.

Chapter 6: Protecting Our Resources

1 For a more in-depth discussion of co-management theory and its practice in Belize, see Goetze (2005).

2 For example, according to the World Bank's website, the theme of empowerment — defined as access to information, inclusion and participation, accountability, and local organizational capacity — has been a plank of its development policy since 2000. See http://go.worldbank.org/WXVIV52RBO (accessed 3 March 2005).

3 In this context local communities' ability to determine their participation in projects is co-opted by development agencies that mobilize a participatory approach to import their own ideas and then attribute them to the community. Rather than empowering communities, this "participation" legitimizes external intervention, limits local protest, and contributes to the expansion of agencies' control. The result is the incorporation of community members into a powerful development apparatus. Moreover, the meaning of *empowerment* is predefined externally, so participation takes place on terms as they are understood by outsiders — it is not really open to local views. Consequently, "empowerment," by masking or validating outsiders' predetermined decisions about the means and goals of development interventions, has a disempowering effect (Rahnema 1992; Gardner and Lewis 1996).

4 The term *power* in this context is used to refer to the capacity of people(s) to make or share in decisions on matters that affect their interests (Dahl 1982; Olsen 1993).

5 During initial informal interviews and later formal one-on-one semi-structured interviews, several informants (government representatives, FON staff and board members, and other co-managing NGO staff) commented on the truly community-based nature of FON as an organization that grew out of community member efforts and continued to actively engage in village consultations.

6 Friends of Nature was one of four case studies featured as part of the project, which was being used to evaluate the diversity of co-management options that may be used under

varying conditions throughout the Caribbean region. Project staff also supported the implementation of these co-management pilot projects through training workshops.

7 Prior to FON launching its own efforts, patrols by the Fisheries Department were sporadic, which contributed in large part to their ineffectiveness (see Goetze 2005).

8 In 2001 the Nature Conservancy organized a debt-for-nature swap in which the US government forgave nearly half of Belize's debt to the United States. In exchange, the government of Belize agreed to protect a designated area of rainforest, support community environmental organizations, and invest in a national protected areas system (Goetze 2005).

9 For more on the socio-cultural significance of fishing in Placencia, see Goetze (2005).

Chapter 7: Globalization, European Integration, and the Nationalities Question

We express our thanks to the Carnegie Corporation of New York for funding our research.

1 Some writers distinguish between and from immigrant groups, and not just because they are generally not voluntarily admitted (Kymlicka 1995). Settlers often come, in significant numbers, at the same time and from the same place and locate in the same region. They tend to think strongly of themselves as a community. Most immigrant groups come as individuals, at different times, from different places, settle in dispersed patterns, albeit sometimes in ghettoes, and, while they may have a view of themselves as a community (such as Muslims in France or Kurds in Germany), are seldom as tightly integrated as settler groups. This, however, is a fluid distinction and depends on judgments about the self-consciousness of groups and contested historiography (Keating 2001a).

2 There is a common, but not universal, distinction between minority nations and national minorities and the rights to which each is entitled. For Seymour, Couture, and Nielsen (1998), a minority nation is a group without a state that is entitled to self-determination. A national minority, on the other hand, is a group that lives within a minority nation's homeland and whose ethnic kin dominate the state. A national minority, in their view, has no right to self-determination, only a right to be fairly integrated into a self-determining unit. This distinction is designed to show that the Québécois have a right to self-determination, but Quebec's anglophone communities have no right to have their regions remain in Canada after Quebec's independence.

3 Virtually all Protestants, however, are unionists (British nationalists).

4 Indeed, even those who did not support an eventual European federation hoped for the transcendence of aggressive nationalism. This is one interpretation of Aneurin Bevan's speech on 22 January 1948, in which he indicated that the British government supported "the closer consolidation and economic development [of Europe] and eventually ... the spiritual unity of Europe as a whole" (cited in McKay 1996, 37–38).

5 Most contemporary versions of this line of argument tend to nod in a postmodernist direction. Followers of this approach emphasize the challenge posed to the nation-state model, with its modernist emphasis on unity, sovereignty, and consensus, by increased likelihood of dissensus (see Kristeva 1995; Bhabha 1990; Ricoeur 1995). However, this view is rarely discussed in the concrete form that is necessary to allow a full assessment of it.

6 The exception to this statement would be a small minority of Basque nationalists who are supporters of political violence.

7 For a strong statement of this position, see Kymlicka (2001, 28-29). Not all "progressives" lambaste minority nationalism. There is a tradition on the left that associates minority nationalism with anti-imperialism. Thus, Tom Nairn insists that we should support

minority nationalism if we think, along democratic and anti-imperialist lines, that people should govern themselves and alien rule should be resisted (see Nairn 1997, 47-48).

8 This argument is frequently made in terms of allowing multiple layers of compatible identification — local, national, and European (see Taylor 1995). For a similar, but much less sympathetic (to nationalism) reading, see Kristeva (1995).

9 This is why Quebec sovereigntists object to the Canadian Charter of Rights and Freedoms, which they identify with Pierre Trudeau's Canadian nation-building agenda. Quebec sovereigntists are not against rights per se, which is how their position is sometimes interpreted. Indeed, the Province of Quebec has its own provincial Charter of Rights and Freedoms, which, while it is a provincial statute and not a constitutional document, has been used to strike down provincial legislation.

10 In Kymlicka's view, the rights that are protected are helpful for those small minorities of 5 to 10 percent or less that are incapable of exercising self-government and that are already well on the road to assimilation — such as those who live in the Czech Republic, Slovenia, and Hungary — but are "largely irrelevant" for sizeable national minorities.

11 Concern for the Roma, however, did not seriously affect the accession process. Sasse (2006, 72) notes that the EU harshly criticized the candidate countries for their treatment of the Roma while simultaneously acknowledging that they continued "to fulfil the Copenhagen criteria." The EU and the candidate countries, she argues, "appear to be acting out a charade on Roma policy."

Chapter 8: Challenging Legitimacy or Legitimate Challenges

1 *Helsinki* in this statement refers to the Conference on Security and Co-operation in Europe, Final Act, 1 August 1975, signed by thirty-four countries. Its Declaration on Principles Guiding Relations between Participating States included a reference to the "self-determination of peoples."

2 This division between ethnic and civic nations, originally proposed by Ignatieff (1994), is somewhat misleading. In particular, given the cultural content of all states, no such clear division exists (see Arel 2001). What this quote highlights, however, is the lack of inclusive terms of belonging reflected in the Romanian Constitution.

3 This assertion resonates with the Supreme Court of Canada's ruling on Quebec's secession. According to the court, external self-determination or secession is only entitled if a people are blocked from a meaningful exercise of their right to internal self-determination (Tully 2001, 31).

Chapter 9: Sovereignty Redux?

1 The commission's members are Gareth Evans (co-chair, Australia), Mohamed Sahnoun (co-chair, Algeria), Gisèle Côté-Harper (Canada), Lee Hamilton (United States), Michael Ignatieff (Canada), Vladimir Lukin (Russia), Klaus Naumann (Germany), Cyril Ramaphosa (South Africa), Fidel Ramos (Philippines), Cornelio Sommaruga (Switzerland), Eduardo Stein (Guatemala), and Ramesh Thakur (India).

2 The consultations were held in Ottawa (15 January 2001), Geneva (30-31 January 2001), London (3 February 2001), Maputo (10 March 2001), Washington (2 May 2001), Santiago (4 May 2001), Cairo (21 May 2001), Paris (23 May 2001), New Delhi (10 June 2001), Beijing (14 June 2001), and St. Petersburg (16 July 2001). Summaries of these meetings are included in the supplementary volume that accompanies the commission's report.

3 Other exclusions are the events of 11 September 2001 and the resulting interventions into Afghanistan and Iraq. These are virtually ignored in the report. While it is true that these events occurred after the consultation period and after the majority of the report had been written, the commission nonetheless argues that these events are not relevant to the framework they have established. Whereas the commission is concerned with military interventions that deal with human protection claims in other states, it claims that the US-led intervention in Afghanistan was something "fundamentally different" (ICISS 2001, viii) in that it was a response to a terrorist attack in one's own state.

4 While the idea of the responsibility to protect has received some of its most enthusiastic support from sub-Saharan African countries, the commission's threshold criteria for military intervention are actually more conservative than instruments that already exist in international humanitarian law in that region. For example, the commission does not include systematic racial discrimination or massive human rights abuses as criteria for intervention (MacFarlane, Theiking, and Weiss 2004, 982).

Chapter 10: From Ethnic Civil War to Global War

1 For a discussion of the need to historicize violence and the difficulty of doing so, see Benjamin (1986) and Jacques Derrida's (1992) critical response to Benjamin.

2 Like Hardt and Negri, Mbembe develops his notion of necropolitics through Michel Foucault's concept of biopower. It seems to me, however, that Hardt and Negri rely on Foucault's *The History of Sexuality* (1978), which largely omits the question of race from its discourse on biopolitics. In contrast, Mbembe appears to draw from and expand Foucault's (2003) lecture series *Society Must Be Defended,* in which he examines the modalities of power that regulate death. Most importantly, Foucault argues that the power of death can be exercised only through the systematic application of racism. Indeed, racism, he argues, "is the indispensable precondition that allows someone to be killed, that allows others to be killed" (ibid., 256). Mbembe, then, transfers Foucault's argument into colonial space — a move, as Ann Stoler (1995) suggests, that is painfully absent from Foucault's work — and, by shifting geo-historical context of biopolitics, the epistemological focus equally moves from life to death. It is, thus, that Hardt and Negri and Mbembe employ Foucault to substantially different ends and effects.

Chapter 11: An Airborne Disease

I am most grateful to the Social Sciences and Humanities Research Council for the funds necessary to conduct research for this chapter and to the Canada Research Chairs Program for the time to write it. I am also grateful to Anthony P. Lombardo and Kristina Bergeron for their assistance in conducting the interviews and to Michael Lisetto-Smith for his research assistance.

1 This and other quotations are translated from the French by the author.

2 This respondent's figures are an underestimate. Africa's share of world merchandise exports in 2000 was 2.3 percent; its share of world merchandise imports in the same year was 2.0 percent (WTO 2004). Africa's share of foreign direct investment in 2003 was 2.7 percent of the world total (UNCTAD 2004).

3 The respondent is referring to the late nineteenth-century scramble for Africa, which divided up Africa among several European colonial powers (Oliver and Fage 1962, 181-95).

4 For views favourable to globalization, see *The Economist* (2001), *Globe and Mail* (2001), Legrain (2002), Bhagwati (2004).

Chapter 12: The World Trade Organization

An earlier version of this chapter appears in the Occasional Papers series of the Munk Centre for International Studies, University of Toronto, July 2006.

1 The description of the naked power play is based on interviews with participants (Steinberg 2002, 359-65).

2 Although the SPS Agreement included a provision for technical assistance, nothing much has happened (Zarrilli 1999, 24).

3 Howard-Hassmann (this volume) similarly uses the term *missing* in reference to the experience of much of Africa, and Africans, under globalization.

4 However, one important new development has been the creation of the NGO called International Lawyers and Economists Against Poverty to provide interdisciplinary advice on trade policy for developing countries. Information is available at the organization's website.

5 See note 2 and Blackhurst (2001).

6 Smith (this volume) similarly notes multiple strands within global civil society.

Chapter 13: Governing the Electronic Commons

I would like to thank the several Canadian government officials who provided background information on the World Summit on the Information Society as well as other aspects of the ICANN issue.

1 An interesting parallel to ICANN is the International Accounting Standards Board (IASB), a private-sector, global standard-setting organization that is working at developing a consistent set of global standards for the profession. Many of the governance debates that centre on the IASB are remarkably similar to those that surround ICANN. See Eaton and Porter (2008). There are other examples of global private-sector regulatory or standard-setting regimes, but they remain rare (Ronit and Schneider 1999; Cashore, Auld, Newsom 2004).

2 For a similar understanding of the dynamic interplay of globalization and autonomy in the context of global governance issues, see the volume *Global Ordering: Institutions and Autonomy in a Changing World* (Pauly and Coleman 2008) in this series.

3 The following pages draw on Pal and Teplova (2004).

4 The technical as opposed to governance aspects of these developments are chronicled in Hafner and Lyon (1996). Most of what follows on the Internet addressing systems is taken from Mueller (2002) and Klein (2002).

5 The United Nations Millennium Development Goals are to eradicate extreme poverty and hunger; achieve universal primary education; promote gender equality and empower women; reduce child mortality; improve maternal health; combat HIV/AIDS, malaria, and other diseases; ensure environmental sustainability; and develop a global partnership for development (United Nations 2000).

6 Pauly (2008) develops a similar analysis of the emerging economic coordination role of the UN as states that lead and states that follow engage in a dialogue over the globalizing economy.

Chapter 14: Contested Globalizations

1   Although this is a key part of the neoliberal ideology, in practice neoliberals seek government intervention to protect private property rights. This kind of intervention can involve massive amounts of public expenditures and infringements on other individual rights.

2   The vision of democratic globalization outlined here parallels Herman Daly's discussion of internationalization. For Daly, *internationalization* refers to the "increasing importance of relations between nations: international trade, treaties, alliances, protocols, etc. The basic unit of community and policy remains the nation, even as relations among nations, and among individuals in different nations, become increasingly necessary and important" (Daly 2002).

3   Following common practice among scholars and practitioners, I use the terms *Global North* and *Global South* to refer, respectively, to the early industrializing countries of the Organization for Economic Co-operation and Development (although OECD membership has recently expanded to include some of the wealthiest later industrializers) and to the later industrializing or Third World countries.

4   Markoff (2004) describes a double democratic deficit as states become increasingly constrained by supranational actors and institutions at the same time that they relinquish traditional authority in the areas of welfare and the economy.

5   For more discussion of the concept of transnational network, see Smith (2008); Keck and Sikkink (1998); and Maney (2001).

6   For examples of movements of this era, see Keck and Sikkink (1998); Finnemore (1996); Boswell and Chase-Dunn (2000); Wittner (1997); and Chatfield (2007).

7   Not only did UN conferences provide substantive focal points and meeting opportunities, international agencies also provided some funding for representatives from poor parts of the world, especially funding to travel to international meetings. Private foundations and civil society groups also helped support travel by under-represented groups to global conferences.

8   I qualify this because large-scale protests against the IMF and World Bank have long occurred in the Global South. What was new in the 1990s was that Northern activists were actively working to disrupt the international meetings of these bodies, which were generally in the cities of the Global North.

9   Trade agreements have superseded other international treaties in practice if not in actual law because the global trade bodies have far stronger enforcement mechanisms than do international organizations, which are often based upon non-binding agreements or on legally binding treaties that lack the resources to punish non-compliance. The huge potential costs of trade sanctions create a chilling effect; therefore, few countries even attempt to challenge the prioritization of trade over other forms of international law.

Chapter 15: Conclusion

The author would like to thank William Coleman for detailed comments and suggestions on this chapter.

Works Cited

Ablin, Eduardo, and Roberto Bouzas. 2002. Argentina's foreign trade strategy: The curse of asymmetric integration in the world economy. In *The strategic dynamics of Latin American trade,* ed. Vinod Aggarwal, Ralph Espach, and Joseph Tulchin, 159-72. Stanford, CA: Stanford University Press.

Adams, William. 2004. *Against extinction: The story of conservation.* London: Earthscan.

Adler, Emanuel, and Steven Bernstein. 2005. Knowledge in power: The epistemic construction of global governance. In *Power and global governance*, ed. Michael Barnett and Raymond Duvall, 294-318. Cambridge: Cambridge University Press.

Agamben, Giorgio. 1998. *Homo sacer: Sovereign power and bare life.* Trans. Daniel Heller-Roazen. Stanford, CA: Stanford University Press.

Agarwal, Manmohan, and Jozefina Cutura. 2004. *Integrated framework for trade-related technical assistance, case study.* Washington, DC: World Bank Operations Evaluation Department.

AIV and CAVV. 2000. *Humanitarian intervention.* The Hague: Advisory Council on International Affairs/Advisory Committee on Issues of Public International Law.

Alcock, Antony. 2001. From conflict to agreement in Northern Ireland: Lessons from Europe. In *Northern Ireland and the divided world,* ed. John McGarry, 159-81. Oxford: Oxford University Press.

Alfred, Taiaiake. 1999. *Peace, power, righteousness: An indigenous manifesto.* Don Mills, ON: Oxford University Press.

—. 2002. Sovereignty. In *A companion to American Indian history,* ed. Philip J. Deloria and Neal Salisbury, 460-74. Oxford: Blackwell.

Ali, Taisier M., and Robert O. Matthews, eds. 1999. *Civil wars in Africa: Roots and resolution.* Montreal and Kingston: McGill-Queen's University Press.

—. 2004. *Durable peace: Challenges for peacebuilding in Africa.* Toronto: University of Toronto Press.

Amin, Samir. 2003. *Obsolescent capitalism: Contemporary politics and global disorder.* Trans. Patrick Camiller. London: Zed Books.

Anderson, Benedict. 1991. *Imagined communities: Reflections on the origin and spread of nationalism.* Rev. ed. London: Verso.

Anderson, Kym, Will Martin, and Dominique van der Mensbrugghe. 2005. Would multi-lateral trade reform benefit sub-Saharan Africans? Washington, DC, World Bank Policy Research Paper 3616.

Annan, Kofi A. 1999. *The question of intervention: Statements by the secretary-general.* New York: United Nations.

—. 2005. *In larger freedom: Towards development, security and human rights for all.* New York: United Nations Secretariat. http://http://www.un.org/largerfreedom/.

Appadurai, Arjun. 1996. *Modernity at large: Cultural dimensions of globalization.* Minneapolis: University of Minnesota Press.

Arasanayagam, Jean. 1995. *All is burning.* New Delhi: Penguin Books India.

Archibugi, Danielle, ed. 2003. *Debating cosmopolitics.* London: Verso.

—. 2004. Cosmopolitan guidelines for humanitarian intervention. *Alternatives: Global, Local, Political* 29 (1): 1-22.

Archibugi, Danielle, and David Held, eds. 1995. *Cosmopolitan democracy: An agenda for a new world order.* Cambridge, MA: Polity Press/Blackwell Publishers.

Archibugi, Danielle, David Held, and Martin Köhler, eds. 1998. *Re-imagining political community: Studies in cosmopolitan democracy.* Stanford, CA: Stanford University Press.

Arel, Dominique. 2001. Political stability in multinational democracies: Comparing language dynamics in Brussels, Montreal and Barcelona. In *Multinational democracies,* ed. Alain-G. Gagnon and James Tully, 65-89. Cambridge: Cambridge University Press.

Asch, Michael. 1997. *Aboriginal and treaty rights in Canada.* Vancouver: UBC Press.

AVERT. 2005. Sub-Saharan Africa: HIV and AIDS statistics. AVERT. http://www.avert.org/subaadults.htm.

Awashish, Philip. 1988. The stakes for the Cree of Québec. In *James Bay and Northern Québec: Ten years after,* ed. Sylvie Vincent and Garry Bowers, 42-45. Montreal: Recherches amérindiennes au Québec.

—. 2002. Some reflections on Eeyou governance and the James Bay and Northern Quebec Agreement. In *Reflections on the James Bay and Northern Québec Agreement,* ed. Alain-G. Gagnon and Guy Rocher, 153-63. Montreal: Québec Amérique.

Axworthy, Lloyd. 2003. *Navigating a new world: Canada's global future.* Toronto: Knopf.

—. 2008. International community has a responsibility to protect Myanmar. *Edmonton Journal,* 13 May.

Axworthy, Lloyd, and Sarah Taylor. 1998. A ban for all seasons: The landmines convention and its implications for Canadian diplomacy. *International Journal* 53 (2): 189-203.

Ayoob, Mohammed. 2002. Humanitarian intervention and state sovereignty. *International Journal of Human Rights* 6 (1): 81-102.

Azueta, James. 2000. Marine Protected Areas Network Initiative (draft). Belize City: Fisheries Department, Ministry of Agriculture, Fisheries and Cooperatives.

Bagwell, Kyle, Petros Mavroidis, and Robert Staigler. 2004. The case for tradable remedies in WTO dispute settlement. World Bank Policy Research Working Paper 3314, Washington, DC.

Baiocchi, Gianpaolo. 2004. The party and the multitude: Brazil's Workers' Party (PT) and the challenges of building a just social order in a globalizing context. *Journal of World-Systems Research* 10 (1): 199-215.

Balakrishnan, Gopal, ed. 2003. *Debating empire.* London: Verso.

Balibar, Étienne. 2002. *Politics and the other scene.* London: Verso.

—. 2004. *We, the people of Europe? Reflections on transnational citizenship.* Trans. James Swenson. Princeton, NJ: Princeton University Press.

Ball, Terence, and Richard Bellamy, eds. 2003. *The Cambridge history of twentieth-century political thought*. Cambridge: Cambridge University Press.

Bandy, Joe, and Jackie Smith. 2005. *Coalitions across borders: Transnational protest and the neoliberal order*. Lanham, MD: Rowman and Littlefield.

Barber, Benjamin. 1995. *Jihad vs. McWorld*. New York: Random House.

Barkawi, Tarak, and Mark Laffey. 2002. Retrieving the imperial. *Millennium: Journal of International Studies* 31 (1): 109-27.

Barker, Mary L., and Dieter Soyez. 1994. Think locally, act globally? The transnationalization of Canadian resourse-use conflicts. *Environment* 36: 12-20, 32-36.

Barlow, John Perry. 1996. A declaration of the independence of cyberspace. http://www.islandone.org/Politics/DeclarationOfIndependance.html.

Barnett, Michael, and Raymond Duvall. 2005. Power in global governance. In *Power in global governance*, 1-32. New York: Cambridge University Press.

Barry, Andrew, Thomas Osborne, and Nikolas Rose. 1996. *Foucault and political reason*. Chicago: University of Chicago Press.

Batt, Judy. 2006. Cross-border minorities and European integration in southeast Europe: The Hungarians and Serbs compared. In *European integration and the nationalities question*, ed. John McGarry and Michael Keating, 169-90. London: Routledge.

Beck, Ulrich. 1999. Democracy beyond the nation-state. *Dissent* 46 (1): 53-56.

—. 2002. The terrorist threat: World Risk Society revisited. *Theory, Culture, and Society* 19 (4): 39-55.

Beier, Marshall. 2005. *International relations in uncommon places: Indigeneity, cosmology, and the limits of international theory*. New York: Palgrave Macmillan.

Beiner, Ronald. 1995. Foucault's hyper-liberalism. *Critical Review* 9 (3): 349-70.

Beitz, Charles. 1979. *Political theory and international relations*. Princeton: Princeton University Press.

—. 2000. Rawls's law of peoples. *Ethics* 110 (4): 669-96.

Bellamy, Alex J. 2003. Humanitarian responsibilities and interventionist claims in international society. *Review of International Studies* 29 (3): 321-40.

Bellamy, Richard, and Dario Castiglione. 1998. Between cosmopolis and community: Three models of rights and democracy within the European Union. In *Re-imagining political community: Studies in cosmopolitan democracy*, ed. Daniele Archibugi, David Held, and Martin Köhler, 152-78. Stanford, CA: Stanford University Press.

Bencivenni, Marcella. 2006. The new world order and the possibility of change: A critical analysis of Hardt and Negri's "multitude." *Socialism and Democracy* 20 (1): 23-43.

Bendell, Jem. 2004. *Flags of inconvenience? The global compact and the future of the United Nations*. Nottingham, UK: Nottingham University Business School.

Benjamin, Walter. 1986. *Reflections: Essays, aphorisms, autobiographical writings*. Trans. Edmund Jephcott. New York: Schocken Books.

Berkes, Fikret. 1999. *Sacred ecology: Traditional ecological knowledge and resource management*. Philadelphia, PA: Taylor and Francis.

Berkes, Fikret., Robin Mahon, Patrick McConney, Richard Pollnac, and Robert Pomeroy. 2001. *Managing small-scale fisheries: Alternative directions and methods*. Ottawa, ON: IDRC.

Bergeron, Kristina Maud. Under review. Global activism and changing identities: Interconnecting the global and the local — Examples from the Grand Council of the Crees and the Saami Council. In *Indigenous peoples and autonomy: Insights for a global age*, ed. Mario Blaser, Ravi de Costa, Deborah McGregor, and William D. Coleman. Vancouver: UBC Press.

Bernard, H. Russell. 1995. *Research methods in anthropology: Qualitative and quantitative approaches.* 2nd ed. Walnut Creek: Alta Mira Press.

Bernier, Julie. 2001. Nationalism in transition: Nationalizing impulses and international counter-weights in Latvia and Estonia. In *Minority nationalism in the changing state order,* ed. Michael Keating and John McGarry, 342-62. Oxford: Oxford University Press.

Bernstein, Steven. 2004. The elusive basis of legitimacy in global governance: Three conceptions. Working Paper Series, Institute on Globalization and the Human Condition, McMaster University, Hamilton, Ontario.

Bernstein, Steven, and Benjamin Cashore. 2000. Globalization, four paths of internationalization and domestic policy change. *Canadian Journal of Political Science* 33 (1): 67-99.

Besley, Timothy, and Robin Burgess. 2003. Halving global poverty. *Journal of Economic Perspectives* 17 (3): 3-22.

Bhabha, Homi, ed. 1990. *Nation and narration.* London: Routledge.

—. 1994. *The location of culture.* London: Routledge.

Bhagwati, Jagdish. 2004. *In defense of globalization.* New York: Oxford.

Bicego, George, Shea Rutstein, and Kiersten Johnson. 2003. Dimensions of the emerging orphan crisis in sub-Saharan Africa. *Social Science and Medicine* 56 (6): 1235-47.

Biersteker, Thomas W., and Cynthia Weber. 1996. *Sovereignty as a social construct.* Cambridge: Cambridge University Press.

Bigo, Didier. 2006. Protection: Security, territory and population. In *The politics of protection: Sites of insecurity and political agency,* ed. Jef Huysmans, Andrew Dobson, and Raia Prokhovnik, 84-100. London: Routledge.

Bishai, Linda S. 1998. Sovereignty and minority rights: Interrelations and implications. *Global Governance* 4 (2): 157-82.

Blackhurst, Richard. 2001. Reforming WTO decision making: Lessons from Singapore and Seattle. In *The World Trade Organization: Millennium Round,* ed. Klaus Gunter Deutsch and Bernhard Speyer, 295-99. London: MacMillan.

Blaser, Mario, Ravi de Costa, Deborah McGregor, and William D. Coleman, eds. Under review. *Indigenous peoples and autonomy: Insights for a global age.* Vancouver: UBC Press.

Blaser, Mario, Harvey A. Feit, and Glenn McRae. 2004a. Indigenous peoples and development processes: New terrains of struggle. In *In the way of development,* ed. Mario Blaser, Harvey A. Feit, and Glenn McRae, 1-25. London: Zed Books.

—, eds. 2004b. *In the way of development.* London: Zed Books.

Bodansky, Daniel. 1999. The legitimacy of international governance: A coming challenge for international environmental law? *American Journal of International Law* 93 (3): 596-624.

Bohman, James. 1997. The public spheres of the world citizen. In *Perpetual peace: Essays on Kant's cosmopolitan ideal,* ed. James Bohman and Matthias Lutz-Bahmann, 179-200. Cambridge, MA: MIT Press.

Boswell, Terry, and Christopher Chase-Dunn. 2000. *The spiral of capitalism and socialism.* Boulder, CO: Lynne Rienner Publishers.

Bown, Chad P., and Bernard M. Hoekman. 2005a. *WTO dispute settlement and missing developing country cases: Engaging the private sector.* Wisconsin: University of Wisconsin Press.

—. 2005b. WTO dispute settlement and the missing developing country cases: Engaging the private sector. *Journal of International Economic Law* 8 (4): 861-90.

Brennan, Timothy. 1997. *At home in the world: Cosmopolitanism now.* Cambridge, MA: Harvard University Press.

—. 2005. The trans-moralists. *Globalization and Autonomy Online Compendium.* http://www.globalautonomy.ca/global1/position.jsp?index=PP_Brennan_TransMoralists.xml.

Broad, Robin, and Zahara Hecksher. 2003. Before Seattle: The historical roots of the current movement against corporate-led globalisation. *Third World Quarterly* 24 (4): 713-28.

Brockington, Dan. 2004. Community conservation, inequality and injustice: Myths of power in protected area management. *Conservation and Society* 2 (2): 411-32.

Brown, Chris. 1992. *International relations theory: New normative approaches.* New York: Harvester Wheatsheaf.

—, ed. 1994. *Political restructuring in Europe: Ethical perspectives.* London: Routledge.

Brown, D. 2004. The fisher organization model of co-management: The case of the Belize Fishermen Cooperative Association (BFCA), Ltd. *Biannual Newsletter of the Caribbean Regional Fisheries Mechanism* (July): 1-2.

Brown, Nicholas, and Imre Szeman. 2002. Michael Hardt and Antonio Negri interviewed by Nicholas Brown and Imre Szeman. *Cultural Studies* 16 (2): 177-92.

—. 2005. What is the multitude? *Cultural Studies* 19 (3): 372-87.

Brubaker, Rogers. 1996. *Nationalism reframed: Nationhood and the national question in the new Europe.* Cambridge: Cambridge University Press.

Bruno, Kenny, and Joshua Karliner. 2002. *Earthsummit.biz: The corporate takeover of sustainable development.* Oakland, CA: Food First Books.

Brydon, Diana, and William D. Coleman, eds. 2008. *Renegotiating community: Interdisciplinary perspectives, global contexts.* Vancouver: UBC Press.

Brysk, Allison. 1996. Turning weakness into strength: The internationalization of Indian rights. *Latin American Perspectives* 23 (2): 38-57.

Buchanan, A. 2000. Rawls's law of peoples: Rules for a vanished Westphalian world. *Ethics* 110 (4): 697-721.

Buchanan, Allen, and Robert O. Keohane. 2004. The preventive use of force: A cosmopolitan institutional proposal. *Ethics and International Affairs* 18 (1): 1-22.

Burchell, Graham, Colin Gordon, and Peter Miller, eds. 1991. *The Foucault effect.* Chicago: University of Chicago Press.

Burnnée, Jutta, and Stephen J. Toope. 2000. International law and constructivism: Elements of an interactional theory of international law. *Columbia Journal of Transnational Law* 39: 19-74.

Buzan, Barry, Ole Waever, and Joap de Wilde. 1998. *Security: A new framework for analysis.* Boulder, CO: Lynne Rienner.

Calder, Gideon. 2003. *Rorty.* London: Weidenfeld and Nicolson.

Calhoun, Craig. 2002. Imagining solidarity: Cosmopolitanism, constitutional patriotism, and the public sphere. *Public Culture* 14 (1): 147-71.

Cashore, Benjamin, Graeme Auld, and Deanna Newsom. 2004. *Governing through markets: Forest certification and the emergence of non-state authority.* New Haven: Yale University Press.

Castoriadis, Cornelius. 1991. *Philosophy, politics, autonomy: Essays in political philosophy.* Ed. David Ames Curtis. New York: Oxford University Press.

CCA, UWI, and MRAG (Caribbean Conservation Association, University of the West Indies, and Marine Resources Assessment Group). 2003. *Summary report of the Project Terminal Workshops held in Barbados, Grenada and Belize on 19, 22, and 28 May 2003.* Report of the Caribbean Coastal Co-management Guidelines Project, Barbados, Caribbean Conservation Association.

Cederman, Lars-Erik. 2001. Nationalism and bounded integration: What it would take to construct a European demos. *European Journal of International Relations* 7 (June): 139-74.

Centre for Development Studies. 2000. DfID support for pro-poor civil society organizations: A good practice guide. Manuscript. Department of Economics and International Development, University of Bath.

Chamberlin, Edward J. 2004. *If this is your land, where are your stories? Finding common ground.* Toronto: Vintage Canada.

Charnovitz, Steve. 1997. Two centuries of participation: NGOs and international governance. *Michigan Journal of International Law* 18 (2): 183-286.

Chase-Dunn, Christopher. 2002. Globalization from below: Toward a collectively rational and democratic global commonwealth. *Annals of the American Academy of Political and Social Science* 581: 48-61.

Chatfield, Charles. 1997. Intergovernmental and nongovernmental associations to 1945. In *Transnational social movements and global politics: Solidarity beyond the state,* ed. Jackie Smith, Charles Chatfield, and Ron Pagnucco, 19-41. Syracuse, NY: Syracuse University Press.

—. 2007. National insecurity: From dissent to protest against US foreign policy. In *The long war: A new history of US national security policy since World War II,* ed. Andrew Bacevich, 456-516. New York: Columbia University Press.

Chenier, Jacqueline, Stephen Sherwood, and Tahnee Robertson. 1999. Copán, Honduras: Collaboration for identity, equity, and sustainability. In *Cultivating peace: Conflict and collaboration in natural resource management,* ed. Daniel Buckles, 221-36. Ottawa, ON: IDRC.

Chomsky, Noam. 2003. *Hegemony or survival.* New York: Metropolitan Books.

Ciaccia, John. [1975] 1998. Philosophy of the agreement. In *James Bay and Northern Québec Agreement and complementary agreements.* Quebec: Les Publications du Québec.

Civil Society Internet Governance Caucus. 2003. Shaping information societies for human needs: Civil society declaration to the World Summit on the Information Society. http://www.itu.int/wsis/docs/geneva/civil-society-declaration.pdf.

Clarkson, Stephen. 2008. Differentiated autonomy: North America's model of transborder governance. In *Global ordering: Institutions and autonomy in a changing world,* ed. Louis Pauly and William D. Coleman. 191-213. Vancouver: UBC Press.

Claude, Inis L., Jr. 1966. Collective legitimization as a political function of the United Nations. *International Organization* 20 (3): 367-79.

Clifford, Michael. 2001. *Political genealogy after Foucault: Savage identities.* New York: Routledge.

Cochran, Molly. 1999. *Normative theory in international relations: A pragmatic approach.* Cambridge: Cambridge University Press.

Code, Lorraine. 2000. The perversion of autonomy and the subjection of women: Discourses of social advocacy at century's end. In *Relational autonomy: Feminist perspectives on autonomy, agency and the social self,* ed. Catriona Mackenzie and Natalie Stoljar, 181-212. New York: Oxford University Press.

Cohen, Joshua. 1989. Deliberation and democratic legitimacy. In *The good polity: Normative analysis of the state,* ed. Alan Hamlin and Philip Pettit, 17-34. New York: Blackwell.

Cohen, Robin, and Steve Vertovec, eds. 2002. *Conceiving cosmopolitanism.* Oxford: Oxford University Press.

Coicaud, Jean-Marc, and Veijo Heiskanen, eds. 2001. *The legitimacy of international organizations.* Tokyo: United Nations University Press.

Coker, Christopher. 2001. *Humane warfare.* London: Routledge.

Colas, Alejandro. 2003. The power of representation: Democratic politics and global governance. Special issue, *Review of International Studies* 29: S97-S118.

Coleman, William D. 2005. Globalization and development. In *International development governance,* ed. Ahmed Shafiqul Huque and Habib Zafarullah, 75-90. Boca Raton, FL: CRC Press/ Taylor and Francis.

Collier, Paul. 2007. *The bottom billion: Why the poorest countries are failing and what can be done about it.* New York: Oxford.

Colomer, Josep M. 2007. *Great empires, small nations: The uncertain future of the sovereign state.* London: Routledge.

Connolly, William. 1984. Introduction: Legitimacy and modernity. In *Legitimacy and the state,* ed. William Connolly, 1-19. Oxford: Basil Blackwell.

—. 1991. *Identity/difference: Democratic negotiations of political paradox.* Ithaca, NY: Cornell University Press.

Conservation International. Conservation strategies. Conservation International. http://?www.conservation.org/xp/CIWEB/strategies/ (accessed 20 June 2005).

Consultative Board. 2004. *The future of the WTO: Addressing institutional challenges in the new millennium.* Report to the director-general, Supachai Panitchpakdi, Geneva, World Trade Organization.

Coon Come, Matthew. 2004. Survival in the context of mega-resource development: Experiences of the James Bay Crees and the First Nations of Canada. In *In the way of development,* ed. Mario Blaser, Harvey A. Feit, and Glenn McRae, 153-64. London: Zed Books.

Cooper, Andrew F. 2004. *Tests of global governance: Canadian diplomacy and United Nations World Conferences.* Tokyo: United Nations University Press.

Cooper, Ian. 2006. The watchdogs of subsidiarity: National parliaments and the logic of arguing in the EU. *Journal of Common Market Studies* 44 (2): 281-304.

Cornell, Drucilla. 2004. Defending ideals: War, democracy, and political struggles. London: Routledge.

Couture, Armand. 1988. Le point de vue d'un promoteur. In *James Bay and Northern Québec: Ten years after,* ed. Sylvie Vincent and Garry Bowers, 50-53. Montreal: Recherches amérindiennes au Québec.

—. 2002. Programs of social and economic development from sections 28, 29 and 30 of the agreement. In *Reflections on the James Bay and Northern Québec Agreement,* ed. Alain-G. Gagnon and Guy Rocher, 63-68. Montreal: Québec Amérique.

Craik, Brian. 2004. The importance of working together: Exclusions, conflicts and participation in James Bay, Quebec. In *In the way of development,* ed. Mario Blaser, Harvey A. Feit, and Glenn McRae, 166-85. London: Zed Books.

Crawford, James, and Susan Marks. 1998. The global democratic deficit: An essay in international law and its limits. In *Re-imagining political community: Studies in cosmopolitan democracy,* ed. Daniele Archibugi, David Held, and Martin Köhler, 72-90. Stanford, CA: Stanford University Press.

Cukier, Kenneth Neil. 2005. Who will control the Internet? *Foreign Affairs* (November-December): 7-13.

CZMAI (Coastal Zone Management Authority and Institute). 2000. *State of the coast report, Belize.* Belize City: CZMAI.

Dahl, Robert. 1982. *Dilemmas of pluralist democracy: Autonomy vs. control.* New Haven, CT: Yale University Press.

—. 1994. A democratic dilemma: System effectiveness versus citizen participation. *Political Science Quarterly* 109 (1): 23-34.

Dahrendorf, Ralph. 1995. Preserving prosperity. *New Statesmen and Society* 13 (29): 36-40.

Dallmayr, Fred. 2005. Empire or cosmopolis? Civilization at the crossroads. *Globalizations* 2 (1): 14-30.

Daly, Herman. 2002. Globalization versus internationalization, and four economic arguments for why internationalization is a better model for world community. Paper presented at "Globalizations: Cultural, Economic, Democratic" conference, College Park, MD.

Danspeckgruber, Wolfgang. 2002. Self-determination and regionalisation in contemporary Europe. In *The self-determination of peoples: Community, nation and state in an interdependent world,* ed. Wolfgang Danspeckgruber, 165-200. Boulder, CO: Lynne Rienner.

Davidson, Donald. 1979. What metaphors mean. In *On Metaphor,* ed. Sheldon Sacks, 29-46. Chicago: University of Chicago Press.

Deibert, Ronald J. 1997. "Exorcismus theoriae": Pragmatism, metaphors and the return of the medieval in IR theory. *European Journal of International Relations* 3 (2): 167-92.

Delanty, Gerard. 2000. *Citizenship in a global age.* Buckingham: Open University Press.

della Porta, Donatella, and Herbert Reiter. 2006. The policing of global protest: The G8 at Genoa and its aftermath. In *Policing transnational protest in the aftermath of the "Battle of Seattle,"* ed. Donatella della Porta, Abby Peterson, and Herbert Reiter, 13-41. Aldershot, UK: Ashgate.

Derrida, Jacques. 1992. Force of law: The "mystical foundation of authority." In *Deconstruction and the possibility of justice,* ed. Drucilla Cornell, Michel Rosenfeld, and David Gray Carlson, 3-67. New York: Routledge.

Deutsch, Karl. 1953. *Nationalism and social communication: An inquiry into the foundations of nationality.* Cambridge, MA: Technology Press of the Massachusetts Institute of Technology.

Deutsch, Karl, Sidney A. Burrell, Robert A. Kahn, Maurice Lee Jr., Martin Lichterman, Raymond E. Lindgren, Francis L. Loewenheim, and Richard W. van Wagenen. 1957. *Political community and the North Atlantic area: International organization in light of historical experience.* Princeton, NJ: Princeton University Press.

Devetak, Richard, and Richard Higgott. 1999. Justice unbound? Globalization, states, and the transformation of the social bond. *International Affairs* 75 (3): 483-98.

Dewey, John. 1927. *The public and its problems.* New York: Henry Holt.

Diamond, Billy. 1990. Villages of the damned: The James Bay agreement leaves a trail of broken promises. *Arctic Circle* (November-December): 24-34.

Donnelly, Jack. 2003. *Universal human rights in theory and practice.* 2nd ed. Ithaca, NY: Cornell University Press.

Douglas, Ian R. 1999. Globalization as governance: Toward an archaeology of contemporary political reason. In *Globalization and governance,* ed. Aseem Prakash and Jeffrey A. Hart, 134-60. London: Routledge.

Dower, Nigel, and John Williams, eds. 2002. *Global citizenship: A critical reader.* Edinburgh: Edinburgh University Press.

Downes, Paul. 2004. Melville's Benito Cereno and the politics of humanitarian intervention. *South Atlantic Quarterly* 103 (2/3): 465-88.

Doyal, Len, and Ian Gough. 1991. *A theory of human need.* New York: Guildford Press.

Drahos, Peter, and John Braithwaite. 2004. *Who owns the knowledge economy? Political organising behind TRIPS.* Dorset: Corner House, Sturminster Newton.

Dunoff, Jeffrey. 2006. Constitutional conceits: The WTO's "constitution" and the discipline of international law. *European Journal of International Law* 17 (3): 647-75.

DUPI (Danish Institute of International Affairs). 1999. *Humanitarian intervention: Legal and political aspects.* Copenhagen: Danish Institute of International Affairs.

Durant, Will. 1962. *The story of philosophy.* 2nd ed. New York: Time Incorporated.

Eaton, Sarah, and Tony Porter. 2008. Globalization, autonomy, and global institutions: Accounting for accounting. In *Global ordering: Institutions and autonomy in a changing world,* ed. Louis Pauly and William D. Coleman, 125-43. Vancouver: UBC Press.

The Economist. 2001. Globalisation and its critics: A survey of globalisation. 29 September: 3-14 (insert).

Edwards, Steven. 2005. Canada sways UN delegates to let US keep control of web. *National Post,* 17 November.

Escobar, Arturo. 1995. *Encountering development: The making and unmaking of the Third World.* Princeton, NJ: Princeton University Press.

Esserman, Susan, and Robert Howse. 2005. The creative evolution of world trade. *Financial Times,* 23 August.

Essid, Yassine, and William D. Coleman, eds. Under review. *Deux Méditerranées: Les voies de la mondialisation et de l'autonomie.* Québec: Les Presses de l'Université Laval.

Etzioni, Amitai. 1993. *The spirit of community: Rights, responsibilities and the communitarian agenda.* New York: Crown.

Evans, Gareth, and Mohamed Sahnoun. 2001. Intervention and state sovereignty: Breaking new ground. *Global Governance* 7 (2): 119-25.

Eyles, John. 1988. Interpreting the geographical world. In *Qualitative methods in human geography,* ed. John Eyles and David Smith, 1-16. Cambridge: Polity Press.

Feinstein, Lee, and Anne-Marie Slaughter. 2004. A duty to prevent. *Foreign Affairs* 83 (1): 136-50.

Feit, Harvey A. 1985. Legitimation and autonomy in James Bay Cree responses to hydroelectric development. In *Indigenous peoples and the nation-state,* ed. Noel Dyck, 27-66. St. John's, NL: Memorial University, Institute for Social and Economic Research.

—. 1989. James Bay Cree self-governance and land management. In *We are here,* ed. Edwin N. Wilmsen, 68-98. Berkeley: University of California Press.

—. 2005. Re-cognizing co-management as co-governance: Histories and visions of conservation at James Bay. *Anthropologica* 47 (2): 267-88.

—. In press. Neoliberal governance and James Bay Cree governance: Negotiated agreements, oppositional struggles, and co-governance. In *Indigenous peoples and autonomy: Insights for a global age,* ed. Mario E. Blaser, Ravi de Costa, Deborah McGregor, and William D. Coleman. Vancouver: UBC Press.

Feit, Harvey A., and Robert Beaulieu. 2001. Voices from a disappearing forest. In *Aboriginal autonomy and development in northern Quebec and Labrador,* ed. Colin H. Scott, 119-48. Vancouver: UBC Press.

Ferguson, James. 1990. *The anti-politics machine.* Cambridge: Cambridge University Press.

Ferguson, Niall. 2005. *Colossus.* New York: Penguin.

Ferree, Myra Marx. 2005. Soft repression: Ridicule, stigma, and silencing in gender-based movements. In *Repression and mobilization,* ed. Christian Davenport, Hank Johnston, and Carol Mueller, 138-58. Minneapolis: University of Minnesota Press.

Ferree, Myra Marx, and Carol Mueller. 2004. Feminism and the women's movement: A global perspective. In *The Blackwell companion to social movements,* ed. David A. Snow, Sarah A. Soule, and Hanspeter Kriesi, 576-607. New York: Blackwell.

Finger, J. Michael, and Philip Schuler. 2000. Implementation of Uruguay Round commitments: The development challenge. *World Economy* 23 (4): 511-25.

Finnemore, Martha. 1996. *National interests in international society.* Ithaca, NY: Cornell University Press.

Føllesdal, Andreas. 1998. Survey article: Subsidiarity. *Journal of Political Philosophy* 6 (2): 190-218.

Foreign Policy. 2005. The Fifth Annual A.T. Kearney/Foreign Policy Globalization Index. May-June: 52-60.

Forsyth, Tim. 2004. Social movements and environmental democratization in Thailand. In *Earthly politics: Local and global in environmental governance,* ed. Sheila Jasanoff and Marybeth Martello, 195-216. Cambridge, MA: MIT Press.

Foster, John. 1999. Civil society and multilateral theatres. In *Whose world is it anyway? Civil Society, the United Nations, and the multilateral future,* ed. John W. Foster and Anita Anand, 129-95. Ottawa, ON: United Nations Association of Canada.

Foucault, Michel. 1972. *The archaeology of knowledge and the discourse of language.* New York: Random House.

—. 1977. *Discipline and punish.* Trans. A. Sheridon. New York: Random House.

—. 1978. *History of sexuality.* Trans. Robert Hurley. New York: Vintage Books.

—. 1991. Governmentality. In *The Foucault effect: Studies in governmentality,* ed. Graham Burchell, Colin Gordon, and Peter Miller, 87-104. Chicago: University of Chicago Press.

—. 2003. *Society must be defended: Lectures at the Collège de France, 1975-1976.* Trans. David Macey. New York: Picador.

Francis, Daniel, and Toby Morantz. 1983. *Partners in furs.* Montreal and Kingston: McGill-Queen's University Press.

Franck, Thomas M. 1995. *Fairness in international law and institutions.* Oxford: Oxford University Press.

Friedman, Elisabeth Jay, Ann Marie Clark, and Kathryn Hochstetler. 2005. *The sovereign limits of global civil society.* New York: State University of New York Press.

Friedman, Elisabeth Jay, Kathyrn Hochsteller, and Ann Marie Clark. 2005. *Sovereignty, democracy and civil society: State-society relations at UN World Conferences.* Albany, NY: State University of New York Press.

Friedman, Jonathan. 2003. Globalization, dis-integration, re-organization: The transformations of violence. In *Globalization, the state, and violence,* ed. Jonathan Friedman, vii-xv. Walnut Creek, CA: AltaMira Press.

Fussler, Claude, Aron Cramer, and Sebastian van der Veght, eds. 2004. *Raising the bar: Creating value with the United Nations Global Compact.* Sheffield: Greenleaf Publishing.

Gagnon, Alain, Montserrat Guibernau, and Francois Rocher. 2003. Introduction: The conditions of diversity in multinational democracies. In *The conditions of diversity in multinational democracies,* ed. Alain Gagnon, Montserrat Guiberneau, and Francois Rocher, 1-15. Montreal: Institute for Research on Public Policy.

Gagnon, Alain-G., and Guy Rocher, eds. 2002. *Reflections on the James Bay and Northern Québec Agreement.* Montreal: Québec Amérique.

Gardner, Katy, and David Lewis. 1996. *Anthropology, development and the post-modern challenge.* London: Pluto Press.

GATT (General Agreement on Tariffs and Trade). 2004. *The results of the Uruguay Round of multilateral trade negotiations: The legal texts.* Geneva: General Agreement on Tariffs and Trade.

Gauthier, David. 1997. The social contract theory of the state. In *Contemporary political philosophy: An anthology,* ed. Robert E. Goodin and Philip Pettit, 27-44. Oxford: Blackwell Publishers.

Gerhards, Jurgen, and Dieter Rucht. 1992. Mesomobilization contexts: Organizing and framing in two protest campaigns in West Germany. *American Journal of Sociology* 98 (3): 555-95.

Giddens, Anthony. 2000. *The consequences of modernity.* Oxford: Polity Press.

Gills, Barry. 2005. "Empire" versus "cosmopolis": The clash of globalizations. *Globalizations* 2 (1): 5-13.

Glasius, Marlies, and Mary Kaldor. 2002. The state of global civil society: Before and after September 11. In *Global civil society yearbook, 2002,* ed. Marlies Glasius, Mary Kaldor, and Helmut Anheier, 3-34. Oxford: Oxford University Press.

Globe and Mail. 2001. The myths about globalization. 12, 13, 14, 16, 17, and 18 April.

Gnarowski, Michael, ed. 2002. *I dream of yesterday and tomorrow.* Kemptville, ON: Golden Dog Press.

Goetze, Tara. 2005. Muddy waters: Conservation discourse and the politics of power in marine park co-management in Belize. PhD diss., McMaster University, Hamilton, Ontario.

Goldberg, David Theo. 1993. *Racist culture: Philosophy and the politics of meaning.* Oxford: Blackwell.

Gorman, Daniel. 2009. Freedom of the ether or the electromagnetic commons? Globality, the public interest, and multilateral radio negotiations in the 1920s. In *Empires and autonomy: Moments in the history of globalization,* ed. Stephen Streeter, John C. Weaver, and William D. Coleman. Vancouver: UBC Press.

Gourdeau, Éric. 2002. Genesis of the James Bay and Northern Québec Agreement. In *Reflections on the James Bay and Northern Québec Agreement,* ed. Alain-G. Gagnon and Guy Rocher, 17-23. Montreal: Québec Amérique.

Grand Council of the Crees (Eeyou Istchee). 1997. Growing crisis over wealth-sharing from resources on Cree lands concerns annual general assembly. Grand Council of the Crees. Article no. 150. http://www.gcc.ca/archive/article.php?id=150.

—. 1998. *Never without consent.* Toronto: ECW Press.

Gurr, Ted. 2000. *Peoples versus states: Minorities at risk in the new century.* Washington, DC: United States Institute of Peace Press.

Gutmann, Amy, and Dennis F. Thompson. 1996. *Democracy and disagreement.* Cambridge, MA: Belknap Press of Harvard University Press.

Haagerup, Neils. 1984. *Report drawn up on behalf of the Political Affairs Committee on the situation in Northern Ireland* (Haagerup Report). European Parliament Working Documents 1983-4, 1-1526/83.

Habermas, Jürgen. 1973. *Legitimation crisis.* Trans. Thomas McCarthey. Boston: Beacon Press.

—. 1991. Discourse ethics: Notes on philosophical justification. In *The communicative ethics controversy,* ed. Seyla Benhabib and Fred Dallmayr. Cambridge, MA: MIT Press.

—. 1996. *Between facts and norms: Contributions to a discourse theory of law and democracy.* Trans. William Rehg. Cambridge, MA: MIT Press.

—. 2001a. Europe needs a constitution. *New Left Review* 11 (September-October): 5-26.

—. 2001b. *The postnational constellation.* Trans. Max Pensky. Cambridge: Polity Press.

Hafner, Katie, and Matthew Lyon. 1996. *Where wizards stay up late: The origins of the Internet.* New York: Simon and Schuster.

Hanagan, Michael. 2002. Irish transnational social movements, migrants, and the state system. In *Globalization and resistance: Transnational dimensions of social movements,* ed. Jackie Smith and Hank Johnston, 53-74. Boulder: Rowman and Littlefield.

Hannum, Hurst. 1990. *Autonomy, sovereignty and self-determination: The accommodation of conflicting rights.* Philadelphia: University of Pennsylvania Press.

Hardt, Michael, and Antonio Negri. 2000. *Empire.* Cambridge, MA: Harvard University Press.

—. 2004. *Multitude: War and democracy in the Age of Empire.* New York: Penguin.

Hart, H.L.A. 1991. *The concept of law.* Oxford: Clarendon Press.

Härting, Heike. 2006. Global civil war and post-colonial studies. Working Paper Series, Institute on Globalization and the Human Condition, McMaster University, Hamilton, Ontario. http://www.globalautonomy.ca/global1/article.jsp?index=RA_Harting_GlobalCivilWar.xml.

Harvey, David. 1990. *The condition of postmodernity.* Oxford: Blackwell Publishing.

Hedetoft, Ulf. 2008. Sovereignty revisited: European reconfigurations, global challenges, and implications for small states. In *Global ordering: Institutions and autonomy in a changing world,* ed. Louis Pauly and William D. Coleman, 214-33. Vancouver: UBC Press.

Held, David. 1995. *Democracy and the global order: From the modern state to cosmopolitan governance.* Stanford, CA: Stanford University Press.

—. 2004. *The global covenant.* Oxford: Polity Press.

—. 2005. At the global crossroads: The end of the Washington Consensus and the rise of global social democracy. *Globalizations* 2 (1): 95-113.

Held, David, Anthony McGrew, David Goldblatt, and Jonathan Perraton. 1999. *Global transformations: Politics, economics and culture.* Stanford, CA: Stanford University Press.

Hesse, Mary. 1987. Tropical talk: The myth of the literal. *Proceedings of the Aristotelian Society* 61: S297-S311.

Hinsely, F.H. 1986. *Sovereignty.* 2nd ed. Cambridge: Cambridge University Press.

Hirst, Paul, and Graeme Thompson. 1999. *Globalization in question.* Cambridge: Polity Press.

Hobbes, Thomas. [1651] 1968. *Leviathan.* Ed. C.B. Macpherson. London: Penguin.

—. [1651] 1996. *Leviathan.* Ed. Richard Tuck. Cambridge: Cambridge University Press.

Hobsbawm, Eric. 1990. *Nations and nationalism since 1780.* Cambridge: Cambridge University Press.

Hochschild, Adam. 1998. *King Leopold's ghost.* New York: Houghton Mifflin.

Hoekema, A. 1995. Do joint decision-making boards enhance chances for a new partnership between the state and indigenous peoples? *Indigenous Affairs* 1: 4-10.

Hoekman, Bernard. 2002. Economic development and the World Trade Organization after Doha. Policy Research Working Paper 2851, World Bank, Development Research Group, Trade, Geneva.

Hoekman, Bernard M., and Petros Mavroidis. 1999. *Enforcing multilateral commitments: Dispute settlement and developing countries.* Geneva: WTO/World Bank Conference.

Holzgrefe, J.L., and Robert O. Keohane, eds. 2003. *Humanitarian intervention: Ethical, legal, and political dilemmas.* Cambridge: Cambridge University Press.

Hooghe, Lisbet, and Gary Marks. 2003. Unraveling the central state, but how? Types of multi-level governance. *American Political Science Review* 97 (2): 233-43.

Horn, Henrik, and Petros C. Mavroidis. 1999. Remedies in the dispute settlement system and developing country interests. http://www.econ-law.se/Papers/Remedies%20990611-1.pdf.

Howard, Rhoda E. 1995. *Human rights and the search for community.* Boulder, CO: Westview.

Howard-Hassmann, Rhoda E. 2005. The second great transformation: Human rights leapfrogging in the era of globalization. *Human Rights Quarterly* 27 (1): 1-40.

Howse, Robert, and Kalypso Nicolaïdis. 2001. Legitimacy and global governance: Why constitutionalizing the WTO is a step too far. In *Efficiency, equity and legitimacy: The multilateral trading system at the millennium,* ed. Roger B. Porter, Raymond Vernon, and Pierre Sauve, 227-52. Washington, DC: Brookings Institution Press.

Hroch, Miroslav. 1985. *Preconditions of national revival in Europe: A comparative analysis of the social composition of patriotic groups among the smaller European nations.* Cambridge: Cambridge University Press.

Hughes, James, Gwendolyn Sasse, and C. Gordon. 2003. EU enlargement, Europeanisation and the dynamics of regionalisation in the CEECs. In *The regional challenge in central and eastern Europe: Territorial restructuring and European integration,* ed. Michael Keating and James Hughes, 69-88. Paris: Presses interuniversitaires européennes/Peter Lang.

Huntington, Samuel. 1993. The clash of civilizations? *Foreign Affairs* 72: 22-49.

—. 1996. *The clash of civilizations and the remaking of world order.* New York: Simon and Schuster.

Hutchings, Kimberly. 1998. The idea of international citizenship. In *Cosmopolitan citizenship,* ed. Roland Dannreuther and Kimberly Hutchings, 3-34. Basingstoke: Macmillan.

Huysmans, Jef, Andrew Dobson, and Raia Prokhovnik, eds. 2006. *The politics of protection: Sites of insecurity and political agency.* London: Routledge.

Hyndman, Jennifer. 2000. *Managing displacement: Refugees and the politics of humanitarianism.* Minneapolis: University of Minnesota Press.

ICANN (Internet Corporation for Assigned Names and Numbers). 2002a. President's report: ICANN — The case for reform. ICANN. http://www.icann.org/general/lynn-reform-proposal-24feb02.htm.

—. 2002b. Working paper on ICANN core mission and values. ICANN. http://www.icann. org/committees/evol-reform/working-paper-mission-06may02.htm.

—. 2003. Sixth status report under JPA/MOU. ICANN. http://www.icann.org/general/status-report-31mar03.htm.

—. 2005a. At-Large Advisory Committee (ALAC). ICANN. http://www.icann.org/committees/alac/.

—. 2005b. ICANN concludes 24th international public meeting in Vancouver with action on Governmental Advisory Committee evolution and internationalised domain names. ICANN. http://www.icann.org/announcements/announcement1-05dec05.htm.

ICISS. 2001. *The responsibility to protect: Report of the International Commission on Intervention and State Sovereignty.* Ottawa: International Development Research Centre. http://www.dfait-maeci.gc.ca/iciss-ciise/report-en.asp.

ICISS Beijing Consultation. 2001. *The responsibility to protect: Regional consultations.* Ottawa: International Development Research Centre.

Ignatieff, Michael. 1994. *Blood and belonging: Journeys into the new nationalism.* London: Vintage.

—. 2003. *Empire lite.* Toronto: Penguin.

IMF (International Monetary Fund). 2005. IMF executive directors and voting power. International Monetary Fund. http://www.imf.org/external/np/sec/memdir/eds.htm.

Inglehart, Ronald. 1999. *World values survey.* Ann Arbor: University of Michigan.

Inglis, J., ed. 1993. *Traditional ecological knowledge: Concepts and cases.* Ottawa: International Development Research Centre.

Internet Governance Project. 2005. Internet governance: Quo vadis? A response to the WGIG Report. http://dcc.syr.edu/miscarticles/IGP-quovadis.pdf.

Internet World Stats. 2009. Internet usage statistics: The Internet big picture — World Internet users and population statistics. Internet World Stats. http://www.internetworldstats.com/stats.htm.

Isin, Engin F., and Patricia K. Wood. 1999. *Citizenship and identity.* London: Sage.

Jackson, Patrick T. 2004. Forum introduction: Is the state a person? Why should we care? *Review of International Studies* 30 (2): 255-58.

Jackson, Robert H. 2000. *The global covenant.* Cambridge, MA: Harvard University Press.

Jacques, Gloria. 1999. Orphans of the AIDS pandemic: The sub-Saharan African experience. In *AIDS and development in Africa: A social science perspective,* ed. Kempe Ronald Hope Sr., 93-108. New York: Hawthorne Press.

Jameson, Fredrick. 1986. Third World literature in the era of multinational capitalism. *Social Text* 15 (Fall): 65-88.

Jurado, Elena. 2006. Liberalising Estonia's citizenship policy: The role of the European Union, OSCE and Council of Europe. In *European integration and the nationalities question,* ed. John McGarry and Michael Keating, 258-72. London: Routledge.

Kaldor, Mary. 2000. Civilising globalisation. *Millennium: Journal of International Studies* 29 (1): 105-14.

—. 2001. *New and old wars: Organized violence in a global era.* Stanford, CA: Stanford University Press.

—. 2003. Global civil society in an era of regressive globalisation. In *Global Civil Society Yearbook, 2003,* ed. Mary Kaldor, Helmut Anheier, and Marlies Glasius, 3-33. London: Sage.

Kanaganayagam, Chelva. 2003. The anxiety of being postcolonial: Ideology and the contemporary postcolonial novel. *Miscelanea: A Journal of English and American Studies* 28: 43-54.

Kant, Immanuel. 1996. Towards a perpetual peace. In *The Cambridge edition of the works of Immanuel Kant: Practical philosophy,* trans. M. Gordon, 311-52. Cambridge: Cambridge University Press.

—. 1999. Grounding for the metaphysics of morals. In *Moral issues in global perspective,* ed. Christine Koggel, 494-502. Peterborough, ON: Broadview Press.

Kearney, J.F. 1989. Co-management or co-optation? The ambiguities of lobster fishery management in southwest Nova Scotia. In *Co-operative management of local fisheries,* ed. Evelyn Pinkerton, 85-102. Vancouver: UBC Press.

Kearney, Richard. 1997. *Postnationalist Ireland: Politics, culture, philosophy.* London: Routledge.

Keating, Michael. 1996. *Nations against the state: The new politics of nationalism in Quebec, Catalonia and Scotland.* London: Macmillan.

—. 2001a. *Plurinational democracy: Stateless nations in a post-sovereignty era.* Oxford: Oxford University Press.

—. 2001b. So many nations, so few states: Territory and nationalism in the global era. In *Multinational democracies,* ed. Alain-G. Gagnon and James Tully, 39-64. Cambridge: Cambridge University Press.

—. 2003. Regionalization in central and eastern Europe: The diffusion of a Western model? In *The regional challenge in central and eastern Europe: Territorial restructuring and European integration,* ed. Michael Keating and James Hughes, 51-67. Paris: Presses interuniversitaires européennes/Peter Lang.

—. 2004. European integration and the nationalities question. *Politics and Society* 31 (1): 367-88.

—. 2006. Europe, the state and the nation. In *European integration and the nationalities question,* ed., John McGarry and Michael Keating, 23-34. London: Routledge.

Keating, Michael, and Zoe Bray. 2006. Renegotiating sovereignty: Basque nationalism and the rise and fall of the Ibarretxe Plan. *Ethnopolitics* 5 (4): 347-64.

Keating, Michael, and John McGarry. 2001. Introduction. In *Minority nationalism in the changing state order,* ed. Michael Keating and John McGarry, 1-18. Oxford: Oxford University Press.

Keck, Margaret, and Kathryn Sikkink. 1998. *Activists beyond borders.* Ithaca, NY: Cornell University Press.

Kelley, Judith. 2004. *Ethnic politics in Europe: The power of norms and incentives.* Princeton, NJ: Princeton University Press.

Keohane, Robert, and Joseph S. Nye Jr. 2001. The club model of multilateral cooperation and problems of democratic legitimacy. In *Efficiency, equity and legitimacy: The multilateral trading system at the millennium,* ed. Roger B. Porter, Raymond Vernon, and Pierre Sauve, 264-94. Washington, DC: Brookings Institution Press.

Key, Carol. 2002. The political economy of the transition from fishing to tourism in Placencia, Belize. *International Review of Modern Sociology* 30 (1): 1-17.

Kingsbury, Benedict. 2007. International law as inter-public law. Unpublished paper, New York University School of Law.

Kissinger, Henry A. 2004. America's assignment: What will we face in the next four years? *Newsweek,* 8 November.

Kitchelt, Herbert. 2003. Landscapes of political interest intermediation: Social movements, interest groups, and parties in the early twenty-first century. In *Social movements and democracy,* ed. Pedro Ibarra, 81-104. New York: Palgrave Macmillan.

Klein, Hans. 2001. The feasibility of global democracy: Understanding ICANN's at-large elections. *Info* 3: 333-45.

—. 2002. ICANN and Internet governance: Leveraging technical coordination to realize global public policy. *The Information Society* 18 (3): 193-207.

—. 2005. An assessment of the WSIS-2/Tunis '05 outcomes. Internet and Public Policy Project. http://www.ip3.gatech.edu/images/Significance_of_WSIS-II_Tunis-05.pdf.

Krasner, Stephen D. 1999. *Sovereignty: Organized hypocrisy.* Princeton, NJ: Princeton University Press.

—. 2001. Abiding sovereignty. *International Political Science Review* 22 (3): 229-51.

Kraus, Peter A. 2003. "Transnationalism" or "renationalization"? The politics of cultural identity in the European Union. In *The conditions of diversity in multinational democracies,* ed. Alain-G. Gagnon, Montserrat Guiberneau, and François Rocher, 241-66. Montreal: Institute for Research on Public Policy.

Kriesberg, Louis. 1997. Social movements and global transformation. In *Transnational social movements and world politics: Solidarity beyond the state,* ed. Jackie Smith, Charles Chatfield, and Ron Pagnucco, 3-18. Syracuse, NY: Syracuse University Press.

Kristeva, Julia. 1995. Strangers to ourselves. In *States of mind: Dialogues with contemporary thinkers on the European mind,* ed. Richard Kearney, 6-13. Manchester: Manchester University Press.

Krut, Riva. 1997. *Globalization and civil society: NGO influence on international decision-making.* Geneva: United Nations Research Institute for Social Development.

Kymlicka, Will. 1989. *Liberalism, community, and culture.* Oxford: Oxford University Press.

—. 1995. *Multicultural citizenship: A liberal theory of minority rights.* Oxford: Oxford University Press.

—. 2001. Western political theory and ethnic relations in eastern Europe. In *Can liberal pluralism be exported?* ed. Will Kymlicka and Magda Opalski, 13-106. Oxford: Oxford University Press.

—. 2006. The evolving basis of European norms of minority rights: Rights to culture, participation and autonomy. In *European integration and the nationalities question,* ed. John McGarry and Michael Keating, 35-63. London: Routledge.

Kymlicka, Will, and Christine Straehle. 1999. Cosmopolitanism, nation-states and minority nationalism: A critical review of recent literature. *European Journal of Philosophy* 7 (1): 65-88.

Laguerre, Michel S. 1998. *Diasporic citizenship: Haitian Americans in transnational America.* New York: St. Martin's Press.

Lakoff, George, and Mark Johnson. 1980. *Metaphors we live by.* Chicago: University of Chicago Press.

357

Lalumière, Catherine, Jean-Pierre Landua, and Emmanuel Glimet. 1998. Rapport sur l'accord multilatéral sur l'investissement: Ministère de l'Economie, des Finances et de l'Industrie. http://www.finances.gouv.fr/pole_ecofin/international/ami0998/ami0998.htm (accessed 22 June 2005).

Landry, Bernard. 2002. Notes pour une allocution du premier ministre du Québec, monsieur Bernard Landry à l'occasion de la signature de l'entente finale entre le gouvernement du Québec et le Grand Conseil des Cris du Québec. Le Secrétariat aux affaires autochtones. http://www.autochtones.gouv.qc.ca/centre_de_presse/discours/2002/saa_dis20020207.htm.

Lane, Jan-Erik. 1996. *Constitutions and political theory*. Manchester: Manchester University Press.

Lawrence, Patricia. 2003. Kali in a context of terror: The tasks of a goddess in Sri Lanka's civil war. In *Encountering Kali: In the margins, at the center, in the west*, ed. Rachel Fell McDermott and Jeffrey J. Kripal, 100-23. Berkeley, CA: University of California Press.

Legrain, Philippe. 2002. *Open world: The truth about globalization*. London: Abacus.

Lijphart, Arend. 1977. *Democracy in plural societies: A comparative exploration*. New Haven, CT: Yale University Press.

Linden, Ronald H., and Lisa M. Pohlman. 2003. Now you see it, now you don't: Anti-EU politics in central and southeast Europe. *European Integration* 25 (4): 311-34.

Linklater, Andrew. 1998a. Citizenship and sovereignty in the post-Westphalian European state. In *Re-imagining political community: Studies in cosmopolitan democracy*, ed. Daniele Archibugi, David Held, and Martin Köhler, 113-37. Stanford, CA: Stanford University Press.

—. 1998b. *The transformation of political community: Ethical foundations for the post-Westphalian era*. Columbia: University of South Carolina Press.

Livezey, Lowell W. 1989. US religious organizations and the international human rights movement. *Human Rights Quarterly* 11 (1): 14-81.

Ludmer, Josefina. 2001. An agenda for the multitudes. *Rethinking Marxism* 13 (3/4): 168-72.

MacFarlane, Neil S., Carolin J. Thieking, and Thomas G. Weiss. 2004. The responsibility to protect: Is anyone interested in humanitarian intervention? *Third World Quarterly* 25 (5): 977-92.

MacLure, Jocelyn. 2003. Between nation and dissemination: Revisiting the tension between national identity and diversity. In *The conditions of diversity in multinational democracies*, ed. Alain-G. Gagnon, Montserrat Guiberneau, and François Rocher, 41-58. Montreal: Institute for Research on Public Policy.

MacMillan, Margaret. 2001. *Paris 1919: Six months that changed the world*. New York: Random House.

Malouf, Albert. 1973. *La Baie James indienne, texte integral du judgement du juge Albert Malouf*. Présentation de André Gagnon. Montreal: Éditions du jour.

Maney, Gregory M. 2001. Rival transnational networks and indigenous rights: The San Blas Kuna in Panama and the Yanomami in Brazil. In *Political opportunities, social movements and democratization*, vol. 23, *Research in social movements, conflicts and change*, ed. Patrick G. Coy, 103-44. Amsterdam: Elsevier.

Markoff, John. 2004. Who will construct the global order? In *Transnational democracy in critical and comparative perspective: Democracy's range reconsidered*, ed. Bruce W. Morrison, 19-36. London: Ashgate.

Marx, Karl, and Friedrich Engels. [1848] 2002. *The Communist manifesto*. London: Penguin.

Mbembe, Achille. 2003. Necropolitics. *Public Culture* 15 (1): 11-40.

McConney, Patrick, Robin Mahon, and Robert Pomeroy. 2003a. *Belize case study: Fisheries Advisory Board in the context of integrated coastal management.* Caribbean Coastal Co-management Guidelines Project. Barbados: Caribbean Conservation Association.

—. 2003b. *Guidelines for coastal resource co-management in the Caribbean: Communicating the concepts and conditions that favour success.* Caribbean Coastal Co-management Guidelines Project. Barbados: Caribbean Conservation Association.

—. 2004. Coastal resources co-management in the Caribbean. Paper presented at the International Association for the Study of Common Property conference, 9-13 August 2004, Oaxaca, Mexico.

McField, M. 2002. *Evaluation of management effectiveness: Belize Marine Protected Areas System.* Belize City: Coastal Zone Management Authority and Institute.

McGarry, John. 1998. Orphans of secession: National pluralism in secessionist regions and post-secessionist states. In *National self-determination and secession,* ed. Margaret Moore, 215-32. Oxford: Oxford University Press.

—. 2006. Europe's limits: European integration and conflict management in Northern Ireland. In *European integration and the nationalities question,* ed. John McGarry and Michael Keating, 273-89. London: Routledge.

McGarry, John, and Margaret Moore. 2005. Karl Renner, power-sharing and non-territorial autonomy. In *National cultural autonomy and its contemporary critics,* ed. Ephraim Nimni, 74-94. London: Routledge.

McGarry, John, and Brendan O'Leary. 2004. *The Northern Ireland conflict: Consociational engagements.* Oxford: Oxford University Press.

McGivern, Brendan. 2004. Decision making in the global market — Consumers International. *Briefing paper on the World Trade Organization.* Brussels: Consumers International.

McGrew, Anthony. 1997. Globalization and territorial democracy: An introduction. In *The transformation of democracy,* ed. Anthony McGrew, 1-24. Cambridge: Polity Press.

McKay, David. 1996. *Rush to union: Understanding the European federal bargain.* Oxford: Clarendon.

McRae, Glenn. 2004. Grassroots transnationalism and life projects of Vermonters in the Great Whale campaign. In *In the way of development,* ed. Mario Blaser, Harvey A. Feit, and Glenn McRae, 111-29. London: Zed Books.

McRoberts, Kenneth. 2003. Managing cultural differences in multinational democracies. In *The conditions of diversity in multinational democracies,* ed. Alain-G. Gagnon, Montserrat Guiberneau, and François Rocher. Montreal: Institute for Research on Public Policy.

Menike, Karunawathie. 1993. People's empowerment from the people's perspective. *Development in Practice* 3 (3): 176-83.

Miall, Hugh. 1992. *New conflicts in Europe: Prevention and resolution.* Current Decision Report no. 10. London: Oxford Research Group.

Miller, David. 1995. *On nationality.* Oxford: Oxford University Press.

Millon-Delsol, Chantal. 1992. *L'état subsidiaire: Ingérence et non-ingérence de l'état — Le principe de subsidiarité aux fondements de l'histoire européenne.* Paris: Presses Universitaires de France.

Mitrany, David. 1966. *A working peace system.* Chicago: Quadrangle Books.

Mohan, Giles, and Kristian Stokke. 2000. Participatory development and empowerment: The dangers of localism. *Third World Quarterly* 21 (2): 247-68.

Moody, Kim. 1997. *Workers in a lean world: Unions in the international economy.* New York: Verso.

Moses, Ted. 2002. Speaking notes. In *Reflections on the James Bay and Northern Québec Agreement,* ed. Alain-G. Gagnon and Guy Rocher, 229-35. Montreal: Québec Amérique.

Mouffe, Chantal. 2000. *The democratic paradox.* London: Verso.

Mueller, Milton L. 2002. *Ruling the root: Internet governance and the taming of cyberspace.* Cambridge, MA: MIT Press.

Murphy, Michael. 2001. The limits of culture in the politics of self-determination. *Ethnicities* 1 (3): 367-88.

Nadasdy, Paul. 1999. The politics of TEK: Power and the "integration" of knowledge. *Arctic Anthropology* 36 (1-2): 1-18.

Nagel, Thomas. 1986. *The view from nowhere.* Oxford: Oxford University Press.

Nairn, Tom. 1997. *Faces of nationalism: Janus revisited.* London: Verso.

Nancy, Jean-Luc. 2000. *Being singular plural.* Trans. Robert D. Richardson and Anne E. O'Byrne. Stanford, CA: Stanford University Press.

Narlikar, Amrita. 2006. Fairness in international trade negotiations: Developing countries in the GATT and WTO. Mimeograph, Centre of International Studies, Cambridge University.

Näsström, Soffia. 2003. What globalization overshadows. *Political Theory* 31 (6): 808-34.

National Intelligence Council. 2004. *Mapping the global future: Report of the National Intelligence Council's 2020 Project.* Washington, DC: National Intelligence Council.

Nature Conservancy. How we work: Our partners. The Nature Conservancy. http://www.nature.org/partners/.

Nedeva, Ivanka. 1993. Democracy building in ethnically diverse societies: The cases of Bulgaria and Romania. In *Minorities: The new Europe's old issue,* ed. Ian Cuthbertson and Jane Leibowitz, 123-55. Prague: Institute for East-West Studies.

Negri, Antonio. 2002. Approximations: Towards an ontological definition of the multitude. Trans. A. Bove. *Multitudes* 9: 36-48.

Neumann, Roderick. 2001. Disciplining peasants in Tanzania: From state violence to self-surveillance in wildlife conservation. In *Violent Environments,* ed. Nancy Peluso and Michael Watts, 305-27. Ithaca, NY: Cornell University Press.

Niezen, Ronald. 1998. *Defending the land: Sovereignty and forest life in James Bay Cree society.* Boston: Allyn and Bacon.

—. 2003. *The origins of Indigenism: Human rights and the politics of identity.* Berkeley: University of California Press.

Nimtz, August. 2002. Marx and Engels: The prototypical transnational actors. In *Restructuring world politics: The power of transnational agency and norms,* ed. Sanjeev Khagram, James Riker, and Kathryn Sikkink, 245-68. Minneapolis: University of Minnesota Press.

Norris, Pippa. 1999. *Critical citizens: Global support for democratic governance.* New York: Oxford University Press.

NTIA (National Telecommunications and Information Administration). 2005. US principles on the Internet's domain name and addressing system. NTIA. http://www.ntia.doc.gov/ntiahome/domainname/USDNSprinciples_06302005.htm.

Nussbaum, Martha C. 2000. *Women and human development: The capabilities approach.* Cambridge: Cambridge University Press.

Nweke, Remmy. 2005. Politics of Internet governance. Working Group on Internet Governance. http://www.wgig.org/docs/Politics-of-Internet-Governance.htm.

Nye, Joseph S., Jr., Jessica P. Einhorn, Béla Kadar, Hisashi Owada, Luis Rudio, and Soogil Young. 2003. *The "democracy deficit" in the global economy: Enhancing the legitimacy and accountability of global institutions.* Task Force Report 57. Trilateral Commission.

O'Brien, Robert, Anne Marie Goetz, Jan Aart Scholte, and Marc Williams. 2000. *Contesting global governance: Multilateral economic institutions and global social movements.* Cambridge: Cambridge University Press.

OECD (Organisation for Economic Co-operation and Development). 2001. Engaging citizens in policy-making: Information, consultation and public participation. Public Management Policy Brief No. 10. Paris: OECD.

Oliver, Roland, and J.D. Fage. 1962. *A short history of Africa*. Harmondsworth, UK: Penguin.

Olsen, Marvin. 1993. Forms and levels of power exertion. In *Power in modern societies*, Marvin E. Olsen and Martin N. Marger, 29-36. Oxford: Westview Press.

Ondaatje, Michael. 2000. *Anil's ghost*. Toronto: McClelland and Stewart.

Ostry, Sylvia. 1990. *Government and corporations in a shrinking world*. New York: Council on Foreign Relations.

—. 1997. *The post-Cold War trading system*. Chicago: University of Chicago Press.

—. 1999. Coherence in global policy-making: Is this possible? Paper presented at "Asia and the Future of the World Economic System," London, 17 March 1999. http://www.utoronto.ca/cis/ostry.

—. 2001. Institutional design for better governance. In *Efficiency, equity, legitimacy: The multilateral trading system at the millennium*, ed. Roger B. Porter, Pierre Sauve, Arvind Subramanian, and Americo Beviglia-Zampetti, 361-80. Washington, DC: Brookings Institution Press.

—. 2002. The Uruguay Round North-South grand bargain: Implications for future negotiations. In *The political economy of international trade law: Essays in honor of Robert E. Hudec*, ed. Daniel M. Kennedy and James D. Southwick, 285-300. Cambridge: Cambridge University Press.

—. 2003. Global integration: Current and counter currents. Walter Gordon Lecture, Massey College, University of Toronto.

—. 2004. *External transparency in trade policy*. Washington, DC: Occasional Paper 68, Group of Thirty.

Paine, Ellen. 2000. The road to the global compact: Corporate power and the battle over global public policy at the United Nations. Global Policy Forum. http://www.globalpolicy.org/reform/papers/2000/road.htm (accessed 21 February 2007).

Pal, Leslie A. 1998. A thousand points of darkness: Electronic mobilization and the case of the Communications Decency Act. In *Digital democracy: Policy and politics in the wired world*, ed. Cynthia J. Alexander and Leslie A. Pal, 105-31. Toronto: Oxford University Press.

Pal, Leslie A., and Tatyana Teplova. 2004. Domain games: Global governance of the Internet. In *e-government reconsidered: Renewal of governance for the knowledge age*, ed. E. Lynn Oliver and Larry Sanders, 43-58. Regina, SK: Canadian Plains Research Center/Saskatchewan Institute of Public Policy.

Palacio, Joseph. 2001. *Identifying past and current methods of coastal resource management in the southern coast of Belize, Central America*. Belize City: School of Continuing Studies, University of the West Indies.

Passavant, Paul, and Jodi Dean, eds. 2004. *Empire's new clothes*. New York: Routledge.

Patton, Michael Quinn. 1990. *Qualitative evaluation and research methods*. 2nd ed. Newbury Park, CA: Sage.

Pauly, Louis W. 2007. The United Nations in a changing global economy. In *Global liberalism and political order: Toward a new grand compromise?* ed. Steven Bernstein and Louis W. Pauly, 91-108. Albany: State University of New York Press.

—. 2008. The United Nations, the Bretton Woods institutions, and the reconstruction of a multilateral order. In *Global ordering: Institutions and autonomy in a changing world*, ed. Louis W. Pauly and William D. Coleman, 23-43. Vancouver: UBC Press.

Pauly, Louis W., and William D. Coleman, eds. 2008. *Global ordering: Institutions and autonomy in a changing world*. Vancouver: UBC Press.

Pease, Kelly-Kate. 2000. International organizations: Perspectives on governance in the twenty-first century. Upper Saddle River, NJ: Prentice Hall.

Penketh, Anne. 2003. Annan pushes for enlarged Security Council. *The Independent,* September 9, 11.

Petersmann, Ernst-Ulrich, ed. 2003. *Preparing for the Doha Development Round: Challenges to the legitimacy and efficiency of the world trading system — Conference report*. Florence: Robert Schuman Centre for Advanced Studies, European University Institute.

Pettit, Philip. 1997. *Republicanism: A theory of freedom and government*. Oxford: Oxford University Press.

Pinkerton, Evelyn, ed. 1989. *Co-operative management of local fisheries*. Vancouver: UBC Press.

Pogge, Thomas. 1992. Cosmopolitanism and sovereignty. *Ethics* 103 (1): 48-75.

—. 2002. *World poverty and human rights*. Cambridge: Polity.

Polanyi, Karl. 1944. *The great transformation: The political and economic origins of our time*. Boston: Beacon Press.

Polletta, Francesca. 2002. *Freedom is an endless meeting*. Chicago: University of Chicago Press.

Posluns, Michael. 1993. *Voices from the Odyak*. Toronto: NC Press.

Power. 1996. Directed by Magnus Isacsson. Montreal: Cineflix Productions, with the National Film Board of Canada and TVOntario.

Power, Roger B., Pierre Sauvé, Arvind Subramanian, and Americo Bevegliée Zampetti, eds. 2001. *Efficiency, equity and legitimacy: The multilateral trading system at the millennium*. Cambridge/Washington: Centre for Business and Government, Harvard University/ Brookings Institution.

Quebec. [1975] 1998. *James Bay and Northern Québec Agreement and Complementary Agreement*. Quebec: Les publications du Québec.

Rahnema, Majid. 1992. Participation. In *The Development Dictionary,* ed. Wolfgang Sachs, 116-31. London: Zed Books.

Rawls, John. 1971. *A theory of justice*. Cambridge, MA: Harvard University Press.

—. 1985. Justice as fairness: Political not metaphysical. *Philosophy and Public Affairs* 14 (3): 223-51.

—. 1996. *Political liberalism*. New York: Columbia University Press.

Razack, Sherene. 2004. *Dark threats and white knights: The Somalia affair, peacekeeping, and the new imperialism*. Toronto: University of Toronto Press.

Read, J. 2006. Axes of projection: Urbanization, globalization, and poetics in Latin America. Paper presented at the Andrew W. Mellon-Sawyer Seminar on Globalizing the Americas, November 2006, Toronto.

Reinicke, Wolfgang H. 1998. *Global public policy: Governing without government?* Washington, DC: Brookings Institution Press.

Richardson, Boyce. [1975] 1991. *Strangers devour the land*. Toronto: Douglas and McIntyre.

Ricoeur, Paul. 1984. The political paradox. In *Legitimacy and the state,* ed. William Connolly, 250-72. Oxford: Basil Blackwell.

—. 1995. Universality and the power of difference. In *States of mind: Dialogues with contemporary thinkers on the European mind,* ed. Richard Kearney, 33-38. Manchester: Manchester University Press.

Riles, Annelise. 2001. *The network inside out*. Ann Arbor: University of Michigan Press.

Ringmar, Erik. 1996. On the ontological status of the state. *European Journal of International Relations* 2 (4): 439-66.

Roberts, Adam. 2003. Intervention: One step forward in the search for the impossible. *International Journal of Human Rights* 7 (3): 142-53.

Robertson, Roland. 1992. *Globalisation, social theory and global culture.* London: Sage.

Ronit, Karsten, and Volker Schneider. 1999. Global governance through private organizations. *Governance* 12 (July): 243-66.

Rorty, Richard. 1989. *Irony, contingency, and solidarity.* Cambridge: Cambridge University Press.

—. 1991. *Objectivity, relativism, truth.* Cambridge: Cambridge University Press.

Rose, Nikolas. 1996. Governing "advanced" liberal democracies. In *Foucault and political reason,* ed. Andrew Barry, Thomas Osborne, and Nikolas Rose, 37-64. Chicago: University of Chicago Press.

Rosenberg, J. 2000. *The follies of globalization theory.* New York: Verso.

Rosenthal, Naomi, Meryl Fingrutd, Michele Ethier, Roberta Karant, and David McDonald. 1985. Social movements and network analysis: A case study of nineteenth-century women's reform in New York State. *American Journal of Sociology* 90 (5): 1022-55.

Rothman, Franklin Daniel, and Pamela E. Oliver. 2002. From local to global: The anti-dam movement in southern Brazil, 1979-1992. In *Globalization and resistance: Transnational dimensions of social movements,* ed. Jackie Smith and Hank Johnston, 115-31. Lanham, MD: Rowman and Littlefield.

Roy, Arundhati. 2001. *Power politics.* Cambridge, MA: South End Press.

—. 2003. *War talk.* Cambridge: South End Press.

—. 2004. *An ordinary person's guide to empire.* Cambridge, MA: South End Press.

Rucht, Dieter. 2000. Distant issue movements in Germany: Empirical description and theoretical reflections. In *Globalizations and social movements: Culture, power, and the transnational public sphere,* ed. John A. Guidry, Michael D. Kennedy, and Mayer N. Zald, 76-107. Ann Arbor: University of Michigan Press.

—. 2003. Social movements challenging neo-liberal globalization. In *Social movements and democracy,* ed. Pedro Ibarra, 211-27. New York: Palgrave Macmillan.

Ruggie, John G. 1982. International regimes, transactions, and change: Embedded liberalism in the postwar economic order. *International Organization* 36 (2): 379-415.

—. 1993. Territoriality and beyond: Problematizing modernity in international relations. *International Organization* 47 (1): 139-74.

—. 2003a. Taking embedded liberalism global: The corporate connection. In *Taming globalization: Frontiers of governance,* ed. David Held and Mathias Koenig-Archibugi, 93-129. Cambridge: Polity Press.

—. 2003b. The United Nations and globalization: Patterns and limits of institutional adaptation. *Global Governance* 9 (3): 301-21.

—. 2007. Global markets and global governance: The prospects for convergence. In *Global liberalism and political order: Toward a new grand compromise?* ed. Steven Bernstein and Louis W. Pauly, 23-48. Albany: State University of New York Press.

Rupert, Mark. 2000. Ideologies of globalization: Contending visions of a new world order. New York: Routledge.

Sachs, Wolfgang, ed. 1993a. *The development dictionary.* London: Zed Books.

—. 1993b. Global ecology and the shadow of "development." In *Global ecology,* ed. Wolfgang Sachs, 2-21. London: Zed Books.

Said. Edward. [1978] 1991. *Orientalism: Western conceptions of the Orient.* London: Penguin.

—. 1993. *Culture and imperialism.* New York: Alfred Knopf.

Salat, Levente. 2003. Southeast European challenges to representative democracy. In *A new balance: Democracy and minorities,* ed. Monica Robotin and Levente Salat, 3-30. Budapest: Open Society Institute.

Salisbury, Richard F. 1986. *A homeland for the Cree.* Montreal and Kingston: McGill-Queen's University Press.

Sandel, Michael. 1982. *Liberalism and the limits of justice.* Cambridge: Cambridge University Press.

Sasse, Gwendolyn. 2006. National minorities and EU enlargement: External or domestic incentives for accommodation? In *European integration and the nationalities question,* ed. John McGarry and Michael Keating, 64-84. London: Routledge.

Sassen, Saskia. 2005. The repositioning of citizenship and alienage: Emergent subjects and spaces for politics. *Globalizations* 2 (1): 79-94.

Scanlon, Thomas M. 1982. Contractualism and utilitarianism. In *Utilitarianism and beyond,* ed. Amartya Sen and Bernard Williams, 103-28. Cambridge: Cambridge University Press.

—. 1998. *What we owe to each other.* Cambridge: Harvard University Press.

Scharpf, Fritz W. 1998. Interdependence and democratic legitimation. MPIfG Working Paper 98/2, Max Planck Institute for the Study of Societies, Cologne, Germany.

Schmitt, Carl, 1985. *Political theology: Four chapters on the concept of sovereignty.* Trans. George Schwab. Cambridge, MA: MIT Press.

Scholte, Jan Aart. 2002. *Globalization: An introduction.* Basingstoke: Palgrave.

—. 2005. *Globalization: A critical introduction.* 2nd ed. London: Macmillan Palgrave.

—. 2007. Civil society and the legitimation of global governance. CSGR Working Paper No. 223/07, Centre for the Study of Globalisation and Regionalisation, University of Warwick.

Scott, Colin H. 2004. Conflicting discourses of property, governance and development in the indigenous North. In *In the way of development,* Mario Blaser, Harvey A. Feit, and Glenn McRae, 299-312. London: Zed Books.

—. 2005. Co-management and the politics of Aboriginal consent to resource development. In *Reconfiguring Aboriginal-state relations,* ed. Michael Murphy, 133-63. Montreal and Kingston: McGill-Queen's University Press.

Scott, David. 1999. *Refashioning futures: Criticism after postcoloniality.* Princeton, NJ: Princeton University Press.

—. 2005. Colonial governmentality. In *Anthropologies of modernity,* ed. Jonathan Xavier Inda, 23-49. Oxford: Blackwell.

Sen, Amartya. 1999. *Development as freedom.* New York: Alfred A. Knopf.

Seymour, Michel, Jocelyn Couture, and Kai Nielsen. 1998. Introduction: Questioning the ethnic/civic dichotomy. In *Rethinking nationalism,* ed. Jocelyne Couture, Kai Nielsen, and Michel Seymour. *Canadian Journal of Philosophy* 22: S1-S61.

Shaffer, Gregory G. 2001. The World Trade Organization under challenge: Democracy and the law and politics of the WTO's treatment of trade and environment matters. *Harvard Environmental Law Review* 25 (1): 2-97.

—. 2006. The challenges of WTO law: Strategies for developing country adaptation. *World Trade Review* 5 (2): 177-98.

Shah, Nisha. 2006. Cosmopolitanizing and decosmopolitanizing globalization: Metaphorical redescription and the transformation of political community. *Globalizations* 3 (3): 393-411.

Shakespeare, William. 2003. *The merchant of Venice.* Ed. M.M. Mahood. New York: Cambridge University Press.

Shapiro, Ian. 1999. *Democratic justice.* New Haven, CT: Yale University Press.

Shaw, Martin. 1999. War and globality: The role and character of war in the global transition. In *The new agenda for peace research,* ed. Ho-Won Jeong, 61-80. Aldershot: Ashgate.

Sidaway, J.D. 2003. Sovereign excesses? Portraying postcolonial sovereignty scapes. *Political Geography* 22: 157-78.

Sivanandan, Ambalavaner. 1997. *When memory dies.* London: Arcadia Books.

Skovgaard, Jakob. 2007. Preventing ethnic conflict, securing ethnic justice? The Council of Europe, the EU and the OSCE High Commissioner on national minorities' use of contested concepts in their responses to the Hungarian minority policies of Hungary, Romania and Slovakia. PhD diss., European University Institute.

Slaughter, Anne-Marie. 2004a. Disaggregated sovereignty: Towards the public accountability of global government networks. *Government and Opposition* 39 (2): 159-90.

—. 2004b. *A new world order.* Princeton, NJ: Princeton University Press.

Smith, Jackie. 2004. Exploring connections between global integration and political mobilization. *Journal of World Systems Research* 10 (1): 255-85.

—. 2008. *Social movements for global democracy.* Baltimore, MD: Johns Hopkins University Press.

Smith, Rogers. 2003. *Stories of peoplehood: The politics and morals of political membership.* Cambridge: Cambridge University Press.

Snyder, Anna. 2003. *Setting the agenda for global peace: Conflict and consensus building.* Burlington, VT: Ashgate.

Soysal, Yasemin. 2001. Postnational citizenship: Reconfiguring the familiar terrain. In *The Blackwell companion to political sociology,* ed. Kate Nash and Alan Scott, 333-42. Malden, MA: Blackwell.

Spivak, Gayatri. 1994. Can the subaltern speak? In *Colonial discourse and post-colonial theory: A reader,* eds. Patrick Williams and Laura Chrisman, 66-111. New York: Columbia University Press.

—. 2004. Terror: A speech after 9/11. *Boundary 2* 31 (2): 81-111.

Staggenborg, Suzanne. 1986. Coalition work in the pro-choice movement: Organizational and environmental opportunities and obstacles. *Social Problems* 33 (5): 374-90.

Steger, Manfred. 2003. *Globalization: A very short introduction.* Oxford: Oxford University Press.

—, ed. 2004. *Rethinking globalism.* Lanham, MD: Rowman and Littlefield.

—. 2005. From market globalism to imperial globalism: Ideology and American power after 9/11. *Globalizations* 2 (1): 31-46.

Stein, Jonathan P. 2002. National minorities and political development in post-Communist Europe. In *The politics of national minority participation in post-Communist Europe: State-building, democracy and ethnic mobilization,* ed. Jonathan P. Stein, 237-68. Armonk: M.E. Sharpe.

Steinberg, Richard H. 2002. In the shadow of law or power? Consensus-based bargaining and outcomes in the GATT/WTO. *International Organizations* 56 (2): 339-74.

Stevens, Stan, ed. 1997. *Conservation through cultural survival: Indigenous peoples and protected areas.* Washington, DC: Island Press.

Stiglitz, Joseph E. 2002. *Globalization and its discontents.* New York: W.W. Norton.

Stoler, Ann Laura. 1995. *Race and the education of desire: Foucault's History of Sexuality and the colonial order of things.* Durham, NC: Duke University Press.

Streeter, Stephen, John C. Weaver, and William D. Coleman, eds. 2009. *Empires and autonomy: Moments in the history of globalization.* Vancouver: UBC Press.

Suchman, Mark C. 1995. Managing legitimacy: Strategic and institutional approaches. *Academy of Management Review* 20 (3): 571-610.

Szeman, Imre. 2001a. Globalization. In *Encyclopaedia of postcolonial studies,* ed. John Hawley, 209-17. Westport, CT: Greenwood Press.

—. 2001b. Plundering the empire: Globalization, mediation, and cultural studies. *Rethinking Marxism* 13 (3/4): 173-89.

—. 2003. *Zones of instability: Literature, postcolonialism, and the nation.* Durham, NC: Duke University Press.

Szeman, Imre, and Nicholas Brown. 2006. What is the multitude? Questions for Michael Hardt and Antonio Negri. *Cultural Studies* 19 (3): 372-87.

Tambiah, Stanley. 1996. *Leveling crowds: Ethnonationalist conflicts and collective violence in South Asia.* Berkeley: University of California Press.

Tarrow, Sidney. 1996. States and opportunities: The political structuring of social movements in democratic states. In *Political opportunities, mobilizing structures and framing: Social movement dynamics in cross-national perspective,* ed. Doug McAdam, John McCarthy, and Mayer Zald. New York: Cambridge University Press.

—. 1998. *Power in movement: Social movements, collective action and politics.* 2nd ed. New York: Cambridge University Press.

—. 2006. *The new transnational contention: Movements, states, and international institutions.* New York: Cambridge University Press.

TASTE. 2001. *Draft report of the Executive Workshop on Co-management (28-29 August 2001) and the Executive Workshop on Education and Outreach (30 August 2001).* Punta Gorda, Belize: FON/CCA.

Taussig, Michael. 1992. *The nervous system.* New York: Routledge.

Taylor, Charles. 1991. *The malaise of modernity.* Toronto: Anansi.

—. 1992. Multiculturalism and the politics of recognition. Princeton, NJ: Princeton University Press.

—. 1995. Nations and federations: Living among others. In *States of mind: Dialogues with contemporary thinkers on the European mind,* ed. Richard Kearney, 23-32. Manchester: Manchester University Press.

—. 2002. Modern social imaginaries. *Public Culture* 14 (1): 91-124.

Thakur, Ramesh. 2002. Intervention, sovereignty and the responsibility to protect: Experiences for ICISS. *Security Dialogue* 33 (3): 323-40.

—. 2003. In defence of the responsibility to protect. *International Journal of Human Rights* 7 (3): 160-78.

Tilly, Charles. 1985. War making and state making as organized crime. In *Bringing the state back in,* ed. Peter B. Evans, Dietrich Rueschemeyer, and Theda Skocpol, 169-91. Cambridge: Cambridge University Press.

Tismaneanu, Vladimir. 1998. *Fantasies of salvation: Democracy, nationalism, and myth in post-Communist Europe.* Princeton, NJ: Princeton University Press.

Tsing, Anna. 2005. *Friction: An ethnography of global connection.* Princeton, NJ: Princeton University Press.

Tully, James. 1995. *Strange multiplicity.* Cambridge: Cambridge University Press.

—. 2001. Introduction. In *Multinational democracies,* ed. Alain-G. Gagnon and James Tully, 1-34. Cambridge: Cambridge University Press.

UNAIDS and WHO (World Health Organization). 2003. *Aids epidemic update.* Geneva: Joint United Nations Programme on HIV/AIDS, December.

UNCTAD (United Nations Conference on Trade and Development). 2004. FDI inflows, by host region and economy, 1970-2003. http://www.unctad.org.

United Nations. 2000. United Nations Millennium Development Goals. United Nations. http://www.un.org/millenniumgoals/.

—. General Assembly. 2005. *Report of the Panel of Eminent Persons on United Nations–Civil Society Relations.* New York: United Nations.

UN Millennium Project. 2005. *Investing in development: A practical plan to achieve the Millennium Development Goals.* New York: United Nations.

US Central Intelligence Agency. 2000. Global trends 2015. http://www.dni.gov/nic/PDF_GIF_global/globaltrend2015.pdf.

Uyangoda, Jayadeva. 1999. A political culture of conflict. In *Creating peace in Sri Lanka: Civil war and reconciliation,* ed. Robert I. Rotberg, 157-68. Washington, DC: Brookings Institution Press.

Vaughan-Williams, Nick. 2005. Protesting against citizenship. *Citizenship Studies* 9 (2): 167-79.

Verba, Sidney, Kay Schlozman, and Henry Brady. 1995. *Voice and equality: Civic volunteerism in American politics.* Cambridge, MA: Harvard University Press.

Verdery, Katherine. 1991. *National ideology under Socialism: Identity and cultural politics in Ceauşescu's Romania.* Berkeley: University of California Press.

Verdery, Katherine, and Gail Kligman. 1992. Romania after Ceauşescu: Post-Communist Communism? In *Eastern Europe in revolution,* ed. Ivo Banac, 117-47. Ithaca, NY: Cornell University Press.

Vincent, R.J. 1974. *Nonintervention and international order.* Princeton, NJ: Princeton University Press.

—. 1986. *Human rights and international relations.* New York: Cambridge University Press.

Vincent, Sylvie, and Garry Bowers, eds. 1988. *James Bay and northern Québec: Ten years after.* Montreal: Recherches amérindiennes au Québec.

Walker, Robert B.J. 1991. On the spatiotemporal conditions of democratic practice. *Alternatives* 16 (2): 243-62.

—. 1993. *Inside/outside: International relations as political theory.* Cambridge: Cambridge University Press.

—. 2003. Polis, cosmopolis, politics. *Alternatives: Global, Local, Political* 28 (2): 267-87.

Walton, John, and David Seddon. 1994. *Free markets and food riots: The politics of global adjustment.* Cambridge, MA: Blackwell.

Waltz, Kenneth. 1979. *Theory of international politics.* Reading, MA: Addison-Wesley.

Walzer, Michael. 1983. *Spheres of justice: A defense of pluralism and equality.* New York: Basic Books.

Warner, Daniel. 1991. *An ethics of responsibility in international relations.* Boulder, CO: Lynne Reinner.

—. 1999. Searching for responsibility/community in international relations. In *Moral spaces: Rethinking ethics and world politics,* ed. David Campbell and Michael J. Shapiro, 1-28. Minneapolis: University of Minnesota Press.

—. 2003. The responsibility to protect and irresponsible, cynical engagement. *Millennium: Journal of International Studies* 32 (1): 109-21.

Washington File. 2005. Word Summit agrees on status quo for Internet governance. http://news.findlaw.com/wash/s/20051116/20051116191452.html.

Waters, Malcolm. 1995. *Globalization: Key ideas.* New York: Routledge.

Weber, Cynthia. 1995. *Simulation sovereignty.* Cambridge: Cambridge University Press.

Weber, Max. 1978. *Economy and society.* Ed. Guenther Roth and Claus Wittich. Berkeley: University of California Press.

—. 1994. *Political writings*. Cambridge: Cambridge University Press.

Weiler, J.H.H. 2000. The rule of lawyers and the ethos of diplomatic reflections on WTO dispute settlement. Harvard Jean Monnet Working Paper 9/00. http://www. jeanmonnetprogram.org/papers/00/000901.html.

Weinberg, Jonathan. 2000. ICANN and the problem of legitimacy. *Duke Law Journal* 50 (1): 187-260.

Weiss, Linda. 1998. *Myth of the powerless state*. Ithaca, NY: Cornell University Press.

Weiss, Thomas G. 2004. The sunset of humanitarian intervention? The responsibility to protect in a unipolar era. *Security Dialogue* 35 (2): 125-53.

Weiss, Thomas G., and Cindy Collins. 2000. *Humanitarian challenges and intervention*. 2nd ed. Boulder, CO: Westview Press.

Weitzner, Viviane, and Marvin. Borras. 1999. Cahuita, Limón, Costa Rica: From conflict to collaboration. In *Cultivating peace: Conflict and collaboration in natural resource management*, ed. Daniel Buckles, 129-50. Ottawa, ON: IDRC.

WGIG (Working Group on Internet Governance). 2005. *Report of the Working Group on Internet Governance*. International Telecommunication Union. http://www.itu.int/wsis/ wgig/docs/wgig-report.pdf.

Wheeler, Nicholas J. 2000. *Saving strangers: Humanitarian intervention in international society*. Oxford: Oxford University Press.

Wieviorka, Michael. 2003. The new paradigm of violence. In *Globalization, the state, and violence*, ed. Jonathan Friedman, 107-40. Walnut Creek, CA: AltaMira Press.

Wight, Martin. 1966. Why is there no international theory? In *Diplomatic investigations*, ed. Herbert Butterfield and Martin Wight, 17-34. London: Allen and Unwin.

Wilkinson, Paul Francis, and Brigitte Masella. 2002. Summary of the Round Table with the Agreement Signatories. In *Reflections on the James Bay and Northern Québec Agreement*, Alain-G. Gagnon and Guy Rocher, 217-31. Montreal: Québec Amérique.

Willetts, Peter. 1989. The pattern of conferences. In *Global issues in the United Nations framework*, ed. Paul Taylor and A.J.R. Groom, 35-63. New York: St. Martin's Press.

—. 1996a. *The conscience of the world: The influence of NGOs in the United Nations system*. London: C. Hurst.

—. 1996b. From Stockholm to Rio and beyond: The impact of the environmental movement on the United Nations consultative arrangements for NGOs. *Review of International Studies* 22 (1): 57-80.

Williamson, Karina. 2004. From heavenly harmony to eloquent silence: Representations of world order from Dryden to Shelley. *Review of English Studies* 55 (221): 527-44.

Winham, Gilbert R. 1986. *International trade and the Tokyo Round negotiation*. Princeton, NJ: Princeton University Press.

Wittner, Lawrence. 1997. *Resisting the bomb: A history of the world nuclear disarmament movement, 1954-1970*. Vol. 2. Stanford, CA: Stanford University Press.

Woods, Ngaire. 1999. Good governance in international organizations. *Global Governance* 5 (1): 39-61.

World Bank. 2007. *World Bank development indicators*. Washington, DC: The World Bank.

World Health Organization. 2000. *Tobacco company strategies to undermine tobacco control activities at the World Health Organization*. Geneva: World Health Organization.

World Wildlife Fund (US). Participation. http://worldwildlife.org/bsp/publications/africa/ biome/participation.pdf.

WSIS (World Summit on the Information Society). 2003. Declaration of Principles. WSIS Document WSIS-03/GENEVA/DOC/4-E. http://www.itu.int/wsis/docs/geneva/official/ dop.html.

—. 2005a. Draft interim report of the third meeting of the Preparatory Committee (Tunis Phase). WSIS Document WSIS-II/PC-3/DOC/10(Rev.1)-E. http://www.itu.int/wsis/documents/doc_multi.asp?lang=en&id=2122|.

—. 2005b. Preliminary report of the Working Group on Internet Governance. WSIS Document WSIS-II/PC-2/DOC/5-E 21. http://www.wgig.org/docs/PrelimReportPrepCom.pdf.

—. 2005c. Tunis Agenda for the Information Society. WSIS Document WSIS-05/TUNIS/DOC/6 (Rev. 1)-E. http://www.itu.int/wsis/docs2/tunis/off/6rev1.html.

WTO (World Trade Organization). 2004. *International trade statistics 2004.* Tables 3.1 and 3.2. WTO. http://www.wto.org/english/res_e/statis_e/its2004_e/its04_byregion_e.pdf.

Young, Iris Marion. 1990. *Justice and the politics of difference.* Princeton, NJ: Princeton University Press.

—. 2001. *Inclusion and democracy.* Oxford: Oxford University Press.

—. 2003. From guilt to solidarity: Sweatshops and political responsibility. *Dissent* 50 (2): 39-45.

—. 2004. Responsibility and global labor justice. *Journal of Political Philosophy* 12 (4): 365-88.

—. 2006. Responsibility and global justice: A social connection model. *Social Philosophy and Policy* 12 (3): 103-30.

Zarrilli, Simonetta. 1999. WTO Sanitary and Phytosanitary Agreement: Issues for developing countries. Trade-related agenda development and equity working paper, Geneva.

Zielonka, Jan. 2006. *Europe as empire: The nature of the enlarged European Union.* Oxford: Oxford University Press.

Žižek, Slavoj. 1989. *The sublime object of ideology.* London: Verso.

Zolo, Danilo. 1997. *Cosmopolis.* Cambridge: Polity Press.

Contributors

Steven Bernstein is an associate professor of political science and the associate director of the Centre for International Studies at the University of Toronto. His current research focuses on the problem of legitimacy in global governance.

William D. Coleman is Center for International Governance Innovation Chair in Globalization and Public Policy at the Balsillie School of International Affairs in Waterloo, Ontario.

Ian Cooper is a senior researcher at ARENA — Centre for European Studies at the University of Oslo. He has a doctorate in political science from Yale and has held fellowships at the University of Toronto and the Université Catholique de Louvain. His research interests include constitutionalism, democracy, and legitimacy in the European Union; global governance; international relations theory; and Catholic social philosophy.

Harvey A. Feit is professor emeritus of anthropology at McMaster University. His research and publication interests include political and narrative ecologies, indigenous co-governance and globalization, relational and indigenous ontologies, and ethnography. He is co-founder of the Indigenous Studies Program at McMaster University.

Tara C. Goetze is an adjunct scholar with the McMaster Institute on Globalization and the Human Condition and a senior policy advisor at the Department of Environment, Government of Canada. She has a PhD in anthropology from McMaster University, where she held a fellowship with the International Development Research Centre. Her research interests include environmental governance, relationalities and discourses of conservation, sustainable conflict management, and the politics of participation.

Heike Härting is associate professor of English at the Université de Montréal. She is the editor-in-chief of *Postcolonial Text*. Her publications and research interests focus on contemporary Canadian literature and postcolonial cultural studies and theory, narratives of global violence, discourses of humanitarianism and capital, and cinematic and literary representations of Africa in the era of globalization.

Rhoda E. Howard-Hassmann is Canada Research Chair in International Human Rights at Wilfrid Laurier University, where she holds a joint appointment in the Department of Global Studies and the Balsillie School of International Affairs. She is also a senior research fellow at the Centre for International Governance Innovation and a fellow of the Royal Society of Canada. In 2006 the Human Rights section of the American Political Science Association named Dr. Howard-Hassmann its first distinguished scholar of human rights.

Michael Keating is professor of political and social sciences at the European University Institute, Florence, and professor of politics at the University of Strathclyde. He has published widely on nationalism, regionalism, public policy, and European integration.

John McGarry is professor and Canada Research Chair in Nationalism and Democracy in the Department of Political Studies at Queen's University. He has edited, co-edited, and co-authored twelve books on ethnic conflict, nationalism, and the politics of Northern Ireland. He is a member of the editorial boards of *Ethnopolitics; Journal of Conflict Studies*; *Irish Political Studies*; *Journal on Ethnopolitics and Minority Issues in Europe (JEMIE)*; and *Peace and Conflict Studies* and a member of the advisory board of the European Centre for Minority Issues. In 2008-9 he served as senior advisor on power sharing to the United Nations (Mediation Support Unit).

371

Margaret Moore is Sir Edward Peacock Professor of Political Theory at Queen's University and author of *Foundations of Liberalism* (1993) and *Ethics of Nationalism* (2001) (both with Oxford University Press). She is currently working on a book on global justice and political communities.

Peter Nyers is associate professor of politics of citizenship and intercultural relations in the Department of Political Science at McMaster University. His publications include *Rethinking Refugees: Beyond States of Emergency* (Routledge, 2006), *Citizenship between Past and Future* (Routledge, 2008), and *Securitizations of Citizenship* (Routledge, 2009).

Sylvia Ostry is distinguished research fellow, Centre for International Studies, University of Toronto. She has a doctorate in economics from McGill University and Cambridge University. Her most recent publications include "The World Trading System: In Dire Need of Reform," *Temple International and Comparative Law Journal* (Spring 2003); "The WTO: Post Seattle and Chinese Accession," in *China and the Long March to Global Trade*, ed. Ostry, Alexandroff, and Gomez (Routledge, 2003); and "Between Feast and Famine: Fixing Global Trade," in *Feeding the Future: From Fat to Famine — How to Solve the World's Food Crises,* ed. Heintzman and Solomon (Anansi, 2006).

Leslie A. Pal is Chancellor's Professor of Public Policy and Administration at Carleton University. He is founder and co-director of the Centre on Governance and Public Management. His research interests include global public policy networks, theories of public policy, and the global movement for public-sector reform.

Nisha Shah is a SSHRC postdoctoral fellow at the Watson Institute for International Studies at Brown University and the Centre for the Study of Global Governance at the London School of Economics. She has published in *Globalizations* and the *International Journal of Media and Cultural Politics* and is co-editor of *Metaphors of Globalization: Mirrors, Magicians and Mutinies* (Palgrave, 2008).

Jackie Smith is associate professor of sociology and peace studies at the University of Notre Dame, where she also directs the Center for the Study of Social Movements and Social Change. Smith writes and teaches about social movements, globalization, and international institutions and is a senior fellow in the university's Gender Studies Program. Her latest books include *Social Movements for Global*

Democracy (Johns Hopkins University Press, 2008) and (with numerous collaborators) *Global Democracy and the World Social Forums* (Paradigm Publishers, 2007).

Julie Sunday completed a PhD in anthropology in 2005 at McMaster University, where she held two research fellowships with the McMaster Institute on Globalization and the Human Condition. She currently works as a senior policy advisor at the Department of Justice, Government of Canada.

Melissa S. Williams is professor of political science and founding director of the Centre for Ethics at the University of Toronto. Her work in contemporary democratic theory and the history of political thought ranges across the themes of representation, citizenship, deliberative democracy, toleration, education, Aboriginal rights, feminist theory, multiculturalism, and affirmative action.

Index

Advisory Centre on WTO Law (ACWL), 269

Africa. *See also* African Union (AU): AIDS epidemic, effect of, 242, 250, 256; countries with UN missions in Geneva, and WTO delegates, 265; economic and social problems, 242; and globalization, as continuation of colonialism, 246, 247, 248, 249; and globalization, as theft of resources, 249-50, 252-53, 257-58; and globalization, as threat to local industries, 246, 252; and globalization, as Western-dominated economic phenomenon, 249; and globalization, trade affected by SPS Agreement, 264; human rights movement, as benefit of globalization, 251; imposed conditions of structural adjustment programs, 247, 250; institutional changes needed for economic development, 255; and international banking organizations, 246, 247, 248-49, 251, 252; interviewee opinions on globalization, 244-53; lack of collective autonomy under globalization, 25, 321-22; lack of participation in dispute settlement in WTO, 267, 269, 270; lack of personal autonomy, 256; limited participation in Uruguay Round of GATT, 264; as "missing" in globalization, 14, 15; need for internal legitimacy of government and institutions, 254, 255, 328; need for legitimate institutions to exercise economic control, 241-42; as passive recipient of globalization, 241, 243, 244, 245; preconditions for poverty reduction, 254; private multinational corporations, as exploiting African labour, 248; privatization of state-owned resources, 248-49; and problems of coordination of international technical assistance, 274-75; sense of abandonment by global community, 252; view of international governance as lacking legitimacy, 253

African Union (AU): promotion of democracy and human rights, 255, 256; as regional organization, 150

Agamben, Giorgio, 198, 233, 236

Agreement on Agriculture (GATT), 264

Agreement Concerning a New Relationship (James Bay Cree and Quebec, 2002), 122-23

Agreement on Trade-Related Aspects of Intellectual Property Rights (TRIPS) (GATT), 262

agriculture: developing countries, lack of role in setting international standards for

Beveridge Plan (UK), 276

Black Bloc, 279

Black July (Sri Lanka, 1983), 222

Blacksmith, Charlie Coon, 105-6, 110, 115, 126

Bodin, Jean, 33

borders: barriers between kin-states and related minorities, 160; and conceptual link between sovereignty and territory, 191; effect of European Union (EU), 158-60; Hungarian minority on Romanian borders, 187

Bosnia-Herzegovina: conflict prevention and economic reconstruction by European Union (EU), 166; dual citizenship agreement with Croatia, 160; international organizations' endorsement of autonomy of, 166; problems of nationalist questions, 154; Serb and Croatian minorities, 150

Boston Social Forum (2004), 313

Brazil, 261, 262

"The Buddha's Fire Sermon" (Arasanayagam), 225

Buddhism, politicization in Sri Lanka, 222

Bulgaria, Turkish minority of, 150, 154, 160, 164

Burgess, Robin, 253

Burma. See Myanmar

Canada, as archetype of globalizing society, 28

capitalism: abandonment of state, and assumption of autonomous power, 90; anti-capitalist protesters, against multinational corporations, 311; as driving force behind globalization, 242; and empire, 90

Caribbean Conservation Association, 134

Castoriardis, Cornelius, 232-33

Catalonia, 155, 157, 173-74

Chamberlin, Edward, 218

China: impact on world trade, 261; against internal intervention, 204; opposition to US domination of ICANN, 299; refusal to join ICISS, 204; rejection of concept of forcible emergency relief aid, 199; shift of balance of power to, 277

Chrétien, Jean, 203

citizenship. *See also* community: and accountability, 39, 47; as agency within communities of shared fate, 49; autonomous, use of information and communications technology (ICT), 284; definition, 33, 39; and democracy, unravelling of connection between, 35-38; denationalized or post-national, 37; denial of, to Tamils by Sri Lankan Sinhalese government, 222; diasporic, 37-38; disaggregation of, through unbundling of territoriality and sovereignty, 48-49, 323; environmental, 37; and freedom, 52; global, 37, 38-44, 87-88, 92; and global liberal internationalism, 3; immanence, and multitude as political community, 93; modern, as bound with concepts of sovereignty and legitimacy, 34; modern, and self-legislation within bounded community, 39; and mutual affectedness, 50-51; prerequisites, 47-48; reformulation of, 37-38, 39-40; roles and activities of citizens, 46-49; self-protection, 46, 47, 48, 49; self-rule, 39, 46-47, 48, 49; and social interdependence, 42-43; territorial loyalty undermined by Internet, 281; and theories of state sovereignty, 33-34; worker, 38

civil rights movement, 36

civil society, global. *See* global civil society

Civil Society Internet Governance Caucus, 292

civility: and democracy, 234; discourse of, as counter to necropolitics of localized transnational warfare, 231-32; longing for, and global dimensions of violence, 221; as opposition of identity politics, 233; politics of, 237; reappropriation of, 233

Coastal Co-Management Guidelines Project (Belize), 134, 135

Code, Lorraine: on perversion of autonomy, 221; on racism, heteronomy, and autonomy, 232

Codex Alimentarius Commission, 266

co-governance: James Bay Cree Nation, compared with neoliberal governance,

institutions, 12, 18, 25-27, 314, 315-16;
and globalization, 1-2, 3, 5-9; government, threatened by citizens empowered
by the Internet, 281; and indigenous
peoples in settler states, 98; of intergovernmental organizations (IGOs), 259;
of Internet governance, concern of
WGIG, 294-95; intertwined with autonomy and democracy, 10, 94; lack of, in
international governance as viewed by
Africans, 253; liberal understanding of,
320; of military interventions, 198, 199-
203, 205-6; political, 5-6, 80; and power,
16; and sovereignty, challenge of unbundling of, 36; state, effect of
globalization on, 86; state, and people's
autonomy, 173; symptoms of weakening
of, 36; understanding of, and role of
metaphor, 77-78
Leslie, Laurence, 138, 140
Leslie, Lennox, 138, 140, 142
Leveling Crowds (Tambiah), 227
liberal internationalism: as basis for political
legitimacy under globalization, 319; as
response to globalization, 2; on sovereign states and collective autonomy, 18;
support for revival of, 27-28
liberalism. *See also* liberal internationalism;
neoliberalism: and citizens' rights, 47;
embedded, 260; on power, 14
Liberation Tigers of Tamil Eelam (LTTE),
222
literary works, and politics in Sri Lanka,
216-38; *All Is Burning* (Arasanayagam),
221, 222, 225; *Anil's Ghost* (Ondaatje),
218, 224; "The Buddha's Fire Sermon"
(Arasanayagam), 225; *Funny Boy* (Selvadurai), 218; "I am an Innocent Man"
(Arasanayagam), 226-28; "Man without
a Mask" (Arasanayagam), 225, 228; *Power
Politics* (Roy), 219; *Reef* (Gunesekera), 218;
When Memory Dies (Sivanandan), 218
Locke, John: and doctrine of popular sovereignty, 34; on the individual, 58

Macedonia, 166
Madrid Convention, 159

Major Collaborative Research Initiative
(MCRI), ix
Malaysia, anti-globalization NGOs, 278
"Man without a Mask" (Arasanayagam),
225, 228
Mapping the Global Future (National Intelligence Council), 277
marine protected areas (MPAs), Belize,
129-48
Metabie, Simon, 105-6
Mbembe, Achille: on the colonial roots of
contemporary warfare, 230; on necropolitics, 229-30; on race, and imperial
population control, 230; on the topography of cruelty, 228, 230
McWorld (Barber), 300
media, use by global civil society for dissent,
278. *See also* Internet
mercenaries: British Special Air Service
(SAS), 228, 230; and criminalization of
localized transnational warfare, 230; in
"I am an Innocent Man" (Arasanayagam),
226-28; and privatization of warfare,
227-28; use of, in new wars of globalization, 222
metaphor: dead, considered as description of
reality, 78, 80; definition, 78; globalization, metaphors for, 81-82; metaphorical
redescription, effect of, 79, 80; metaphorical status of terms *cosmopolis* and
empire, 84-85; as normative and legitimating, 80; role of, in understanding
legitimacy of political communities,
77-78
military intervention. *See also* responsibility
to protect (R2P) doctrine: as challenge
to state's autonomy, 201; and difficulties
of post-intervention reconstruction, 213;
as exceptional measure, 202, 210; goal
of, 210; question of authorization of, 205
Millennium Development Goals, 284
Millennium Report *(We, the Peoples)*
(Annan), 203
minorities. *See* indigenous peoples; minority
nationalist movements
minority nationalist movements. *See also*
identity: claims of autonomy, 173, 174;

differing goals of, 150; as distinguished
from immigrant communities, 151;
engagement of global forces to further
claims for autonomy, 191-92, 193-94;
free trade, and accommodation of, 168;
issues of territorial jurisdiction and legitimacy, 324-25; and limits of liberalism,
326; minority rights protections, international regime of, 162-67; mobilization
facilitated by new communications technologies, 155; nationalism, viewed as
dangerous and conflict-ridden, 153-54;
nationality, definition, 150; under new
European institutional arrangements,
156-61, 167; not necessarily illiberal and
ethnocentric, 155; not necessarily secessionist, 156; as re-emergence of ethnic
and nationalist politics, 154; relations
with host state, 23, 150, 155, 168; stateless, traditional negative view of, 153;
viability because of weakening of
nation-state, 154-55
Moldova: attempted conflict resolution by
OSCE, 166; international organizations'
endorsement for autonomy of, 166;
problems of nationalist questions, 154
multiculturalism, in European Union (EU),
165
Multilateral Agreement on Investment
(MAI), 267, 278
multinational corporations. *See also* multinational enterprises (MNES): attempts to
increase influence in UN, 312, 314; exploitation of African labour, 248; power,
and unaccountability of, 36
multinational enterprises (MNES). *See also*
multinational corporations: as catalyst
for anti-corporate globalization movement, 263; and US agenda in WTO,
261-62
Multitude (Hardt and Negri), 75
Myanmar, 199

Nancy, Jean-Luc, 224
nation-state. *See also* sovereignty: assumptions about congruence of nation and
state, 153; and authority of international

organizations, 12; minority nations
within, recognition as secession or independence, 161; rogue, and new wars of
globalization, 222; unbundling of territoriality of, since end of Cold War, 35
National Fisheries Advisory Board, Belize,
137
National Intelligence Council, 277
National Science Foundation, 285
nationalism. *See* minority nationalist
movements
natural resources. *See also* environment:
Belize, co-management by CNGOS
and fishers, 129-48; Belize, as important
for eco-tourism, 142; Quebec, co-
governance with James Bay Cree Nation,
97-127; sustainable resource management, and local empowerment, 131-33
Nature Conservancy, 140, 141
Ndoho Ouchimauch status, of James Bay
Cree Nation members, 105-8, 124-25
necropolitics: definition, 220, 229-30; mutation of politics into violence, 231
neocolonialism. *See* colonialism
neoliberalism. *See also* liberal internationalism; liberalism: emphasis on economic
dimension of globalization, 300-1, 315;
and feminist view of individual autonomy, 10; and Foucauldian tradition,
17-18; governance, compared with Cree
co-governance, 125-28; neoliberal
globalization vs. democracy, 302, 303,
304-6; private corporations, transfer of
government responsibility to, 122; resource development in Quebec, and
co-governance with James Bay Cree
Nation, 17, 102, 114, 116-18; response to
democratic pressures, 314-15; WTO as
symbol of, to anti-corporate globalization movement, 278
New International Economic Order
(NIEO), 277
New Partnership for Africa's Development
(NEPAD), 274
non-governmental organizations (NGOs).
See also conservation non-governmental
organizations (CNGOS); Friends of

Shapiro, Ian, 41
Sinhala Only Act (Sri Lanka, 1956), 222
Sinhala Only Movement, 223
Sinhalese, in Sri Lanka, 221-23
Sivanandan, A., 218
Slovakia: Hungarian minority, 150; Hungarians, minority rights of, 164; problems of
   nationalist questions, 154
social compact: as alien to US economic
   philosophy, 276; renegotiation, as difficult process in Europe, 277
social connection model (Young), 41, 49-50
Social Sciences and Humanities Research
   Council of Canada (SSHRC), ix
South Tyrol, 157, 159
Southern countries: new coalitions, 277;
   social movements, central roles in transnational organizing, 313-14
sovereignty. See also autonomy; legitimacy:
   and cosmopolitan-communitarian
   debate, 60; definition, 74-75; empire,
   under globalization, 90-92; and legitimacy, as roots of localized transnational
   wars, 224; limitations of, for minority
   nationalist movements, 168; norm,
   change to commitment to democratic
   governance, 191; pooling, by European
   Union (EU), 150, 157; state, and autonomy, 83, 86; state, erosion under
   globalization, 8, 283; state, overruled by
   intervention to protect human rights,
   11-12, 203, 205, 214; and territorial
   borders, 158-60, 191; unbundling, as
   challenge to legitimacy, 36
Soviet Union, breakup along national lines,
   152, 154, 165
Spain, 154
Spinoza, Baruch, 89, 91
Sri Lanka: civil war, globalization of, 222;
   civil war, grounded in colonial history,
   217; civil war, international dimension
   of, 216, 219, 222; civil war, as localized
   transnational war, 237; colonial roots of
   Buddhist Sinhalese and Hindu Tamil
   relations, 221-23, 234-35; as country in
   permanent state of emergency, 229; denial of rights to Tamils under Sinhalese

government, 222; literature, and politics,
   216-38; postcolonial governance, 99
Strong, Maurice, 310
subsidiarity, principle of: definition, 158; in
   practice, 69, 70; as support for regional
   minorities, 158, 159
Sudan, 199
supraterritoriality, and globalization, 242,
   244
sustainable resource management. See
   natural resources
Sutherland Consultative Board, 276

Tambiah, Stanley, 221, 227
Tamils: denial of rights under Sinhalese
   government, 222; perceived as colonial
   collaborators in Sri Lanka, 221
Technical Barriers to Trade (TBT) Agreement, 266
Tennessee Valley Authority, 69
territoriality, unbundling and decentred
   economic relations, 35
Thakur, Ramesh, 206
Third World Network, 278
Third World solidarity, as transnational
   activism, 308
Tokyo Round, of GATT, 262
Trade and Competitiveness Act (US, 1988),
   262
Trade Policy Review Mechanism (TPRM),
   272-73
transnational activists: democratic globalizers,
   as against neoliberalism, 305; global
   justice movement, 311-14; historical
   roots of, 306-14
Transylvania: history of border changes
   between Hungary and Romania, 170; as
   regional concentration of Hungarians in
   Romania, 169
Treaty of Rome, 153
Trudeau, Pierre Elliot, 112
Tunisia. See also World Summit on the Information Society (WSIS) (Tunisia,
   2005): resolution on World Summit on
   the Information Society, 286; suppression of civil society protests demanding
   freedom of communication, 299

Printed and bound in Canada by Friesens

Set in Syntax and Bembo by Artegraphica Design Co. Ltd.

Text design: George Kirkpatrick

Copy editor: Lesley Erickson

Indexer: Annette Lorek